The Six Black Presidents

Black Blood: White Masks

USA

Auset BaKhufu

PIK² Publications
Washington, D.C.   Maryland   California

ISBN: 1-880187-00-0

Published by: PIK² Publications

                   Washington, D.C.

Distributed by: A & A Distributors
                   P.O. Box 1113-AA
                   Temple Hills, MD 20757-1113

Mail all inquiries to A & A Distributors c/o PIK² Publications

Library of Congress Catalog Card Number: 91-90486

BaKhufu, Auset   3 3113 01260 3660

The Six Black Presidents: Black Blood, White Masks/
by Auset BaKhufu

Bibliography
Includes index.
International Standard Book Numbering: 1-880187-00-0 (pbk): $12.95

Subjects: a. United States' Presidents. b. Jefferson, Thomas.
c. Jackson, Andrew. d. Lincoln, Abraham. e. Hamlin, Hannibal.
f. Harding,Warren. g. Eisenhower, Dwight. h. Biography.
i. African-Americans. j. Ourstory. k. History.

1993   CIP: 91-90486

Cover design concept by the Author

First Edition
First Printing   January, 1993

Printed in the United States of America

10 9 8 7 6 5 4 3 2 1

*This book is a special dedication
to my Daddy, Fred T. Barber*

1923 - 1991

(picture taken during the Eisenhower years)

The Six Black Presidents

Black Blood: White Masks

USA

TO preserve and retain the flavor and writing style of the author, all editing lies exclusively with the publisher and author.

DISCLAIMER: Within the confines of this book, there are several references to alternative medicines, herbs and herbal remedies. The author is in no way prescribing medical or herbal remedies here. If you are interested, for any reason, in the herbal references herein, please do contact or see your medical, natural, or herbal doctor first. However, it is your constitutional right as an intelligent person, a human being, to prescribe for yourself alternative medicines/herbals as you see fit for your mental and physical well-being.

FRONT COVER: *Ida Stover Eisenhower and her son, Dwight*

CONTENTS

ACKNOWLEDGEMENTS

I thank my parents and family for the full Black, and therefore African, life that they have given me unpretentiously and lovingly. Love goes to my husband and child, and any combination of words would not be enough to express to them the affection I have for them for simply Being. I thank my M'zee and mentor-like, Dr. John Henrik Clarke, for his encouragement whenever I became apprehensive while writing this book. I thank him for never, ever being too busy to listen to my chit-chat and to talk with me about my writing and research efforts. Much appreciation goes to the late J.A. Rogers for his in-depth research and writings. I am especially grateful for his research pamphlet, *The Five Negro Presidents*, 1965. I thank my students who asked so many questions about the presidents mentioned in Rogers' pamphlet that they propelled me into feeling the necessity of this present work. I thank Stephen B. Oates and the late William Henry Herndon for their in-depth writings on Abraham Lincoln. I also acknowledge the libraries and librarians in Hillcrest Heights and Oxon Hill, Maryland, and also the Durham County library in Durham, North Carolina. Special thanks also go to the Martin Luther King Memorial Library and Howard University library and Medical College in Washington, D.C. I am grateful to the Library of Congress' existence. Here, I was able to research and find much undercover information. Whenever I visited the Thomas Jefferson Building, which is situated within the Library of Congress, to gather my research and write, I was always tickled Black.

FOREWORD

by Dr. Wade Nobles

Dr. Auset BaKhufu's *"The Six Black Presidents: Black Blood, White Masks"* is a psychobiography of six presidents of the United States who are believed by some historians to be of African Ancestry. Na'im Akbar and I have suggested that "psychology" is the study of the illumination of the human spirit. A "psychobiography" would, therefore, be a study of the illumination of the spirit through the written (graphy) analyses of a life or living organism. Dr. BaKhufu attempts to analyze the lives of Thomas Jefferson, Andrew Jackson, Abraham Lincoln, Hannibal Hamlin, Warren G. Harding and Dwight D. Eisenhower as living organisms and in so doing illuminates the hidden spirit that was theirs to live and America's to hide. Auset BaKhufu has met the challenge of calling forth the illumination of that which most social scientists would deny and all theorists would prefer not to deal with. Some would even go as far as to say "what's the point or so what?" And while I am of the opinion that if these Presidents perceived themselves as White and in their thoughts and deeds served the interest of White supremacy, then illuminating their Blackness is meaningless.

Thankfully, Dr. BaKhufu saw greater significance in this effort and proceeded not just to prove that a few USA presidents were Black. In fact, after reading this work, the reader should realize that the value of this book is not in the historiography of racial ownership. Clearly each reader will have the opportunity to judge whether or not this is a believable book. However, in my opinion that is not where its value lies. The value of this book is in its ability to reframe the question as the simultaneous study of the task of illuminating the spirit of the nation and the key men who served as its heroic icons. In effect, the value of *"The Six Black Presidents: Black Blood, White*

Masks" is in its ability to enlarge the venue of analyses. This book, in effect, suggests that the hidden African spirit buried in the social reality of "Whiteness" must be factored in the historical explanations of White rulership and governance. One, therefore, should not read this book with an Oprah Winfrey or Geraldo Rivera exposé perspective. It is not a scholarly "National Inquire." Its importance really doesn't lie in publicly discussing the unmentionable or documenting how much "Black Blood" these men had or whether or not they had mental problems or what strange things occurred in their marital/family lives.

Dr. W.E.B. Dubois' recognition of "two warring idols in one dark body" is equally true even if the dark body is light enough to pass for white. The acceptance of an influential African Spirit hidden in the beingness of those "who are passing" calls for a reanalysis of these men and the decisions of their time which shaped and reinforced the developmental path of this nation. Dr. BaKhufu's treatise forces us to reconsider the choices made and chances taken by Thomas Jefferson. How should Jefferson's relationship with the enslaved African Sally Hemmings be interpreted? What was the real motivation for his interest or need to devise a mathematical formula for determining who is Black and who is not or to write the Jefferson Plan for African Resettlement? Akbar's notion of "Anti-Self Disorder" coupled with the life stories of these men is intriguing. Does the Anti-Self Disorder inform BaKhufu's research and better explain Andrew Jackson's psychopathic hatred and slaughter of Blacks and Indians? Similarly, the information shared by Dr. BaKhufu also calls for a reanalysis of the historical events surrounding David Walker and Nat Turner during the Jacksonian era. Clearly the information found in "The Six Black Presidents: Black Blood, White Masks" also raises questions in the lives of Hamilton, Hamlin, Harding and Eisenhower.

The newly classified African Centered Movement challenges the hegemony of the existing scientific paradigms and the supremacy of an Eurocentric epistemology. Dr. Auset BaKhufu's "The Six Black Presidents: Black

Blood, White Masks" will further this scientific revolution. The book will, without a doubt, gender controversy, criticism and debate. In so doing it will serve as a welcomed stimulus for clarifying a new historical method and as such will stimulate new research and analyses. When all is said and done, *"The Six Black Presidents: Black Blood, White Masks"* will serve all of us by expanding the frontiers of knowing and the boundaries of truth.

Wade W. Nobles
November, 1992

Dr. Wade W. Nobles, Psychologist
Center for Applied Cultural Studies
& Educational Achievement
San Francisco State University
San Francisco, California

A PRELIMINARY TREATISE
(Psychobiographies of Six Black Presidents, USA)

Instead of an Introduction (*I don't particularly care for them*), I thought I'd start you off on your reading adventure with a Prime Treat. Although I'm treating you to foregoing the reading of an introductory chapter, familiarizing you somewhat to what the book entails is essential. You will be treated and enlightened to some of the instructive thoughts of the African and respected elder (M'zee), Dr. John Henrik Clarke. One of the main treats, I hope, in this section is the definition of terms as we (Black People) should define ourselves — and others.

The "impossible to be authorized" psychobiographies of the six presidents of the United States said to be of African ancestry is written in such a way that it places a new sense of direction and understanding in the his-story of "passing-for-white" in America. Hopefully this book is also an example of utilizing new ideas, new points of view, and unveiling the masks of significant and important history (his-story) and ourstory. Old sociology and new social psychology have been closely intertwined in order to understand the significance and importance of the psychology behind the *sociology of color* in America.

The Lincoln chapter was the last to be completed, but the first to be recognized, noted and recorded. Lincoln's insanity is referenced throughout this chapter because his mental problems were developed in childhood and grew into adulthood. Lincoln has been an idol, savior and genius to many. Many older people have attested to the fine line between genius and insanity. I immediately saw that this chapter would be very emotionally charged, time-consuming, technical and psychological, not to mention anguishly demanding. It necessitated my professional skills in the specializations of psychology (Sakku) and sociology. But, this chapter could not have been written to my satisfaction without the writing and study of some medical inquiry, and of course, old politics. I learned too late that Abraham Lincoln did not like the nickname "Abe;" therefore this name is used thoughout this work. I believe that any soul should be called by the name that they prefer, especially if the person on the receiving end simply does not like the name for which they're being labeled or called. Going into the print and changing the name throughout the book would have been too time consuming and costly. Actually at times the sound of the name simply fitted in so perfectly with the content that it would have demeaned the literary arts, Goddess Muse, and the art of writing creativity not to have used "Abe" some of the time. From this point on though, I would hope that we as writers/ourstorians will respect Lincoln's choice and refer to him by the name or names of his choice, Abraham or Lincoln, or both combined.

The book is written mostly in chronological order although I do tend to deviate from this order for more clarity on a particular subject or statement if need be. I've found through my readings that knowing the dates of births and deaths of other historical figures gives me a better sense of ourstory/history. Therefore, information about other famous people is mentioned throughout the book. In this book/biography, small but interesting detail is given to make up a more engaging whole. There are also interesting tid-bits given throughout the book about the different ourstorical/historical happenings during various periods. Many African stories and histories about African culture from all over the world, ancient and modern, went into the research and study for the writing of this book. There are many references quoted throughout this work. This in-depth process was necessary for the benefit of the reader who might be interested in the first-hand references. Most of the information pertaining to the possible African ancestry of these presidents comes from documented literature and reports written and stated by white people. And although in-depth information may not be given on any particular subject of your *personal* interest, there is enough information provided in order for you to find and obtain more knowledge on any of the subjects mentioned. Note paper is provided in the back of the book for your convenience.

If I have misunderstood and quoted anyone's work or writing out of the content in which it was intended, I apologize; but if I have reinterpreted in my own opinion as to what I think was meant or what the quote could xii

mean, then it stands as is. If I have misquoted anyone period, please inform me. I am not a politician, and I'm proud not be a his-storian; therefore it is safe for you to believe that I'm sincere in my endeavor to make the reader know the truth and to also understand the points being made herein and from all sources. Although I am not a politician, I am political-minded enough to understand survival tactics for my people.

Although it may be exhausting to perceive sometimes, this book is not anti-anyone; it is however, pro-truth. After extensive research, it was difficult to have anything totally positive to say about any of these presidents. They all had negative feelings about African people, although some of their actions demonstrated that they were actually mental victims — victims of the prejudice and insensitivity of this society. In essence, the two parallels of being Black and White deemed very mental and therefore dangerous people, in these cases.

Multiracials or mulattos need an approach to sociology and psychology that they can relate to, an approach to take into consideration the entities they share with non-mulatto people, in addition to the things that make them different from non-mulatto peoples psychologically, and even socially. A more understanding knowledge of differences in everybody's cultural and biological life is needed. The point here though is not to overemphasize differences between mulattoes and non-mulattoes psychologically and socially, but to place experiences in their proper perspectives. A mulatto person should not have to choose one part of themselves over the other. This makes for an unhealthy personality. But in a racist society, a choice is almost imperative.

Our problem of disunity as a black people is of the most prevailing magnitude over any other race in the world, therefore, it must be stressed that I am not trying to claim any people or persons as an African if they do not wish to be an African or to claim their Africanness. What I'm documenting here is that many sources, research, and study point to the likelihood that these presidents had black blood running through their veins. They, perhaps by no choice of their own, claimed white and continued to do so throughout their adult life — *outwardly*. Their *inward* feelings is the story being told here.

These presidents lived very Dr. Jekyll/Mr. Hyde lives. This phenomenon of alternate selves in earlier times seems to have been too complex to be addressed into the methods of psychological science. Because of the times, the problems were not dealt with adequately. Even today, the methods of psychological science will not be able to deal with this phenomenon properly unless scholars study the ancients and learn to understand and to know that any visible entity can also be an invisible entity. For example, just because the presidents mentioned in this book may not have been told by their parents verbally that they possessed a certain amount of African blood, this certainly does not mean that they did not know it, or better yet, did not feel it. This feeling, this entity is an invisible known — visible only to the mind, the knowingness in all of us. This school of thought will have to be dealt with very carefully. I would hope that the psychoanalysis of this psychohistory, and the scientific personalogy will lead us to be more interested in and concerned about the different syndromes and phenomena of multiracials, i.e., mulatto peoples, especially those people who may not have known from their parents that they had black blood running through their veins — although, as mentioned, something innate in them led them to know and understand that there was "something" unique and different about their lives as they *tried* to live white. I find this especially true of Abraham Lincoln, Hannibal Hamlin and Warren G. Harding. Their personal beliefs and political careers were closely intertwined. I tend to think that Abe Lincoln mentally dissociated himself in personal dilemmas in order to effectively deal with his political life, and also in order to be loyal to his unconscious or conscious mind as to who his true "self" really was. In the book, *New Dimensions in African History*, by John Henrik Clarke and Yosef ben-Jochannan, Dr. Clarke mentions that if a person does not understand who they are, if they are searching for their identity, and they are not sure where they should put their loyalty, or who they should be committed to, they represent a danger within the cultural mainstream of their society (pp. 24 & 25). Lincoln, Hamlin, and perhaps Harding represented a danger to white America's status quo. Included in the book are psychological and mental ramifications of a person trying to be or trying to utilize themselves as two, i.e., split selves.

Dr. Clarke told me that he knew J.A. Rogers when he was writing the pamphlet, *The Five Negro Presidents.* He said that they were pretty good friends, and he told Rogers that most of the presidents mentioned aren't worth talking about. Dr. Clarke mentioned to me that he used to golf caddy for Dwight D. Eisenhower. He said that Ike was a man who could not look him in the eye. I suggested to Dr. Clarke that maybe Eisenhower was fearful that he may see something of himself in Dr. Clarke's eyes if he had looked at him directly. Dr. Clarke laughed and said, "It's all conjecture anyway, and the white race can have all of them [the six black presidents]." Dr. Clarke said that Eisenhower had a wide mouth and a wide nose, but this certainly doesn't mean that he is an African man, and that it also doesn't mean that he is not. Although this is my sentiments exactly, there has been indications that these men may have African Ancestry, and this information is documented by white people. Because the information is documented by whites is not an indication that the information is true. Dr. John Henrik Clarke said that he could care less, or he "could give a damn about who has a drop of black blood in them" [if they're claiming white only]. We agreed that for any person who wants to claim white, even if they do have a drop of black blood, then let them be white, because that is one less mouth that we [Africa peoples] have to feed!" Dr. Clarke laughed and said "We didn't make that rule anyway" [the rule or law that a drop of black blood deems a person a whole Black person] — June 4, 1991 - 7:00 pm.

This book is written not for the amusement and appeasement of white people in general. It is necessary to make this clear, because so many people Black, white and otherwise tend to automatically assume, though sometimes unconsciously, that most literature is written for this purpose and to this particular audience — especially if the selected content is on the presidents of the United States, simply because most people think that all of these presidents have all been white. This book is written to and for my people. They are Africans all over the world, and especially to Africans living in America; however, the book is readable and teachable for and to anyone, anywhere in the world. It is also written for the learning, interest, amusement, and satisfaction (conscious rising) of anyone interested, but is especially written to Africans living in America who have never been treated as "American." The latter could be a blessing in disguise — giving strength, reverence and recognition to the originators of the earth. When Africans gain the respect, economic power, political power and their true place in history, then a statement such as the one just written may not be appropriate. This is not an anti-American book; this is a pro-American book, in hopes for future improvements and truth.

DEFINING OURSELVES — AND THEM
(DEFINITION OF TERMS)

Ourstory = A chronological record of true and significant events of the world — the universe, including real and true explanations for their causes. A true account of the backgrounds of all peoples. In essence, a branch of knowledge that records and explains past, present, and future events, through specific past events and circumstances. **Our** shows a comradery — unitedness, togetherness. Ourstory is the true account and backgrounds of every race in the world. *The Six Black Presidents: Black Blood, White Masks (USA)* is not an ourstory book, although related and interesting ourstorical events are mentioned throughout this work.

History/his-story = is a form of taking away ourstorical events, just as *hys*terectomy is the procedure of taking the uterus away from a woman (a procedure that has been recently found to have been unnecessarily performed on many women, Black, White, Indian, Jewish, etc.) *His*tory has taken away much of the culture, and in essence, the lives of zillions of Black people. *Hiss*, To make a harsh sound, often an expression of disapproval. *His* will always be someone else's, not *Ours* or *Everyones.*

De-coding = the science of reading between the lines of his-story in order to get to the truth; to assimilate fact; to be able to read prejudice, attitudes, lies and truths where they are *supposedly* not written.

Necro = means dead. Place a line down the right side of the "c" and you get Negro. This definition is a very good reason for Black peoples to understand that they are Africans, *not* Negroes. Africans are very much alive when they understand their ourstory and his-story.

Go-on-to-the-Ancestors/Journey-on-to-the-Ancestors = To pass away. Die/Death.

Swarthy = means Dark. A word used by white people to describe the skin color of a person whom they are claiming to be white.

Majority = Black peoples who are 9/10 of the whole world population; they include Africans, Spanish, Hispanics, Latinos, Japanese, Indians, Jews, Mexicans,

Koreans, etc. Etc. is for those of you who belong here, but have not been placed in this very proud group due to time and space. The most recent percentage: 93%.

Minority = The 1/10 of the world population of people proclaiming to be white. The most recent percentage: 7%.

Political Prisoners/Enslaved persons (instead of slaves) = One who has been forcibly enslaved to aid in someone else's economic, social and political well being. A people enslaved in order to aid in the mental strength of another group, e.g., white supremacy.

Prisoner, a person deprived of his or her liberty and kept under involuntary restraint, confinement or custody. The African people of America were never slaves within themselves. A slave or slave people would have never wished to be nor would they have become free.

In an article written by John Hope Franklin, he states that the "happy slave syndrome" is a myth. This fictitious syndrome was only in the heads of the so-called "slave owner" who could not accept the fact that enslaved peoples were continuously freeing themselves everyday, sometimes at the expense of the so-called slave owner's life. "Records abound with instances of violence in the master-slave relationship that belie any claim that the plantation was a place of surpassing tranquility." (Franklin, J., *American Visions*, "Runaway Slaves," February/March, 1991, pp. 30-31). Today Africans in America are by law, free. But one day soon, we will be FREE. And I don't mean that old church, Negro spiritual song, down-in-the-grave, free; I mean ALIVE AND FREE!

M'zee (Mezee) = is the Swahili word meaning *elder* or the respected *grand old man*. I'll take this opportunity to point out that Swahili was chosen by members of the Pan-African conference in 1974 as the official and Pan-African language which petitions all Africans to learn Swahili so that all Africans will be able to understand each other and be able to communicate with each other no matter were Africans may be in the world. This act of learning is essential toward our survival; it's also fun. I've discovered that in most classes, our children learn much faster than the adults; it's up to us to send them to the classes.

Sakku = The study of ancient African psychology and philosophy. Psychic universality. Dr. Nobles states that Sakku is to master what's real and what isn't real. What's real is sometimes invisible. Understanding that the invisible and the visible are one and the same, and understanding that the invisible is far greater than the visible. "Beingness." The use of metaphor is important in this school of thought. Nobles asserts that the use of metaphor is the key to "seeing." To be able to de-code. To engage oneself in service and protocol that speak to the spirit. To be in touch with intuitions and emotions. Sakku is not a Jungian theory. For more information on the study of Sakku, please see the works of Wade Nobles, Ph.D., psychologist, San Francisco, California.

[1]*Fail-for-white* = Being African/Black/multiracial but personifying whiteness, i.e., their actions, culture, etc. (Fell-for-white = falling for the trick, the con, of thinking that white is better.) Falling for a con; a trick.

Pass-for-white = Operational definition for this book: A very light-complexioned African/Black person who uses their light-skin to enpower the African race by listening to and/or procuring plans and information from whites who wish to exploit Africans. The purpose of this light-complexioned person to "pass-for-white" would be to infiltrate white organizations in order for Africans to counteract the efforts of people who aspire to harm melanized people (i.e., people of color). Pass-for-white is also a term, used up until now, which describes a person who is pale enough in complexion to look white and lives their very existence as a white person, ignoring their African Self. This is *usually* a very light-complexioned person of African descent.

europenisized = when a man because of psychological barriers cannot function properly sexually. Impotency. Usually a man whose mind is of the paternalistic nature, causing him not to understand the needs of himself, much less the needs of a woman. This "paternalistic" mind set can render a man physically and mentally —

---

[1]All bold-italic faced terms are penned and defined exclusively by the author.

impotent, i.e., europenisized. (Europe was named for an African princess, Europa, but Europe or Euro has been so closely associated and parallelled with people or things of a white persuasion that no further discussion of the word need be analyzed.)

Europhobia = fear or hatred of white people.

Mutaphobia = (from mutation) Having a keen awareness of and a healthy fear (not an inferior fear) of the character of white people — a character of which, for many whites, ourstory and history have shown, is of brutality, violence, and mental cruelty against people of color — usually Blacks (which shows whites' own phobias and fears in the process). An example of a healthy fear is for Africans to fear and be concerned about their plight in a racist society to the degree of understanding that there is an immense need for self-reliance, ourstorical study, economic empowerment, and a new and much need spiritual comradery in the African community — all over the world. *Mutaphobics* are intelligent beings who are concerned about their mental and physical security in a society were racists abound in every sector of government, state, business, church, and other professional and nonprofessional sectors.

jambalaya (or djambalaya, the "d" is silent) = An ourstorical operational definition. A variety of distinct and concrete elements, mostly of a psychological or sociological Africentric nature (e.g., Africentric research scientists have a *jambalaya* of sociological and psychological factors to resolve.)

idiogenio = An intellectual idiot. A genius with no faculties for common sense; where perception and ignorance cross. (See Thomas Jefferson.)

IT'S A COLOR THANG

Introductory and True Tales

Story 1: Last year, a friend's husband, Jerry, was stopped in a southern United States city for driving too fast. The police who wrote him the speeding ticket was very polite and cordial toward Jerry. The police gave Jerry the ticket and asked him to slow down. Later, when Jerry examined the ticket, he noticed that the police had written "white" in the race area on the ticket stub. Jerry is a very light-skinned Black man who could fail-for-white. Now this tells us what color the police was. Anyway, many Black people have been failing-for-white for years. Jerry is smart and fortunate; he has the good sense to pass-for and be Black and proud!

Story 2: Adam Clayton Powell, Jr. was the 1940's thru 1960's political figure from New York City's Harlem. When Powell attended Colgate college, he decided to simply attend school and let the administration and the students think whatever they wished to think. Therefore, he found himself living in the white dormitories and relishing in all the freedom and social life of any other white student on Colgate's campus. When Powell, Jr. decided to join a white fraternity, the fraternity checked his background and found that Powell, Jr. was a Black man. The fraternity, of course, did not grant Powell his wish to become a member. Powell's white roommate requested that Powell, Jr. be removed from their room immediately. The college administrators concurred. The white students ceased their communication with Powell, Jr. altogether, while many of the Black students were simply appalled that Adam Clayton Powell, Jr. had "fell"-for-white at all. One Black student who looked even more white than Powell, Jr. was so disgusted with Powell that he, like the white students, stopped speaking to Powell completely. The Black students, of course, felt thatPowell, Jr. most definitely should have never denied his heritage.

It was said of President Warren Gamaliel Harding that no one believed the "fine-looking, hawk-nosed, gray-eyed" man had "Negro" blood. Anyway, Adam Clayton Powell, Jr. learned from this experience and many more to come, and became one of the first Black/African-American people to advise and vocalize, "Black Power!" Harding stayed white.

Story 3: Before Alex Haley, the author of the famous *Roots*, journeyed-on-to-the-ancestors in January of 1992, he had began work on *Queen*, a six-hour David Wolper miniseries for CBS-T.V. This is the story of his father's mother who Haley said "looked absolutely white." The psychological ramifications of looking white, and actually being Black is the drive behind the story. Haley's grandmother was born into slavery, fathered by the white slaveholder. Haley said that he feels that the "biggest challenge will be casting the lead." He said that it's a must that the lead be a Black woman, or the African-American community would be "upset." He said that although he feels that Jasmine Guy, from the television show *A Different World*, or Lisa Bonet, former *Cosby Show* daughter would do very well as actresses, he feels that they are too dark to play the part. Of course, there are many very light-skinned, white-looking sisters in the African community who could play the part to the hilt even without acting lessons (we don't usually need them). But the show must go on, and the person who has been cast in the part is Halle Berry. Ms. Berry made an interesting and sensible statement when she asserted: "I'm black. I realized very early in my life that I wasn't going to be this mulatto stuck in the middle, don't know if I'm black or white" (*U.S.A. Today*, 1992; *Emerge* Magazine, November, 1992, p. 42). She is just as beautifully dark as Jasmine and Lisa. The point I'm making here is that the late Elder Haley made a request. The request was for a very light-skinned African woman from the community. He simply wants the story authentic. Why can't he get his dying wish? The request is not hard to grant. Jasmine, Lisa, and Halle are all multiracial (so is the Fresh Princess of Bel Air, Karyn Parsons). All are extremely talented, African sisters. Haley did say that "...Makeup should help" (*T.V. Guide*, January 25, 1992, p. 16). So I suppose that this is what will be done. Such a waste of cosmetics when authenticity lives in the community.

Story 4: J.A. Rogers writes an interesting story. This is the case of an African-American, who went over to the white side, then to the Black side again. This story attracted national attention. This African-American was Attorney

T. John McKee. His picture appeared on the front page of the *New York Daily News* on February 20, 1948 along with this story. McKee was to become a millionaire.

T. John McKee, as a white man, attended Yale University, studied law, became an attorney, married him a white woman, had some children with Mrs. McKee, then, I am sure, shocked her by becoming a Black man. After living as a white person for forty-five years, this successful Wall Street lawyer saw an advertisement issued by an Orphan company in Philadelphia for any living grandsons of an African-American millionaire named McKee. Grandfather McKee had left in his will $800,000 to found a Military School for Black and White Orphans with the condition that if this request did not go through, then the money along with interest should be given to the last living grandson. Attorney McKee discovered that he was indeed the last living grandson of Grandfather McKee. Attorney McKee promptly became, again, Black and proud "to the tune of $1,240,000 plus interest on the original sum" (Rogers, *The Five Negro Presidents*, p. 4).

****

This book of psychobiographies exposes and analyzes the mysteries surrounding the African ethnicity of six of the United States most well-known and influential presidents. The book will read like a psychological thriller to some white people. How much Black blood did these presidents have? How deep were their mental problems? And why did they all have rather strange marriages? The lives of these presidents including their wives and family, their careers, and their friends and enemies will be briefly examined. Three of these presidents had documented mental problems. Three also had wives who had mental problems. They all had friends who turned into foes, and foes who turned into friends. They all had interesting lives and some told many lies.

I've lived in the minds of these men for three years and with the last word written, I packed my books, my typing fingers, and my truth and left them. This book is based on fact, not fiction. I hope you enjoy your journey through the psyches of *The Six Black Presidents*.

Auset BaKhufu

> *The speaker stated that Thomas Jefferson*
> *was a "low-lived fellow, the son of a*
> *half-breed Indian squaw sired by a*
> *Virginia mulatto father." After the*
> *speech, it was voted that no one*
> *should vote for the "half-Injun, half-nigger ..."*

—From: *The Jonny Cake Papers*

THOMAS JEFFERSON

3rd President U.S.A.

Thomas Jefferson was the 3rd President of the United States. He was in office from March 4, 1801 to March 3, 1809. Before his term as president of the United States, he served as vice president to the second president of the United States, John Adams. This service was from March 4, 1799 to March 3, 1801.

JEFFERSON'S EARLY LIFE

Thomas Jefferson was born April 13, 1743. He was born in Shadwell, Coochland County, now known as Albemarle County, Virginia. His father, Peter Jefferson was said to be half-Black, half-Indian (Rogers, *The Five Negro Presidents*, p. 6). Apparently Peter Jefferson looked or acted white enough to father white enough children in order to to rear them in a white enough neighborhood. Peter Jefferson was said to be a very strong man who was very fond of the Indians in his community and found much pleasure in their company. Thomas Jefferson would never match the size and strength of his father who was said to be of African ancestry. Peter and Thomas Jefferson found Indians fascinating and worthy of respect.

The Jeffersons enjoyed talking with the Indians, and Thomas felt that he could learn a lot from them. (Brodie, *Thomas Jefferson: An Intimate History*, p. 55; Bumann & Patterson, *Our American Presidents*, p. 15. More than a thousand interesting items and manuscripts exist on Thomas Jefferson and his life in the Duke University Library, Durham, North Carolina).

THOMAS JEFFERSON'S MOM

Thomas Jefferson's mother was said to be from one of the most prominent landowning families in Virginia. Isham Randolph, her father, was a rich seafaring, slaveholder well known throughout the colony of Virginia (Adler, *Thomas Jefferson: Father of Our* Democracy, pp. 10-11, 1987). There is much literature about the ancestry of Jefferson's mother, but not a lot at all about Jefferson's father. Even in the 1981-*Facts About the Presidents: From George Washington to Ronald Reagan*, and *Jefferson*, by Arthur M. Schlesinger, Jr., there is no documentation of his birthplace. His mother's birthplace is listed as London, England (Kane, p. 25, and Schlesinger, p. 16). Fawn Brodie states in her book, *Thomas Jefferson: An Intimate History*, "We do not know if Jane Randolph Jefferson felt superior to her husband because of her English birth..., whereas Peter Jefferson knew nothing of his own ancestry.... Jefferson's *Autobiography* about his mother's ancestors hints at such a conflict." Jefferson wrote to a friend that life with his mother was like "colonial subservience" (Brodie, p. 44 & 46). Does this mean that Jefferson felt enslaved under a white supremacist attitude, and that perhaps his mother's attitude toward him was indeed an indication that she felt her son also to be beneath her? Thomas was after all the son of a man who was half-Black and half-Indian (?). So why did Jane Randolph marry Peter Jefferson? It is possible that he had deceived her by "failing-for-white" until she got the scoop on his ancestry from the "hood" and saw his *strange* fondness for Blacks and Indians. Of course, Mrs. Jefferson could have been aloof and uncaring toward her children because she was under tremendous stress and strain. Thomas Jefferson's sister, Elizabeth, was mentally retarded.

THOMAS JEFFERSON'S DAD, PETER

Even though it is likely that Peter Jefferson was of African ancestry and had a fondness for Blacks, still at the time of his death, he owned approximately ninety political prisoners (slaves). His son would own over one-hundred political prisoners at his death.

Later in Thomas Jefferson's life when asked if he remembered his first years at Shadwell, he said in his squeaky voice that he remembered nothing. His earliest memory is of being lifted onto a horse at age two, and riding with a Black slave for three days from Shadwell to Tockahoe (Schlesinger, p. 13). Who was the so-called slave? A relative of whom Peter Jefferson trusted with his young son?

THE MANY-FACED MAN: JEFFERSON'S ADULT LIFE

By the time Thomas Jefferson became a man, he was already over six feet tall with large hands and feet, but he still did not reach the large size of his father. One interesting feature was Thomas Jefferson's red hair which he wore in a ponytail like many young African and white youth of today. Jefferson's unique look deemed him the nickname of "Red Fox" (Bumann & Patterson, p.15). Redd Foxx, the late comedian of television fame, was also nicknamed for his red hair.

Thomas Robinson Hazard wrote a book called, *The Jonny Cake Papers*, 1867 & 1915. This book was titled after the delicious jonny cakes of a slave woman by the name of Phillis who Hazard's grandfather proclaimed to own. She was from Senegrambia or Guinea. (See page 18). It is noted in this book that Hazard interviewed an old man by the name of Paris Gardiner who had been present at the 1796 campaign election of Thomas Jefferson. Gardiner stated that a tree-stump speaker for the campaign informed the listeners that he knew a secret about Jefferson that would certainly convince no one to elect Jefferson to be President of the United States. The speaker stated that Thomas Jefferson was a "mean-spirited, low-lived fellow, the son of a half-breed Indian squaw, sired by a Virginia mulatto father." After the speech, it was voted that no one should vote for the "half-Injun, half-nig-

ger, half-Frenchman, with a touch of bullfrog." (Hazard, pp.
233 & 237; Coyle, *Ordeal of the Presidency*, p. 69. Also see: *Jefferson*, by Albert J. Nock, p. 233, 1926, and David S. Browder,
New York Times Magazine, September 9, 1964.) Famous psychoanalyst and popular figure in the study of human development, Erik Erickson, stated at the second annual Jefferson
Lectures in 1973 that "His [Thomas Jefferson's] parentage
was obscure." He asserted that Jefferson was a man with a
"conflicted personality" with "contrasting images in identity formation." There's more. Erickson labeled Thomas Jefferson the "Protean President" in one section of his lecture.
This, Erickson said, shows "a man of many appearances, a
many-sided man of universal stature....But it can also mean
a man of many disguises." Thomas Jefferson was a man of
"contradictory modes of action." He was the grand statesman one day, and the simple, secluded, farm-type man the
next. Erickson wanted to know what was behind the
facade? What was behind the mask of the many-faced man?
Perhaps in trying to validate himself as a whole, normal
identity, Jefferson was known to "demean" those who had
less than himself by calling them all "half-breeds." Others
he designated the name, "pretenders," (Erickson, *Dimensions of a New Identity*) as if he were not.

Jefferson was interested enough in the question of race,
race mixture, and "half-breeds" (Jefferson's expression) to
devise a mathematical formula of possibilities that constitutes who is black and who is not. Of course he used the
capital "A" to express pure white blood, and the small "a"
to express pure black blood, and any given mixture of either
as "MS." He said let the first crossing of "a", pure black
blood, with pure white blood, "A" which is half and half be
called a mulatto. If a mulatto "crosses" with a pure whiteblooded person, then the offspring will be of one-fourth
black blood and called a quarteroon. Yet he doesn't say
whether he would consider this person (offspring) black or
white. But since the person is called a quarteroon in his
mathematical terminology instead of a white person, then
it is supposed that the person is considered Black/African
(especially according to the laws of America, which postulate that just one drop of Black blood makes a person
Black/African). Jefferson said that the third cross "clears"

the blood (as if something is wrong with black blood). His formula shows that if the quarteroon crosses with a pure white person, then their offspring will now have only one-eighth of black blood, and since their blood is virtually clear, then they are white. He calls these offspring octoroon. His statements and his formula show the quarteroon as still being considered a mulatto (Black). And, as mentioned, he states that the octoroon is "cleared" and therefore is a white person (Brodie, p. 433-434 [see these pages for the full mathematical formula]; Dennis, *Black History*, p. 60, and *Writings*, L & B., XIV, pp. 267-271 — Jefferson said to Francis Gray). Jefferson calculated and reworked this formula over and over again, probably trying to determine and decide what he should consider himself to be. He also stated that, "Our canon considers two crosses with the pure white, and a third with any degree of mixture, however small, as clearing the issue of negro blood" (Brodie, p. 433 and *Writings*, L & B — see above). Well, Jefferson's canon duped him, because his constituents have proven in their discriminatory actions that they consider one drop of black blood as a Black and therefore an African person. Jefferson's formula makes no sense, that is to the laws of America. The only way Jefferson's formula can be legitimized is if the mulatto, quarteroon, octoroon subjects decide to fail-for-white ("pass"). And many of them could not "pass" because of their beautiful dark skin color and superb broad features, fortunately caused by the overpowering substance of their melanin and black blood — no matter how small. *(From this point on, "pass- for-white" will be called "fail-for-white" as explained in the Preliminary Treatise chapter under Defining Ourselves — And Them.).* Notice how Jefferson's formula is a continuation of mixed bloods mating with "pure" whites. According to his formula, of course, if a mixed blood were to mate with the "pure" Black blood, then the offspring is definitely considered Black, African. It is a well documented fact that many mulattos, quadroons, and octoroons were sold into slavery more often than not (Rogers, *Sex and Race*, p. 194 and Harper's Weekly magazine, January 30, 1864).

JEFFERSON AS A MULTITALENTED MULTIRACIAL

Thomas Jefferson is said to have been multitalented. For example, he spoke fluent Greek, and at the age of nineteen, he built himself a flatboat and fantasized about sailing it all the way to Egypt (Brodie, pp. 55-56). The Kemetians (Egyptians — an African people) sailed to the Old World (Americas) in boats thousands of years before Columbus "stumbled upon" this land. Jefferson being the genius that many writers have claimed him to be understood this, and therefore probably knew that it was possible for him to sail his way back to Kemet. Kemet is known as Egypt today.

Jefferson, good at any profession or talent that he set his mind to, won great acclaim in 1776 at the age of thirty-three as author of the Declaration of Independence. This author would like to take this opportunity to note that when a people have brutalized and enslaved another people, whether that brutalization be mental or physical, and forced them to wash for them, cook and feed them, cultivate for them, be sexual with them, and in essence be a SLAVE for them, then the so-called genius isn't really so genius; it's a simple matter of time; it's just that the so-called genius have had plenty of leisure time to think, study, read, play, have good sex, create, and invent. Even though Jefferson advocated independence for the people, he still had in captivity many slaves (political prisoners) at his death. Some free Blacks did own slaves/political prisoners because as mentioned above, many Blacks lived in Old "America" before Columbus was even born. Many of Jefferson's so-called slaves were willed to him from his father, Peter, who is said to be part Black. After Thomas Jefferson's wife's death, Jefferson was also left with her "property," enslaved people, some of them Martha's relatives. Seventeen years after his wife's death, Jefferson became Vice President and later President of the United States.

THE BONAPARTES DURING THE JEFFERSON ERA

It was during Jefferson's first year as Vice President of the United States that Napoleon Bonaparte was reeking havoc in Kemet by blowing off the nose of Her-em-aKhet/the

Sphinx because he noticed that this beautiful female sculpture was built in the image of an African. Napoleon's attitude about race was apparently much different from the attitude of his sister, Pauline Bonaparte, who was reputed to be very fond of Africans. Joel A. Rogers states in some of his literary and historical works that Pauline preferred African men to her own white husband. While in Haiti, she was known to have had an intimate relationship with more than one African man. Thomas Jefferson was known to have had an African mistress. According to Robert Beverley, a colonial leader, "Thomas Jefferson dreamed of the intermingling of blood as a public policy" (Steiner, *The Vanishing White Man*, pp. 185-186). Jefferson didn't just dream; he made his wishes come true with action as a personal policy.

WEBSTER SAID IT

Thomas Jefferson's public service spanned forty interesting years. He was legislator, governor, congressman, diplomat, Secretary of State, Vice President, and President of the United States. He also founded the University of Virginia, which was in 1991 running rampant with drugs, drug dealers, and many drug addicts. Many of the young white males at this University were jailed for their crimes. Jefferson was never jailed for his. Besides becoming President, Jefferson managed his leisure time well enough to also be a successful lawyer, farmer, philosopher, writer, architect, scientist, musician, inventor, slaveholder, and womanizer. Forrest McDonald, from the University of Alabama, stated on a 1991 television special that Thomas Jefferson was a great manipulator. (But, perhaps not as slick as Napoleon Bonaparte. Napoleon "owned" the territory of Louisiana! Jefferson bidded with Napoleon to sell Louisiana to the U.S. for ten million dollars. In 1803, they finally negotiated at fifteen million dollars, and this was only because Napoleon needed the money for war.) Thomas Jefferson, who was not known to show up for Congressional meetings, however, gave magnificent parties and manipulated Congress into getting whatever he wanted when he was President of the United

States. McDonald said that Jefferson was the gentlemen's gentleman — the country squire.

From research collected, it has been determined that Jefferson had affairs with at least three married women, which is engaging in illegal sexual intercourse. He also had children with his Black mistress (a slave/political prisoner named Sally Hemmings) and other African women on his plantation. Some of his mulatto children were sold as slaves, which means that Jefferson also engaged in sexual intercourse for pay. The word that describes the *"actions of Thomas Jefferson"* is *"whore"* (Webster's Dictionary, Second Edition - Deluxe, Simon and Schuster publishers, 1955 & 1983; The American Heritage Dictionary, Dell Publishing Co., Inc., N.Y., 1976. See any well published dictionary). Look it up. Who has ever said that a whore could, should, or would *only* be attributed to a woman? And who is so arrogant as to think that they have the right to make such a decision or determination? A man? The definition and position accept anyone. Pauline Bonaparte would probably be happy to agree.

JEFFERSON'S WIFE

Thomas Jefferson thoroughly enjoyed his life as a single man until he met and fell in love with Martha Wayles Skelton. Thomas Jefferson and Martha were married January 1, 1772 in Williamsburg, Virginia at the Wayles' estate. They were married a short 10 years, 248 days. They had 5 children; 3 died at very young ages. His two daughters, by Martha, who lived into their adult ages were willed all of Jefferson's possessions. Thomas Jefferson had children with Sally Hemmings, his African [Black American] mistress, and these offspring received nothing. Martha died at the young age of 33. Jefferson vowed never to marry again. He did not. But he did have a serious, long thirty-eight year relationship with his wife's half-sister who just happened to have been none other than Sally Hemmings.

GEORGE WASHINGTON

The year 1776 was also an interesting year for another slave-holder and signer of the Declaration of Independence, George Washington. Washington would become the first President of the United States in 1789. *(This will be the same year that the Great Seal of the U.S. will be adopted. This seal would eventually appear on dollar bills and important government documents. One side shows the eagle holding Egyptian olive branches. On the other side is a pyramid with the symbol of the Eye of Heru [or the All Seeing Eye] inside the cap of the pyramid. However, with the cap being detached from the pyramid suggests a nation disconnected, incomplete, and unspiritual.)*

George Washington, in 1776, sold one of his African slaves, Tom, for a keg of molasses and a barrel of liquor. The politically imprisoned brother Tom was sent to Barbados (Rogers, *100 Amazing Facts About the Negro*, pp. 4 & 18; Writings/Letters of George Washington, Vol. II, p. 211, N.Y., 1889). Washington also had several intimate relationships with some of his beautiful African slaves; one of them was impregnated by Washington and gave birth to an African male child (Rogers, *Sex And Race* and *The Five Negro Presidents*, p. 6).

In another interesting 1776 factstory, Washington used to frequent a tavern owned by a black man, Sam Fraunces; he was known as "Black Sam." His daughter, Phoebe ran the tavern. Phoebe was in love with a white Irishman by the name of Hickey. Hickey was one of Washington's body guards and also a spy for Washington's enemies, the British. He was pe titioned to poison Washington. Hickey asked Phoebe to serve Washington a bowl of poison peas. Hickey's hickies and lovemaking must not have binded love and loyalty from Phoebe, because she broke her promise to Hickey and warned Washington not to eat the peas. Washington threw the peas into the front yard of the tavern, and every chicken that ate the peas died. Hickey was hanged. (Rogers, *100 Amazing Facts*, p. 17; *Philadelphia Bulletin*, Feb. 22, 1934, p. 8c; *Evening Star* [Washington, D.C.], Aug. 11, 1916, p. 10).

BENJAMIN BANNEKER

In 1792, Benjamin Banneker, the African-American scientist, a real mathematical genius, inventor and the architect who layed out the District of Columbia (Washington), U.S.A., wrote to Jefferson who was then the Secretary of State, charging Jefferson with violating the moral principles of the Declaration of Independence by owning slaves (*The Banneker Almanac*; Kondo, *A Crash Course in Black History: 150 Important Facts About the Afrikan Peoples*, p. 5). Banneker's mother was a mulatto; Banneker's grandmother was white, his grandfather an African with a Royal background. Banneker's mother married an African. So, Banneker being three-fourths Black, was Black and proud, i.e., African and it showed.

Jefferson was the first president to be inaugurated in Washington, D.C., better known to many African-Americans as Banneker City. Thomas Jefferson was very impressed with the accomplishments of Benjamin Banneker, who made the first time clock in 1754. Jefferson wrote to a friend in Paris, France, stating that: "we now have in the United States a Negro, the son of a black man born in Africa and a black woman born in the United States, who is a very respectable mathematician. I procured him to be employed … in laying out the new Federal city on the Potomac...." Jefferson went on to state that: "I have seen very elegant solutions of geometric problems by him" (Dennis, E., *The Black People of America*, p. 52, 1970). Yet 16 years after the signing of the Declaration of Independence, Jefferson, the so-called "father of democracy" still owned slaves.

While working as a teacher in California, a mulatto/multiracial student (he is Jewish and white) said emphatically, "But, Dr. BaKhufu, that's just the way it was back then!" He was referring to the preconceived notions of most whites that Blacks were inferior, and the fact the many white people thought it their right to own people — so-called slaves. Thomas Jefferson even likened the Black woman to an Orangutan. So this educable-deprived student has been taught well, arrogantly and ignorantly so, by his ancestors and relatives, for both his parents' people owned and dehumanized political prisoners (slaves) in America. Many of these same people now spend much of their time trying to justify what they have done in the past, lie, or forget it. I feel it the duty of African-Americans to never forget and to remind anyone listening, looking, or reading that the biggest holocaust in world history is the death of more than one hundred million (100,000,000) Africans during, and after, the Middle Passage — the En-Slave Trade of Political Prisoners!

ALEXANDER HAMILTON

Thomas Jefferson was also criticized by Alexander Hamilton, who was at the time Secretary of the Treasury. Alexander Hamilton is said to be of African ancestry also (Rogers, *The Five Negro Presidents*, pp. 14 & 15). The two multi-racials initially had a friendly relationship. They disagreed on many issues and soon became fierce political antagonists. Hamilton was 10 years Jefferson's junior. He was just as ambitious and brilliant as Jefferson and was also a lawyer. Hamilton was a military-minded person; Jefferson was not. Jefferson claimed to be appalled by some of the political statements and theoretical suggestions of Hamilton. So started the rivalry between the Republicans and the Federalists (Schlesinger, pp. 65-66). Both men were probably trying to psychologically deal with the secrets of their backgrounds — one trying to be "better" than the other. Many people during this time may not have known or thought about the personal (not political) negative energy between these two men said to have black blood running through their veins. Joel A. Rogers states in his many books that Alexander Hamilton's mother was mixed. In early census, Hamilton's mother's grandfather was listed as having four Black daughters. Alexander Hamilton was West Indian born in the Leeward/Virgin Islands. Native Virgin Islanders said that Hamilton was black. The most positive proof that Hamilton was of African ancestry, says a Rev. Charles D. Martin, is that Hamilton's brother, James, who had the same mother and the same father, migrated to the United States as did his brother Alexander. The difference is that James was treated as a Black person because of his heavily melanized skin color and hair, but Alexander could fail-for-white somewhat. James was a businessman and was once refused a seat in a Broadway riding coach because of his dark complexion. He sued the coach company for serious damages. Rev. Martin stated in an article that Alexander Hamilton was not considered Black only because of the general belief that all West Indians are Black, but because of statements made by eye-witnesses who knew the boy before becoming a man. Rev. Martin said that Hamilton's father was invited by the government to the United States, but his mother was not invited because her skin was too dark. She would cause too much trouble as a colored woman at a white convention. *Beth-Tphillah,* August, 1916 stated that Mrs. Hamilton was "… too typically Negro." The magazine, "The Spokesman", January, 1925, stated that Alexander Hamilton was definitely "of Negro extraction" and that this has never been successfully disputed. "The statesman had Negro blood, his mother being a Negro woman." "When questioned about his birth, Hamilton said, "My blood is as good as those who plume themselves on their ancestry." Joel A. Rogers feels that this is interpreted by some writers as reference to Hamilton's alleged Negro strain. The real truth about Alexander Hamilton's ancestry, Rogers feels, can be found in the earliest and least known pictures of him. Rogers states that these portraits show Hamilton's "negroid features," i.e., hair and mouth (See: *The Five Negro Presidents,* J.A. Rogers, pp. 16 & 18, 1965). See the portrait on page 28. "According to persistent reports, Alexander Hamilton … had some "'Negro Blood."' "'If Hamilton was not a Negro, he certainly brought two Negro sons into the world,"' according to the writings of Professor Maurice R. Davie of Yale University. He goes on to say that "'One married a very light-colored wife; the other married into a white family and lived as white"' (Bennett, *Before the Mayflower,* p. 258). So an African man married a white woman, perhaps trying to get his just due of equal rights. The Declaration of Independence proclaimed equality, but not for slaves. Thomas Jefferson's original draft of the Declaration of Independence contained a clause accusing George III of England of pushing and coercing the slave trade on America. Chase-Riboud, the author of *Sally Hemings,* wrote that Hemings probably had an influence on Jefferson's political thoughts during the writing of the Declaration of Independence. However, Jefferson was forced to strike the clause on slavery from the final draft because it would have obligated the colonists to abolish slavery after gaining their independence" (Kondo, p. 6, 1988. Also see: Dennis, R.E., *The Black People of America*, p. 56, 1970; Whitney, David C., *The American Presidents*, p. 31, 1978; Chase-Riboud, *Sally Heming;* and the U.S. Constitution). Chase-Riboud also feels that it probably hurt Jefferson to have to   strike the clause. The confused Jefferson then turns around and argue for the ignorant position of biological inferiority of Africans. He wrote: "I advance it, therefore, as a suspicion only, that the blacks, whether originally a distinct race, or made distinct by time and circumstance, are inferior to the whites in the endowment both of body and of mind" (Gosset, *Race: the history of an idea in America*, p. 44, and Gould, *The Mismeasure of Man*, p. 32). The man needed help.

A GENIUS YOU SAY?

Having a thinking, but contradictory, two-sided type personality and intellect such as that of Thomas Jefferson's, is what I've termed an "idiogenio." Ingenuity was always creeping into his brain from somewhere. Jefferson was witty and creative, and he did understand that vaccinations and other damaging medications were not a necessity for healthy people who are taught to eat the right foods and to understand the correct use of herbs and herbal formulas. But Jefferson was still fascinated by the research on vaccinations, and "sought to vaccinate his own family" anyway.

An herb, the Twin Leaf (Rheumatism Root), was even named after Thomas Jefferson. It was officially named the *jeffersonia diphylla.* Jefferson was an avid believer in herbs and plants. He tested and grew over one-hundred herbs on his Monticello plantation. He is said to have had a very unique way of growing vegetables also.

Jefferson was so prone to migraine headaches and depression that he would sometimes close himself up in a dark room. His headaches were sometimes so painful that he would fall to the ground, motionless and mourning. Jefferson became a vegetarian late in his life — something he probably should have become earlier. Meat doesn't do the head any good, mentally nor physically. With his knowledge of herbs, I hope that he ordered himself a good, soothing cup of peppermint tea with a little ground ginger to put a health check on both maladies (BaKhufu, notes from: "Herbs: Healing, Health and Spirituality." The exact publication date is pending).

It was during the Jefferson era that a full-blooded African man by the name of John Chavis was petitioned to be a part of a white-man experiment to ascertain as to whether a Black/African man could comprehend and master a college education just as well as a white man. Of course, we know that the Brother "blew them away" with his intelligence, articulation, dignity, and style. Mr. Chavis later ran a school for white people in North Carolina, preparing white girls and boys for college. Chavis was also a preacher, and was forbidden to preach after the "Nat Turner Rebellion For Freedom." So being the true genius that he was and living in such a racist society, he decided to write sermons. These moving sermons were all best sellers. In 1831, at age 68, he journeyed on to be with the ancestors.

Thomas Jefferson continued his foolish thoughts and utterances; he said, "Never yet could I find that a black had uttered a thought above the level of plain narration ... never saw an elementary tract of painting or sculpture." (Kush, *What They Never Told You In History Class,* 1983). Jefferson's stupidity carried over into this generation. While visiting Jefferson's Monticello home in Charlottesville, Virginia, I had the unpleasant experience of listening to a white tour guide regurgitate to us tourists that Jefferson was between a rock and hard place when it came to the question of slavery. She said that he was really against slavery, but was afraid to free his slaves because it would have been like freeing children. She said this with such sincerity. It takes a fool to stand face-to-face with intelligent Black and White people and utter such nonsense without even a wink of, *"It's-just-my-job; I-have-to-say-it."* She went on to give the names of some of the "slaves" that Jefferson did free, but she never mentioned that they were the half-black, half-white relatives of his girlfriend, Sally Hemmings.

In giving Jefferson the benefit of the doubt, maybe he made some of his tasteless, tactless, moronic statements before meeting Banneker. And maybe he never had heard of a John Chavis or anyone like him. It is to Jefferson's misfortune that he had never met such African people, for they certainly existed. Jefferson just couldn't see them even when he was looking at them. Still he went on to say in his letter to his friend in Paris: "... I shall be delighted to see these instances of moral eminence so multiplied as to prove that the want of talents observed in other Negroes is merely the effect of their degraded condition, and not proceeding from any difference in the structure of the parts on which intellect depends" (Dennis, R.E., *The Black People of America*, p. 52, 1970). Jefferson proved this statement to himself by seeing to it that some of his children by African women be educated, especially Sally Hemmings' children. Yet they were not mentioned in his last will and testament.

SALLY HEMMINGS, THOMAS JEFFERSON'S SOUL MATE

As we read about these presidents, we must keep in mind that they behaved like (in most cases) and wished to be considered white men. Thomas Jefferson, with Black blood running through his veins, was a man who apparently liked Africanness for his own reasons whether those reasons be genetics, love or lust. He is said to have fathered several mulatto children. One of his most important and well-known African mistresses was one of his slaves by the name of Sally Hemmings, as mentioned above. Sally Hemmings was the half-sister of Jefferson's deceased wife, Martha. Martha's father was the lover of one of his African political prisoners who became Sally Hemmings' mother. Sally was called "Black Sal" by the political media — An African Venus (Whitney, p. 28; Rogers, *Sex and Race, vol. II*, p. 197; Brodie, p. 345, and Oates' work. See old 1800's newspapers, such as: *the Richmond Examiner, the Richmond Recorder* [Virginia], and *the Boston Gazette* [Mass.] and *the New York Evening Post*). Did Jefferson see Martha in Sally? Perhaps.

In the early 1950's, two professors from North Carolina Central University, Pearl M. Graham and W. Edward

Farrison, Durham, N.C. "subjected the rumors and reports
to modern research methods." Professor Farrison was very
impressed by "'the only absolutely authoritative source of
truth concerning the paternity of Sally Hemmings' children
— from Sally Hemmings herself....'" From the mouth of
Sally Hemmings, she has told her children their biological
background, and they in turn told their children. The "'family history has flowed on through four generations.'" "In
September, 1948, Professor Farrison interviewed three sisters ... each of whom was more than sixty-five years of age,
and who traced their lineage directly to Sally Hemings
through her daughter Harriet." Harriet Hemings was born
in May of 1801, and these sisters had been told that Harriet's
father was Thomas Jefferson. These three old sisters looked
very white, according to Professor Farrison. The other
research scholar, Pearl M. Graham has proven that Sally
Hemings bore Thomas Jefferson "'at least four children,
possibly six.'" Sally and her children by Thomas Jefferson
are listed in his farm book as: Hemings, Sally, 1773; Beverly,
1798; Harriet, 1801; Madison, January, 1805; and Eston, May,
1808. Ms. Graham also interviewed Sally Hemings' great-
granddaughter. Graham wrote that "'These ladies descent ...
is further substantiated by the Mendelian Law of Heredity.'"
Ms. Graham also said that she was shown a daguerreo-type
of Ms. Kenney — Harriet Hemings' daughter — which
resembles many of the painted pictures of Jefferson himself
and that this daguerreo-type could easily be mistaken for
Jefferson himself — during his middle years. A daguerreo-
type is an original photograph processed by early American
methods on a light sensitive metal plate and developed by
mercury vapor. Graham went on to state that Jefferson's
hair was a sandy red color, and many of his African descendants had this same type and color of hair. Gertrude Harriet
(Kenney) Watson was nicknamed "Jefferson Hair Gertie"
because her hair was so much like ancestor Jefferson's hair
(Bennett, pp. 257-258).

THE PRICE OF FREEDOM

A white man by the name of A.M. Ross tells of the many
slave sales that he witnessed and the obscene examinations

of female slaves by ignorant white men. Ross stated that many of these women were sent to houses of prostitution as sources of income to white people. On one slave auctioning block that Ross witnessed was the mulatto daughters of Thomas Jefferson. Ross said that Thomas Jefferson put in his will that his slave offspring be freed, but it is well documented that many of Jefferson's mulatto slave children were sold before his death, and white visitors to his home have stated that many of them looked just like Jefferson (References: Rogers, *Sex and Race* & *Nature Knows No Color Line*). Two of his mulatto daughters were taken from Virginia to New Orleans after Jefferson's death and sold in the slave market for $1,500 each. They were educated, very light complexioned, with long hair and blue eyes. The youngest daughter escaped from her so-called master and killed herself by drowning rather than face the type of life her older sister unfortunately had to face (*The Liberator*, vol. VIII, p. 152, Sept. 21, 1838, Rogers, *Sex and Race*, vol. II, p. 197). If there's black blood running through your veins, in American society (and most others), you're considered black, no matter how many mathematical formulas Jefferson concocted. Science, biology and genetics attest to black gene dominance.

Thomas Jefferson was openly attacked by the media and politicians of his time for having an intimate relationship with Sally Hemmings. Visitors to America had liberal, open conversations about Jefferson's black children (Rogers, *Sex and Race*, vol. II, p. 221). Captain Marryat wrote, "It is a well-known fact that a considerable portion of Mr. Jefferson's slaves were his own children" (Marryat, F., *Dairy in America*, vol. l, p. 251, 1839 and *Social History of the American Family*, vol. II, p. 300, Calhoun, A.W., Cleveland, Ohio, 1918). Historian Alf Mapp states that these children were the children of some of Jefferson's other male relatives. Sally Hemings had no reason to lie to her children about who their father was, but it is not doubted that some of the other politically imprisoned children running around the plantation were the children of some of Jefferson's male relatives as well as Thomas Jefferson's. Much of the history on Jefferson is written as if he were never sexually intimate with anyone after the death of his wife. Sally Hemmings was Jefferson's intimate soul mate for a long 38 years. Ms. Hemmings was like the dark, beautiful mistress of Monticello; although one who is not of the African persuasion would have to look twice to see that either Jefferson or Sally was graced with Black Blood. Research shows that Jefferson never had a *serious* relationship with any other woman during his relationship with Hemmings. However, Jefferson wasn't always so true-blue. Although Jefferson had his days of don-juaning, literature attest to his love for Sally Hemmings. Jefferson never freed her. This could have been his way of keeping Sally safe under his guarded and protective personal attention. Two years after his death, the beautiful 53 (some say 57) year old Hemmings was auctioned off as one of his Monticello possessions for a mere $50. You see, Jefferson died broke. He said that it was one of the worst feelings to have during his dying days. He was embarrassed to tell friends and relatives that if they stayed too long at Monticello, it would be a burden on his household account. He was forced to sell his cherished personal library to Congress for $24,000 in order to have some cash and to run his home as he was accustomed. His library, of course, became the Library of Congress. Chase-Riboud states many true accounts in her fictional account of the Sally Hemmings and Thomas Jefferson affair. She states in her book, *Sally Hemings,* that the census bureau listed Sally Hemmings as white possibly in order to protect Jefferson's honor as a *white* man. If only the Census Bureau knew the many secrets of Thomas Jefferson. Perhaps they did know.

Madison, Thomas Jefferson's and Sally Hemmings' mulatto son, resided in Washington, D.C. Jefferson, however, according to his mathematical formula, would label his son a quarteroon. Madison Hemmings was a lawyer and an accomplished violinist (Hemings, Madison, "Pike County [Ohio] Republican", 1873; Rogers, *Sex and Race*, vol. II, pp. 221-222, 1965; Brodie, F., p. 438). Frederick Douglass' son was also a violinist. His violin still sits on top of the piano in the living room of the Frederick Douglass home in Southeast Washington, D.C. (See the Lincoln chapter for more information on Frederick Douglass [Douglass was Mulatto — having a white father and Black mother]. Madison Hemmings tells the story of his sister, also Thomas Jefferson's child, saying that, "[Harriet] married a white man

… in Washington City….She raised a family of children, and so far as I know they were never suspected of being tainted with African blood in the community where she lived or lives….She thought it to her interest…to assume the role of a white woman…." (Graham, Pearl, *"Thomas Jefferson and Sally Hemings, "Journal of Negro History*, XLIV, 1961, pp. 89-103). Harriet was easily able to fail-for-white, even though both of her parents had African blood. Please note how Mr. Hemings states their family blood as being African. It is sad that today so many young Black people, young and old "try" to disassociate themselves from their Africanness — their wonderful African heritage. Much of this denial is due to the continuous brainwashing in our educational system and the society in general. There are not enough parents taking control of their children's educational lives. Private schools and after school programs are now essential. It is pertinent that we teach our children the truth. There will be a few embarrassments, but many, many proud accomplishments if we simply take control of our own lives and destiny.

JACOB AND OTHER AFRICANS

"Give me liberty, or give me death's," Patrick Henry, had a son by one of his favorite African (Black American) women. The couple named their son Melancton (Bennett, p. 258; Fairbank, C., *How the Way was Prepared*, p. 196, Chicago, 1890, and Rogers, *Sex and Race*, vol. II, p. 222). Melancton? An athlete with melanin? He probably was. He was said to be very intelligent (melanin) and taken good care of by his father. Information such as this is documented in this book to show and update once again, that to have presidents with black blood running through their veins is not so astounding. Benjamin "Electricity" Franklin, also one of the signers of the Declaration of Independence, is well-known for his liaisons with older women and with beautiful African women (Ross, S. *Fall From Grace*, pp. 7-11, 1988, and Rogers, *Sex and Race*, Vol. II, p. 221). It is not felt that the appropriate word to use for Ben's sexual encounters with the African women can be called affairs. History shows that many women during the slave era were actually raped, sometimes brutally. Although many may not have fought the rapist off, their submissiveness was due to their enslavement as political prisoners and could be considered a survival tactic. But lest we forget, it must again be pointed out that many proud African women and men did fight for their rights and dignity in these slave sheds. Many died, but some lived through it. So-called masters with broken necks were found in many instances in slave history. One piece of interesting ourstory was found in *Judicial Cases Concerning American Slavery and the Negro*, Tennessee, 1842:

> Jacob (an enslaved person) was indicted for the murder of his master, Robert Bradford. The slaves were supposed to be working, but Jacob was playing around, not working very hard. Bradford threatened to whip Jacob. Jacob told Bradford that he was as tired of him as he was of him. Bradford attempted to whip Jacob. Jacob took the whip from Bradford, broke it into pieces and ran. In a day or so, Jacob returned. Bradford ordered Jacob to get a rope. Bradford told Jacob that he would be tied and whipped. Jacob refused. Jacob left after being given food and clothing from Bradford, because Bradford said that he did not want Jacob stealing from the neighbors. Bradford then went and got his brother Frederick; they planned to whip Jacob when Jacob returned the next day. Of course, Jacob wasn't one to carry weapons, but he had prepared a large butcher knife; he hid it in his clothing. The next day when the two brothers proceeded to beat Jacob with a stick given to them by a *slave*, the two white men seized Jacob by the collar. Frederick gave Jacob two hard blows to the head. Jacob told the brothers that they would have to kill him because he was fighting back! The two whites jumped on Jacob's back. He threw both off with little effort. He took out his knife and stabbed Robert to death. Once again, he ran ... because "the law cannot recognize the violence of the master as a legitimate cause of provocation" from a so-called slave.
>
>   (Revised from pp. 516-517 of *JCCASN*)

THE JEFFERSON PLAN

Thomas Jefferson stated that slavery was "barbarous, cruel, and shameful." "In the late 1770s Jefferson came up with a plan for the eventual resettlement to Africa of all children born to slaves; they could be replaced, he said, by free white colonists from Europe. The scheme was quickly rejected by Jefferson's fellow planters" (Schlesinger, p. 44). Jefferson proposed that young slaves be educated. He proposed that when the men became 21 and the women became 18 that they be given tools, cows, seeds, *and guns!* He said that they should be set free, but taken back to Africa. Was this because he didn't want them around, or was it because he felt that a people should be in their own cultural environment? (Jefferson is not the only President who wanted Blacks sent back to Africa; Abraham Lincoln, one of the six black presidents, made the same proposal almost 100 years later. See Chapter 3.) But with an afterthought, Jefferson stated that if the slaves were given their freedom, they would still harbor much anger, and would eventually turn on white people. Abraham Lincoln made a similar statement. With all Jefferson's talk and plans, he would later have 200 slaves of his own that he "inherited" from his and his wife's parents. He's known to be a so-called good master, but was criticized for not freeing his slaves (Adler, p. 13). Naturally, Jefferson was criticized by many blacks during this time for not making a positive effort toward freedom for Africans in America.

Run Away from the subscriber in Albermarle the advertisement stated in a Virginia newspaper. "A Mulatto (part white) slave called Sandy. The advertiser, who offered a reward for the return of the 'artful' and 'knavish' Sandy" was none other than Thomas Jefferson.
Schlesinger, p.45, 1986

Jefferson had affairs with many African slaveheld, politically imprisoned, women. These affairs took place before and after the death of his wife. She begged him to stop his carousing, but to no avail. Jefferson is also known to have had affairs with two white women who were married. One of these women's husband was a friend of Jefferson's. The other husband was an acquaintance of Jefferson's and bisexual.

Jefferson is said to have been a very private man. He kept 18,000 letters that he wrote, and filed 25,000 that he received. He destroyed all correspondence that he may have had with his wife, Martha — and his mother. Research, analytical assessments, and psycho-historical theory tends toward the notion that Jefferson was more than likely aware of his father's background, but perhaps never really asked anyone about it. Little is known about Jefferson's marital life, except that he supposedly adored and loved his wife very much. It is speculated that his intimacies with other women were separate from his love for his wife. It is here theorized that if he could separate himself and make himself white and black; then it is also possible that he could also mentally separate and make himself married and single. Jefferson's wife, Martha, died September 6, 1782 — 10 years after their marriage.

MUCKRACKERS AND MUDSLINGERS

From Shelly Ross' book, *Fall From Grace* (1988), she states that the media press was pretty lenient on Jefferson until 1802 when an old acquaintance and ally of Jefferson's — against Alexander Hamilton — became disloyal and eventually turned on Jefferson. This man's name was James Callender, an alcoholic muckracker who was very accurate in his published slandering of public figures. This man fled from Scotland to America in 1793 on sedition charges which derived from his vicious, but true, attacks against the British government. There is much documented proof that many criminals from Europe were shipped to America.

Callender criticized John Adams when he was the president of the United States, calling Adams "weak, ignorant, ferocious, and deceitful." Thomas Jefferson, then the vice president *and* an Adams opponent, gave Callender high marks for such negative publicity, and told Callender that, "Such papers cannot fail to produce the best efforts." However, Callender was still arrested for violation of the 1798 Sedition Act, and Jefferson defended Callender, providing a strong defense for freedom of speech. They lost. An anti-Jefferson judge found Callender guilty. Later when Mr. Jefferson became President of the United States, he fired this judge, and granted Callender his freedom. This is more than he did for his own mulatto children; Jefferson could not see it fit (or appropriate for a "white" man) to legally free his own children until after he was dead. Some of Jefferson's children ran for their freedom — within his eyesight; he sometimes smiled, said nothing and did nothing. Many of the Jefferson children ran and eventually failed-for-white.

Jefferson's trouble started when Callender wanted a job in the White House. When he was refused a job, he decided to take revenge. Sex scandals became Callender's specialty, and he was good at his work. He uncovered an affair that Jefferson started in 1768 with a married woman by the name of Betsey Walker. Betsey was the wife of one of Jefferson's closest friends, John Walker; Jefferson was an usher at their wedding. This seduction went on for years.

John Walker got word of the affair. He later wrote to a friend (an enemy of Jefferson's) stating that at a neighbor's overnight gathering, when the women retired for bed, Jefferson pretended to be ill, and went to bed also. But Jefferson did not go to his own bed; he went the Betsy's bed with me [John Walker] in the house, in close proximity!

JEFFERSON'S WHITE WOMEN

According to CNN News reporter, Andrea Reynolds, when she interviewed Saddam Hussein, she asked him if he had a mistress and an illegitimate child. He answered her indirectly that, "compared to some of your U.S. Presidents, I'm a very virtuous man" (*Geraldo* Talk Show [U.S.A.], "Portrait of a Madman," March 1, 1991).

Thomas Jefferson's virtue was brutally attacked in *the New York Evening Post* ("The Betsy Walker Affair") on April 5, 1805. Jefferson was called an outcast of America. He admitted his guilt to friends that he had an affair with a white woman named Betsy Walker during the summer of 1769. History shows that these old Americans did not necessarily consider Jefferson an outcast because of an affair (many of them were doing the same thing), but probably more because of the publicity surrounding his ancestral background and later his love affair with Sally Hemmings. These people did not label George Washington an outcast (he seduced his next door neighbor's wife, and had affairs with several of his female political prisoners [slaves]). They did not call Benjamin "Electricity" Franklin an outcast, who seduced several older women, and had affairs with many beautiful African slave women (Rogers, *Sex and Race*, vol. II, p. 221, and Ross, *Fall From Grace*, pp. 12-17.) And even in these old, conservative days, none of these men were subjected to a Government/Congress/Senate Hearing! They should have been, because these African women were sexually harrassed. Well, times change, and certain people have to be used as examples.

A few years before Jefferson became minister to France, thousands of Africans were in the Revolutionary War. Most of these Africans were escaped slaves (ex-political prisoners) whom the British had promised their freedom after this war. In 1783, many of these Africans were shipped to Nova Scotia; they settled a Black town. Many slaves in New York City took advantage of this cruise opportunity and boarded ship in order to get away from the brutality of America. Many of these same Africans later settled in Sierra Leone, West Africa.

Before Jefferson became President, while serving as minister to France, he had another affair, with another married white woman. Her name was Maria Cosway. She was 27 years old with blond hair, blue eyes, and an Italian accent. Thomas Jefferson is said to have fallen in love with her as soon as he laid his eyes on her. Maria was talented, and Jefferson loved her all the more for this. She was introduced to high class society by none other than the sexy Angelica Church, the sister-in-law *and* lover of Alexander Hamilton.

For Jefferson, at age 43 and thinking that all his emotional feelings were buried with his wife, discovered that he had very strong emotions for this young woman. Jefferson disregarded the presence of her bisexual husband, Richard. Thomas and Maria shared many beautiful moments and afternoons together. Even Richard began to encourage the relationship. Whenever Jefferson visited the couple in their home, Richard would always leave Maria and Jefferson alone. These occasions were probably good times for Richard's own liaisons. At the time, neither Jefferson nor Maria were aware of Richard's bisexuality.

In September, 1786, it was time for the Cosway's to return to London. Jefferson expressed that he felt "more dead than alive." He wrote 12 pages of love to Maria called: *My Head and My Heart* (This poem can be found in Helen D. Bullock's book, *My Head and My Heart*, N.Y., 1945 and other more up-to-date literature on Jefferson).

In August, 1787 Maria returned to Paris, France. She returned to visit Jefferson for a 4 month period, and her husband was not with her. Things had changed. On December 8th when she left Paris to return to London, she stood Jefferson up for their farewell breakfast. They never saw each again, but they did continue to write each other for the rest of their lives.

John Callender, the muckracker, claimed that the reason the romance took a downfall was because Jefferson had begun that same summer to have an affair with a young seventeen year mulatto (Black American) female, Sally Hemmings. Hemmings was the mother of six of Jefferson's mulatto children. Sally went along on this trip to help Jefferson care for his daughter by Martha. As mentioned, Sally Hemmings was the half sister of Jefferson's wife, Martha Wayles Jefferson. Martha's father had taken an African woman named Betty as his mistress after the death of his third wife. They had six children; Sally was one of these children, and she was willed to Martha after her father's death (Ross, S., pp. 35-41, and Hemings, Madison, "Pike County [Ohio] Republican", 1873). At no time during his lifetime did Thomas Jefferson divulge any useful information on the Sally Hemmings subject nor his ancestry.

In 1808, at the ripe old age of 65 before leaving his presidential post, Jefferson did have a brief bed affair, while Sally Hemmings dutifully cared for their newborn baby, Eston. This affair was with the fourth President of the United States' wife. James Madison was a good friend of Jefferson's — perhaps too good. Madison admired and respected Jefferson. Madison was a sickly man who stood a short 5'4 1/2" and weighed only 99 pounds. He was shy and insecure, especially when it came to love and women. He did, however, luck up and marry a beautiful, sexy woman named Dolley.

Madison adored his wife, and perhaps wanted to satisfy her no matter what it took. Knowing of Jefferson's sexual prowess, James Madison offered Jefferson his wife in return for political favors. Jefferson, being the dutiful gentleman, took Madison up on his offer and had a mutual seduction session (or more) with Madison's very well-endowed 39 year old wife. She was the same age as Sally Hemmings, so old Jefferson was probably just looking for a little white action here *connecting* with his other Self.

DECLARATION OF DEMISE

Twenty-six years after Thomas Jefferson's death, Frederick Douglass said in a 4th of July speech for Africans:

> What, to the American slave, is your 4th of July? I answer; a day that reveals to him, more than all other days in the year, the gross injustice and cruelty to which he is the constant victim. To him, your celebration is a sham; your boasted liberty, an unholy license; your national greatness, swelling vanity; your sounds of rejoicing are empty and heartless; your denunciation of tyrants, brass fronted impudence; your shouts of liberty and equality, hollow mockery; your prayers and hymns, your sermons and thanksgivings, with all your religious parade and solemnity, are, to him, mere bombast, fraud, deception, impiety, and hypocrisy — a thin veil to cover up crimes which could disgrace a nation of savages.

Speech at Rochester, New York, July 5, 1852

Thomas Jefferson died on Independence Day, July 4th 1826, exactly fifty years after his writing of the Declaration of Independence — a declaration of false claims, written by a slaveholder. With everything about Jefferson's life said and done, his mulatto father, Peter Jefferson, would still be proud of his son. Thomas did do many interesting things during his lifetime, and he aspired to satisfy his father.

1789 Jean Antoine Houdon's bust of **Thomas Jefferson** (*Paris*).

Maria Cosway, Thomas Jefferson's girlfriend.

Alexander Hamilton, drawn from life, although J. A. Rogers contends that Hamilton was darker than this picture shows. Rogers also suggests that we note Hamilton's *"wool-ish hair."*

Monticello, Sally Hemmings' and **Thomas Jefferson's** home.

Ancient America (African head found in San Lorenzo before Columbus).

ANDREW JACKSON

7th President U.S.A.

Andrew Jackson was the 7th President of the United States. He served as president from March 4, 1829 - March 3, 1837. Andrew Jackson said that his position as President of the United States was "a situation of dignified slavery." (Medved, M., *The Shadow Presidents*, p. 12, 1979).

BIRTH QUESTIONS

Andrew Jackson was born March 15, 1767 on the settlement of old Warhaw, the border of North and South Carolina. His mother and father were said to have been very poor immigrants from Ireland. Their birthdates are not known. Jackson was the third child in a family of three children.

Some historical documents state that Andrew Jackson, Senior was not the biological father of Andrew Jackson. Jackson's supposed father, Andrew Jackson, Sr. died before Jackson was born and is said to have been conceived after the senior's death. It is said that the father of Andrew Jackson was an African slave (Rogers, J.A., *The Five Negro Presidents*, p. 6, 1965). Rogers also writes that the Virginia Magazine of History, vol. 29, p. 191, says that Andrew Jackson was the son of a white female who had intermarried with a Black man and that Jackson's oldest brother had been sold into slavery in Carolina. Rogers points out that what gives an air of truth to this was that Jackson, Sr. died before Andrew was born, and that his widow went to live on her sister's farm, Mrs. William Crawford, where there were many male African slaves (or political prisoners) and that one of these men was the father of Andrew Jackson. Jackson felt defenseless when the tabloids "attacked" his ancestry. One newspaper article read: "General Jackson's mother was a *common prostitute* ... brought to this country by the British soldiers! She afterward married a *mulatto man*, with whom she had several children, of which number General Jackson is one!!!" (Remini, Robert, *Andrew Jackson*, p. 13, 1966; Coyle,

David C., *Ordeal of the Presidency*, p. 127, 1960; Rogers, Joel A., *The Five Negro Presidents*, p 6, 1965; Jacobson, D., "Affairs of Dame Rumor," p. 190, 1943; the "Telegraph", Jan. 26, Feb. 16, Mar. 13, May 20, July 2 & 28, 1828, and the "National Journal" [a Washington publication], Sept., 4, 1828 & June 16, 1827).

In David Whitney's book: *The American Presidents*, it is stated that Andrew Jackson, Sr. died only a few days before Andrew's birth. Coit (*Andrew Jackson*, p. 2, 1965) states that Jackson, Sr. died a few days after the younger Jackson was born, and Schlesinger, *Jackson*, p. 23, states that Andrew Jackson's father died one month before his birth. The literature on this subject is very scarce giving credence to wonder and speculation. There isn't even a specific day or date as to when Jackson, Sr. died, and Andrew Jackson did have many living relatives who should have known. The reader should note that most of Andrew Jackson's known relatives were from his maternal side.

YOUTH

During Jackson's young years on the farm with his mother and brother, Jackson is said to remember days when he would read newspapers to the whole community. Some historians state that Jackson especially remembered reading the words of Thomas Jefferson's "Declaration of Independence" when a copy of that document first reached Waxhaw in the summer of 1776. Andrew Jackson was 9 years old at the time (Whitney, p. 67). Remini states in his book that this is a nice story, but very untrue. He said that some overzealous historian added this to his writings to enhance the tales of Jackson's life story (p. 189). Nonetheless, neither of these mulattos (Jefferson nor Jackson) realized that he would one day be the President of the United States.

Jackson grew up a poorly educated orphan, but he was a fast, non-traditional learner, who fought as a boy-militiaman in the Revolutionary War. He also squandered away a small inheritance as a teenager then finally settled down enough to become a lawyer.

One of the main psychological forces in Jackson's life was his unmitigated hate for the British. His mother used to tell horror stories to Jackson and his brothers about the suffering the family endured under British rule in Ireland. In the spring of 1780 during the American Revolution, these feelings of hate and revenge were escalated. Jackson had once refused to polish a British soldiers boots; the soldier attacked Andrew Jackson with a sword. Jackson raised his hand so that the sword would not cut his face; his hand was slashed to the bone. He was to carry these mental and physical scars with him for the rest of his life. Andrew was thirteen (Remini, p. 18) or maybe twelve at the time.

His brother Hugh died an eighteen year old soldier in 1780 from heat exhaustion; his brother Robert died the same year at age 15 from a very high fever; Jackson's mother died in 1781 of cholera (Remini, p. 19; Schlesinger, p. 26). Her last words to Andrew, before she left to care for American soldiers were, "None will respect you more than you respect yourself; avoid quarrels as long as you can ... but sustain your manhood always....The law offers no remedy for such outrages that can satisfy the feelings of a true man" (Schlesinger, p. 26). As stated earlier, historian Joel A. Rogers mentions in his writing that one of Andrew Jackson's brothers was sold into slavery (*The Five Negro Presidents*, p. 6). Another account of the "brother sold into slavery" story can be found in David C. Coyle's, *Ordeal of the Presidency*, p. 127, 1960. The research deduced on this particular subject has not corresponded with this particular story as being fact. But with the many inclusions and exclusions in history, who knows, it could possibly be true.

LAWYER

Seven years after the death of his mother (1787), Andrew Jackson was admitted to the bar to practice law in Salisbury, North Carolina. During his student years, he was said to be absolutely wild. Many Salisbury residents were shocked years later when they heard that this barbaric-type boy was running for the presidency of the United States. One Salisbury woman said, "Well, if Andrew Jackson can be President, anybody can!" (Remini, p. 23 and Coit, p. 9).

Attorney Andrew Jackson moved to Nashville, Tennessee in 1788. He was a boarder in the home of a socially prominent widow by the name of Mrs. Rachel Stockley Donelson. Mrs. Stockley Donelson had a married daughter by the name of Rachel Donelson Robards. She was married to an insanely jealous lawyer by the name of Lewis Robards. Andrew Jackson fell in love with this married woman immediately. Different from Thomas Jefferson and his married women relationships, Andrew Jackson would eventually marry Rachel.

A ROUGH MARRIAGE

Andrew Jackson had a tough enough childhood and teenage life without the headache of what was to come after he was finally married at age 24 to the feisty, intelligent lady, Rachel Donelson, minus the Robards. They were married in 1791.

Rachel, at age 18, had married Lewis Robards who was from a so-called good family. It was later discovered that Robards was mentally ill (Remini, p. 190, #3). After Rachel and Lewis were married, Lewis would sometimes go into insane rages, accusing Rachel of flirting with men, when she really had not. In one case she had only offered some man a glass of water. But Rachel was flirtatious on some occasions. Robards' insaneness got to be too much for Rachel. She thought it best to leave him for her own sanity and good. She left Robards more than once; she always went back to him. By age 23, she finally left him for good; she was also dating Attorney Andrew Jackson by this time. She finally divorced Lewis Robards, so Rachel and Jackson thought.

After Rachel and Jackson were married, they discovered three years later that Robards never filed the divorce papers; the papers were null and void. It is rather strange that Jackson who was now a lawyer himself did not check into the detailed technical legalities of his fiance/wife's divorce papers — especially since the mental faculties of her husband/ex-husband were questionable. Robards then sued Rachel for divorce, stating that she was still his wife, and saying that Rachel was a prostitute, sleeping with another man. This upset the Jacksons very much. Andrew Jackson stated that he would not marry Rachel again just to appease society, because in his eyes, he and Rachel were really married, and he loved her. But he finally consented, and they had another wedding, yet smaller than the first. From this point on, the media had a field day with the Jacksons.

BLACK BLOOD

During the Jackson years, tabloids were widespread about Jackson's black blood, and his wife, the prostitute. They said that Andrew Jackson had stolen another man's wife directly from his bosom. The Jackson's true friends, and Rachel's family knew better. They knew that Robards was an insanely jealous man who himself had committed adultery while still married to Rachel. Robards' affair was with one of his political imprisoned African/Black female slaves. Old his-story literature indicates that this type of behavior for white males was not a social taboo; it was not considered rape or adulterous. Many white women went into jealous rages, but they were not in positions to do anything else.

MURDERERS

In May of 1805, the now socially prominent Andrew Jackson brought into the Jackson's prosperous home the distinguished murderer and former Vice President of the United States, Aaron Burr. Burr slayed mulatto Alexander Hamilton in 1804. Afterwards, Burr was wined and dined in many socially elite settings as a hero for killing Alexander Hamilton. Westerners held duels in high esteem; they did not hold Hamilton as high (Coit, *Andrew Jackson,* p. 26, 1965; Remini, *Andrew Jackson,* p. 47, 1966; Schlesinger, p. 43, 1986). It seems that it was appropriate conduct to invite Burr-types into the Jackson home, since Jackson is destined to be such a murderer himself. The years between 1812-1817, Jackson will slaughter and kill many Indians and Africans. One year (1806) after Burr's social visit to the Jackson home, Jackson also killed a man. His name was Charles Dickinson. It is said that Dickinson had made verbal slurs about his beloved Rachel and her alleged prostitutism (Coit, pp. 24-25, 1965 and Kane, *Facts About the Presidents,* p. 55). Jackson would later defend a political friend whose wife was being dishonored in the media also.

In 1815 when the British and the Americans were fighting on the west bank of the Rodriquez Canal, 2,057 British soldiers lay dead and only 13 Americans; all of the "Americans" were Black. These African men fighting for Americans, barely free, of course were put on the front line. Jackson said, of these African men that they "were so anxious for glory that they could not be prevented from advancing over our breast works and exposing themselves. They fought like desperadoes..." (Remini, p. 72). With the shackles of slavery in mind, it is a possibility that some of these brothers may have gone overboard in their efforts to appease the "master," and it is also just as equally a grand possibility that while these men fought on the front line, the white soldiers stood by laughing and watching them die. For men such as these Blacks, all one white man had to do was yell, "Get down!" But, living in an America such as it was then, many of these Black men probably knew exactly what they were doing; it was just like jumping over the ship rails during the Middle Passage. But no matter what, Jackson still thought them stupid, and understood perfectly well why these African men might do such a thing ... trying to please "massa." Please readers do note that the Webster dictionary defines a desperadoe as a bold and reckless CRIMINAL! Why did Jackson say that these men fought like desperadoes? But during the War of 1812, some Africans had fought so superbly and gallantly that Jackson could not help but commend them.

DANIEL WEBSTER

Another note: Daniel Webster, who was a Statesman, and an acquaintance of Jefferson's and Jackson's, was also known to have had black blood. A white acquaintance of Daniel Webster's before Webster became famous saw Daniel Webster one day and exclaimed "What....that little black stable-boy that once brought me the horses?" (Rogers, *Nature Knows No Color Line*, p. 235 and Harvey, P., *Reminiscences of Daniel Webster*, p. 77, 1882). Daniel Webster was known as "Black Dan." It is said that Webster was so dark that a General Butler in a letter to Stanton, who was Secretary of War, likened Webster to the Black race. In the

September, 1862 letter to Stanton, Butler wrote: "I shall have within a few days a Regiment 1000 strong of Native Guards, colored, the darkest of whom will be about the complexion of the late Mr. Webster." (Rogers, *Your History*, p. 79).

A RAGE IN JACKSON

Andrew Jackson was not a fan of George Washington. He said that George Washington should be impeached for signing a treaty with England (Coit, p. 16). Jackson was a man who hated the British, Indians, blacks, whites, and this research and psycho-history shows that he seemed to have hated himself to a certain degree. It can be deduced from the literature, however, that Jackson did love his wife, Rachel. With his biological family gone, her love and her family were very much needed to keep him as mentally stable as possible. He is said to have loved children — in his "normal" frame of mind. Jackson's frame of mind was not only questioned by John Adams, but also by Thomas Jefferson.

Although Jackson and Jefferson had their differences, they both still had to make their public appearances. In the Spring of 1815, Thomas Jefferson was a guest at Jackson's Hermitage home. Jefferson was now 72 years of age and travelled all the way from his Monticello home, of which he shared with his African mistress, Sally Hemmings, to join in the tribute to the slaughter hero. When Jefferson was asked to give a toast to Jackson, he said, "Honor and gratitude to those who have filled the measure of their country's honor." (Remini, p. 77). From the political history gathered about Jefferson's feelings toward Jackson, the statement Jefferson made bordered toward sarcasm. Several years before this occasion, these two men had met at a conference. Jefferson was then Vice-President of the United States and was presiding over a federal government conference. Jefferson noted that every time Jackson would rise to speak, "Jackson would become so choked with rage he could not say one word." Thomas Jefferson decided that the young Senator Jackson was a passionate and "dangerous" person (Coit, p. 21). Forrest McDonald remarked on a recent television special (1991) that Jackson sought the approval of the rebel, the common man.

LINCOYER

In 1813, Jackson had savagely assaulted another community of Indians, burning villages, plundering their food — and killing. He systematically slaughtered these Indians in Talluschatches. After this horrible massacre, Jackson found a dead Indian mother still clutching her baby. He asked some sad, hurt Indian women to take the child. Remini tells the story like this:

> "'All of his relations are dead,' they [the Indian women] said, 'kill him too.' The General [Jackson] rejected this solution and afterward took the boy, named Lincoyer, back to the Hermitage and provided him with every advantage, including a good education'" (p. 58).

Any reader can conclude from this statement how some historians write to make white political "criminals" sound like the nicest, kindest, most honorable people in the world. Historical biographer, Margaret Coit goes further by stating that Jackson was "tender and gentle." Look and listen to the statement: "General *rejected* this solution." A white supremist personality: *"I can't do anything you ask; who do you think you are?"* These feeling women knew how to keep the child alive — at least a little longer. They were mourning their own and probably thought that a "savage" like Jackson was bound to kill them in a few moments anyway. Historian Robert V. Remini stated that, "When Andrew Jackson hated, it often became grand passion. He could resort to petty and vindictive acts to nurture his hatred and keep it bright and strong and ferocious" (Schlesinger, *Andrew Jackson*, p. 26). Lincoyer lived a short life of 17 years. It's difficult to stay alive living among your enemy. Even the youngest of children can feel it. Thomas Jefferson felt the same — living with a mother who held an attitude of superiority toward her own son. Lincoyer died of tuberculosis (Remini, p. 58) and perhaps mental anguish. Jackson made a statement during one of his political speeches in reference to Indians: "What good man would prefer a country covered with forests, and ranged by a few thousand savages ..." (Steiner, p. 117). Did he really feel any differently toward Lincoyer?

BLACKS AND INDIANS

During this time, it bothered the "Americans" (white people such as the ones who were honoring Jackson for wild massacres) that Indians revolted against white people taking their land by raiding white settlements in the United States. This commonsense approach that the Indians were taking was also attracting runaway slaves (ex-political prisoners in America who had freed themselves) from the whole southern region. "Hanging tough" with the Indians (many of whom were and are black themselves) was a haven for these Africans. In fact, a band of ex-slaves (white historians call them fugitive slaves) from South Carolina and Georgia seized a fort on the Apalachicola River in northern Florida and encouraged other brothers and sisters (escaped political prisoners) to join them. Since this new Black fort "menanced" all slaveholders, white Americans felt that the fort had to be wiped out. Jackson gave the "go-ahead" to blow up the fort. He killed 270 African men, women, and children, i.e., Africans in America, African-Americans or Blacks; these people were your ancestors. These were Black people trying to live free in America. Have you ever asked yourself what African children learn in "school" about Andrew Jackson. Are they given this information? Or is it in the past, over and done — unimportant? (For more information on the massacre of these 270 Black people see: Remini, *Andrew Jackson,* p. 78, 1966 and other Jackson historical documents and history books.) It was around this time that the "Star-Spangled Banner" was written. How quaint.

Whites continued to migrate to the coastal region, and there were repeated instances of forceable Indian removal from their own lands. In revenge, the Indians attacked white settlements then fled to Florida for safety. President James Monroe thought that by purchasing Florida from Spain it would solve this problem. But his solution was rejected.

In 1817 a Scottish trader by the name of Alexander Arbuthnot arrived in Florida to trade with the Indians.

Remini stated in his book that, "Arbuthnot was one of those rare white men who genuinely sympathized with the Indians and tried to help them." Later in the same year, another Britisher arrived in Florida; he was Robert Ambrister. He too was an Indian sympathizer. He, like Arbuthnot, understood that no one should brutally take away what belongs to someone else. The difference in these two men was that the latter suggested to the Indians that they fight the Americans. This was not news to the Indians. White historians state in their writings that when Andrew Jackson was around, the Indians would tremble and perish where they stood. This is questionable. Jackson gave permission to fire bomb these Indians' fort. The Indians were forewarned by Arbuthnot, so when the Americans arrived, the Indians had left. Ambrister, not knowing what was going on, stumbled into the Indian camp and saw that it was now occupied by crazy Americans. Both Arbuthnot and Ambrister were tried for inciting the Indians into war against the United States and providing them with guns. The court found both men guilty and sentenced Arbuthnot to be hanged until dead, and Ambrister to be shot to death. But, when the members of the court asked for a reconsideration of Ambrister's sentence, since the former British soldier was just an adventurer, the court changed his sentence to fifty slave-type lashes on the bare back and one year in prison with hard labor. Andrew Jackson said, "No way!" About the Indians, Jackson admonished, that it would not be fair to punish the "poor ignorant savages," and not the men who incited them. He said he had no mercy for such "criminals." He arrested Armbrister and Arbuthnot as "unprincipled villains." He also accused them of being spies for the Spaniards. So, Jackson reimposed the initial sentence and ordered Ambrister "to be shot to death" and Arbuthnot to be "suspended by the neck with a rope until he is dead." These sentences were carried out on April 29, 1818 (Remini, pp. 81 & 82). Arbuthnot was hanged from the yardarm of his own ship, and Armbrister was blindfolded with his own necktie, then shot (Coit, p. 69). Many racist murderers thrive on this type of sick killing behavior. They insult, humiliate, then kill. Stories of whites requesting that Blacks crawl, sing, dance, or run before they are killed are not forgotten.

It would not be improbable that Jackson took his hate for British people out on these two British men. Andrew Jackson considered Arbuthnot and Ambrister criminals for not allowing him to kill people. If Jackson could be questioned today about his thinking in such matters, he would probably say, "But, the Indians were on our land! I didn't know Indians and Africans were people." Who had ever told Andrew Jackson and others with attitudes like his that anything they wanted was theirs, and that if the owners did not comply, it was all right for them to kill, massacre, and take? It is a well-known historical attitude, i.e., supremist. It is a well-documented fact that the white people who came from Europe/England to America were the outcast and criminals. They got off the ships on what is known as American land today, from Europe and violently demanded land. Most people do not know that Africans in fact were in Ancient America many years before white people ... and Indians (Reference Books: Van Sertima, Ivan, *They Came Before Columbus* and Fell, Barry, *America B.C.*).

During this time, the Treaty of Fort Jackson, and the stealing of Indian and African land, made Andrew Jackson a hero to most white people throughout the South and West (Cotterill, R.S., *The Southern Indians*, p. 189, 1814). But in the April 15, 1991 *Jet* magazine, p. 19, it is stated that some eighth graders in Plantation, Florida did not think he was so heroic. They organized a drive to convince the federal government to remove Jackson's face from the twenty dollar bill after researching and finding that he traded slaves and aided in forcibly removing the Indians out of the Eastern United States. "Plantation," Florida? Anyway, the very intelligent students are now appealing to major corporations to back their campaign against this bill, and in essence, against Andrew Jackson. It is important for these students to note that there were also many successful "slave & Indian" revolts during Jackson's time and afterwards (references: Stampp, *The Peculiar Institution*, 1956; Quarles, *The Negro in the Making of America*, 1969, and other pertinent literature pertaining to this subject matter. Also see indexes: Fugitive Slaves and Seminole Indians). Many African ex-political prisoners (slaves) and Indians cohabitated for years — sharing survival and cultures in an otherwise beastly society.

Ourstorical/Historical note — for the children: On January 21, 1824, Ashanti leader, Osei Bonsu, defeated white Britain at Assamaka, Ashanti, Africa.

JACKSON AS INCOMPETENT

One historian said that General Andrew Jackson was a patriot and a traitor, a great general, but entirely ignorant of the art of war. This historian said that Jackson was an eloquent writer, but totally unable to compose a correct sentence, or spell words of four syllables. He said that Jackson was the most candid of men (Remini, p. 14). John Quincy Adams said that Jackson was "incompetent both by his ignorance and by the fury of his passions." He concluded that Andrew Jackson was not a scholar (Schlesinger, *Jackson*, pp. 58 & 24). Everyone who knew Jackson, especially in his youth, never forgot his temper, even though his close friends felt that Jackson was always in control of himself. They said that Jackson would put on grand acts of emotion just to get what he wanted (Schlesinger, *Jackson*, p. 23). Jackson never hesitated to disobey his superiors. He has been referred to as an "urbane savage. An astrocious saint" (Remini, p. 14); however, his wife, Rachel, adored this man who was known to get so drunk that he had to be carried out of wild parties.

RACHEL JACKSON

Rachel's mental and physical health had been failing during Jackson's turbulent, savage, and political career. It was 1828, the same year when Shaka Zulu, the Great Zulu King, was killed in Africa and Nat Turner had a Vision, when Rachel became very ill. All her feistiness was gone. She was plagued with irrational fears for herself and her husband. There is a letter, which is now a part of the Hermitage museum, that reveals her clinging, childlike behavior toward Jackson. She was unstable and terrified whenever Jackson would leave her for the battlefield, and now she was just as terrified when he left her to perform his political duties. Jackson begin to consciously or unconsciously seize every opportunity to escape his wife's neurotic behavior. "Never would he have admitted, even to himself, how

Rachel's almost hysterical overprotectiveness must have irked him." After witnessing one of Jackson's separations from his wife, a friend of the family wrote a peculiar paragraph: "'History will never record how many men have performed great deeds because they were driven out of their homes by some unbearable trait of their wives....'" (Coit, p. 67). This sentence can *somewhat* be applied to Abraham Lincoln, Warren G. Harding and Dwight D. Eisenhower (See the chapters on Lincoln, Harding and Eisenhower).

Rachel used to cry so often that she herself didn't even realize she was crying (Remini, p. 47). Friends had gotten to the point where they had to stay close by her side at social events, so that she would not speak irrationally and embarrass her now distinguished husband. Rachel slipped into a serious depression during the campaign, and her health worsened. After the election, she gave up. Jackson's 1828 presidential win was an empty one for him. Rachel was by his side on election night, but she died before he took the oath of office. He blamed the media for her depression, stress, and untimely death. He called them murderers — as if he were not. He wore a black armband during his oath of office ceremony symbolizing his mourning. Jackson never had eyes for another woman, although he enjoyed the social company of Creole women (Remini, p. 65). Old New Orleans was famous for its annual Quarteroon/Creole balls. Only the African women of this type were invited; African men of the same type and their full-blooded (the beautiful chocolates) African brothers and sisters were cordially uninvited. The annual ball was for the entertainment of whites only (Rogers, *Your History*, p. 67).

One year before Jackson's election, the World Anti-Slavery Convention opened in London. This was a convention of necessity to debate and oust political figures with racist attitudes like the soon-to-be-elected Andrew Jackson in the United States. During the 1832 election, bells rang out for Jackson. He was triumphant. He won, but there were many non-colored men and women in the South who continued to detest Andrew Jackson. Many detested his arrogance and his ignorance; others did not like the fact that he was a Mason. He stated that South Carolinians were free to talk and agitate as much as they wished. He promised, "But, if one drop of blood be shed there in defiance of the laws of the United States I will hang the first man of them I can get my hands on to the first tree I can find" (Coit, p. 107). Sounds familiar? This type of behavior was recreation for Jackson and others. Earlier in the summer of 1813, a future Senator, Thomas Hart Benton, shot Jackson almost to death (Whitney, p. 71). Years later this Senator warned a congressman: "When Jackson begins to talk about hanging, [men] can begin to look for ropes" (Coit, p. 109). For a while, the respectability of the country was behind Andrew Jackson. John Quincy Adams and Mulatto (or Black) Daniel Webster also praised Jackson. While Jackson was being praised, a young man of 23 was brooding over Jackson's ideas and the new proclamation. Although he did not know that he would be president one day, he did remember his feelings of the past when he composed his First Inaugural Address in 1861. This man was Abraham Lincoln. In the meantime, Andrew Jackson went on to win his 1832, second term in office.

DAVID WALKER AND NAT TURNER

During the Jackson years in 1829, David Walker, a strong African man who advocated that slavery was against the will of God, wrote an appeal to this effect and created mass alarm for white people in the slaveholding states. His call to the Africans to resist slavery was intolerable to white supremists like Andrew Jackson. David Walker was later killed by militant white people. Nat Turner fulfilled Walker's call on August 21, 1831. Turner read and felt the spirit of Ra (the sun) to determine the best day to free himself and his people. The revolt was swift — no holds barred; he wanted freedom for himself and his people by any means necessary. Turner had only six revolutionaries accompanying him. Within a few hours, there were seventy. Turner started with his so-called master and the master's family. They were slain. Sixty white people were killed within a twenty-four hour time span. Two warships and the U.S. Marines were sent to subdue Turner. The Turner revolt and quest for freedom against a people who had treated his people totally inhumane was a sign that things had to change. Nat Turner is considered an honorable hero in the

African/Black communities of America, for his revolt was
not against a people simply because of their skin color nor
because he wanted to take something from them that did
not belong to him; his revolt was for his dignity, his freedom
and the freedom of the Black, that is African, race.

THE ASSASSINATION ATTEMPT
AND THE LITTLE DARK MAN

The first attempt to assassinate a President took place in
1835. Andrew Jackson was attending the funeral of an
acquaintance in Washington. As Jackson walked by the casket, a "deranged" man, who some historians described as
short and dark, pulled out a pistol and fired it at Jackson at
point blank range. The President was shocked into silliness
and stillness for a second, then Jackson lunged at the little
dark man with his cane. The man dropped the pistol and
immediately pulled out another one, and fired. Was this
man deranged? This guy was serious. The gun, amazingly,
misfired again! Then a young army officer subdued the dark
man (Remini, p. 171; Coit, p. 121). The President lived; the
little dark man went to the crazy house. And who knows
what happened to him there?

THE OLD MAN IS DEAD

Andrew Jackson lived until the age of 78. On June 8, 1845,
Andrew Jackson dying of old aches and pains, mental and
physical, told his family and servants that he would meet
them above. He said, "I'll see you all in heaven, whites and
blacks." His eyes then closed; his head drooped to the side;
his breathing stopped. Outside were a crowd of Blacks peer-
ing through the window at him and moaning (Remini, p. 148)
… or acting. These people were Jackson's "slaves." Many of
these same political prisoners, so-called slaves, had the same
blood and spirit running through their veins and soul as
Shaka Zulu, David Walker, Nat Turner, and Harriet Tubman.

Andrew Jackson had campaigned and won his place as
the seventh President of the United States, and he has also
won his place as the second President of the United States
said, by white people, to be of African ancestry.

Andrew Jackson *(Library of Congress)*.

Jackson's wife, **Rachel.**

Nat Turner, One of the Chosen Ones

Black Seminole Indians.

Why do people always expect authors
to answer questions? I am an author
because I want to ask questions.
If I had answers I'd be a politician.

Eugene Ionesco

ABRAHAM LINCOLN

16th President U.S.A.

The so-called official book of facts on United States Presidents said that Abraham Lincoln's ancestry was English. Lincoln described himself as having "a dark complexion and coarse hair." William Henry Herndon, Lincoln's law partner, said that Lincoln had "very dark skin." The contents of one book written in 1863 state that Lincoln's "mother was of the Ethiopian tribe." Old 1800's white southerners said that Lincoln was "of Negro ancestry." But, "Woodrow Wilson wrote that Lincoln '"came of the most unpromising stock on the continent, the 'poor white trash,' of the South'" (Wilson's statement: Simon, *A House Divided*, p. 2). So, some say that he was a Black president; others say he was not.

Abraham Lincoln was from the newly formed republican party. This party became the dominant party during the Civil War and the subsequent Reconstruction period. Lincoln was the 16th President of the United States. His term was from March 4, 1861 until his death on April 15, 1865 from an assassin's bullet. His murder was a conspiracy. He was killed by people who disagreed with him on such political issues as slavery, "saving" the Union between the North and South, and inevitably — economics. It is my contention that Lincoln's obscure ancestral background may have played a major part in the easy decision to assassinate him.

Abraham Lincoln had not been in the White House very long when he realized that he had a combination of a military and a social war on his hands. Lincoln is the Civil War president, the president said to have freed the slaves and joined the states. This war had many names: Mr. Lincoln's War, The War Against Slavery, The War of the Sixties, The Brother's War, and others.

THE MYTHOLOGICAL MAN

Abraham Lincoln has been dead for 125 years now. Yet many of us know his birthday by heart. Most get a free day from school or work. Ninety percent of the literature on Abraham Lincoln states that he was a great man, a great leader, and a great president. He is, however, the man who sent hundreds of African-Americans off to Haiti because he felt that colonization would be the best living environment for both Blacks and whites. These African people were sent to this Island with menial food supplies, and most of them died. Lincoln did, however, one year and two months later, send for the survivors. Well, so much for good ole honest Abe — whatever color he was. Whether Lincoln believed in freedom for African-Americans or not, he still did not want to live with nor near them. This, of course, implies that he must have had a difficult time living with himself.

I was 11 years old, riding on a big old orange school bus when I thought, "Do I trust Abe Lincoln? Was he really honest? Did he free Black people?" Our sixth grade teacher had been teaching "a fictitious" (I know this now) Abe Lincoln story that day. This "school" lesson was around 10 O'clock that morning, and here it was 2:45 p.m. and I was still thinking about this lesson. I had some serious doubts that Lincoln *really* freed Black people. Of course, I learned later that there were many factstories about incidences on the plantation whereas many a so-called master was found dead, beat to death or strangled by a strongwilled and tired enslaved African determined to be free. Whites were beginning to be afraid that all enslaved persons/Blacks/Africans would began to plea, flee, and ultimately fight for their God-given birthright to be a free people. We remain in a continuous struggle for freedom even today. So I know that the freedom we do have, we acquired ourselves. I didn't feel that Lincoln was what teachers, historians, politicians, the media and others said he was. As far as I was concerned, he was probably more *or* less than what they said he was. Lincoln couldn't even free his own mind, so it is unlikely that he could free a whole race of people.

Jehuti Amen Ra, the author of *Shattering The Myth Of The Man Who Freed The Slaves*, says that as long as we accept the myth of the man who freed the slaves, we will always be victimized by mental enslavement. He deplores that when our children grow up thinking that Lincoln, Honest Abe, freed people who had been enslaved, then African-Americans grow up thinking that the white man liberated them. Abraham Lincoln did not free the slaves; the African peoples freed themselves.

In the preface of Stephen B. Oates, book, *With Malice Toward None*, p. xv, he writes about the Lincoln of mythology and the folk hero:

> He comes to us in the mists of legend as a home-spun "rail splitter" from the Illinois prairies, a saintly commoner who called himself "Abe," spoke in a deep, fatherly voice, and cared little about material rewards and social station. He also comes to us as Father Abraham, the Great Emancipator who led the North off to civil war to free the slaves and after the conflict ended offered the South a tender and forgiving hand.

Lerone Bennett, Jr., the famous historian/ourstorian, says that Lincoln had a "wonderful sense of the ironic and ridiculous" and that all of the mythical and mysterious things that have erroneously gone down in history about his political beliefs, Lincoln would find amusing. Bennett states: "In the general literature, Lincoln is depicted as an eloquent and flaming idealist, whaling away at the demon of slavery. This view is almost totally false. In the first place, Lincoln was a opportunist, not an idealist" (Bennett, *Ebony*, "Was Abe Lincoln a White Supremist?" 1968). Abraham Lincoln asserted, "Whatever you are, be a good one." When it came to the necessity of being a whole person who had a good sense of identity, Lincoln was *not* a good one, but when it came to the business of being mentally ill, but functional in the political arena of a racist 1800's America, he was pretty good. But who is Abraham Lincoln?

THE HUE-MAN

It is said that Abraham Lincoln was born February 12, 1809 in Hardfin County, Kentucky — a slave state. Abraham Lincoln is the immortal president who is admired by many. His mother was Nancy Hanks Lincoln, and his father is said to have been Thomas Lincoln. "Questioning surviving Kentucky pioneers, Herndon found some who doubted that Thomas could have fathered the president — or anyone else for that matter" (Simon, p. 2). According to Herndon, Thomas Lincoln was castrated at some point during his lifetime; however, he could not ascertain as to the exact date that this emasculation took place (Herndon, *The Hidden Lincoln*, pp. 139 & 205; Ross, *Fall From Grace*, p. 98). Was Herndon, or some surviving pioneer who knew the Lincoln family, lying? If so, why? Was Thomas Lincoln castrated before or after his marriage to Nancy Hanks? Or, more precisely, was he castrated before or after Lincoln's birth? Seeing it written that Thomas Lincoln was castrated, gives more prudence to questions surrounding Abraham Lincoln's birth. Was Lincoln's biological father an African man as some 1800's white southerners and the well-known African-American anthropologist and writer J.A. Rogers contend? Or was the father one of the white men mentioned in the article, "The Many-Sired Lincoln (1899)," the book, *The Genesis of Lincoln* (1899), or a more recent work, *White House Tales* (1989), by Webb Garrison? Abraham Lincoln began his life in a log cabin under suspicious circumstances (Oates, pp. 3-7, 1977).

Lincoln witnessed the burial of his little two year old brother. The grave was located directly outside the cabin window. Again, it is not known who may have sired this child. In Herndon's and Lamon's literary works about Lincoln, it is written that Thomas Lincoln once caught his wife with another. Thomas and the man fought so violently over this matter that Thomas Lincoln ended the fight by biting off the man's nose (Lewis, p. 323). This story sounds a little farfetched, and somewhat reminiscent of a true Napoleon

Bonaparte story. Napoleon and his gang tromped over to Kemet and proceeded to knock and shoot the noses off many of the magnificent statues there because the statues' magnificence did not favor them in facial features.

Lincoln's beloved mother Nancy died when he was only nine years old. While the coffin was being built, the deceased mother lay in the same room where the entire family cooked, ate, read, and slept. Other close relatives with whom little Abe loved died around this same time in 1818. A year later, Abe was kicked by a horse, and as Lincoln puts it, this injury "killed him for a time."

More trauma: As a young boy, Lincoln almost drowned and was saved by a neighborhood teenager. As a young teenager himself Lincoln witnessed the initial dementia of a young male neighbor. Lincoln wondered for the rest of his life why this young man lost his mind. Lincoln was so moved with wonderment and sadness over this episode that he wrote a poem about its occurrence. At the age of nineteen, Lincoln lost his older, adored sister Sarah. She died trying to have a baby. The stillborn baby (Lincoln's niece or nephew) was buried in her arms. Lincoln also lived to bury two of his own children.

Lincoln was called ugly by his peers, and his father was forever picking on him. Abraham Lincoln and his "father," Thomas Lincoln, never had a good healthy relationship. Some form of child abuse is suspected. Throughout this chapter you will notice that Lincoln exhibited many of the symptoms typical of an adult survivor of child abuse. Some symptoms are: depression, psychosomatic illness, self-destructive thoughts and/or behavior, eating problems, anxiety, personal and intimate relationship difficulties, sense of unreality, intrusive thoughts and images, sleep disturbances such as nightmares, and abrupt switches in personality and thought.

You will read within the confines of this chapter, including new theories, old theories, and many references, that Lincoln was a manic-depressive, tending toward dissociative states of mind and multiple personalities. His melancholia is a well-known fact. Lincoln has recently been said to have been a victim of Marfan's syndrome. He was a hypochondriac bisexual tending toward homosexuality who always

thought of death. He was a fatalist. White people said that he
had "Negro blood," and was called names such as Africanus
the First from Liberia, The Ancient, sooty and swarthy, i.e.,
black. He had black blood running through his veins. He did
not have all of the problems mentioned above because he
had black blood. No, to the contrary; he had these problems
because he lived in a racist, fatalist society with red, blue,
and white blood who thought that having a little black blood
would "sooty" up their America. Dr. Kenneth Clark contends that the negative effects of white American racism on
the personality development and psychological harmony of
African-Americans are "unmistakable" (Clark, *Dark Ghetto*,
p. 81). The thought of Lincoln openly revealing his true
ancestry probably made him tremble. Over 10,000 Blacks a
year "pass-for-white" (operational definition: fail-for-white)
every year in the United States in order to get away from
racism, discrimination, and prejudice (Television program:
Tony Brown's Journal, 1988). Of course, Lincoln's many
bizarre and puzzling problems and personalities do not
exclude the problems he acquired from his obscure family
background and his chaotic, and possibly abusive childhood.
Literature written by Lincoln and others attest to the fact that
Lincoln was an extremely melancholic person and possibly a
manic depressive. There was something more to Lincoln's
lifetime of brooding, suffering, sadness and melancholic personality than the death of his mother. There was something
more, much more in-depth. Sigmund Freud points out "that
such an individual hates himself only a little more than he
loves himself" (Menninger, p. 41). Lincoln's problems and
traumas were doubled and tripled. Dr. Kenneth Clark states
that dark-skinned children are taught at an early age to hate
themselves. Very few ever "lose that sense of shame and self-
hatred" (p. 65).

Multiple Personality Disorder or syndrome is usually
caused by traumata of life. These are mental injuries which
the primary personality simply could not handle, so the mind
disconnected and the traumata no longer longer existed
(BaKhufu, *A Comprehensive Study of Multiple Personalities: Why
Aren't Blacks in Therapy?* p. 7, dissertation, 1985). It should be
noted, however, that people with multiple personality disorders or dissociative tendencies can function normally (as far

as we can see). They can certainly function well enough to become President of these United States, which it was then as today, an absorbing joke. Lincoln, although a melancholic and sad person most of the time, had another Self who liked bawdy stories, songs and jokes.

Another mask? Lincoln was a minstrel show, "Negro" ditties, dirty joke-telling, smutty poetry writing enthusiast. He would often ask his lawyer, biographer and banjo-playing friend, Ward Hill Lamon to sing a very demeaning *song*, if you will, about a young African servant entitled, "The Blue-tailed Fly." They would then commence to stamp their feet to ignorance: *They used to have tails you know.* Lincoln was also fond of listening to songs about mulattos (Quarles, *Lincoln and the Negro*, p. 40, 1962). Why?

Lincoln was an overcompensating multiracial who went to extremes to try to prove himself worthy and white. His show of racism was a sign of this sickness — his confusion. His racism was minus the direct physical violence, perhaps because such an act would have been totally against his African nature. This side of the African is usually used for survival reasons, or when an African or Africans have been provoked and demeaned into a type of mental illness — killing one another in senseless societal defeat, and sometimes, but not often, killing others (See: Kenneth Clark's *Black Ghetto: Dilemmas of Social Power*, 1965, and Amos Wilson's *Black-on-Black Violence: The Psychodynamics of Black Self-Annihilation in Service of White Domination*, 1990, for additional information).

NANCY HANKS

When Lincoln was a young boy, his mama died. Nancy Hanks Lincoln was Abraham Lincoln's mother. She was the daughter of Lucey Hanks. Lucey did not know who her father was, and Nancy did not know who her father was. So Lucey's background is just as obscure as Nancy's background. The Hankses were aware, however, that they had an ancestor by the name of Abraham.

Abraham Hanks traveled the mountainsides finding his way through the wilderness until he reached Kentucky County, the unsettled part of Virginia. He travelled with

William Calk, and after working with Calk on the surveying and the layout of the town of Boonesborough for Daniel Boone in the Spring of 1775, he returned to Virginia to be with his wife, Sarah Harper, and the rest of his family (Baber, *Sarah and Abe*, p. 5). So when Nancy named her son Abraham, it could have been for maternal and not *paternal* reasons. (Thomas Lincoln's father's name was Abraham also.)

Nancy was an illegitimately born child (whatever makes a *child* "not legal?") who never knew who her father was. Nancy Hanks' birthdate is listed as February 5, 1784 — born in Campbell County, Virginia to Lucey Hanks and an unknown man. From interviewing people who knew Nancy, William H. Herndon, who would become Abraham Lincoln's law partner, described Nancy Hanks Lincoln: "She was above the ordinary height in stature, weighed about 130 pounds, was slenderly built … Her skin was dark; hair dark brown; … forehead prominent; face … with a marked expression of melancholy which fixed itself in the memory of everyone who ever saw or knew her" (Herndon, *Herndon's Lincoln*, p. 5).

Nancy was born during a time when white indentured slavery was running rampant. Many of these slaves were white and multiracial women. Many of these women (some free and some otherwise) had children with and ran away with African men. Those who remained enslaved, but had mulatto children were sometimes beaten for their "crime" (Catterall, vol. 4, p. 478) and sold away or banished to another county. One such white female indentured slave who birthed two mulatto children was banished all the way to Barbados. Of course, some of these women had children by their so-called slavemasters also. During these times, "certain white slaveholders used to buy the white women, marry them off to Negro slaves, and thus be able legally to hold the white women slaves for life and their mulatto offspring slaves until they reached the age of thirty" or twenty-five (Rogers, *Sex and Race*, vol. II, pp. 232-233; Ortiz, p. 19). "Free white women who had children by Negroes were sold at public auction[s]. '"We notice, … the sale, as servants of a white woman and her bastard mulatto child in 1790; and of white women for having colored children in 1793 and 1794", (Rogers, *Sex and Race*, vol II, p. 234 — from a book written by J.R. Brackett,

1889). A preacher from Kentucky, John Rankin, wrote that he knew of "several instances of slaves actually *seducing* [author italics] the daughters of their masters. Such seductions sometimes happen in the most respectable families," said Rev. Rankin (Rogers, *Sex and Race*, vol. II, p. 234, from: Abdy, E.S., *J. of Residence and Tour in the U.S.*, vol. 3, p. 27, "Letters of Slavery, p. 69). In Richard Grant Whites' work, *Book of the Prophet ... Wherein Marvelous Things are Foretold of the Reign of Abraham*, 1863, he writes that Abraham Lincoln's mother is "of the Ethiopian tribe of Hanks" (Donald, p. 307).

As stated earlier, not a lot is known about sad, dark-skinned, dark-haired Nancy's family background, although much literature states that she came from "lowly" surroundings. Meaning what? Lincoln acknowledged the fact that his mother was "illegitimate." Others state that he may have been mistaken. Nancy Hanks' background is vague, and any question asked of it would be a legitimate one. She was a frail, sensitive woman who although "uneducated" was intelligent. Although Lincoln's grandma Lucey could write, her daughter, never learned to write her name. Nancy did, however, memorize many passages from the Bible which she would later recite to her children.

Nancy was living with "guardians" in Kentucky when she met a young man who is said to have hated slavery, but came from a family of slaveholders; his name was Thomas Lincoln. He associated himself with people who thought slavery was wrong. He once stormed out of a Baptist church meeting during an argument over slavery. In 1806 Nancy supposedly would marry, or become the servant to, Thomas Lincoln. Fifty-two years later, Abraham Lincoln will claim: I am opposed to "the niggers and the white people marrying together."

In the winter of 1816, the Lincoln family moved to Indiana. They lived in a three-sided cabin. In 1817 Nancy's relatives, The Sparrows, moved to Little Pigeon Creek, Indiana also. Dennis Hanks, the illegitimate son of one of Nancy's aunts, relocated to Little Pigeon Creek with the Sparrows. He was a nineteen year old semi-illiterate. "For some reason," Dennis Hanks disliked Thomas Lincoln tremendously, and he would speak negatively of Abraham Lincoln's "father" for the rest of his life. He said that Thomas Lincoln was "shiftless" and "neglected his family" (Oates, p. 8, 1977). Dennis and Abe had a noble and friendly relationship. A year after the Sparrows' arrival, Nancy Hanks died at the young age of thirty-four from an illness that caused death from drinking milk from sick cows. Some months later, the Sparrows, whom Lincoln loved, died from this same sickness, so Dennis moved in with the Lincolns. When Lincoln's mother died, Thomas Lincoln did not give her a proper burial. There was no funeral service, but Thomas Lincoln did build her a black coffin. And especially appalling to young Abe was that no prayer was said over his mother's grave. This upset Abraham Lincoln immensely. So when a travelling preacher came through town, the young nine year boy asked this holy stranger to pray over his beloved mother's grave. This made Lincoln feel better.

Now why didn't Thomas Lincoln feel it necessary to bury the lady properly? Was Nancy or her mother mulatto, or a white indentured slave? Did Thomas Lincoln "rescue" Nancy from a life of brutal slavery — an institution of which he supposedly condemned. Did he neglect his responsibility to bury her properly because he saw her as not equal to himself? Did his very nature (the son of slaveholders) reveal itself after "his wife's" death? In 1805 Thomas Lincoln had worked as a slavecatcher, called "patrollers." His job was to seize suspicious-looking white characters [Mullatos?] and "Negroes" who were roaming around without permits (Sandburg, pp. 22-23, 1925). As you will read later, Thomas was a man with problems. How deep did his problems run? Almost a short one year later, Thomas Lincoln returned to Kentucky to call on a widow with whom he used to date when he was younger. She had however, for some unknown reason, broke off the relationship and married someone else. She was Sally (Sarah) Bush. She married a man named Johnston instead of Thomas Lincoln. Mr. Johnston left Sally Bush Johnston with three children plus property. So when Thomas called on her, she really had nothing to lose. Whether Thomas was able to father children or not probably did not matter, because she already had her children — and some money. So why not help out a friend who is trying to rear two innocent children? Sally Bush Johnston was a good woman. She married Thomas Lincoln and returned to Indi-

ana with him to help care for his family and household
which was beginning to deteriorate. The children appreciated this gesture, and they loved Sally who was also called
or named Sarah, like Lincoln's sister. But Abe Lincoln would
never forget Nancy Hanks, the mother he loved so much.

Abraham Lincoln had no records of his "parents'" marriage certificate. It has been claimed and "later research has
confirmed (author italics) the fact that Thomas Lincoln and
Nancy Hanks were [really] married … in Washington
County, Kentucky, on June 12, 1806, and that Abraham Lincoln was the second child born to this union" (Wilson, R., p.
180). What research? Are there certificates? One author
wrote that: "Lincoln himself doubted his legitimacy and had
hunted in vain for legal proof of his parents' marriage.
Another source states, "After his death *sufficient* (author's
italics) records of the event were found in a Kentucky courthouse where Lincoln had never searched" (Lewis, *Myths
After Lincoln*, p. 323, 1929). Lincoln was mentally ill, not stupid. There is a difference. He was a lawyer. Why wouldn't
he search where "his parents" were said to be married and
where he was said to be born? And the marriage "proof"
was *sufficient* to whom? Any diehard Lincolnite could have
conjured up a piece of paper, or any lie to protect a man
who is held in such high esteem as the late, great Mr. Lincoln. Of course, many his-storians will criticize these allegations as preposterous, but as far back as the time of George
Washington, CIA tactics were being erected and used to
deceive the general public about the true operations of
American government in history. For example, according to
G.J.A. O'Toole, author of the book, *Honorable Treachery*, and
a former CIA employee, George Washington instructed his
spys on the use of invisible ink. In 1777 George Washington
organized a network of spys, an intelligence service, to spy
on the British in order to win the war. That was then. And
today anyone who continues to believe and trust any information coming from the Warren Commission needs help.

It is said that Nancy and Thomas had one child in 1807
and one in 1809, Sarah and Abraham respectively. Lincoln
adored his sister Sarah. She died trying to give birth at the
young age of twenty-one. Lincoln's sister was buried with
her stillborn child in her arms. Lincoln was nineteen. We do

not really know the true ages of Abraham Lincoln nor his sister. If Sarah is supposed to be older than Lincoln, and so many attest to Lincoln not being the child of Thomas, then why would Sarah be the child of Thomas? It is doubtful that Nancy married Thomas, had a daughter with him, then slept with a Black man (or whomever) and conceived then birthed Abraham.

Sarah and Abe did not resemble each other at all. Sarah was said to have been short and stout with confined features. Her brother, Abe, was tall, skinny, and not so pretty. (Of course, in the African community not resembling a sibling or having a different skin color doesn't mean anything. In just one family alone, one can see every community [tribe] of Africa, and in all its sizes, shapes, and colors.) Lincoln was often called "ugly" by his peers. A child who felt the sting of sharp retorts was likely to remember these negative names forever. A childhood acquaintance of Lincoln's recalled that because of his appearance, they always made fun of him. She said, he "didn't mind because he was such a good fellow." Of course the impressionable boy was bothered — and stayed bothered until his death — about many things.

It can not be doubted that Nancy could have brought into this "marriage" two children from another man or other men, possibly African. Lincoln's mother nor his grandmother knew their fathers, and Sarah and Abe possibly never knew their biological father(s) either. William Herndon wrote "that Lincoln too, was a bastard" (Ross, p. 10; Donald, p. 307). The old 1800's Lincoln biographers said that Dennis Hanks was very protective of Lincoln and his mother. He was very careful not to divulge too much ancestral and family information to the media. And do we really know the truth behind the death of other important political figures such as Patrice Lumumba, Martin Luther King, Malcolm X, Abdul Nasser, and others? We can not continue to trust the stories of his-storians and government officials who make endless efforts at trying to deceive the public about the personal lives, family lives, and deaths of political figures — and especially those of Presidents in America.

"Around 1850, as Lincoln and William H. Herndon rode in a buggy toward the courthouse in Menard County, Illinois,

Lincoln spoke of his mother, praising her for his own best qualities of mind and character, crediting in turn the unknown Virginia gentleman who had fathered her. "'God bless my mother;'" Lincoln concluded" (Simon, p. 2). Lincoln is known to have said: "All that I am, and all that I hope to be, I owe to my mother." Some feel that Lincoln attributed this statement to his stepmother, Sarah (Sally) Bush. She encouraged Abe to read, and he did love Mrs. Bush; however, these sentiments, many of us feel, were meant from the heart to his biological mother, Nancy Hanks.

Lincoln's mother was intelligent, sensitive, and sad much like Abe himself. She is the woman who, after Lincoln became president of the United States and especially after his assassination, many writers crowned her ... and her son saints, likening them to Mary and the baby Jesus, the Black Madonna and child. Of course a marriage certificate would have to be "found" for such a remarkable woman, and it is not doubted here that she was not wonderful and remarkable. She was probably a magnificent person. However, writer John T. Morse thought it ridiculous that so many biographers wrote about the Lincolns as if they were saints — as if Nancy were some sort of "Madonna in the wilderness" (Simon, pp. 2-3). Poetry and songs have been written about Abraham Lincoln and his biological mother, Nancy. Although this poem was not written for nor about Lincoln and his mother, it does fit here.

Maát

I searched
Deep
for Mary
and
found
The Black Madonna

by: Auset BaKhufu
(Published in the Amer. Poetry Anthology, © 1988)

THOMAS LINCOLN

Abraham Lincoln's earliest known ancestor (biological or not) was Samuel Lincoln, a weaver who migrated from Norfolk, England in 1637. He later moved to Salem, Massachusetts. His descendants later relocated to New Jersey, then to Philadelphia, and later on to Virginia. They became a very prosperous family in Virginia. After selling their land, Thomas Lincoln's father Abraham (called "Abe") and some other family members moved to Kentucky. Abe was killed when Thomas Lincoln was ten years young. Young Thomas witnessed the whole thing. This killing took place in 1788. Abe was killed by some Indians who were probably fighting for what initially belonged to them (and others) — their land. Thomas Lincoln's mother was left to raise her boys alone. The boys eventually grew up and went their respectful and separate ways. Thomas Lincoln subsequently spent part of his life living with a young boy with an ambiguous masked background who would become the President of the United States.

The relationship between Abraham Lincoln and his father was an awfully painful one. Although Lincoln and his father could be quite humorous at times, they still could not get along most of the time. The Lincoln father/son topic has not received the attention it craves and deserves. Lincoln's very silence on the subject demonstrated that he may have liked someone to figure this mess out. But the little information that Lincoln provided (or rather did not provide) was very revealing — to me. One Lincoln lecturer feels that when Lincoln said he owed his existence to his mother that this was an indirect judgement against his father, "a man for whom he never had a single recorded word of praise" (Simon, p. 2).

Most writers of history books state that Thomas Lincoln was Abraham Lincoln's father. Most contend that Thomas Lincoln was a lazy man, and Abraham said as much himself about Thomas Lincoln. Many historians say that Thomas became a good workman, but sometimes was a little shiftless. Some feel that this is an overstatement imploring that Thomas was not lazy and shiftless. It is documented that around 1816 Thomas Lincoln's finances began to dwindle. Abe was seven (or nine) years of age at the time.

William H. Herndon stated that if Lincoln ever discussed his parents or his background at all, it was with much reluctance and reserve. Herndon said there was something about Lincoln's origin he [Lincoln] never cared to discuss. John Locke Scripps, senior editor of the *Chicago Press & Tribune*, was petitioned to write a short biographical sketch on Lincoln's family background. Scripps pointed out that Lincoln "seemed to be painfully impressed with the extreme poverty of this early surroundings, and the utter absence of all romantic and heroic elements." Lincoln "told Scripps a few things about his ancestry, but warned that he did not want them published....There was much about himself he would never reveal ... much about his parents and their backgrounds and *deficiencies* (author italics) he refused to make public for the opposition to exaggerate and use against him." Not so much as a "glimpse" of who Lincoln really was revealed itself in his short autobiographical sketch (Oates, p. 4, 1977) unless you are a diligent, undeniable, unrelenting, insightful and penetrating, ninja-like reader of any discipline, profession or position, ourstorical writer, researcher, Sakku psychologist or psychiatrist and can comprehend the invisible which is inside the visible, then you will not see it. Many possess this gift.

Thomas Lincoln did not seem to be Abraham Lincoln's "father" in any sense and definition of the word. It is possible that Thomas harbored resentful tendencies toward Abraham Lincoln and Nancy Hanks, because Nancy had biblically slept with an African man (or at least some other man), and had this child, Abe. Thomas Lincoln seemed to have been an angry man left to rear the child of a masked man after Nancy's death. Abraham Lincoln's personality, his mental history and his behavior point to the possibility of some facet of serious abuse. On the *Donahue Show,* June 5, 1991, NBC, one of the guests stated that, "We have a nation who wants to castrate rapists." Whether Thomas was castrated before or after Lincoln's birth, doesn't matter. The George Washington University Medical Center in Washington, D.C. stated that just because a person may have been castrated, doesn't mean that they do not have sexual urges. And in many cases a castrated person can still perform sexually to some degree, whether they can have a child or not.

William Herndon could not pinpoint when Thomas was castrated. Dennis Hanks said that Thomas Lincoln had lost his ability to have children when he was a young boy from mumps complications. Or could Thomas have been castrated by some of the same people with whom he had served the Lord? Two years before Nancy's death, Nancy and Thomas Lincoln had joined a group called the separist church; here they prayed, sang, and talked of a non-slavery society with their antislavery preachers. Thomas Lincoln was known to be "taken with spasms of religion." He was a recurrent religious fanatic who was not loyal to any one denomination. He was apt to join two or three religious groups in rapid succession (*World Book Encyclopedia*, p. 4009, 1937) then leave them. Did the church/religious fanatics or some concerned neighbors, or any one person who might have discovered Thomas abusing his child have emasculated him? Dennis Hanks took many secrets to his grave. Two facts that are known, however, is that he disliked Thomas Lincoln, and only associated with the man for survival reasons when he was younger. Did Dennis Hanks know something? Did young Abe Lincoln reveal more to Dennis Hanks than he did to the world? The perpetrator(s) would not have known that little Abe had black blood running through his veins; it is possible, though, that a closer family member, such as Dennis Hanks, could have known. No stone must be left unturned; Lincoln did have deep in breeded mental problems, and his father seemed to have had some emotional problems as well. Thomas Lincoln, as a young boy, saw his father killed. He was probably deranged from that point on with no impending psychological help to be found anywhere. Just because it was 1788 doesn't mean that the act would not affect him just as it would affect a child today in some form or fashion. It is pertinent that these stories be told and analyzed. Questions must be asked. It is time for myths and lies to be dispelled.

This is total speculation: Had knowledge of Lincoln's ancestral background been known by the perpetrator(s) of Thomas Lincoln's possible castration, he may have gone unharmed, or at least not harmed as harshly. Thinking that young Lincoln was totally white, the perpetrator(s) could not understand why any father, and especially a biological one, would do such a thing to his *own* child. This is a fact: Incest is one of the primary causes for a person to disconnect their psyche, or to develop multiple personalities (MPD). The action (incest) and its consequences (multiple or alternate selves) are the Ultimate Secrets.

Multiple personality has been recognized by psychologists since the 1700's although it was forgotten until recently. Freud was about to embark upon a study on alternate personalities when his colleagues forced him to cease his psychological investigations into this scientific arena. Freud's young female patients/clients were beginning to relate to Freud that they were being molested by their fathers or some other adult, usually a relative. Many of these young women had "taken flight" from their dominant selves and mentally split causing them to possess two or more "selves" or personalities. These young women were not understood nor were they able to be treated. There were surely young boys too who were not asked about their problems during this time. And with societal stigmas of "manliness" being placed and urged on young boys during the 1800's, it is highly unlikely that they could discuss this problem with anyone.

One out of every 15 males was, is, and will be raped at some point during their lifetime. The "cover-ups" of these hideous crimes were even more covered during Lincoln's lifetime. Herndon said there was something about Lincoln that Lincoln never cared to discuss. "Lincoln had a secret preying on his mind. Was it his race? His enemies harped on it. Herndon says of it, '"Lincoln often thought of committing suicide. Why? Did the knowledge of his mother's origin or his own press the thought of suicide upon him?'" (Rogers, p. 8; Herndon, *The Hidden Lincoln*, p. 412). Or was being Black that bad? Or was it something more traumatic to a young boy? Lincoln physically left home in his early twenties. Lincoln was twenty-two when he "finally '"separated from his father" (Oates, p. 17).

IMAGES OF MULTIPLE SELVES

For the person experiencing dissociative mental symptoms, it is possible for the mind and the body to be divided in such a way that several diverse lives are quite separate from one another. But they can still exist concurrently in, and as one human being. Therefore in trying to be a white man in a black man's body or mind, but subconsciously or consciously perceiving that there is black blood running through the veins, the body wouldn't necessarily always know what the mind was going to do, and the mind wouldn't always know what the body was going to do. Multiple personality (or dissociative tendencies) is not a disorder that is incapacitating. Some multiple personality victims maintain responsible positions. They complete graduate degrees, obtain law degrees, they get married, they have children, and do other "normal" things. These mulatto presidents' dominant selves were their white selves. This dominant self was reared to be white since early childhood, i.e., to have a white mentality. Studies have shown that when African children are reared in a racist society, they often fantasize about being white, because white seems to be easier to live with than being Black. "The obsession with whiteness continues past childhood and into adulthood" (Clark, *Dark Ghetto*, pp. 64 & 65).

In the book, *Sybil*, written by Dr. Flora Rheta Schreiber, the main character, Sybil, split into many personalities because of continuous sexual abuse when she was a child. The book was made into a movie. When Lincoln was a young boy, he almost drowned in a creek; an older neighbor boy saved his life. Eve Black from "The Three Faces of Eve" (the movie), and I'm Eve (the autobiographical book), saw a drowned man pulled from a creek near her home. And although she already had some childhood problems, this incident caused her first mental split — causing her to develop multiple personalities. The Lincoln's had a third child, a boy; at the young age of 2, he died of some undisclosed sickness. His grave was in direct eyesight of the Lincoln's living quarters (Oates, p. 5, 1977). Nancy Hanks Lincoln's dead body stayed in the family living quarters while her casket was being built. What can these circumstances do to the psyche of young people's minds as they try to grow into healthy and mentally stable adults?

Lincoln experienced two serious mental breakdowns during his lifetime. Herndon, who has, of course, been slandered for some of his writings on Lincoln, stated in a letter to a friend that Lincoln had most definitely been insane in Menard County in 1835. Lincoln was then twenty-six years of age, that is if he was born in 1809. The neighbors there said that Lincoln was crazy. Herndon stated that Lincoln suffered "a burden of wild despair." Lincoln had a "crazy spell." In his desperation, Lincoln wrote a book on *Infidelity* (*The Hidden Lincoln*, pp. 36-37); a sign that he was possibly scribbling with self-pity as he thought about the backgrounds of his biological father, mother, grandmother, great grandparents, or whomever.

"Storms and deaths, his mother would say, were part of the workings of God, mysterious and incomprehensible." Nancy reared Abe and Sarah "with a melancholy affection." Unable to read, she recited prayers for the children and quoted memorized passages from the family Bible. Although she could not write her name, Nancy was capable of indoctrinating her children with primitive Baptist utterances of christian "fatalism in which she glorified" (Oates, p. 5, 1977). William Herndon said, "Mr. Lincoln held to a firm belief that he was doomed to a sad fate; he held firmly to the philosophy of fatalism all of his life; he said to me more than once: '"Billy, I fear that I shall meet with some terrible end"' (Herndon's Notes and Monographs, *The Hidden Lincoln*, p. 410). Lincoln was in a constant state of fragmented thinking, going back and forth to the past and then again to present, and even *channeling* to the future. Perhaps the future was brighter — or better yet, darker.

Lincoln always believed that dreams possessed hidden meanings. He was right. Psychiatrist Carl Bell and other social scientists contend that dreams are oftentimes connected to unseen or internal conflict. He says that today there are ways to teach people to use their dreams to their advantage. One aspect of this procedure, Bell says, is to "scan" yourself internally — and often. He states that it is pertinent to talk aloud about your states of "frenzy." As Herndon said, "Lincoln was a very "shut-mouthed" person. Lincoln was tense, and needed to relax. Even as a child, Lincoln held the belief of hidden meaning in dreams, and these beliefs continued on into his adulthood.

Abraham Lincoln would often work late into the night. Sometimes while waiting for sleep to come to him, he would read a book of Shakespeare's Tragedies. He loved reading *Hamlet* and *Macbeth*. He would recite stanzas of morbid poems about graves and death. Lincoln would finally go into a fitful sleep filled with dreams of war, water and phantom ships (Oates, p. 250, 1977). Lincoln's son, Willie, died while Lincoln was President. Willie Lincoln died on February 20, 1862. He was only twelve. After his death, Lincoln would sometimes dream that the boy was still alive. He would see Willie playing in the yard and call out to him, only to wake up and find himself in his own house of darkness ... it was only a dream. "Ultimately it was Lincoln's own fatalism that eased his sorrow the most and helped him cope with his dreams and memories. After Willie's death, he talked more frequently about God than he had before — about how the Almighty had taken Willie and how He controlled the fates and destinies of everyone." Some people wished that Lincoln was a religious man so badly that they have written that he found God after Willie's death, that Lincoln had a devotional of daily readings. Lincoln was not a religious man, and people close to him confirmed that Lincoln hardly ever read this little book. He did, however, respect the Bible and enjoyed many of its passages. He received a Bible from a group of African-Americans from Baltimore, Maryland. He told them that receiving such a book was like a gift from "God." Lincoln stated decisively, "There is a divinity that shapes our ends."

By 1862, Lincoln saw himself as '"an instrument of Providence"' who had been put on Earth, during the Civil War, "for God's own designs." Lincoln dreamed of corpses, guns flashing in the night, and of soldiers too tired to move (Oates, pp. 292-293 & 331-332, 1977). The war and Lincoln's secrets wrecked Lincoln's already fragile mentality. Lincoln continued to have fitful sleep and dreams. One day before Lincoln was assassinated, he awakened, opened the Bible, and every page he flipped to were passages about fantasy or dreams. It isn't such an impossible feat when dealing with the King James Bible to flip to pages of fantasy and dreams. The book is filled with these types of stories. Mary Todd Lincoln said that her husband sometimes frightened her. She thought that something had possession of him. Lincoln told Mary that he dreamed that people were mourning, and that he actually thought that he had left his bed and went

THE LETTER ON THIS PAGE WAS WRITTEN BY A MR.
A. G. FRICK TO ABRAHAM LINCOLN ON FEBRUARY
14, 1861. HE WROTE FOR THE STATES OF TENNESSEE,
MISSOURI, KENTUCKY, VIRGINIA, NORTH CARO-
LINA AND ARKANSAS THAT THEY WOULD ALL
SECEDE IF MR. LINCOLN DID NOT RESIGN FROM
THE PRESIDENCY "glory be to god on high." THE LET-
TER INCLUDES:

   Sir
Mr Abe Lincoln
if you don't Resign [sic] we are going to put a spider in
you [sic] dumpling . . . . you are nothing but a goddern
Black nigger

                     Yours TC"(?)
                     Mr. A.G. Frick

LINCOLN FOUND THIS LETTER ON THE TABLE IN
HIS SUITE (#6) AT THE WILLARD HOTEL IN WASH-
INGTON, D.C.

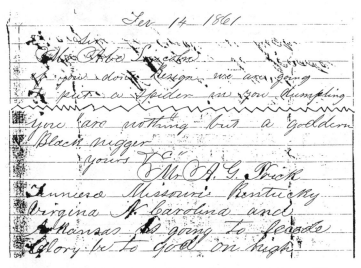

Abraham Lincoln Collection, Archives and Manuscripts Dept., Chicago
Historical Society.

LINCOLN'S CONFUSED STATE OF MIND REVEALS ITSELF ONCE AGAIN WHEN IN MID-1862 HE WROTE IN AN EMANCIPATION PROCLAMATION DRAFT "gradual *adoption*" OF SLAVERY. THE LETTER ON THIS PAGE SHOWS HIS HASTY CORRECTION TO "gradual *abolishment*" OF SLAVERY . . . LINCOLN'S WHITE SELF WAS DEFINITELY DOMINANT IN THIS PARTICULAR INSTANCE.

(*New York Public Library*, **Reference: Sanders, G.,** *Abraham Lincoln Fact Book,* **Eastern Acorn Press, 1982)**

Important: The reading of the Preliminary Treatise & the Defining Ourselves section.

downstairs. He told Mary that downstairs people were crying, but the criers were invisible. Lincoln told his wife that he wandered from room to room; things looked familiar, but where were the mourning people? When he arrived in the East room of the White House, there was an eerie surprise a — corpse. Soldiers were guarding the corpse. Lincoln then saw the crowd, and asked who is dead in the White House? A soldier answered him, "The President; he was killed by an assassin!" A Lincoln biographer said that when Lincoln thought about this dream, he was "grave, gloomy, and at times visibly *pale*" (Oates, pp. 425-427, 1977). The insane have sense buried within their nonsense.

BLACK AND WHITE

As President of the United States from 1861 to 1865, Abraham Lincoln received a lot of hate mail laced with death threats. Lincoln's family and friends were worried. Lincoln received over 100 visitors at the White House on a daily basis. He was warned by many that he was in danger. One sure sign was that of broken windows at the front door of the White House.

Just after the first election, one day while immersed in his fear and tiredness, Lincoln glanced in the mirror and distinctly saw "two images of his own face." Shocked, he got closer to the mirror and the two images had disappeared. He looked again and the two images had returned; the images were very clear now: one swarthy, one pale. Mary Todd Lincoln told him that the swarthy, dark face meant "life" and good, that he would be elected to a second term in the Presidential seat. (No president since Andrew Jackson had served more than four years, so Lincoln wanted to win his second term badly, although many felt that he was not as sophisticated and culturally refined as Jackson. But if he did win, it would prove to himself and others that the decisions he had made in the past were acceptable.) There had been many occasions when Mary Todd thought that Lincoln "was not himself." Mary continued; she told Lincoln that the light, pale face meant death and evil, "an omen" that he would die during his second term in office. "It puzzled him that the second image was pale, much like the face of a dead

man." (References: Whitney, p. 144; Garrison, p. 62; Sandburg, *Mary Lincoln*, p. 44, 1932; and Oates, p. 196, 1977). Lincoln was murdered by a white man named John Wilkes
Booth during his second term in office as President of the
United States, 1865. Understanding his dreams, rejecting a
totally white mentality, and accepting his Black Self could
have saved Lincoln's life.

Abraham Lincoln had many internal conflicts and stressful periods of indecision, especially during the Civil War.
Abe Lincoln also had self-destructive thoughts because of
more intimate reasons. He thought that he would be killed.
We know from the study and understanding of the *power of
thought* that this man, perhaps not by his own hand, possibly mentally killed himself before the bullet collided with
his brain from the racist assassin's gun. These self-destructive thoughts caused him to have fear and panic. Panic for
what? Panic because he may be found out one day. Lincoln
was known to have mused: "You can fool some of the people some of the time, but you can't fool all of the people all
of the time." What did he really mean? Did Lincoln feel, or
hope, that someone would figure his complex problem out
one day? He had to deal with the internal conflicts with and
within himself which essentially was caused by the attitude,
discrimination and sickness of white America. At no point
during Lincoln's lifetime could he be HimSelf in America.

The author of *The Three Musketeers*, Alexandre Dumas
was an African man living in France, when in 1847 he wrote
a letter to a white southern Democrat in America. In this letter, he told the democrat that his mother was an African
woman. He wrote that he was not ashamed that his very
looks attest to his ancestry and lineage. He went on to say
that he was anxious to visit America, but there was only one
thing that stops him. He wrote: "I am told that my African
blood will subject me to inconvenience in your country, and
that I may even be taken and sold as a slave, according to
[your] existing laws" (Dennis, *Black History*, p. 77).

While travelling with his family in 1847, lawyer Lincoln
heard many slavery and anti-slavery stories. One story that
he remembered was that of a young woman by the name of
Eliza, who had 1/64 Black blood, with the rest of her being
white. She was a slave and considered Black, African. She

had jet black hair, brown olive skin and dark glowing eyes. She was being auctioned off between an American minister and a Frenchman. The auctioneer wanted all he could get, so he first pulled the young woman's dress top down exposing her breast. The greedy auctioneer then said, "Now who is going to lose a chance like this!" The two bidders bidded higher. The auctioneer then pulled Eliza's dress up to the waist and patting her thighs, he cried, "I'm going to sell this girl! Who is going to be the winner of this prize?" The American preacher "won" the "prize" by five dollars, at $1,585.00. The preacher, Calvin Fairbank, immediately set Eliza free. This gesture made a lot of Blacks and Whites happy (Sandburg, p. 163, 1925). Lincoln must have liked this anti-slavery story enough to later relate it to friends. It was not discussed in Sandburg's work, but it is possible that there was debate between whites as to whether this woman was actually African or white. No matter, Lincoln and many other "whites" were on shaky ground when these questions of blood percentage arose.

A caucasian man by the name of Timothy White, the American minister who was held hostage for five years in Beirut, Lebanon, said on the television show, *20/20*, April 17, 1992 that anyone, and it doesn't matter what color or race you are, who thinks that they have a right to hold another person, of any race or color, in bondage, is "uncivilized." His statement holds true for anytime during his-story (history).

STILL TRYING TO FIGURE OUT LINCOLN

Dennis Hanks' claims that the estrangement between Lincoln and his father was widened even more when Lincoln was beat by Thomas for reading books. Thomas told Lincoln that he was ruining himself with education (Oates, p. 13, 1977). Dr. Carl Bell from Chicago, Illinois contends that children are naturally eager to learn, and they should be rewarded for their efforts and encouraged, not the opposite. Is it possible that Thomas Lincoln felt that Abe should not be taught to read and learn because he knew of the child's true ancestral background? During this time, Blacks were not allowed to learn and to read in American society.

Young Abe learned to read in spite of Thomas Lincoln. How else had young Abe been ruined?

Lincoln was a large child for his age, "gawky" looking, and mostly introverted. Thomas Lincoln could not understand why Abe always wanted to read and he felt somewhat threatened by this act (*World Book Encyclopedia*, p. 4011, 1937; Oates, p. 13, 1977). Was he afraid that he may lose his mental hold on the child, and the child may one day come into his senses — and tell? Lincoln's very demeanor during his youth and adult life exhibits that of an abused child. Lincoln was never psychologically screened for victimization.

The development of children has been analyzed and questioned by parents, educators, and psychologists alike. We sometimes marvel at and sometimes get confused by children's everyday troubles and mental problems — assuming that they are too young for such deep problems, especially in 1800's psychology. Since parents are known and said to be role models for their children, children reflect the behaviors, attitudes, ideals and ideas of the parents. In the case of Andrew Jackson, his mother had told him before she died to always stand up and be a man. Now what does that mean to a child? She also told him never to forget that the British were very brutal towards them. As recorded, Jackson seemed to have held a personal vendetta against the British for the remainder of his life. Lincoln, however, held his personal vendetta against his father — and himself. Nancy adored her children and was, of course, their prime careprovider. She left a lasting impression, but Lincoln had many problems after her death. He was only nine (ten or eleven) when she died. This was not a happy time for young Abe. This unhappiness lingered throughout his life.

There is a deep interconnectedness with all beings which causes a person to want to be happy unless there is something so morbid or extraordinarily sad about his or her life (usually stemming from childhood) that a person would choose not to be happy. Abraham was a very sad man, bordering soundly toward manic depression, borderline personality disorder, and dissociation. Lincoln had a tendency to stare off into space even in mid-sentence. He was also prone to the habit of "forgetting" to eat. Maybe the other Self wasn't hungry. Lincoln was also so apt to change from one mood to another with such quick force that it was as if he were a different person. To the people in the room with him, it was as if they were suddenly in the room with an entirely different person. Mary Todd Lincoln was known for saying that "Mr. Lincoln doesn't seem himself today." Mary said that Lincoln's quick disposition and personality transformations scared her. Lincoln had mood swings. Mary did not like his habit of withdrawing into himself. He would sometimes become distant and glummy when she wanted to have a discussion. "She did not understand his [sickness] hypo any more than his friends did and was irritated by his spells of abstraction. They might come at the dinner table, where he would stare into space, impervious to conversation and Mary's glances. Or he would go off and sit in his rocking chair, immersed in himself as he mulled over some law case or the state of the Union, mulled over the meaning of life and the inevitability of death, his death and that of his wife and children, until he would shake such thoughts away and pull himself back to his house, this room, his playing sons, his anxious wife. Once a spell even came over him while he pulled one of his boys in a wagon. Lost in thought [or another Self], he tugged the wagon over an uneven plank sidewalk and the child fell off. But Lincoln was oblivious to the fallen boy and went on with his head bent forward, hauling the empty wagon around the neighborhood" (Oates, p. 66, 1977). What a sight this must have been to the neighbors. Of course, they wondered about Mr. Lincoln's sanity.

The behaviors and personality changes referred to above are exhibited by people known to have multiple personality disorder (MPD). Whether Lincoln liked it or not, and whether he was Black or White, it is deduced that he had at least a White personality and a Black personality, and an extraordinarily moody personality and an odd and mysterious humorous personality within his sudden transformations of Self and divisions of psyche. Ninety-seven percent of multiple personality victims (people with dissociative states) report a history of childhood trauma, most commonly a combination of emotional, physical and/or sexual abuse. The personality that is dominant at any particular time determines the individual's behavior, actions, and words.

When dealing with multiracials, especially those who suffer from a dissociative state of mind, it would be necessary to sometimes (not always) separate the whole person in order to understand and deal with certain aspects and actions of the person in general. For example, if Lincoln had decided consciously or unconsciously that he was going to be a black person, then he would more than likely say black enough things to make black people think that he freed the slaves, and if he decides that he is going to be a white person, then he would say negative things about black people, such as Blacks are not equal to white people. You will notice in Chapter 7 that Dwight D. Eisenhower's actions bordered toward this phenomenon. Although it is not felt that Eisenhower was a multiple personality, I do feel that he put himself in the shoes of Blacks, Jews, and Whites given certain situations. Please allow me to reiterate that these presidents' dominant personalities were that of a white personality living in America. Each personality of a person with multiple personality syndrome is real. But, I repeat, I'm referring to personalities here and not the actual, real or whole person — biologically speaking.

Some old biographers alluded to, and a few recent biographers have said that Lincoln was possibly homosexual, bisexual, or least had the tendencies. He could have been anything considering all of the problems he carried around with him with no type of therapeutic outlet. So the subject of homosexuality is another Lincoln mask that must be addressed. He did dread the company of women, unless they were unavailable, e.g., not white, old, married, or whatever. Did he think that he would have to perform? Could he not imagine himself with a woman? What happened to Lincoln as a child? Were Lincoln's problems physical, mental, or both?

In the winter of 1850 when Thomas Lincoln was dying, Abraham Lincoln would not see nor write to his father, but he did take the time to write back to John Johnston, Sally Bush's son, explaining to him that there was really no need for him to see, talk with, or write his father. Finally Lincoln did write a short note to Johnston, and asked him to tell his dying father to call upon the "Maker; who will not turn away from him ..." (Oates, p. 95, 1977). Lincoln was not present at his father's funeral. Maybe Lincoln was protecting his already fragmented Self from reverting to regressive states of mind.

Everything being pure, real in its own right or space, and everything being bio (right/left, up/down, good/bad, Upper Nile/Lower Nile), and everything having a universal interconnectedness, surely there has to be a connection to the fact that Abe Lincoln choose not to even sit by his father at his deathbed when his father specifically requested that he visit him. Perhaps the old man wanted to verbally mend his ways or to tell Lincoln who he really was. Even after Thomas Lincoln's death, Lincoln decided that he did not even want to see the man's face, much less anything else that *may* have been on his person. Abraham Lincoln choose not to attend "his father's?" funeral. There has to be some deep imbedded reasons why a person would choose not to attend their own father's funeral unless they were totally incapacitated themselves; Abe Lincoln was not incapacitated, and could have attended his father's funeral. It is highly improbable that Lincoln did not attend this funeral because he simply loved his father too much to handle it. Is it possible that another personality became dominant and decided not to attend? Had Lincoln been treated like a real son, and especially if Lincoln had been Thomas' biological son and with Abe being the type of personality that his dominant self was, he would have attended a kind father's funeral.

On the other hand, Lincoln could have been still depressed from the death of his young son, Eddie. He died on February 1, 1850; he was only four. Going to Thomas Lincoln's funeral could have proven too much for an already distressed man and mind. But a year had passed, "the Lincoln's had learned to live with Eddie's death, Mary finding what solace she could in religion and Lincoln in his professional work." Mary was pregnant again also. The baby was born on December 21, 1850. Lincoln's father died on January 17, 1851. Too many outstanding memories of his mother could cause a breakdown. Perhaps not attending the funeral was a way to keep the little sanity he had intact. Nine years later, in 1860, Lincoln visited his "father's" grave. There was no headstone. Lincoln ordered that an appropriate headstone be placed by the grave.

There has been much speculation about Abraham Lincoln's mental health, physical health, family background, and his birth. There will be even more speculation in the future, especially now, and after the 1991 CNN news announcement.

LINCOLN AND RECENT MEDICAL THEORIES

On May 7, 1991 on U.S.A. - CNN News, Atlanta, Georgia, it was announced that DNA testing was being carried out on Lincoln's blood and hair. It was stated that researchers are trying to determine if Lincoln had Marfan syndrome. Marfan syndrome is a blood disease of the heart and arteries that kills at an early age. At any time the arteries might burst if the victims of this disorder are not careful. The victims are usually very tall and skinny. Marfan syndrome is also a disease which affects the blood vessels in the eyes. We do not know how long Lincoln would have lived. He was around fifty-six when he was killed. Studies show that some victims of the Marfan syndrome and its variants sometimes exhibit mental and antisocial behavior *(Current Medical Diagnosis and Treatment,* A Lange Medical Book, 1992, Appleton and Lange, Norwalk, CA, p. 835).

On this same CNN news report, it was also stated that Lincoln was a Black man — that it is possible that he had African ancestry. When I contacted the researchers who are conducting this research on Lincoln, they stated that they were unaware of this news report. To tell truth, it did fly by fast. When I contacted CNN in Atlanta, they could find nothing. The young lady I spoke with said that she did remember that there was some news report on Lincoln, but that it had been erased from the computer. Then I started getting phone calls from people who knew that I was writing this book; they heard the report also, and the rest is our-story.

The Walter Reed Medical Library, that is the Walter Reed Hospital, is responsible for the DNA testing being done on Lincoln. They report that they are trying to determine whether Lincoln had Marfan syndrome. I talked with Mr. D.L. at the Walter Reed Medical Museum. He told me that the DNA testing on Lincoln has not been completed and that they are testing Lincoln's dried blood, hair, as well as some of his extracted bone. Mr. D.L. volunteered to me that they have discovered a way to clone Lincoln's blood so that they can do more testing. I asked Mr. D.L. if there had been any testing on the DNA or the genetic makeup of Lincoln to determine whether or not Lincoln was Black. I went on to explain that an acquaintance had heard news on CNN, Durham, North Carolina that researchers had conducted some DNA testing on Lincoln, and that they think that Lincoln may have had an African heritage — Black blood. Mr. D.L. said that the experts and scholars on Lincoln, as far as they have "discussed," plead no basis for this belief. I then questioned to Mr. D.L., "So there has been some conversation or some discussion about this?" Mr. D.L. answered, "Well, no; it hasn't been."

Many whites still cannot accept the fact that there is a possibility that they and/or their forefathers, have elected a black man, or several, into the White House. "Lincoln experts" have a great propensity for evading the question of Lincoln's ancestry. Many Lincoln biographers, writers, and "experts" know more than they write or say.

Flo Hyman, an African-American Olympic volleyball champion, died suddenly from Marfan syndrome in 1986. Chris Patton, a young African-American basketball player from the University of Maryland also died from this disease. It is said that this disease affects about 1 in every 15,000 people without racial or ethnic predilection. "The *marfanoid habitus* may be seen in some patients with sickle cell disease, the Klinefelter syndrome." *(Cecil Textbook of Medicine,* Wyngaarden & Smith, W.B. Saunders Co., Philadelphia, Pa, 1988, p. 1178; *Current Medical Diagnosis.* 1992, p. 804).

In spite of the vast amount of information on the sickling process, American doctors and researchers have not been able to develop a general treatment for the disease that causes sickling. This sickling disease, which mostly affect Africans, is called sickle cell anemia. There are a large number of people who are afflicted with sickle cell anemia. People develop the sickle disease or inherit the sickle hemoglobin gene from just one parent and a normal hemoglobin gene from the other parent. Of course, both parents can have this sickling disease which would make their child highly susceptible. Sickle cell anemia has associated problems in blood circulation (See: Edelstein, The Sickle Cell, pp. 3-4. 48. 63. & 150). Dr. Sunday Fadulu states that the sickle cell disease is a disorder that comes from inadequate oxygen transported by an abnormal hemoglobin molecule in the red blood cells. Dr. Fadulu, a professor of Microbiology at Texas Southern University, has developed the only drug in existence that controls this painful disease and reverses its symptoms. This healing drug comes from the chewing stick in Dr. Fadulu's home of Nigeria, Africa (The Washington Afro-American, August 24, 1991, A5).

The sickling trait (or carrier) has been said to be an advantage in some medical cases. As a result of this genetic advantage that carriers have over noncarriers, in those regions of Africa infected with malaria, more and more carriers have survived malaria in each generation over thousands of years. Today in certain regions of Africa, twenty to thirty percent of the population are carriers. Carriers are effectively free of the symptoms of malaria. This, of course, does not negate the seriousness of the disease.

At sixteen, Lincoln was more than six feet tall. He was a large dark boy with high cheekbones, dark, deep set eyes, like his mother's, and coarse, unruly hair. His legs were so long that some say he seemed to have stood on stilts. Lincoln is said to have been an exceptionally good athlete. He was one of the fastest runners and one of the best fighters in the neighborhood. "His arm muscles were like cables, so strong that he could seize an ax by the end of the handle and hold it straight out at arm's length" (Oates, p. 13, 1977) like Hercules. He was strong, but as he matured, worked and studied, he acquired a rigorous profession. With his profession and mental instability, he sometimes forgot to eat. Not eating aggravated his stomach and his nervous system which caused him to be extremely prostrated. The Marfan's person tend to grow exceptionally tall; they are usually skinny people, with long hands and feet. The chest and spine are likely to be deformed and the joint capsules are basically weak, though from observation many people with Marfan syndrome seem rather athletically strong. Marfan victims are usually double-jointed with a protruding stomach. Most usually do not live beyond age fifty, although this is changing. Death is usually caused by sudden heart failure or the bursting of arteries. There is a fifty percent chance that Marfan victims' children will develop the disease (Professional Guide to Diseases, 3rd ed., Springhouse Corp., PA, 1989).

Seventy-five percent of Marfan's sufferers have eye problems; they are usually myopic. Abraham did wear glasses occasionally, but he was hyperopic, not myopic like most

Marfan's victims. He bought his eyeglasses in Bloomington, Illinois for $.38 (thirty-eight cents). Years after Lincoln purchased his "expensive" glasses, it was found that the prescription was "three times more powerful than he needed" (Garrison, p. 88).

In eighty-five percent of the Marfan's sufferers, family history shows Marfan syndrome in one parent as well. In the remaining fifteen percent, a negative family history suggest fresh mutation, possibly because of advanced paternal age, i.e., the parents were old when the child was conceived. "Because no specific test confirms Marfan syndrome, diagnosis rests on typical clinical features ... and a history of the disease in close relatives. And as for Lincoln, "A distant relative had Marfan syndrome, but the relationship spanned about eight generations — not a strong family history" (*JAMA*, Oct. 3, 1990, p. 1645). Did Nancy Hanks have Marfan syndrome? Improbable. However, as mentioned, she was a tall, rather slim woman. Nancy Hanks did die young, but historians have written that she died from milk sickness. Tallness and slimness doesn't always mean that one has the Marfan syndrome. It would be good, however, to at least check with a doctor if you are exceptionally tall and skinny. Thomas Lincoln was only thirty-one years old when Lincoln was born. Was Lincoln's biological African father a tall, distinguished- looking man of sixty or so with a Mali or Zulu King appearance? Maybe. Or did Lincoln get his Marfan syndrome from Nancy's mother, Lucey, or Lucey's father or mother — or whomever? If scientists wish to say that Lincoln had Marfan syndrome (and they have not, yet), then they are also implying that Thomas Lincoln definitely may not have been Abraham Lincoln's biological father. Thomas Lincoln did not have Marfan syndrome. His age nor Nancy's was advanced enough at Lincoln's birth to cause Lincoln to develop the disease from this particular union. Of course, it is possible in some way that Lincoln could have had this disease. But if Lincoln were fat and short, today's white researchers, scientists, and his-storians would look for a disease to fit the fat/short description. They would likely test Lincoln's DNA for thyroid problems. Almost any reason could be given to the general public as an excuse to search Lincoln's DNA for his true ancestry. Of course, they're curious. What scientist or politician in America, and the world for that matter, wouldn't be? We're all curious. America runs its motor on race, color, prejudice, discrimination and the American dream. I do not feel that researchers and the Government care whether Lincoln had Marfan syndrome. I do think they care if he were Black. Professor William Pearce, Associate professor of surgery at Northwestern University stated that if it could be determined whether Lincoln had Marfan syndrome, it "would give a big psychological boost to the 40,000 Americans with this condition, as well as people with other fatal inherited diseases" (*Washington Post*, Forum, p. 7, Oct. 22, 1991). Just imagine what it would do for the Black race if the DNA showed that he was actually Black? Many have already agreed that Lincoln was a mixed-blood white supremist. Many whites and a few blacks still think that Lincoln was a really great man. When the truth is ultimately and widely revealed about Lincoln's mental illness, his abuse, and his basic (real and raw) thoughts and actions regarding politics, race and life, more people of all races (some Blacks included) will unfortunately be willing to accept Lincoln's Africanness as a bad President. No one will wish to claim him any more.

BLACK AWARENESS

Lincoln was said to be the illegitimate son of a Black person by Nancy Hanks (J.A. Rogers, *The Five Negro Presidents*, p. 8, sentence 1, 1965). Lincoln himself described his father as having a dark complexion, black, coarse hair, and brown eyes. Was he referring to Thomas Lincoln or someone else? Did Nancy Hanks disclose significant information to her young son before her death? Lincoln described himself as "Of dark complexion with coarse black hair and dark eyes." He said that he was six feet, four inches tall, dark skinned, with dark coarse hair. His hair was thick. Lincoln's barber was a Haitian-born African by the name of William Florville. When Lincoln was in his late twenties, he petitioned Florville to be his barber. Lincoln had just begun his double career as lawyer and politician. Florville cut Lincoln's hair for more than twenty years, while Lincoln in turn handled the law requirements of Florville's real estate business. "Billy the Barber," as Florville was called, owned a farm and plenty of town land considering it was 1830's America. Lincoln's background gave rise to many caricatures and cartoons. One such cartoon was depicted in a drawing in *Vanity Fair* in 1861. The artist drew Lincoln adorning a semi-curly Afro. See page 150. Why did Lincoln have to wear those big, tall top hats? Was it because he couldn't always get his hands on some grease and water to slick a beautiful dark mane down? Had the 1861 *Vanity Fair* cartoonist seen Lincoln's hair in its natural state? When reviewing unofficial pictures of Lincoln in the Library of Congress, James Madison Building, I noticed that in many of these pictures his natural coarse hair was captured. It looks as if when Lincoln knew that his picture was going to be taken, he prepared his hair with some type of "slicker," e.g., hair grease and water, or something.

Lincoln's behavior and sometimes his words and actions indicated that he was aware of his Black Self to some degree. This "awareness" has been termed a "melanin receptor" by some social scientists. We are not blessed onto this Earth without some genetic memory of who we are. This Black self, though a part of his dissociative or multiple selves, was a persistent part of Lincoln, the man. For a metaphoric example, he made a comment about white people in one of his speeches and referred to whites as "them," as if he were not a part of the white race. All of Lincoln's "selves" would sometimes confuse and confound people, making it difficult to understand some of Lincoln's tactics, antics, and answers to certain political questions. Lerone Bennett asserts that Lincoln's public speeches on the subject of race, especially in the 1830's and 1840's, were two-sided or two-faced. He said that Lincoln was very careful to be for and against slavery. In J.A. Rogers, pamphlet he mentions a statement by Chauncey Burr, who said in reference to Abraham Lincoln: "It would not rebound to Lincoln's honor to have it proved that he is part Negro. For then on the ground of a natural sympathy with his own race we might find excuses for facts which we could never pardon a white man." (Coleman, Wim. "The Evidence that Abraham Lincoln was not Born in Lawful Wedlock," 1899; *The American Mercury*, "The Many-Sired Lincoln, pp. 129-135). The 1800's white feminist and crusader for human rights, Jane Grey Swisshelm, referred to Lincoln as the "Prince of Darkness," a man who was "incapable of understanding, or believing in the wickedness, the cruelty, and barbarism of the Southern [white] people ... in defense of their right to whip women and rob cradles" (Larsen, Arthur J., pp. 289-290). Many of the ex-enslaved people during Lincoln's reign called him "half-Moses, half-Yankee" (Donald, p. 369). Did they know something? William Herndon, Lincoln's law partner, said not only was Lincoln's hair coarse, and not only was his skin dark, but Lincoln had "very dark skin." White southerners said that Lincoln was "of Negro ancestry" (Donald, p. 370). They said his skin color was "sooty" (Black), so they called Abe, "Africanus the First from Liberia." It is also written that Lincoln's mother, Nancy Hanks Lincoln, had African blood, that is, "Ethiopian ancestry" (Donald, p. 307; also see White, Richard Grant).

During Lincoln's presidential campaign, he and his running mate, Hannibal Hamlin, were said to be Black men. Of course the statements were meant to be "smears" against them. Many southerners said that Lincoln was "sooty" and a "scoundrelly creature" (Handlin, p. 137). They thought that Lincoln must be a lunatic to want freedom for Blacks. Herndon said that when Lincoln signed the Emancipation Proclamation, "there was no heart in the act" (Bennett, p. 42, 1968).

On April 14, 1887, twenty-two years after Lincoln's death, a splendid monument of Lincoln was unmasked. Many high officials were in attendance singing Lincoln's praises. One high official here did not sing Lincoln's praises, and he pointed out to the crowd that Abraham Lincoln was not the Black race's ideal of a man. Within the confines (invisibility) of Frederick Douglass' speech, he admits his knowledge, conscious or unconscious, that Abraham Lincoln wasn't necessarily a white man himself, but his "habits of thought" were that of a white man. Here's the speech (author italics):

> Long after his departure to the solemn *shades, the silent continent of eternity,* it must be admitted, truth compels me to admit, even here in the presence of the monument we have erected to his memory, Abraham Lincoln was not, in the fullest sense of the

word, either our man or our model. In his interests, in his associations, in his habit of thought, and in his prejudices, he was a white man. He was preeminently the white man's President, entirely devoted to the welfare of white men.... In all his education and feeling he was an American of the Americans.

Frederick Douglass

And if Africans living in America had been considered Americans in the mind of Frederick Douglass, then Lincoln would have been named as their president, too. Lincoln was the white man's president. Africans living in America have some "Lincolns" living in their communities and working in the courts and educational institutions today. Frederick Douglass never said that Lincoln was a white man, per se; he said that Lincoln's actions and philosophies were white, and therefore, he was the white man's president. For lack of a better example for understanding this particular theory, it is submitted to you that Lincoln was an Uncle Tom. (Ourstory is in the process of correcting the Uncle Tom view. Many have misunderstood Uncle Tom's motives in the book, *Uncle Tom's Cabin;* however, the old theory still holds regarding Lincoln).

Frederick Douglass said that Abraham Lincoln was white in his interest, associations, and thoughts, not his skin color nor his race. Now we must look to the *many* hues of a now *determined* continent that will always be eternal to all life for understanding the invisible.

HIDING BEHIND A CLOWN'S MASK

Abraham Lincoln's clown personality may have been his ISH, inner self-helper, or what (or more appropriately who) is termed the Protector/Protective personality for victims of Multiple Personality Disorder. Lincoln's clown Self would joke around in order to hide emotional problems and keep hurt and embarrassment in check.

After telling a joke, Lincoln was known to sometimes fall to the ground, crinkle up his prominent nose, grin, give a loud, high-pitched, howling laugh, then commence to scratching his elbows (Oates, p. 50, 1984). "When he was around girls, he covered up a painful shyness by acting the clown." Lincoln also loved joking around with the men in his community store when he was a young man. Later as a lawyer and President of the United States, he enjoyed clowning around with his young assistants, John Nicolay and John Hay. They thought it funny when the President would visit them in the White House bedroom that they shared and joke and show them laughable caricatures. Nicolay and Hay thought it hilarious that Lincoln would laugh and poke fun at caricatures when he looked just as funny as many of the caricatures himself. They too thought Lincoln was a clown. Many of the flyers that circulated during Lincoln's presidential campaign depicted him as a clown. One such caricature was titled *Under the Veil,* drawn by Volck, 1862.

When Lincoln ran for President, some campaign circuits contended that Lincoln was an infidel, a clown. (Oates, 13 & 76, 1977). "Even conservative Southern papers continually referred to Lincoln as a '"gorilla"' or a '"clown"' (Du Bois, p. 165). In the book, *Ordeal of the Presidency,* Chapter VI is entitled, "Baboon In The White House," referring to Lincoln. The caricature of Lincoln as a veiled clown was circulated throughout his political career. Psychologist Na'im Akbar postulates in his book, *Chains and Images of Psychological Slavery,* that the holder of enslaved persons (the so-called master) "prided himself in his superiority by being entertained by the slave. Writers have long pointed to the **jester,** the **clown,** or the **fool,** as the inferior one who was responsible for making his [so-called] superior laugh. Using a person for your clown has always been one of the major ways to assert your dominance over a person. Mockery is one of the more sophisticated forms of humiliation" (Akbar, p. 20). In essence, to many of these white people during the Lincoln Era, to mock Lincoln was to say, "you are are beneath me; you are black."

During the summer of 1860, Lincoln and Stephen Douglas were Republican and Democratic candidates for President of the United States. Their campaigns and their debates, as in their 1858 Senatorial debates, would prove to be politically explosive. They had been debating each other for years. Frederick Douglass joined in the fight against the racist "Little Giant," Stephen Douglas. A few years after Lincoln was admitted to the bar, he ran for the U.S. House of

Representatives from Illinois. As the campaigns of 1840's continued, Lincoln and Douglas debated one another from one end of Illinois to the other. In one campaign confrontation, Lincoln mimicked a Democratic opponent, imitating the way the man talked and walked. Lincoln carried on with hilarious gestures, and facial expressions. He sent "the crowd into paroxysms of laughter. That sort of thing enraged Douglas's paper, the *Illinois State Register*, which berated Lincoln for his '"assumed clownishness"' and '"game of buffoonery,"' ... Lincoln, hoping that he had not offended anyone, apologized" (Oates, p. 51, 1977). He lost then, but he didn't lose in 1860.

LINCOLN'S DARK RUNNING MATE, HANNIBAL HAMLIN

Lincoln was pleased when he learned that Hannibal Hamlin would be his running partner. He felt that his very peculiar wife, Mary Lincoln, would even like Hamlin. Lincoln couldn't wait to tell Mary the good news.

Just before his inauguration in November of 1860, Lincoln was threatened with plans of secession from several states. He said that he did not have time to worry about the South right now. He was more concerned about the selection of Cabinet members. So he called a meeting with Hannibal Hamlin. They met in Chicago. Lincoln wanted to get Hamlin's opinion about who should be the Cabinet member from New England. This meeting took place on November 22, 1860. It was the first time the two men had met. Lincoln, of course, had heard that Hamlin was a mulatto. Lincoln noticed that Hannibal Hamlin was "tall, slump-shouldered, and olive-skinned" (Oates, p. 197, 1977) much like himself. They had an amicable and productive meeting. In the meantime, Lincoln continued to hope that this thing with the South would not be a problem.

When Lincoln found it necessary to release a Mr. Salmon Chase from his Treasury duties, Chase sympathizers objected. Lincoln told them that if they did not like what he had done, then the Senate could have his resignation and have Hannibal Hamlin as their president. This sounds like a threat. Did Lincoln mean it to sound this way? Maybe not.

Giving Lincoln the benefit of the doubt here, the man was probably just sick and tired of all of the problems. Let someone else have the problems for a change.

In March of 1861, Hannibal Hamlin pleaded with Lincoln to rid General George McClellan of his military and interior duties. McClellan had become a joke during the Civil War. Some said that McClellan was an absolute imbecile, a traitor who knew nothing about military strategy. Lincoln confronted McClellan, but defended him by stating that he was not saying that McClellan was a traitor, but he was repeating what others had said. McClellan was reduced to tears stating that he was not a traitor; he said that he was still loyal to the Union. Lincoln visited the indecisive McClellan's military headquarters once. Lincoln noticed some soldiers working on something, and asked what they were building. A soldier answered the President. He informed Lincoln that it was a toilet for General McClellan. Lincoln said, "Is it a one-holer or a two-holer?" He answered the President, "It's a one-holer." Lincoln later said to his assistant, "Thank goodness it's a one-holer, because if it were a two-holer, McClellan would shit on himself before he could make up his mind which hole to use." Lincoln's exact words were: "Thank God it is a one-holer, for if it were a two-holer McClellan would beshit himself before he could make up his mind which hole he should use" (Hyman, Dick, pp. 64-66). President Lincoln released McClellan as General in Chief from his Civil War duties. McClellan was fired on November 5, 1861.

Later when George McClellan ran against Lincoln in the 1864 Presidential Election, McClellan wrote to his wife declaring that Lincoln was nothing but a "well-meaning baboon." He wrote in another letter that upon visiting the White House, he found the "original gorilla" there. Lincoln, though being ever the gentleman, felt that General McClellan was inept in his duties and said of him, "McClellan is a pleasant and scholarly gentleman; he is an admirable engineer, but he seems to have a special talent for stationary engineering" (Gross, *Lincoln's Own Stories*, p. 164). Of course, Lincoln did not know that McClellan had called, or would call him a gorilla; otherwise Lincoln probably would have made a more bawdy and smutty remark about McClellan, only if to his closest friends.

McClellan promised to restore the Union and slavery. During this campaign the Democrats advertised with posters showing Republican men dancing with Black women; they headed the poster "the Miscegenation Ball." They said that under Lincoln, interracial relationships would flourish. One Democratic paper in Wisconsin declared that: "If he [Lincoln] is elected to misgovern for another four years, we trust some bold hand will pierce his heart with dagger point for the public good" (Oates, p. 397, 1977). Postmaster General, Montgomery Blair, gave a speech in Maryland, admonishing that to allow Blacks to vote means that Blacks would one day be able to sit in Congress. The manumission of slaves would mean the "infusing of their blood into our whole system" (Oates, p. 370, 1977). These white men went as far as to fear that Black men would take all of their white women and their jobs. This fear is a demonstration that many whites already knew and have always known the strength and intelligence of African peoples. One of white man's greatest fears was (and is) that of Strong, mentally and physically, African Black Men. (For more information on this age-old sociological and psychological phenomenon, see works by: Cress-Welsing, ben-Jochannan, Julia and Nathan Hare, Kunjufu, Akbar, and Carmichael & Hamilton, *Black Power*).

"Because of Lincoln's dark complexion, one newspaper, the *Register* hailed him as the lion of the Whig *tribe* (author italics) who came originally from Liberia" (Oates, pp. 51-52, 1977).

EDUCATION/EDDICATION

I suppose that Abe is still
fooling hisself with eddication.
I tried to stop it, but he has
got that fool idea in his head,
and it can't be got out.

Thomas Lincoln

As a young boy, Abe Lincoln started his "schooling" when he was about 9 years old. He attended whenever he could and stated that he learned only in increments — "in littles," he remarked. His teacher was a fifty-two year old Catholic slaveowner (Oates, p. 7, 1977). Lincoln took pride in learning. (Thomas Lincoln's statement on the education of Abraham Lincoln can be found in Henry C. Whitney's *Life of Lincoln*, 1908, and Simon's, *A House Divided*, p. 6, 1987.)

From menial reading materials, Young Abe Lincoln read enough about George Washington and Thomas Jefferson to view them as heroic men who shaped and changed the course of history; he idolized them (Oates, p. 11, 1977). Penmanship was also important to Lincoln. Sally (Sarah Bush) took up where Nancy Hanks unfortunately had to leave off by teaching Abe the importance of learning. Lincoln borrowed *Kirkham's Grammar* from a friend named Graham. One month after Lincoln's death, Graham bragged that he was Lincoln's mentor, and that Lincoln was one of his best "schollars" [sic]. Lincoln labored over Graham's English book until he was able to scribble well enough to become known for the eloquent writing of Lincoln's Gettysburg Address. "A new computer software package called the RightWriter, which analyzes documents for style, grammar and readability" said that Abraham Lincoln should have used shorter sentences in his writing and more positive wording. The computer program also calculated that Lincoln was "overly descriptive," using too many adjectives. It computed, why use "Four score and seven years ago?" Just say, "Eighty-seven" (Boritt, p. 65). It's all a matter of literary opinion. Most spell "potato" and one spells p-o-t-a-t-o-e. At any rate, Harriet Beecher Stowe thought that Lincoln's writing was ingenious.

There were many who were politically against Lincoln, but Harriet Beecher Stowe defended Lincoln to the end. She thought that he was a good and respectable President, and she also admired his literary style. When Beecher Stowe met Lincoln in the White House, he chauvinistically kidded, "So you're the *little woman* who wrote the book that made this great war." He, of course, was referring to Uncle Tom's Cabin. This book sold 300,000 copies in its first edition during a time in his-story when the national population was about 23.9 million.

Harriet Beecher Stowe and Abraham Lincoln had a cordial conversation. Lincoln communicated his melancholy to Ms. Stowe by disclosing to her that he didn't think he would live through the Civil War. Lincoln related this feeling to so many people. It is unfortunate that no one noticed his call for help. Being an artist, Ms. Stowe left Lincoln's omnipresence touched by his "suffering," but adjourned by doing nothing, and so did many others.

In her biographical evaluation of Lincoln, she stated that Lincoln was a "patient pain;" she wrote that he was a "man of peculiar strengths" (Oates, p. 389, 1977). Lincoln was a determined, self-taught person; he was a hard worker, who was determined to succeed.

LINCOLN AND RELIGION

Thomas Lincoln was a church man. Young Abe would sometimes attend church. Immediately after returning home, he would mimic the minister verbatim, planning never to return. "Lincoln never joined that or any other church" (Simon, p. 7). Lincoln was not a religious person, and sometimes spoke out against Christianity. Lincoln saw "false selves" at the church. Below is a modern-day example as to why some people rebel against church and religion:

Salley is a college educated woman in her late 30's. She showed classical symptoms of multiple personality disorder. Her score on a dissociative psychology scale was also high. It is also possible that she is a borderline personality. She reported internal voices that were fighting for dominant control of her body. When successful, they are usually self-harming and self-defeating. She was reared by strict and disapproving Christian fundamentalist parents. Salley, therefore, renounced traditional religious dogma at an early age after observing hypocrisy in her church. Several false-selfs developed, and these false-selfs would alternate to meet the demands of significant others in her life. Internally, Salley continued to waiver in the

absence of a connected sense of identity or an acceptable
belief system.

From: *DISSOCIATION: Progress In The Dissociative Disorder* - The Official Journal of the International Society for the Study of Multiple Personality and Dissociation, "...Role of Exogenous Trauma in the Etiology of MPD and its Variants," by Ganaway, George, p. 213, vol. II. no. 4, December, 1989.

Lincoln considered himself a spiritual person, not a religious person. Although Lincoln was not a christian, he was a frequent reader of the Bible. He was certain that voices and visions could "reveal hidden truth." Lincoln read many books on spiritualism stating "that he always had a strong tendency toward mysticism" (Garrison, p. 68). At one White House seance, it is written that the psychic-medium gave Lincoln detailed messages from Daniel Webster. Webster supposedly told Lincoln to stop dragging his feet, and go on and sign the Emancipation Proclamation. Lincoln concurred — though with shaky hands.

One witness to the signing of the Emancipation proclamation said that Lincoln's hand shook and trembled so violently that he could hardly hold the ink pen steady. Lincoln's White House aides said that this problem was entirely physical and had nothing whatsoever to do with second thoughts about signing the Emancipation Proclamation. Lincoln had been shaking hands much of the day in celebration of New Year's Day events. Lincoln said, "Three hours' hand-shaking is not calculated to improve a man's chirography." This was more than likely the truth, for the Emancipation Proclamation, when read critically and carefully, did not free enslaved peoples anyway (*Ebony*, "Was Lincoln a White Supremacist?" Bennett, L. Jr., p. 40, 1968; Garrison, p. 190).

An 1800's spiritualist by the name of Ordway related to Herndon, Lincoln's friend, that Lincoln was a participant in several seances. Lincoln was a religious skeptic, for how could his cold, uncaring father consider himself religious? Herndon said that Lincoln "did not believe that Jesus was God nor the son of God" (*The Hidden Lincoln*, p. 64). Did they discuss this?

Some say that Lincoln attended psychic meetings and seances only to see what garbage the psychic was feeding to Mrs. Lincoln's already fragile mind. Mary Todd Lincoln had emotional problems, and sometimes turned to spiritualism for comfort. So did Lincoln.

BOUND FOR NEW ORLEANS AND VOODOO

A popular story exists that Lincoln was warned as a young man, while on a trip to New Orleans, that he would one day fight the institution of slavery. However, the man who started this rumor was not on this trip with Lincoln, so Lerone Bennett asserts that "the story is of dubious value."

On January 6, 1831, the World Anti-Slavery Convention opened in London, England. In this same year, a young single twenty-two year old Abe Lincoln received, what he considered, his first real chance in life from a relative of his biological mother. This relative was named John Hanks. He petitioned Lincoln to help him take a boatload of provisions and merchandise to New Orleans, Andrew Jackson's old stomping ground. Lincoln enjoyed and learned much during this trip down the Mississippi. Herndon states that Lincoln believed too much in the philosophies and theories of the common people. He tended to believe in these people more than he believed in scientists. And who are the common people? Were Blacks a part of this "common" group during this era in his-story? While on his New Orleans trip, Abraham Lincoln visited a voodoo doctor (Lewis, p. 31). It would do Africans and others a world of good to learn more about the art of voudou (voodoo) rather than to immediately assume that there is something weird and scary about this Ancient African Science. The roots of Voudou or Voudouism come from Ancient Kemet. Many ancient medical treaties written on papyri have been found in Kemet. These medical treaties were sometimes headed: *Medicine and Magic.* The Ancients did have some faith in medicine, but not without the help and purity of the spirit or spirituality, e.g., the so-called supernatural. This concept was not detrimental to healing; it was beneficial mind medicine. These very spiritual practices are unique in that if you are not spiritually connected, then most of the practices will not work anyway. It takes a pure, genuine and spiritual glow of the connected mental and physical to practice voudouism. Psychiatrist Carl Bell argues that whether you are healing yourself mentally, or receiving help, it is important to realize that there are many folk cures in African-American culture. Harriet Tubman was exceedingly connected in her actions with the Underground Railroad system. Her mental and physical was a must, and she had it down to such a science that many of the people that she freed didn't even understand what was going on. But they did understand that this woman, called Moses, and the ancestors were responsible for their freedom. Some cried that they did not want to go; they didn't want to be free. Tubman knew that they were delirious with fear, but not crazy. She decided to be the sensible One for them. So she threatened to kill them herself if they didn't get up off their behinds like the Gods and Goddesses, Kings and Queens they were (are) and live free! She psyched herself and the fearful ones out — in a word, voudouism. She had to become more than Herself in order to get through this horrific ordeal. She did it with a positive voudouristic spirit (BaKhufu, notes from: "The Mystery Teachings of the Temple of Ast." Publication date pending).

Lincoln made his visit to the Voudou Doctor before he knew Mary Todd. Lincoln had a notion that he would one day die a horrendous, sudden death. So the allegations that he visited spiritualists and psychics *only* because he was concerned about Mary and her emotional problems isn't entirely true. Lincoln, especially being in the frantic frame of mind that he carried around with him continuously, was only believing in himself and his ancestors during this visit — and rightly so. It is unfortunate, however, that Abraham Lincoln did not realize and understand the benefits of his spiritual visits in New Orleans. If he had realized and understood, perhaps he would not have felt it necessary to wear a white mask while swimming blindly in wonderful Black Blood. One year later, Abraham Lincoln felt confident enough to announce his candidacy for the Illinois legislature.

THE POLITICIAN IN THE MAKING

Lincoln went into politics, while Africans continued to struggle for their political rights all over the world. Jamaican hero, Samuel Sharpe was hanged on May 23, 1832. Life went on. The first passenger train in the United States ran between Augusta, Georgia and Charleston, South Carolina in 1834, the same year that Lincoln was elected as one of Illinois' state representatives. New technology and ways to travel made governmental negotiations and conferences easier.

People liked and could relate to the opinions and plans of Abraham Lincoln. There were slave markets in Washington, D.C. during this time. Lincoln supposedly did not like this. But Congress could not change the slavery law. Then Abe thought, *"D.C. is not a state; it is a District — the capitol of the United States."* So he went about the business of trying to change the slavery laws in Washington, D.C. Congress would not budge. Lincoln did not relent. He used his frantic mind and agitated nature to energize him toward his political goals. Lincoln is essentially referred to in many historical articles as a melancholic person like his mother. Literature shows that he was also an opportunist *(Ebony,* "Was Lincoln a White Supremacist?" Bennett, L.). He became President of the United States. Ken Burns, the producer of the television special *The Civil War,* stated that if Lincoln were to run for President of the United States today, he would not win because he would be too mentally unstable. Herndon states that Lincoln walked a fine line between sanity and insanity, and was said by many of his neighbors to have been in a mental institution or least needed to be in one, especially when he was about aged twenty-four or twenty-six (Herndon, *The Hidden Lincoln,* p. 36).

DISSOCIATIVE STATES BOUND FOR THE WHITE HOUSE

"Multiple personality is an adaptive behavior to traumatic childhood abuse experiences; it is a defense mechanism and the goal is survival." Dissociation, splitting, or multiple personalities are modes of survival usually in the face of severe child abuse (BaKhufu, *A Comprehensive Study*

of Multiple Personalities: Why Aren't Blacks in Therapy? p. 26,
Dissertation, 1985).

As far as American psychology "scholars" are concerned,
the psychology and the understanding of psychology
wasn't developed until the 1800's, or more like the 1900's
because it was 1890 when white people decided that psychology was even a discipline. By this time, Jefferson, Jackson, and Lincoln were all deceased taking their psychosis,
neurosis, or whatever other mental problem they possessed
with them to the grave.

*Africans have been studying and utilizing the discipline of psy-
chology for ages. Psychology for Africans was and is the spiritual;
psychology for Africans is philosophy; psychology to most
Africans from the school of Sakku is herbal medicine, body over
mind, and principally mind over body. Psychology and philosophy
to Africans have always been important, highly exercised disci-
plines in the understanding of all peoples ... and animals
(BaKhufu, notes from: "Healing: Herbs, Health and Spirituality,"
and "The Mystery Teachings of the Temple of Ast"). Dr. Wade
Nobles explains Sakku as understanding that the psychology of
Invisible and Visible is being one and the same. It is "Beingness."
The invisible is far greater than the visible. Sounds Jungian? No.
Psychologist Carl Jung "borrowed" many ancient philosophies
from Africa.*

Abraham Lincoln possessed what is called a split-brain.
To some psychological professionals, this phenomenon is
designated the name: divided mind, in essence multiple personality. Research shows that it wasn't until the 1970's that
cognitive science began to understand the importance of
consciousness and unconsciousness in the study and discipline of psychology. Seeing as how the study of multiple
personality had not developed itself until the 1980's, it will
not be unusual for Abe Lincoln to have actually been a mild
dissociate or a multiple personality with two to three different personalities who knew each other well enough to
always remember what the other did, making him a person
functional enough to become the president of the United
States. While this syndrome is usually not diagnosed until
adulthood, 89% of multiple personality victims have been
misdiagnosed at least once. Common misdiagnoses include
depression, borderline and sociopathic personality disorder,

schizophrenia, epilepsy, and *manic depressive* illness. Lincoln is known to have been a depressed person with manic depressive proclivity. Lincoln may have also been a borderline and sociopathic personality because of the ways in which he socialized, or better yet, did not socialize with other people. Another self was a wiz at work. Lincoln was a well-known, sought-after lawyer.

LAWYER LINCOLN

Lincoln knew as a young boy that he wanted to do great things with his life. He was an early opportunist. He never attended a college or university; he was, however, as most lawyers during this era in time, a self-taught attorney with very few law books. Lincoln was good in his profession, although Lincoln's greatest achievement seems to have been that of business and economy in the United States, for slavery and the elicit slave trade was America's main source of wealth. But ...

In 1841, when Lincoln was an Illinois lawyer, he won the court case for an African woman named Nance who had been illegally sold in a state where slavery was illegal. The woman was freed — again.

In another case, which it is presumed he deliberately lost, Lincoln represented a slaveholder who was suing abolitionists for hiding and protecting an enslaved family and others. This slave family had escaped the slaveholder's threat when they learned that he planned to sell the wife and children to the South. When Lincoln lost the case, the slaveholder refused to pay Lincoln.

Lincoln was defending attorney in numerous judiciary cases. He was a busy lawyer, but he found the time, as if he were motivated by some force, or as a mission, to be "prosecutor" and handled a case against a man accused of raping a seven-year-old. Lincoln was triumphant — relieved and elated when the rapist/child molester was convicted (The above stories can be found in Garrison's, *White House Tales,* pp. 226-228).

During Lincoln's reign as lawyer and prosecutor, there were other legal battles going on of enormous importance but with little notoriety. The Amistad Revolt occurred from

1839 to 1842. This revolt started when approximately 55 Africans were forced from their homeland of Sierra Leone, Africa and shipped to Cuba. Here they were held captive — enslaved. They were later to be taken to Puerto Principe. The day came, and on the "voyage," Singbe Pieh led a serious revolt. The Africans seized their captors' weapons and took over the ship. They killed the captain, forced much of the crew overboard and told the remaining crew of white Spaniards to sail them back home — to Africa. The Spanish crew, however, sailed the ship straight to the U.S. mainland. These angry white men argued that the Africans should be tried for murder and mutiny. The trial of these brave Africans was successful in uniting Africans in America and white abolitionists. It was unmentioned history such as this that helped lead toward a Civil War. A sculpture of Sengbe Pieh (p.k.a., Joseph Cinque) now stands in front of City Hall in New Haven, Connecticut. These Africans were chained and enslaved, but returned home to Africa as heroes.

As a defendant, Lincoln handled the case of a young African male who was free. Upon arriving in the "free" state of New Orleans without special freedman's papers, he was apprehended as a slave and put in jail. This is a perfect example of the black code tactic. After a while, the young African man would have been sold as a slave in order to save the state prisoner expenses. The young man's mother went to attorney Lincoln for help. After nothing positive happened in the court procedures, and after exhausting all of his legal methods, Lincoln told the Governor, "By God, Governor, I'll make the ground in this country too hot for the foot of a slave, whether you have the legal power to secure the release of this boy or not." In order to get the young African out of jail, Lincoln had to resort to collecting funds in order to buy the young man's freedom. Polly, the young African man's mother, was delighted that her son was free again *(Herndon's-Life of Lincoln,* pp. 308-309, 1892). These are some of the true stories about Lincoln that have come down over the years confusing and confounding African-Americans and whites alike. Lincoln was not the man he seemed to be. In Lincoln's very defense of this African man, his prejudice shone in his stereotypical remark that the Africans' feet are more agreeable to the hot and can withhold the heat from the ground better than a white man's. Now this could be true and not so stereotypical, but that's another story — melanin. Of course, Lincoln referred to the young African man as a boy. Well his court tactics in these particular cases were good. These court cases that Lincoln won were not necessarily a moral thing; they ring toward something personal.

LINCOLN IN THE HOUSE OF REPRESENTATIVES

In 1846, Lincoln defeated Clay in Illinois, making him the only Whig elected from Illinois. Lincoln was saddened when Henry Clay died in 1852. In a speech in Springfield, he said that Clay was "my beau ideal of a statesman." His personal feelings for Clay overshadowed their political views. In some cases, Lincoln respected the political views of Henry Clay who was said to be anti-slavery (Oates, p. 105, 1977).

From March 4, 1847 to March 3, 1849, Lincoln served in the U.S. House of Representatives, Illinois. During the summer of 1846, right after he defeated Clay, Lincoln rode horseback to Indiana to campaign. While there, he visited his old neighborhood. He had not seen this place in fourteen years now. Of course, he experienced feelings of melancholy, but still felt creative and thoughtful enough about his experiences here to be moved to prose. This visit was somewhat therapeutic for Lincoln. This trip perhaps give Lincoln an opportunity to get rid of some of the resentment he concealed under his mask of bitterness about childhood experiences and upbringing under Thomas Lincoln. Lincoln wrote, "...things decayed and loved ones lost,..." He said that the memories of this place were like "dreamy shadows" (Oates, pp. 68-69, 1977).

In 1847, while Lincoln served the House, Frederick Douglass and Martin R. Delaney served their people well when they launched the publication of the very famous *North Star* anti-slavery newspaper. This is the same year that a young enslaved woman by the name of Cassily was indicted for cooking broken glass into gravy and serving it to her so-called master, John Hamilton and his wife. Africans were sick and tired of white people thinking they could hold them like prisoners, make them cook for them, farm for them, and then turn around and rape them as if this is a normal and civilized thing to do. They needed a teacher. Was Cassily a teacher? Frederick Douglass contended that white people in this era in his-story did not seem to understand anything else. Talk was cheap to them. Action spoke louder than words.

CRAZY AS A LOON WITH HOMOSEXUAL TENDENCIES

As stated earlier, Lincoln learned to live with death and madness and the bizarre at an early age. At sixteen he witnessed an otherwise intelligent nineteen year boy suddenly go mad. The boy's eyes bulged then he tried to mutilate himself. Lincoln watched as the boy attacked his father then his mother. Witnessing this scene depressed Lincoln to no end, yet, Lincoln had a morbid fascination for the boy's condition. Lincoln would sometimes sneak off in the middle of the night and listen as the boy yelled, cried, swore, and prayed. Lincoln would never forget this incident, and he would always wonder what "killed the boy's mind." As an adult, Lincoln set this tragedy to verse (Oates, p. 12, 1977). Lincoln was obsessed with insanity, madness and death. His thoughts and conversations were almost always on these subjects. Below is an excerpt from the poem, "The Maniac," a twenty-three stanza conto by Abraham Lincoln:

> But here's an object more of dread
> Than ought the grave contains —
> A human form with reason fled,
> While wretched life remains...

> O death! Thou aw-inspiring prince,
> That keeps the world in fear;
> Why dost thou tear more blest ones hence,
> And leave him ling'ring here

Relatives of Mary Todd Lincoln's asserted that Lincoln was "crazy as a loon" (Oates, p. 57, 1977). They said that he had feelings that he could not please a wife. His intimate friend, Joshua Speed, who was engaged to be married, wrote Lincoln stating that he had "intense anxieties" about getting married also. Lincoln told Speed that he was his special friend and that he could feel his suffering as if it were his own. "You love your fiance; so marry her; you'll be alright," Lincoln told him (but not in these exact words). Writing to Speed was almost like therapy for Lincoln. He wrote that he was certain that he was hypo (i.e., a hypochondriac — depressed and anxious with feelings of illness, imagined or real) In reference to other feelings, he wrote that he felt like "quite a man" (Oates, p. 60, 1977). Speed got married. He wrote Lincoln and told him he was doing fine. Lincoln wrote back telling Speed that their worrying was sheer nonsense. We are "peculiar" (See: Oates, p. 60, 1977).

SO THEN, WAS LINCOLN BI-SEXUAL?

Abraham Lincoln and Mary Todd had a disturbing courtship. They had an on-again, off-again engagement. Lincoln had cold feet — icy cold feet, and at one point, lost his mind over his impending matrimony. He was forever running to Joshua Speed, with whom he once shared a bed, for comfort and reassurance about his relationship with Mary. Peter Gefter, a white modern-day novelist who admits to being bi-sexual, but more homosexual, said that, "Love between two men is usually more intense than between a man and a woman."

"Though laconic by nature, he [Lincoln] hungered for male companionship....When he was around girls, he covered up a painful shyness by acting the clown." Lincoln also "avoided eligible young women..., he was insecure in their presence and was afraid of failure and rejection in love" (Oates, pp. 13 & 19, 1977). Lincoln seems to have been psychologically confined in a phallic stage of confusion, possibly as a result child abuse — mental or physical from some authoritative figure, whether that figure be Thomas Lincoln or not. Children can grow into adults sheltering extremely resentful feelings toward the adult who was responsible for taking care of them and rescuing them from harm or abuse. Many studies reveal the resentment and hurt that many women feel toward their mothers for not rescuing them from sexual abuse from their fathers or stepfathers — whether the mother was aware of the abuse or not. Studies show that in most cases, these mothers were aware of the abuse. Recent and more studies are being researched and completed on the abuse of young boys.

Well-known developmental psychologist, Erik Erickson, surmises that children have to decide who they are and what they want out of life. Erickson doesn't explain to parents, teachers, psychologists, and significant others in a direct way, that it is their responsibility to teach the children that they are to gain a healthy identity by voicing early-on their concerns as well as any abuses. He does not explain very well how one is supposed to teach this behavior and other behaviors to the children. If children are not protected to the best of the "significant others'" ability, then the child may never have a true and normal identity; on the other hand, they may have many identities, though not normal ones. The persona must be healthy, because Erickson writes, the process of acquiring an identity for Self is a difficult one. According to his theory, when one suffers psychologically from the process of trying to obtain his or her wants, needs, and identity, and becomes fixated in a particular place during her or his growth period, then the person suffers from identity crisis. Forming an identity and self-concept in a racist society is difficult enough without the added problem of abuse. Lincoln's fixation in Freud's phallic stage, which is Freud's third stage of personality development, may have been real. Freud maintains that it is here when the child obtains gratification from genital manipulation. It is also the stage where males develop the Oedipus complex of love for their mothers and hostility toward their fathers. An imposing fear of punishment and/or castration is also present. Lincoln was possibly very familiar with the subject of castration. If Dennis Hanks were aware of Thomas Lincoln's physical propensities, then Abe could have been aware also, and in many ways. Literature does not point to either mother as being suspects in abuse toward Lincoln. The love Lincoln had for both of his mothers, and the resentment Lincoln harbored toward his father/significant other has already been discussed. In this surmise, please keep in mind that I am dealing with the Lincoln reared to be white with a white mentality. Therefore the use of Eriksonian and Freudian theory is appropriate in some places. Many of the theories and practices of these men are so dated that they no longer even fit the psychics of white people. But with the underlying understanding of Sakku psychology, one learns where and how these theories, and they are theories only, can be used appropriately for general understanding — I hope. Lincoln's family background could have generated many unhealthy behaviors and attitudes.

Although it is not felt that Abe Lincoln was a woman hater, he could not relate to a woman on a real healthy and intimate basis. Although it is true, or has been fabricated that he had a love life with a woman named Ann Rutledge who died while they were dating, it is also a fact that Lincoln was a married man with children. Even so, Mary Owens, another woman Lincoln is said to have dated, wrote to Herndon, "Mr. Lincoln was deficient in those little links which make up the great chain of womans [sic] happiness." So she did not marry Lincoln (Herndon, *The Hidden Lincoln*, Correspondence: May 23 and July 22, 1866; Donald, p. 188). It has also been rumored and written that Lincoln was perhaps homosexual. Of course, he could not "come out of the closet" considering the times and especially because of his political career. From the close friendships that he did have with certain men, I would label him a man lover. He was always surrounded by young men with whom he could genuinely relax and confide. One author recently opined, "Lincoln was surely an emotional homosexual at the very least" (Sullivan, *Presidential Passions*, p. 215, 1991). Lincoln's entire life history, his mysterious behaviors and his weary nature indicate that of victimization.

Homosexuality took place in the White House just as it did any other place in the world. Many allude to the possibility that the actual sexual performance did not occur in the early days of his-story because of the social taboo. It is usually stated that these people only had very serious tendencies and inclinations. These "tendencies" and "emotions" are usually performed behind closed doors. So do we know if these social taboos actually occurred or not? No, we do not. But there is one thing for certain: Many of the white men during this early era were not too far removed from homosexual Greek ancestry.

The president preceding Lincoln was said to be gay, i.e, homosexual. It isn't as if this subject matter is something new and alien.

JAMES BUCHANAN,
15TH PRESIDENT OF THE UNITED STATES

James Buchanan was said to be a homosexual who shared his life intimately for 28 years with a Senator from Alabama. Buchanan is the only president who never married. Andrew Jackson penned the President and the Senator Aunt Fancy and Miss Nancy. Jackson said that Senator William Rufus De Vane King, from Alabama, was Buchanan's "better half."

Buchanan grew up in a family of five girls; he was the only boy. So he was reared surrounded with femininity. His father was obnoxious, therefore Buchannan attached himself to the local preacher, a pastor John King. He later said that he had great reverence for John.

Later when he went to college, he attached himself to one of the professors, a Mr. James McCormick. Buchannan, being the Material Girl that he was, was bent on being successful. He had extravagant taste, goals, and objectives, so he tried to court and date a young rich girl named Ann. She had emotional problems. There were a lot of women in America with mental problems in those old days. (That's another book — with white man as culprit.) Ann's parents figured this dainty boy was after something; they didn't know what, but he certainly wasn't going to get their money. The "nervouss" Ann agreed. She also had a *secret* on Buchanan. Eventually Ann broke off the engagement, left town, went crazy, and died.

After this tragedy, Buchanan attached himself to Senator King. The two shared rooms for over twenty years. A Mr. Aaron Brown wrote of "Mr. Buchanan & *his wife*," referring to William King. In several letters from King to Buchanan, King made such statements as: I hope that you do not find as a partner someone who will cause you not to miss me. I shall be lonely without you here in Paris. Here "I shall have no Friend with whom I can commune as with my own thoughts." King also suggested to Buchanan that "the United States would be better represented in Paris '"by someone who has more the spirit of a man"' (Ross, p. 89). The implication in his writing here is that he did not feel "the spirit of a man."

They say as Buchanan matured, he became handsome, tall and broad shouldered. Buchanan was forever claiming to have a relationship with a woman. However, most of these women have complained of his unaffectionate and cold ways. Whenever he would get close to having to make physical contact with a woman, he would withdraw, then make silly excuses. Later he became "close" to another Ann, that is Ann Payne. She was Dolley Madison's niece. Another excuse: He said that he could not marry her because she was too young. Give us a break; during those days, white men would marry a woman as young as ...

As he became closer and closer to the presidential seat, he began to have enough confidence to actively and openly associate with young men. **A.** "There is absolutely no proof that James Buchanan ever led an actively homosexual life.... A latent homosexual, as Buchanan most likely was, could never actively explore his sexuality and successfully rise in the world of politics. The dangers were far too great" (Sullivan, p. 210). But we don't know, do we? **B.** "Today there is evidence that President James Buchanan was a homosexual" (Ross, p. 86).

Buchanan was the fifteenth president of the United States. When Lincoln was going into office, Buchanan told him that he was happy to be leaving. Lincoln later wrote that being in the White House was like "a *white* elephant on my hands ... I wish I had never been born!" With no support from Congress and with all the other problems it's like "a fire in my *front* and *rear*; ..." (All italics in this paragraph are supplied by the author.) Had Lincoln heard the rumors about Buchanan's homosexuality? Of course, he had. So whether Lincoln was gay, Black or both, he had role models — for he probably knew more about Thomas Jefferson's ancestry and James Buchanan's sexual preferences than we will ever know. Read this again and calm down, because I have not said that if you are a Black man you're gay or vice versa. I am referring to Abraham Lincoln here, and no one else.

ELEANOR ROOSEVELT TOO?

Eleanor Roosevelt resided in the White House from 1933 to 1945. Mrs. Roosevelt refused to be a victim to America's imagined strict conservatisms, even though the time in regard to American conservatism and prejudice were not that much different from Lincoln's era. She "was classless by conviction" (Whitney, *Eleanor Roosevelt*, p. 1). Eleanor Roosevelt had no room nor desire for prejudice. Abraham Maslow, the well-known psychologist, named Eleanor Roosevelt and Abraham Lincoln as self-actualized people. Others on his list were Thomas Jefferson and Albert Einstein. He named Adlai Stevenson as a potential case. These are people who know how to use their full potential and creative talents to better the world and self. Maslow admits to finding only one person though who was fully self-actualized. How did he know?

Eleanor Roosevelt is better known in the Black community as the woman who in 1939 withdrew her membership from a white women's group called Daughters of the American Revolution because this clan of women refused to allow the great African soprano Marian Anderson to sing in Constitution Hall. What we didn't know was that during that very same year, Eleanor Roosevelt was sleeping with a white woman named Lerona Hickok.

Eleanor was outraged when the Daughters of the American Revolution would not allow Howard University to rent Constitution Hall in order for Marian Anderson to sing. Eleanor refused to remain a member of such a racist group. Marian Anderson was relegated to singing on the steps of the brother Lincoln's Memorial. She first sang "America," and ended appropriately with: "Nobody Knows the Trouble I've Seen."

Eleanor turned the trouble she ran into around when information begin to leak that she was a lesbian. She was, and did not try at all to hide the fact. There are so many historians who try to deny this by stating that Eleanor was simply an affectionate woman in all aspects of her life.

This year was an interesting one for the Black community. In late 1939, a popular theater group offered a prize to the man who mostly resembled Abraham Lincoln. Pictures were to be submitted to the theater group. The winner would be an honored guest at the premiere movie entitled "Abe Lincoln in Illinois." Thomas Bomar was the winner. He was asked to make an appearance for identification. The judges were even more amazed at the resemblance now that the man stood directly in front of them. They told him that he was even more like Abraham Lincoln than the actor Raymond Massey. Before the premiere opening of the movie, someone noticed the N.W. on Bomar's address. Bomar lived at 136 S Street, N.W., Washington, D.C. This is a Black neighborhood!, the white person thought. After an investigation, it was discovered that Bomar was an African-American. All publicity about the contest immediately stopped. Bomar was still allowed to attend the premiere, but not a word was spoken about the contest (Rogers, Sex and Race, vol. II, pp. 377 & 379).

Eleanor Roosevelt had no reason to change her last name when she got married at age twenty. She married her cousin Franklin Delano Roosevelt, the 32nd President of the United States. Eleanor was a shy girl, but with maturity and life's experiences, all of that changed. She discovered that Franklin was having an affair. This may have been Eleanor's way out, because she admitted "that she never liked having sex with a man." Could she have meant that she didn't like having sex with her cousin? Eleanor may have felt incestuous while having sex with Franklin — the blood a little too close for comfort. Although their familial blood was five times removed, they were both related to Theodore Roosevelt. Eleanor gave Franklin the option of divorce when she discovered that he was having an affair. He refused to "release" her, as they said during Lincoln's era. He wasn't going to jeopardize his political career. Eleanor and Franklin already had their children so Eleanor stopped having sex with her cousin-husband. Eleanor confessed that she had only consented to sex as her "wifely duty." Anyway, she had been his cousin 34 years now — since birth, and his wife only 14 years. So be it. Franklin continued having affairs. Through intelligence and will, Eleanor became known as an assertive, spirited, masculine-looking woman. Some said that Eleanor Roosevelt had a "whim of iron."

Eleanor Roosevelt had not been as a wife to her husband in fourteen years when she met and fell in love with a woman named Lorena Hickok. It was Franklin's 1932 Presidential year. Ms. Hickok was an Associated Press reporter who was assigned to assist Eleanor during Franklin's Presidential campaign. Lorena was more masculine and mannish acting than Eleanor. These two women were mentally and physically liberated in the wrong era, and they didn't care. After Franklin Roosevelt won the election, Eleanor insisted that Lorena Hickok live in the White House. The two women often slept in the same bed. Franklin D. Roosevelt called his wife's female friends "she-males."

Through the years Eleanor and Lorena Hickok wrote over three thousand letters to each other. In them, they did not try to hide the fact that they were lesbians. Eleanor *affectionately* nicknamed Lorena, Hicky. After Hicky gave Eleanor a ring, Eleanor wrote her a letter saying:

> Hick darling, All day I've thought of you … Oh! I want to put my arms around you, I ache to hold you close. Your ring is a great comfort. I look at it & think she does love me or I wouldn't be wearing it!

In another letter when the two women had to be separated due to Lorena's workload, Eleanor wrote:

> I can't kiss you so I kiss your picture goodnight and good morning. Don't laugh! This is the first day I've had no letter and I miss it sadly …

Excerpt from a fourteen page letter: Lovestruck Eleanor wrote to Lorena:

> Most clearly I remember your eyes, with a kind of teasing smile in them, and the feeling of that soft spot just northeast of the corner of your mouth against my lips.

Eleanor's nose (or something) was wide open. She loved this woman. There were many letters of this type between the women. These letters Lorena Hickok kept. She asked that they not be opened until ten years after her death. Some white historians are still saying that there was no homosexual affair between Eleanor and Lorena.

Mrs. Eleanor Roosevelt and Ms. Lorena Hickok were intelligent, well-read women who dedicated the other part of their lives to humanitarian causes. They had some ground and sensitivity to understanding, somewhat, the problems that the people called the "underdog" may have. Childhood traumas: (1) Eleanor had been called "ugly duckling" and unattractive by close relatives. She didn't feel a familial part of the family household that she was reared in as a young woman. (2) Lorena Hickok was an incest victim. She had been raped by her father.

Eleanor died in 1962. Hicky died six years later. Although the two women had had an intense, close, understanding and intimate relationship, they were not intimate companions (dating) at the time of Eleanor's death. Eleanor had become tired of Hicky's untidy appearance. And Eleanor being the somewhat "proper" lady, did not approve of Hicky referring to her as "darling" in the presence of people with whom they socialized.

Eleanor Roosevelt claimed that when she lived in the White House, she sometimes felt the *spirit* of Abraham Lincoln, but she never actually saw him. Relative Teddy Roosevelt said that he often saw Lincoln's ghost.

For more information on Eleanor Roosevelt and Lorena Hickok, see the recently published book, *Eleanor Roosevelt,* by Blanche Cook.

J. EDGAR HOOVER

In 1972, ten years after Eleanor Roosevelt's demise, death came to J. Edgar Hoover, the long-time chief of the Federal Bureau of Investigations. Political sex files were found in his office at the time of his death. Some feel that this was simple abuse of power; while others felt that he used the information and tapes for his own personal enjoyment. "Hoover was preoccupied with homosexuality in the government ... homosexuality runs through the files like a connecting thread." Hoover, himself, "had a lifelong intimate relationship" with one of his FBI workers. When Hoover died,

Clyde Tolson was so upset that he wouldn't even accept condolences from the Bureau office. He resigned on the same day of Hoover's death. Hoover left Tolson most of his half-million dollar estate. He left nothing to his relatives. No one knows for sure if Tolson and Hoover were "practicing" homosexuals. The two were nicknamed "J. Edna" and "Mother Tolson" (Ross, pp. 216-218).

JOSHUA SPEED AND ABE LINCOLN SLEPT TOGETHER

Lincoln was a young attorney in Springfield, Illinois living in "Joshua Speed's General Store, where he and Speed lived together." When Speed first met Lincoln, he knew that Lincoln was a very sad person. Speed liked the melancholy "attorney and invited him to share a double bed in the upstairs room." Even with Lincoln tending to be a "gloomy" and "sad" person, he was still able to make Speed laugh. Speed was also a single man from Kentucky. Speed had his own problems, and he "soon became Lincoln's '"most intimate friend."'" "They not only slept together, but confided in one another about their fears, their feelings, and their problems with women." Herndon said that Lincoln was the most '"shut mouthed"' man that he had ever known. "Said another: '"He made simplicity and candor a mask of deep feelings carefully concealed"'" (Oates, pp. 45 & 99, 1977). But Lincoln wasn't so "shut mouthed" with Speed. Lincoln and Speed shared their feelings on personal and political issues for years. Lincoln never shared such deep feelings with anyone else. Years later, the two men wrote about and shared their differences on one very important political issue. Speed wrote Lincoln that he would rather give up the Union than give up slavery and the ownership of "Negroes." Boom! Lincoln wrote back: "Who is asking you to give up your right to own slaves? Very certainly *I* am not." Owning slaves is your own business, Lincoln told Speed. But '"I confess I hate to see the poor creatures hunted down, and caught, and carried back to their stripes, and unrewarded toils; but I bite my lip and keep quiet"' (*Ebony*, Bennett; Oates, p. 122, 1977). It is true, Lincoln did not make great efforts to aid in the plight of the enslaved people in America as a whole. When Lincoln became President, he hired Speed's brother, James, a prominent Kentucky lawyer who had been successful in keeping Kentucky from leaving the Union.

When Joshua Speed sold his store and decided to move back to Kentucky, Lincoln was devastated. He had just broken off his engagement with Mary. Lincoln took a vacation from his job for a long miserable week. He said, I made "the most discreditable exhibition of myself in the way of hypochondriaism." He forced himself back to work, to the legislature. Carl Sandburg said that some of Lincoln's friends (acquaintances) shared no strong sympathy for Lincoln's "hypo." He wrote that these "friends" acted as if Lincoln was "recovering from punishment received in the tangles of an ancient trap" (Sandburg, p. 45, 1932).

In August of 1841, Lincoln was still experiencing hypochondria, so he went to Kentucky to visit Speed and his parents on their slave plantation — to rest up. Upon meeting the lanky Mr. Lincoln, Speed's mother thought he was much in color like a mulatto. "Speed's mother was much impressed with the tall and swarthy stranger her son had brought with him" (*Herndon's Lincoln*, p. 75). Lincoln enjoyed his visit, getting pampered and served in bed by the Africans who were forced to live on the Speed's plantation. When Lincoln and Speed were alone, they would discuss the depression that they often felt, and the anxieties they had about getting married. Speed pondered the question to Lincoln as to whether he was really capable of love? Could he make the woman happy with whom he was to marry soon? "[Lincoln] doubted his ability and capacity to please and support a wife" (Ross, p. 96) also. However, Lincoln visited Speed's fiance, Fanny Henning, and found her to be delightful. He said that she had the most "heavenly *black eyes.*" He noticed that she had the unfortunate mental and/or physical problem of "melancholly" too. Fanny had been sick, and Speed was obsessed with thinking that this woman would die on him. (Oates, p. 59, 1977). Why did Speed ponder so adamantly about Fanny's death? Was it wishful thinking because he was already placed in a position of having to go through with his marital plans, although he knew his heart (or whatever) wasn't in it? He didn't get married. Instead Speed followed Lincoln back to Springfield — to think. He stayed and reprieved with Lincoln for six months. Speed returned to Fanny in January, 1842.

"He [Lincoln] and Speed were haunted by the approaching wedding" of Speed and his fiance (Sandburg, p. 55, 1932). Why? There were many married men around. Did they need an "intimate" friend experience to determine whether or not they could succeed in a marriage with a woman? There is something awfully strange here. Speed got married in February of 1842. Lincoln wrote him a letter stating that "our forebodings (for which you and I are *peculiar)* are all the worst sort of nonsense" (Sandburg, p. 56, 1932). Now does this mean, perhaps, that they had figured that they were actually bisexual? The question is arguable, but the two were surely experiencing some serious and confusing personal dilemmas. Of course, today men have telephones and they can discuss such matters without having to write down every little thing. The numerous letters between Speed and Lincoln doesn't necessarily mean that anything kinky was going on, but they did sleep together. Speed replied: "words are forgotten — misunderstood — passed by — not noticed in a private conversation — but once put your words in writing and they stand as a living and eternal monument against you." (Sandburg, p. 333, 1932).

There is no problem with the fact that Speed, Lincoln or any- one may have been or is homosexual or bisexual. There is, how- ever, a problem with the fact that Speed advocated slavery. Mr. Lincoln's alleged sexual preferences can do much for the social and economic status and understanding of homosexuals and bisexuals today, I think.

Speed's store clerk, who just happened to be William Herndon at the time, said that, "Speed and Lincoln slept in the same home, and Lincoln sleeps with Speed" *(The Hidden Lincoln: Letters From Herndon,* pp. 65-66). Herndon was knowledgeable of many Lincoln secrets regarding love and relationships, and Lincoln's hunger for male friends was and is a fact. Michael Sullivan writes in his book, *Presidential Passions* that, "Whether or not there was a sexual relationship between the two men can never be definitely known..., it is very apparent [however] that Lincoln was surely an emotional homosexual at the very least. [Lincoln was] much closer to men" (Sullivan, p. 215). It was necessary in this era of time that one's sexual feeling be repressed — especially if these feelings were for the same sex. Then, as it is today, if one is in the political arena this personal revelation could be damaging.

A year after Lincoln's death, in 1866, Joshua Speed wrote a letter to William Herndon disclosing to Herndon that if he (Speed) had not been happily married himself, Lincoln would have never married anyone (Sandburg, p. 60, 1932). Why is this? What would Speed's getting married have to do with whether or not Lincoln would or should marry? It is presumed that Lincoln needed to see for himself that if a good and cherished "intimate friend" could be married and happy, then so, perhaps, could he. Mary Todd gave Lincoln hell before and after they were married.

MARY TODD'S AND ABE LINCOLN'S STORMY COURTSHIP AND MARRIAGE

Nancy Hanks had warned her son about the storm, but surely, he didn't expect a hurricane Mary. According to many, the lady scared him crazy.

Lincoln stood Mary up on their wedding day. Some say that he had fallen in love with one of Mary's house guests. Her name was Matilda Edwards. Many say Lincoln was still in love with a dead woman named Ann Rutledge. Others say that this is sheer fiction. Anyway it is written that the reason for Lincoln's failure to attend his own wedding was "insanity." "In his lunacy he declared he hated Mary and loved Miss Edwards." He was called a "crazy man" (Ross, p. 96). The day in January 1841, when Lincoln missed his wedding to Mary Todd, would later be called the "Fatal First." A year later on November 4, 1842, Abraham and Mary were married. Lincoln still harbored doubts about this marriage. It is said that he only got married because Joshua Speed got married. Lincoln wrote to a friend that he would probably be "less miserable" living with Mary Todd than living by himself. Anyway, he couldn't "openly" live with a man even if he wanted to (See: Sullivan, *Presidential Passions*, pp. 215-217). No matter, Abraham Lincoln wasted no time in impregnating Mary Todd — immediately after the ring was placed on her finger. They had their first child on August 1, 1843. Now according to medical experts at

Howard University, there are, technically, forty (40) lunar weeks from the time of conception until the birth of a child. That is, there are really 10 months of pregnancy instead of the very familiar 9 months. If Abe and Mary Lincoln had a honeymoon baby in 1843, then this presupposes that Mary was pregnant 268 days, which is only thirty-eight (38) lunar weeks. Mary and Mr. Lincoln either had sexual intercourse two weeks before their wedding, or their first son was born a little early. The latter is very possibly the case. They had three more sons.

Lincoln adored his four sons, although he wasn't as close to his oldest son Robert Todd as he was with the younger three. Lincoln would usually let his four boys get by with things for which they should have been disciplined. By the time the Lincolns reached the White House, one son had died. Eddie died at the young age of four in 1850.

The White House staff said the children were a terror. They would climb all over Lincoln when he was doing his work and used his ink pens for darts. He was lovingly overcompensating in many areas with his boys — a kind of love that he did not receive as a child, and he certainly wasn't going to allow his young boys to be cheated out of a more loving and special type of love from him. He knew from personal experience that an unhealthy father/son relationship breeds many mental and physical problems for years to come.

NICOLAY AND HAY, LINCOLN'S YOUNG POLITICAL AIDES

John George Nicolay was born in Germany in 1832. His parents moved to the United States in 1837. Nine years later, his father died, leaving the family destitute. Thus began the young man's journey toward a career in the backgrounds of politics. He began his career by working in a printer's office cleaning. By the time he was in his early twenties, he was the owner and editor of the printing office for which he cleaned. The paper was called the *Free Press*, located in Pittsfield, Illinois. This was a very small, amateurish newspaper whose news was sometimes one or two weeks late. Nicolay wrote ninety-five percent of the news reports himself, and one-hundred percent of the unsigned love poems that one could sometimes read within the confines of the paper's four pages. He was extremely interested in the politics of the city and the surrounding areas. So, Nicolay sold his newspaper and moved to Springfield, Illinois in order to be closer to the political action. He became the Illinois secretary of state. Nicolay was possibly the first person to publicly suggest that the young lawyer from Springfield, Abraham Lincoln, run for President of the United States. John Nicolay was a sensitive person. Once while giving his political opinion, he came close to tears. In 1858, Nicolay was employed as Lincoln's full-time office aide. Nicolay was responsible for many menial and important assignments. He was single and "living alone in a hotel room that Lincoln provided for him." He was engaged to a girl back home, but the engagement was already four years long. Nicolay's finances were small, and furthermore, he extended all of his energies toward the Lincoln campaign; there was little time for a personal life (Medved, p. 17). As Abraham Lincoln, the political figure grew, so did Nicolay's work load. It became necessary to get help for Nicolay. This help came in the form of one John Hay who was destined to become a very good poet, a best-selling novelist, and a respected Secretary of State. While Lincoln and Nicolay were laid-back and self-taught, Hay was twenty-two years old and a sophisticated graduate from Brown University. Lincoln felt a special closeness for both of these young men.

When it was necessary for Lincoln and Nicolay to relocate to Washington, D.C., Nicolay said no way could they do this and not take Hay along. So it was arranged that both young men accompany Lincoln to the nation's Capitol. Hay's parents were against their son being an assistant to the President-elect because it would interfere with their son's law studies. Nicolay had begun to depend on the academic abilities and the "high spirits" of Hay too much to be without him. Nicolay tended to be just as gloomy as Lincoln at times. What Nicolay perhaps did not know was that while a student at Brown University, Hay was an adamant "Hasheesh-Eater." Hay told a friend in a letter that the drug took him to far away places and allowed him to dream dreams. Soon after his far out experiences, he was working side by side with Nicolay and Lincoln. Upon arriving at the

White House, the two young men were given a "nice large bedroom." It did not take long for the Washington elite to gossip and describe Nicolay and Hay as "snobby and unpopular." They were very protective of their boss. Although the two were not getting very large salaries, they still took their jobs exceedingly seriously. They were responsible for screening Lincoln's mail as well as other duties. "When Lincoln signed the Emancipation Proclamation on New Year's Day 1863, it was Nicolay who handed him the pen" (Medved, p. 21).

As the Civil War continued, so did Nicolay's and Lincoln's depressions. Lincoln was in a constant state of depression during this time. He would often turn to Nicolay and Hay for solace. The President would look for a light under the door of the young men's bedroom that they shared. He would enter, and they would stay up half the night reading depressing poetry. The two men gave Lincoln playful pet names. One name they enjoyed calling him was "The Ancient." They all enjoyed going to the theater together. Mary Todd Lincoln did not like these two boys at all. John gave Mary Todd Lincoln a special pet name; he called her "the Hellcat." William Herndon often referred to the two young assistants as "the boys."

On November 9, 1863, Lincoln and "the boys" enjoyed a play called, *The Marble Heart.* The title fit the star perfectly. The star of this play was John Wilkes Booth. Hay related to his diary that Booth's acting was rather docile. The three men had an exceptionally special relationship. Lincoln loved telling ribald jokes. He enjoyed telling the bawdy jokes with sexually explicit detail. He also savored in poems and chants with racial overtones. Lincoln especially liked the song: "Sally is a bright Mullatter, Oh, Sally Brown. Pretty gal, but can't get at her. Oh, Sally Brown." Of course, it was the duty of Nicolay and Hay to guffaw at Lincoln's silliness.

In March of 1865, when the position of Consulate in Paris became vacant, Lincoln immediately sent in Nicolay's name. Nicolay was elated. Lincoln knew that Nicolay and Hay could not be without each other. Why not? Anyway, Lincoln felt it necessary to go about the business of finding a job for John Hay in Paris too; he did. If Lincoln was sweet, then it is not difficult to understand how young ambitious men of certain tastes might cling to attorney/President Lincoln like maggots to further their own political and travel careers.

However, Nicolay now thought about finally marrying his fiance, but he first set out for a cruise to Cuba. He thought this little vacation might untangle his nerves. While sailing from Cuba to Chesapeake Bay, a pilot came on board and said that the President had been shot. Nicolay disregarded the news as more rumors. Of course, he later learned the horrific truth and felt utter despair and guilt for not being by his intimate friend's side. Lincoln was killed in the theater box that they had often shared. Upon returning to Washington, Nicolay was a lost, depressed wreck. He couldn't even write to his fiance. He wrote later that he did not realize what a terrible blow his good friend's death would have on his "personal relations." Nicolay's "personal life had been shattered." He decided to postpone his wedding again, but while visiting Therena Bates, his fiance, in Illinois he was talked into getting married; so he did. (Medved, p. 26).

Nicolay idolized Lincoln for the rest of his life. His subsequent writings show the depth of closeness he felt toward Abraham Lincoln. John Nicolay was never without his old White House desk. Nicolay's daughter later declared that Nicolay could imagine seeing the tall Mr. Lincoln standing by the desk whenever he was writing. "This desk seemed to bring old days close." Author, Michael Medved said that Nicolay was the self-appointed keeper of the Lincoln flame. It is not clear as to what type of relationship Lincoln really had with Speed, Nicolay, nor Hay. But there are other famous men in history where the literature points to nothing other than sheer masculinity.

Frederick Douglass respected women as human beings and felt that they had just as much right to life, liberty, happiness and respect as any man. The women who frequented the company of Frederick Douglass knew this. He loved women, and he was clear in stating his position as a man when he made a speech to the Woman Suffrage Association — *The Woman's Journal*, April 14, 1888:

> When I ran away from slavery,
> it was for myself;

when I advocated emancipation,
it was for my people;
but when I stood up for the rights
of women,
self was out of the question.

TIDBITS FROM 1850'S — AFRICANS IN DIASPORA

On January 25, 1851 Sojourner Truth was the very distinguished speaker addressing the first African-American Women's Rights Convention in Akron, Ohio. Four months later on May 28, 1851, Truth attended the Women's Rights Convention.

The Meaning of the Fourth of July for Black Folks according to Frederick Douglass, July 5, 1852, Rochester, New York: Go where you may, search where you will, roam through all monarchies and despotisms of the Old World, travel through South America, search out every abuse, and when you have found the last, lay your facts by the side of the everyday practices of this nation, and you will say with me that, for revolting barbarity and shameless hypocrisy, America reigns without a rival.

While reading court cases that took place during the Lincoln era, I came across this piece — which subsequently moved me, a few days later, to poetry (I think). I couldn't get this sister out of my mind. In 1855 a white man in Jones, North Carolina was convicted for murdering an elder free African woman. He shot her in the head, then raped her corpse. This is a true account from court records (December, 1855 — Jones, North Carolina, which is now Jones County, near Trenton, in the Fayetteville and Jacksonville, North Carolina vicinities). The actual court record reads:

> State vs. Sewell, 3 Jones, N.C. 245, December, 1855. "Indictment for murder, … [sic] the prisoner had shot an old free Negro woman (aged about 60) in the eyes and face with a pistol … afterwards he was found on a pallet with her, and there were indications that he had ravished her as she lay insensible … on the way to jail, he begged the persons about him not to hurt him, … [sic] [247] verdict … [sic]

115

guilty of murder. Judgement ... [sic] pronounced,"
Affirmed.

Judicial Cases Concerning Slavery
North Carolina Cases, p. 192

Below, in poem-form, is just one piece of ourstory that
existed in diaspora(ed) Africans' lives during the lifetime of
Abe Lincoln:

KNOWINGNESS

I'm not your property
I's Free
I dates back in history.
Come on Lady Slave? Let me
'fore I's ties ya to a tree!
Let me! he plea.
No. Massa Sewell, I will
not 'low you to fray my body
— not hardly
I'm 60, I's Be
I have a sense of God-like
Knowingness
you see
Through my good times and Lordy,
the bad
Over the turmoil
and through the calm,
My sense of Pride-Worth is
Mighty Strong!
Mercy! I dates back to the Nile Valley
This is Ourstory
So, No, Mr. white man,
I will not let you hardy
yr'self on my body!
he Grabbed!!
No! I fight you good 'fore I
'low you to touch my
Body to get
your jolly.
Defeated! Deleted.

he took out his metal gun
and shot her dead.
he took out his little gun
and shot Her in the Head.

by: Auset BaKhufu
© 1992

(To understand the persistence of sexual violence toward African women perpetrated by white males, read papers and articles by Dr. Frances Cress Welsing. Also read Deborah Gray White's book: *Ar'n't I a Woman? Female Slaves in the Plantation South.*)

On May 5, 1857, the Dred Scott decision was made, stating that: A slave is not a citizen, so he can't sue in court. This decision was a grave violation against the Constitution. The jury must have sent some of their descendants to Simi Valley, California. Scott was a former enslaved person who had resided in "free" states for many years. He tried to sue the man who thought of himself as Dred Scott's former master. Justice Taney stated in the courthouse, "Negroes have no rights which the white man is bound to respect." Harriet Scott, Dred's African wife, stood by his side throughout this sadistic mental ordeal. Both husband and wife died on the eve of the Civil War.

The first play written and published by a Black was William Wells Brown, June 27, 1858. Brown also wrote a book patterning his main characters after the lives of Thomas Jefferson's African lover and her mulatto daughters. The name of the book is: *CLOTEL, or The President's Daughter*, 1853, by William Wells Brown — A Classic.

On October 16, 1859, John Brown raided Harper's Ferry in the name of freedom for the slaves. John Brown was a hyper white businessman, who had seen enough brutality against African people, and who had enough guts to try to do something about the uncivilized, ludicrous and barbaric-acting operations of his race.

Five of the 21 heroes who took part in the John Brown raid on Harper's Ferry, on October 16, 1859, were African men. They were: John Copeland, Osborn Anderson,

Dangerfield Newby, Lewis Leary and Shields Green. Leary and Green were killed during their rebellion for freedom (Rogers, *Your History*, p. 76).

MARY TODD LINCOLN

Lincoln was often ill while campaigning against his political rivals during the late 1850's and the early 60's. "He complained of a sore throat and headache." Before Lincoln had been inaugurated for his presidential seat in 1861, there was a great deal of animosity between whites. There are hundreds of books and other literature which record that there had been vague rumors and suspicions afloat concerning a conspiracy to assassinate the president-elect while he was on his way to Washington, D.C. It was February, 1861, and personal friends employed by spys or detectives were assigned to follow up on some clues and prevent the assassination plot. This assassination was to take place as Lincoln was passing through Baltimore, Maryland. Someone was supposed to start a fight, taking the attention away from Lincoln, and during this brief distraction, Lincoln was to be murdered. Lincoln was informed of this plot as he arrived in Philadelphia; he re-routed (References: Brooks, pp. 294, Reprinted in 1978, Amen Ra, p. 28).

Lincoln had many illnesses and ups and downs in his personal life as well as his political life. His son Willie had a bad case of scarlet fever. Lincoln thought that he might have the same malady. Lincoln tended to be a sickly man, and Mary Lincoln was worried about her child and her husband constantly.

Young Willie Lincoln died in the White House on February 10, 1862, a year after plots were made to assassinate his father. Willie died from an attack of malaria. In Africa, malaria takes the lives of over one million children annually. Although malaria is caused by parasites, the person who has an iron deficiency is more likely to develop this disease than one who is not iron deficient, no matter where one lives (Reference: Edelstein, pp. 24, 61 & 63). In the 1800's it was felt that because of Washington's warm, moist climate, and the watery marshes, the region was filled with the disease (Lehrer, p. 246).

Lincoln loved Willie with all of his heart. His precious child lay in the Green Room of the White House for many days before his funeral, mummified with a "new" embalming procedure (Garrison, p. 69). The child's metallic casket was covered with magnificent flowers. February 24, 1862, Mary Todd Lincoln was unable to attend the actual funeral; her nerves were out of control. She and her husband spent a quiet one-half hour with their beloved dead child. While they sat there, a terrible storm began; it fit the grief of these parents. At 2:00 p.m. funeral attendants gathered in the East room to pay their last respects to this innocent child. Many political figures attended Willie Lincoln's funeral. Vice president Hannibal Hamlin attended. Even George McClellan came to pay his respects and wrote Lincoln a note of sympathy.

Many sympathized with the Lincolns and their forever brewing troubles, but sympathy did not cease gossip. Mary Todd Lincoln was heartbroken over the "ugly things" that were being said about her Mr. Lincoln, especially coming from the South. Many southerners were openly calling her beloved husband a Black man, a negro, a nigger!

THE 1860's AND THE 54th

Sojourner Truth said it was time for African-American men to take up weapons to save the Union and assist in rectifying the sins of white men. She said that the white man does not know God, and God does not know him. Sojourner Truth's attacks on racial injustice in the Nation's capitol boosted the morale of the Black community tremendously.

When Lincoln won the presidential election in November, there was wide-scale rebellion in the South. By February of 1861, seven states had seceded from the Union and formed their own confederate government. Soon after, four of the other enslaved states joined the Confederacy and the war was on between the North and the South.

Frederick Douglass was going to Haiti in early 1861 to start negotiations to see whether Blacks in America might be able to eventually relocate and live in Haiti instead of America. But the war began and Douglass ceased his plans in hopes that the war would lead to the freedom of African-Americans. Lincoln had advocated that this was not a war to end slavery, and most whites agreed. White soldiers said, "We ain't fo' the nigger, but we is fo' the war." The debate over slavery had reached its boiling point. When Abraham Lincoln was the Illinois Congressman, he said that a "House divided against itself can not stand." Lincoln also said that he believes this "Government can not endure permanently half-slave and half-free" (Krass, p. 131).

The Civil War started on April 12, 1861. That was when the Confederate Army attacked the Union troops stationed at Fort Sumpter, in Charleston, S.C. This was a confusing war because as mentioned, Blacks and the anti-slavery people thought that this was a war to end slavery, whereas for other Americans they viewed this thing as mainly a battle to reunite the states or the country.

Sojourner Truth decided to tour the midwest in support of the Union's war efforts and the freedom of slaves. Of course, during this lecture tour, she was greeted by many angry people. Then there were also those who supported her lectures and war efforts.

Three months before Lincoln's speech on colonization, Congress had, on April 10, 1862, passed a joint resolution stating that federal financial aid should be given to any state that adopted a plan for the gradual abolition of slavery (Quarles, p. 113). This same year, while traveling through the midwest, Sister Truth was confronted by an anti-war group who threatened to burn down the lecture hall where she was to speak. She retorted, "I do not care if you do burn the place down; I will then stand upon its ashes and say what I have to say!" It was around this time that Truth's health began to give her some problems. Her health was momentarily restored when President Lincoln signed the Emancipation Proclamation which declared that all slaves in the rebellious confederate states would be free on January 1, 1863. After Harriet Beecher Stowe wrote an article on Sojourner Truth about an 1853 meeting that they had together, Truth's popularity rose. This account was published in the April of 1863 *Atlantic* magazine. People who had never heard of Truth were introduced to this amazing woman who Stowe called the African Sybil, a priestess in Ancient Africa.

In 1862, General Hunter of the Union Army had issued a proclamation freeing the slaves of Georgia, Florida, and South Carolina (Rogers, *100 Amazing Facts About the Negro*, p. 17). In volume II of the *Complete Works of Abraham Lincoln*, 1920, Lincoln wrote, "Gen. Hunter is an honest man ... He proclaimed all men free within certain states. I repudiated the proclamation."

April 16, 1862 was the day when slavery in Washington, D.C. was supposedly abolished, giving freedom to African-Americans in the District of Columbia. In May of this same year, General David "Black Dave" Hunter enlisted African-American men for combat in South Carolina, and in October, the first Kansas African-American volunteers fought a winning battle at Island Mound, Missouri.

August 14, 1862: "You are intelligent," Lincoln said to a group of African-American men and women, "and know that success does not as much depend on external help as on self-reliance. Much, therefore, depends on yourselves." This was Lincoln's lecture and meeting with Black leaders on Colonization. Lincoln questioned why the so-called free Negroes seem more determined to live near their slavemasters' children rather than embarking on a journey to a new land to live among their own people? Lincoln said, "I do not know how much attachment you may have toward *our* race." He continued, "It does not strike me that you have the greatest reason to love *them*, but still you are attached to *them* at all events." If you will notice, Lincoln stated in his own words that "You seem to be attached to our race (white people), but then he goes on to say *twice* and refer to the white race as *"them."* Why does Lincoln twice refer to the white race as them, as if he's not white? Is it because his innate self spoke for him in this speech, relating the truth of his ancestry to all? Why is Lincoln so adamantly impressing upon these African men and women that they are intelligent. Did Lincoln express this sentiment to them because he understood himself to be an intelligent being with black blood, therefore the group who stood before him now must also be intelligent? Or was he simply referring to *them* as slaveholders because he felt that he had never actually owned slaves? He's gone; we can't ask him. But it can be said with certainty that Lincoln talked out both sides of his mouth, mind, or genes all of his life. Lincoln muddled over the minds of white people just as much as he did Black people's minds. In his famous speech about race and superiority, he said on one occasion, "I am in favor of having the superior position assigned to the white race." Then on another occasion Lincoln stated, "I am in favor of the race to which I belong having the superior position" — not specifying to which race he belonged. Lincoln and the other presidents in this book, did tend to have the propensity to talk out of both sides of their mouths, brains, heads, genes or whatever. Amen Ra, author of *Shattering the Myth of the Man Who Freed the Slaves*, described this act as masters of double talk (p. 30). In Lincoln's case, he had mastered his multiple personalities, be that consciously or unconsciously.

Four weeks after his speech to African-Americans on colonization, Lincoln said on September 13, 1862, "We didn't go into the war to put down slavery, but to put the flag back." Lincoln's allegiance was first to the restoration of the Union which meant unity for the northern and Southern whites (Amen Ra, pp. 6 & 7). So why were Blacks fighting?

In the meanwhile, in everyday life in the South, African men and women still enslaved by white southerners, were haplessly helping the Confederacy survive. These enslaved persons' **free** labor was indispensable and essential to Confederacy survival. The southern so-called white slavemasters (slaveholders) could join the armed forces and fight since the enslaved persons were taking care of everything at the plantation. Unlike the North, the South did not use Africans as soldiers until later on in the war.

COLONIZATION: LINCOLN SAID SEND THE BLACKS AWAY

Henry Clay was a member of the American Colonization Society and advocated gradual emancipation followed by colonization. Lincoln agreed with his old friend on this issue. Lincoln said, Let's return the "Negro" to their native land, "Pharaoh's country," so that we will no longer have to be bothered. He said, by doing this we may "succeed in freeing our land from the dangerous presence of slavery; and, at the same time, in restoring a captive people to their

long-lost father-land, with bright prospects for the future"
(Oates, pp. 106-107, 1977). Now this is where Garvey and
Lincoln may have gotten along. Even Lincoln knew and
understood from whence Africans originated. It is exceptionally sad when Africans living in America today do not
realize and understand the truth nor the locale of their own
origins. But the Africans or African-Americans during Lincoln's heyday did know that they came from Africa, and
there were many who did want to return, no matter what
his-story says. Lincoln did not know if Southerners would
agree to Africans' return home, but at one point, after the
Nat Turner revolt, some Southerners definitely agreed with
the notion of colonization. Frederick Douglass did not agree
— not on their terms anyway. He also lambasted Lincoln for
his "hypocrisy in government policies."

Frederick Douglass and William Lloyd Garrison
demanded that Lincoln issue an emancipation order (Oates,
pp. 312 & 155, 252, 356, 1977). They said nothing about colonization — at this time. Frederick Douglass said that the
only way to reach whites was with their fear of personal
danger. Let them know that death is all around them —
their deaths. But since the Blacks had calmed down again,
they said, "No!" "We want our slaves!" Whites were against
freeing Black people to roam around on their *white* land;
they said the decision not to free Africans is called: "race
control in a region brimming with Negroes." Lincoln was
hoping that at least three million Africans would be shipped
back to Africa (Oates, Malice, p. 107). It didn't happen.

Abraham Lincoln said in 1862 that it was "a great movement of God to end slavery and that the man would be a
fool who should stand in the way" (Oates, p. 297, 1977). Lincoln knew that he and others tried desperately to keep slavery alive, therefore, Lincoln assumed, it must have been
God who eventually freed enslaved people, the slaves.

Lincoln's plan for the freeing of Blacks was not limited to
his idea of colonization. He also proposed a strategy called
Compensated Emancipation which Benjamin Quarles in his
book *The Negro in the Making of America* said that "Lincoln's
response to the social revolution was to develop two plans,
one for the slaves, one for the free Negroes, and that is that
this plan was for the gradual compensation — freeing

African people gradually over a period extending to some thirty years and paying their so-called masters out of the national treasury. Many white people were against this because it would take too much money (Quarles, p. 113, 1969). Yet there were still many African enslaved people who didn't even know they were free after they were "free." Anyway, these enslaved people remained on white people's plantations for thirty and forty years working for nothing. The so-called masters didn't tell them they were free. How were they to know?

It is said that in the Frederick Douglass monthly of September, 1862, one month after Lincoln's meeting with the so-called free Blacks to discuss colonization, Frederick Douglass thoroughly criticized Lincoln for showing his inconsistencies and his two-facedness, his schizophrenic personality, his contempt for Black people in his hypocrisy (Zilversmit, p. 100; Amen Ra, p. 38).

There were many tired, enslaved people who took up Lincoln's offer to leave America and they were very happy to leave. But they were sent to an island with no provisions for survival. There was no prosperity nor food there, and a lot of these African people died (Rogers, *Africa's Gift to America*, p. 140; Amen Ra, p. 39). Lincoln wanted to colonize Africans to Liberia and Haiti. This possibly could have worked had everybody, Black and White, been more organized and with the appropriate types of resources. Then many Blacks should have been happy to leave America even though they had built the place. Africans built America and still have not been paid for their labor.

WHITE PEOPLE LOOTED AND KILLED SENSELESSLY

Many African-Americans worked for the Union Army fighting and building roads and bridges even before the Emancipation Proclamation was signed. Lincoln drafted the Emancipation Proclamation to legally announce that *some* Africans *in certain areas* of America were free. But Lincoln never intended to make a cemented change in the power structure of the racist nation of America (Reference: Amen Ra, p. 31).

After the Emancipation Proclamation was signed on January 1, 1863, Congress almost immediately opened their armed forces to Africans by way of segregated facilities and military activities. More African regiments were formed and officially led by white officers, but actually led and run by many ingenious Black men. By the end of the war, about 180,000 African men trying to live free in America had served in the northern armies.

By March of 1863, there were more recognized Black (African) military regiments in the North and South. Some of the southern African military personnel helped Union prisoners escape. In Charleston, South Carolina, Robert Smalls and other enslaved persons seized a Confederate boat. They sailed the boat past southern gunfire and met their destination safely at the Union grounds.

African soldiers demonstrated that they still possessed their Warrior selves and their pure African blood by fighting bravely and gallantly. They took part in over 450 battles. One of these battles took place in July of 1863. The 54th African Regiment attacked Fort Wayne. This fort protected Charleston, South Carolina. These military warriors overran the first wall and planted the flag of their African regiment there. The cannon fire against them was heavy. Some were killed and many were wounded. They finally had to retreat.

The Fifty-fourth "Colored" Infantry was from Massachusetts; they were under the command of Robert Gould Shaw. Within eight months after Lincoln signed the Emancipation Proclamation, about fifteen African-American regiments were in the army fields from the North and the South. And Frederick Douglass and others were forming other regiments.

The summer of 1863 was turbulent not only for the soldiers, but also for the average citizen trying to live a peaceful life. There were several race riots. White folks were afraid that their power would diminish if Blacks were freed. (They didn't have anything to worry about did they?) Nevertheless, during this beastly summer, a group of barbaric-acting white people charged a Black community in New York City setting fire to an orphanage. They then proceeded to hang Blacks from street lampposts and set them afire! Others they whipped or clubbed to death, and any white person who got in the way of this sick group got killed too. One modern-day white his-storian described this nonsense as a "civil distur-bance." The old 1800's writers, Black and White, termed it what it was: a race riot. These white people burned down the draft office because Blacks were being accepted into the mili-tary. These whites also *looted* jewelry stores and saloons (Oates, *With Malice Toward None,* p. 357). Now what did bracelets, earrings, necklaces, pearls, diamonds, rubies, and liquor have to do with it? Nothing! It's just that whites were not getting everything they wanted, and they rebelled (?) — No, rioted. Whites rioted because they did not want Blacks to be free, and Blacks rebelled because they wanted to be free. Now who is more sensible? A few years later the news on and around Washington D.C.'s Pennsylvania Avenue was: A Negro with a razor kills a white man on Pennsylvania Avenue in the Nation's Capitol! Now, why did this brother find it necessary to do this? It is ninety-nine percent assured that he had a reason. Without a razor, he would probably have been the casualty. Anyway, one old-time white White House official said of this incident that: "The negroes last night acted is if the Devil had possessed them, ... the white people will soon rise in their majesty and expel the colored race from the city. I am almost convinced that giving them freedom has given them so exalted an estimate of themselves that it will be hard to keep them in their proper places." This statement was written in the diary of Benjamin Brown French. Having written this statement in his personal diary, he probably wasn't trying to impress or satisfy anyone by saying this. So his prejudice stands as it is, and he was said to be a "liberal white." Notice how he capitalized the "d" in devil, and lower-cased the "n" in the word white people use(d) to describe African-Americans. He also feels that whites are *majestic* and that Blacks are to be kept in some par-ticular and/or inferior *place.* These were the sentiments of a liberal?

WHITE HOUSE BUDDIES

On August 10, 1863, Frederick Douglass visited Lincoln at the White House. "Hello, Douglass; you don't have to introduce yourself," Lincoln said, "I know who you are." In this meeting, Douglass said that he was initially willing to have Blacks fight in the war, but since Lincoln was not allowing Blacks to get equal pay to white soldiers, he had come to the White House to complain. Lincoln told Douglass that some of the white soldiers were against having Black men enlisted at all, and the other group of white soldiers, though they didn't care if Blacks were enlisted, thought that the Black soldiers should at least get less pay because they felt that the Blacks were inferior (voicing their own subconscious inferior complex). Lincoln went on, "We had to make some concession to prejudice; but in the end they shall have the same pay as white soldiers." Lincoln told Douglass that he appreciated his help in recruiting "Negro" soldiers. Douglass left the White House with conscientious respect for Abraham (Hanks-Link Horn) Lincoln.

Douglass said that Lincoln is "the first great man that I talked with in the United States freely who in no single instance reminded me of the difference between himself and myself, of the difference of color." Douglass said that he was glad when he could forget that his skin was dark and his hair was crisped (McFeely, p. 77). It is certain that Douglass may have had these sincere feelings because both men were standing there mirror-like, one just as swarthy as the other.

Frederick Douglass' son Lewis became a first sergeant major of Colonel Robert Gould Shaw's 54th African-American regiment. His other son, Charles, was a private in Company F. Charles got sick. So on August 29, 1863, Frederick Douglass wrote President Lincoln asking him to release his son from his military services. Abraham Lincoln wrote back on September 15th, scribbling simply, "Let the boy be discharged. A. Lincoln" (McFeely, pp. 224-235).

Mary Church Terrell, educator and U.S. delegate to the International Peace Conference, was born during the Civil War. She was born on September 23, 1863 in Memphis, Tennessee.

Two months after Terrell's birth, Lincoln delivered his famous Gettysburg Address on November 19, 1863. After the address, Lincoln came back to the White House sick again. The doctors diagnosed his sickness as a case of smallpox, "varioloid" (Oates, p. 367, 1977).

A few days after Lincoln's Gettysburg Address, Sojourner Truth traveled to Camp Ward, an Army base near

Detroit, Michigan, where 1,500 African-American troops were stationed. She brought with her food that was donated by her neighbors in Battle Creek, so that the soldiers might enjoy a decent meal for a change. It was Thanksgiving day, a white man's holiday that is enjoyed by them on the blood of the Indians. Rev. Barashango from Silver Spring, Maryland has dutifully and rightfully termed this day: Misgiving Day. Truth resorted to whatever means necessary and whatever day was available to feed her people. Use these "holidays" to help yourself and others in your community, or go to work and make some money. Upon Sojourner Truth's arrival there, these soldiers understood that they had in their presence a respectful Elder of Wisdom, and they stood at attention in her honor.

FREDERICK DOUGLASS AND HIS AFRICAN WIFE, ANNA

Upon visiting Douglass' home in 1990, I was not surprised to see a picture, bigger than any other picture that he has in his entire beautiful home, of Abraham Lincoln firmly secured on the living room wall. Lincoln never paid a visit to Douglass' home, so Anna didn't have to worry about serving this masked brother. The tour guide said that the room where Lincoln's picture was so symmetrically affixed was for family and guest gatherings. The picture of Douglass' African wife, Anna, hangs serenely on the wall across the hall from the guest gathering room, while a smaller picture of his white wife hangs lower on the opposite wall. Douglass married his white secretary seventeen months after the death of his first wife, Anna. His children, and especially his daughter, Rosetta, were mortified and asked what had he been preaching all of his life? They said that his actions were a contradiction to his philosophy which was African unity and pride. He stated to a friend that he does not apologize for marrying a woman who was only a shade lighter than himself (Harris, et.al., *The Black Book*, p. 24).

It was Anna Murray who finally convinced Frederick Douglass that he could indeed escape from enslaved servitude, slavery. She was born free to pure African parents, and raised to make her living as a servant. Although free, there was not much else for a beautiful dark-skinned African-

American woman to do workwise during this very racist era. Anna was a smart, common-sense woman. Frederick Douglass married Anna in 1840, during Lawyer Lincoln's heyday. Anna and Frederick were married a long forty-two years, until her death. With all of his travels, Douglass never worried about his wife taking care of herself; she was a survivor — a strong woman. Anna's husband had career goals and ambitions that she was not particularly interested in taking a part. "She was not comfortable in the presence of white people." Douglass disregarded Anna's discomfort which caused some arguments. When he had white visitors, Anna would welcome them properly and carefully. She would then proceed to the kitchen, serve everybody, and leave her "ambitious" husband to his white acquaintances (Huggins, pp. 154-155 & McFeely, pp. 154-155). Some thought Anna was just shy; her husband knew better. Anna was simply and purely a mutaphobic. She heeded to the ways and eccentric whims of white people and did not want to be around them. Rosetta, the Douglass' eldest daughter, later said that her mother always remained psychologically tied to the Black community. More of us should be so smart. Anna had already persuaded Douglass to free himself, now she was probably, in her own silent, Goddess-like way, trying to think of more prudent ways for them both to be even freer, i.e, without tying themselves onto the coattails of white people. Freddy was good for tying himself, or something, to white women. One white woman, Ottilia Assing, wrote: "If one stands in so intimate a relationship with a man as I do with Douglass, one comes to know facets of the whole world, ... especially if it is a man whom the entire world has seen and whom so many women have loved." Ottilia's psychologist wrote Douglass that the woman was having emotional problems. So she lived with Frederick and Anna Douglass for three or more months — to calm her disturbed mind. Ottilia wrote her sister that Douglass was thinking of having an extra wing built onto their home so that she could live there indefinitely. She told her sister that she would love this, but that the "illiterate creature" (referring to Anna) had Frederick Douglass hexed, as if the only way for an African woman to keep the attention of a man like Frederick Douglass was to use voodoo, hoodoo or voudou. Anna did not need to use her knowledge of voudouism (unconscious or not) to keep the love of any man. Here's this white woman living in, and writing letters out of this African woman's house and labeling Anna, the woman of the house, an "illiterate creature" and a "bewitcher." This is one reason perhaps why Anna did not want to socialize with white people. Anyway, when Ottilia's shrink learned of the possible intimate relationship between his patient and Frederick Douglass, he said that she must be fantasizing. It was more likely his "fantasy" that they were not intimate. And whether they were intimate or not, this white woman apparently wished that they had been.

TRUTH AND DOUGLASS MEET UP WITH THE PRESIDENT

On August 19, 1864, Douglass was sitting in the White House waiting to see Abraham Lincoln. There were also two other men in the waiting room. Their names were Joseph T. Mills and Alexander Randall, both from Wisconsin. Mills said to the President when he saw him, "I was in your reception room; it was dark; I suppose the clouds and darkness necessarily surround the secrets of state. There in the corner, I saw a man quietly reading who possessed a remarkable physiognomy. I was riveted to the spot; I stood and stared at him. He raised his flashing eyes and caught me in the act. I was compelled to speak, he told Lincoln. "Are you the President?" I asked him. "No, replied the stranger, "I am Frederick Douglass." Lincoln's and Douglass' frizzy hair, swarthy, olive complexions, and their beards could cause one to think that they may be brothers. Mills asked Mr. Lincoln if he was in favor of miscegenation. Lincoln's answer to the question was: "That's a democratic mode of producing good Union men, and I don't propose to infringe on the patent" (McFeely, p. 232).

Many Blacks felt that Lincoln was going a little too slow with this Union and war problem. So, Sojourner told her friends and neighbors that she was going down to the White House to advise the President. Sojourner Truth arrived in Washington, D.C. in September 1864. It was during this time that citizens were trying to decide whether or not Lincoln should be given a second term in office. On October 29, 1864, Sojourner Truth was joined by a group of visitors waiting in the White House reception room for an appointment with President Lincoln. She was pleased to see that Lincoln tended to treat his Black guest with the same courtesy as he treated his white visitors. As soon as she saw Lincoln, she gave him the "Look-you-up-and-down" treatment. She looked this dark man in the face and said, "I had never heard of you until you became President." He laughed and told her, "I had heard of you years before I thought of ever becoming President." She wanted to meet Abraham Lincoln at his office in order to give him some moral support regarding the war, and to give him some advice. She advised him not to worry about all of the attacks that he was getting from racists and otherwise. She also thought that Lincoln might need some encouragement. She thanked Lincoln for what he had done for African-Americans. While at the White House, Abraham Lincoln looked through Sister Truth's book entitled, *The Book of Life.* He then signed it To: Aunty Sojourner Truth — the old stereotypical "Aunty."

On January 31, 1865, the 13th Amendment was passed supposedly giving total freedom to enslaved African peoples in America. January 10, 1864, one year and three months before this Amendment was passed, George Washington Carver, the famous African scientist, was born. This is just a tidbit to aid in placing ourstory into perspective.

INAUGURATION DAY, MARCH 1865

As inauguration day got closer, Lincoln declared to his intimate friend, Joshua Speed, "I am very unwell. My feet and hands always cold — I suppose I ought to be in bed." Speed sympathized with Lincoln that with all of the excitement of the re-election, with people asking all kinds of favors, and with all of the problems that comes with being the President of the United States especially during the trying times of the 1860's, and "with my knowledge of your nervous sensibility it is a wonder that such scenes as this don't kill you" (Oates, p. 409, 1977).

Ward Hill Lamon, who would become another Lincoln biographer, came to the White House armed with guns, knives, and blankets during the heat of the Civil War. He had grave notions that Lincoln was going to be killed. Maybe Lamon was one person who took Lincoln's worries about death to heart. Maybe this was one friend who heeded to Lincoln's cries for help. Lamon lay outside of Lincoln's door as he slept because he felt now that Lincoln had been re-elected that someone might try again to assassinate the President. A few weeks after the election, Lincoln was looking much older than his fifty-five years. The strain of his 1864 re-election into the White House had taken its toll. Mary said that she was very concerned for the health of "Mr. Lincoln," as she so affectionately called him. She said that he seemed "so broken hearted, so completely worn out" (Oates, p. 409, 1977).

Heavy, dark clouds hung over Washington, D.C. on March 4, 1865, and the morning rain poured as political enthusiasts prepared for Lincoln's inauguration. The new Vice President, Andrew Johnson arrived at the inauguration on the arm of outgoing vice president Hannibal Hamlin. At noon Lincoln rode in a carriage up Pennsylvania Avenue toward the Capitol. Finally Lincoln took his place on the beautifully prepared platform. He was still sick and unhappy. Vice President Hamlin sang a short song, full of 1800's political and sentimental soul. Then with much dignity, he introduced the intoxicated Andrew Johnson. Everyone in the audience was shocked at Johnson's drunken speech. Mr. Lincoln held his composure, and looked and listened sadly and sickly. Lincoln remained calm throughout his new vice president's affliction. Finally, Johnson seized a Bible in his hands, and gave it a loud, sloppy kiss. Then he said suddenly and just as loudly, "I kiss this book in the face of my nation of the United States" (Bishop, pp. 33-34). It sounded as if he wanted to say something else. Anyway, Johnson really showed his basic instincts on this important day.

There were many spectators and officials. As Lincoln looked down, he saw a face in the crowd that he could not help but notice; it was his brother, Frederick Douglass. There was another face that the President probably did not notice; it was the face of a murderer, John Wilkes Booth. John Wilkes Booth would later admit to someone that he could have killed Lincoln at this inauguration if he had chosen. He had his derringer (gun) in his pocket.

It was a dark, cloudy, and rainy day. As Lincoln stepped up to the speakers' podium, a brilliant sun suddenly burst through the clouds surrounding Lincoln and the crowd in a ray of warmth. As the sun Ra beat down on Lincoln's weary sick head, he eloquently lamented to the crowd that the troubles he'd seen were due to the cruelty and sin of slavery. He said that God had visited the guilty white people of the North and the South (Oates, pp. 409-410, 1977). Such a contradiction in words and actions when the historian/ourstorian Lerone Bennett, Jr. and Frederick Douglass would assure us that Lincoln was actually a white supremacist in thought and actions. (*Ebony*, "Was Lincoln a White Supremacist?" p. 35). Lincoln did not understand his melanic powers at all. He just wasn't in touch with his Black Power.

After Lincoln's inauguration ceremony in 1865, Douglass went to visit Lincoln at the White House again. "Here comes my friend Douglass. I am glad to see you," Lincoln said upon Douglass' arrival. "I saw you in the crowd today, listening to my address. There is no man in the country whose opinion I value more than yours. I want to know what you think of it." Douglass listened to all of this buttering and replied, "I was impressed; it was a sacred effort." Lincoln smiled, "I am glad you liked it!" He admired Douglass. Lincoln felt that there were some Blacks who were very intelligent (Oates, p. 424, 1977). He thought that these particular Blacks (like himself and Freddy Douglass, I suppose) should be allowed to vote.

MARY LINCOLN, THE HELLCAT

Herndon said that when Lincoln got into some of his depressed moods, "sluggishness" and "vague dreams," Mary would push him into motivated action. Herndon said that her tongue was like a "whiplash" and Lincoln would come out of those melancholy states of mind (Sandburg, p. 77, 1932) fast! "Mrs. Lincoln and Herndon hated each other" (Sandburg, p. 255, 1925).

Lincoln liked to lie down on the floor and read with his shoes off. But Mrs. Lincoln wouldn't hear of it! She told him to put his shirt and tie back on, and some shoes. "Your feet do not need to breathe!" she told him. "And sit up!" With all of this nagging it's a wonder that Mr. Lincoln did not wish that the days would *speed* up. He usually took Mary's temperment lightly, but one day Lincoln got sick of it. Lincoln was not yet president, and they were living in Springfield, Illinois where Lincoln had a law practice. Lincoln pushed Mary Todd out of the door one Sunday, and shrieked, "You make this house intolerable, damn you, get out of it!" Lincoln's high-pitched cry became his vocal trademark during his political campaigns. Some lady acquaintance admonished that: "It was an outstanding characteristic of Mary Todd Lincoln that she wanted what she wanted when she wanted it and no substitute!" (Sandburg, pp. 71 & 90).

By the time Lincoln reached the White House, Mary Lincoln was already nicknamed the "Hellcat". She was not a very likeable first lady. She was not trusted by the North nor the South. She came from a southern slaveholding family, so many northerners distrusted her, and since she deserted the cause of the southerners, they did not trust her either. She seemed to work diligently beside her husband and his political agenda, but she was later accused of being a confederate spy and was investigated for treason. Her three half-brothers were confederate soldiers. Lincoln protected Mary by attending a meeting to vindicate his wife, stating that he knew for a fact that no family members of his were involved in any unlawful acts. The committee members were so moved with the boldness yet sensitivity of the President that they dropped the issue immediately.

After Willie's death on February 20, 1862, the Lincoln family was despondent and sad. Tad, the Lincoln's fourth boy, had been a jovial child, now he was apt to break out crying any moment. Mary suffered a nervous breakdown. It got to the point where Lincoln took her to the window, and pointing to a white building, he said, "Mother, try to control yourself, or you will go mad, then we may have to take you there." "There" was an insane asylum. With the help of her good Black friend, Elizabeth Keckley, Mary Todd improved a little, but any reminder of her dead child would send her into sobbing fits. Elizabeth Keckley was the Black servant who stayed by Mary's side and helped her through very trying times. It is ironic that Lizzie worked first for Jefferson Davis and then for Abraham Lincoln. Mary Lincoln was no longer the social Hellcat-butterfly, and she lived in seclusion with "Lizzie" by her side. She said that her closeness to Lizzie was for "all of the oppressed colored people." Lizzie helped Mary Lincoln tremendously in advocating her new-found abolitionist viewpoint. Mary Lincoln reached out to spiritualism for she could not handle the grief of her son's death alone. She went to every seance she could find around the Washington, D.C. area. She was elated when some psychic or spiritualist would draw back the mask/"veil" which splits us from the ones gone on to the ancestors. Oh hallelujah! Mary could now communicate with Willie.

As time passed, Mary was not so compelled to reach out to the psychic. Instead, she used the therapeutic approach of visiting injured soldiers, giving them food and flowers. But Mary Todd Lincoln was still very mentally ill. She had her own strange set of mood swings spiked with temper outbursts that would make the Hulk cringe. Mary yelled at Lincoln's associates and their wives whenever she felt like it. Some took it with humor, others did not. She provoked General O.C. Ord's wife to tears for sitting beside her Mr. Lincoln. Lincoln was very angry with "Mother" for this. And General Grant's wife, Julia tried to stay away from Mary because she didn't want to be around when Mary "needed" to explode. They had been friends, but no more.

Elizabeth "Lizzie" Keckley and Mary Todd Lincoln did not remain friendly either. Lizzie wrote a book detailing and revealing many personal matters about Mary Lincoln. Mary Lincoln was disappointed to say the least.

LINCOLN'S ASSASSINATION

The issue of Reconstruction and the dissemination and organization of political and economic power among white Americans prompted the assassination of Abraham Lincoln in 1865. In July of 1864, the Radical republicans had retaliated with a bill written by Senator Ben Wade of Ohio and Representative Harry Davis of Maryland. It outlined a much harsher Reconstruction plan than Lincoln's plan, which included a provision for military rule of the defeated Confederacy.

Lincoln's own party was against him on many issues during his second term, especially because of the Emancipation Proclamation and his Reconstruction plans. Lincoln's agenda for Reconstruction was not satisfactory to Confederate sympathizers. These sympathizers, who disagreed with Lincoln, were from his own Republican party. Lincoln's continuous argument on the slavery issue hoaxed Blacks and Whites into thinking that he was in favor of ending slavery and saving the Union. Lincoln's social and political views were serious threats to white America. They were interested in maintaining the white status quo. Lincoln's policies represented drastic measures of presidential power of which the Congress felt powerless to tolerate.

Many of the white people, Northerners and Southerners, who exploited Africans and poor whites in the South were in it for the business. Northern bankers and commercial property was constructed, ships were built, and much of what was manufactured was constructed and built by the Africans, so-called slaves. The manufacturers of shackles and chains to bound the Africans' feet and hands were manufactured by the Northern businesses (References: Works of Bennett, DuBois and Amen Ra).

Slaveholders and plantation owners shipped much of the cotton, tobacco, sugar and other raw materials produced by slave labor to the North to be manufactured. History and research shows that the Democratic party in the South and the North accumulated a great deal of wealth from the institution of slavery also (Windsor, *The Valley of the Dry Bones*, p. 28).

Northern commercial magnates ran for office in the U.S. Congress or backed other politicians who supported their business interests. In the South, many slaveholders held important offices in the House of Senate and the United States Congress. One such slaveholder was Senator Jefferson Davis from Mississippi who owned a ten thousand acre plantation with many slaves. Holding high positions in the government from the Presidency down, these Democrats in the North and the South made the abolition of slavery very difficult.

Although Lincoln did sign the Emancipation Proclamation, he did so only as a last alternative and a military strategy to weaken the Confederate states in rebellion during the Civil War. Africans were duped and forced into building

America by the so-called founding fathers of America, such as George Washington, James Madison, John Adams, Thomas Jefferson, and Andrew Jackson. These presidents and their white male counterparts became wealthy as slave-owners and merchants, while African-Americans still await their reparations for their labor.

These observations, these truths makes it plain to see that the so-called slave is indeed not a slave, but an enslaved person, a political prisoner, because behind the so-called institution of slavery many white people held political positions and owned businesses — all in the name of slavery and the work that Africans performed for them — FREE. Whites held tight to their self-interest and their barbarism in America (References: Amen Ra, p. 26; Windsor, pp. 26-27).

When we begin to read and understand the tensions that mounted among white people during this era, it becomes relatively easy to comprehend why Abe Lincoln was killed less than one week after General Lee surrendered, which marked the end of the Civil War. "White agriculturalists and industrialists who had previously worked together to divide, conquer and enslave African people at home and abroad were struggling for economic, political and social dominance over each other" (Amen-Ra, p. 28).

Lincoln lived as a white man, and was shot by his own people. Did some feel that because Lincoln was possibly Black that he may some day in his old age, perhaps on his dying bed defect to his proper race, and embarrass them, especially since the Civil War was over? Lincoln was viewed as a threat to America. They thought that he was a sensitive, honest, and insane man. To many whites, he was a man who could be a threat to their security, their selfish prosperity, and their very existence, revealing their racist psyches. Who was this masked Lincoln man anyway? They really didn't know. Horace Greeley of the "New York Tribune," 1861, stated that, "There are thousands who do not yet know Abraham Lincoln." His statement still holds true today.

During Lincoln's last public speech on April 11, 1865, he made a vain attempt to defend his policies for Reconstruction (Amen Ra, p. 30). *Lincoln's last public address:*

We all agree that the seceded states, so called, are out of their proper practical relation with the Union, and that the sole object of the government, civil and military, in regard to those states, is to again get them into that proper, practical relation. I believe that it is not only possible, but in fact easier, to do this without deciding or even considering whether these states have ever been out of the Union, than with it. Finding themselves safely at home, it would be utterly immaterial whether they had ever been abroad.

Last Public Speech of Abraham Lincoln, from the White House Balcony, April 11, 1865

THADDEUS STEVENS

Thaddeus Stevens was livid over the assassination of President Lincoln, a man he loved. He said afterwards, "Grind down the traitors; grind the traitors in the dust!" I suppose he was referring to Wilkes and the others who had conspired to kill the President. Many writers, historians, and recent documentarians have contended that Jefferson Davis as well as Stanton were participants in this conspiracy of at least forty-eight others to assassinate Lincoln.

Congressman Thaddeus Stevens, Republican of Lancaster, and a zealot radical was over seventy years old, but he still possessed an air of power. Neither his severe looks, his club-foot, nor the hideous-looking dark brown wig could diminish his political strength. Stevens championship of the rights for Black people was linked to his affair with the House-keeper who was said to be "mulatto" (Jakes, p. 9). Many people were furious when they learned that Lincoln had been assassinated; they thought that Jefferson Davis might have had something to do with it, and some people said that they were not content that Jefferson Davis might be held in irons at Fortress Monroe Prison; a lot of them wanted him dead (Jakes, p. 11). Thaddeus Stevens said that he wanted the Confederate president executed. "Andrew Johnson had accused Jefferson Davis of acting to '"inspire"' and '"procure"' the assassination at Ford's Theatre. Andrew Johnson made the obligatory harsh statements about the South, but he also insisted that he would carry out Lincoln's Presidential program (Jakes, p. 7). He lied.

MARY LINCOLN, AFTER LINCOLN'S DEATH

Mary Todd had always been an extravagant spender. After her husband's death (her provider) was killed, Mary Todd Lincoln was plagued by an extreme fear of losing her money. Mary Todd Lincoln was left with an estate of about $142,000, but she still felt that this amount was not enough. Later, she went to New York under the name of "Mrs. Clarke" to sell all of her clothing in order to obtain *Mo Money.* This scheme would later be called the "old-clothes scandal." She tried to sell dirty clothes and everything. Mary's bizarre behavior was uncovered and exposed to the public. Out of embarrassment, she set sail for Frankfurt, Germany. She left in 1868 and returned in 1871. Upon her return, her youngest son, Tad died from a lingering cold. To add to her troubles, William Herndon had began his lecture tour uncovering Lincoln's dark background, and his lack of love for Mary Todd. He "insinuated that Lincoln, too, was a bastard" (p. 98, Ross, Fall). He wrote that, "Lincoln's married life was a domestic hell on earth" *(The Hidden Lincoln: Letters From Herndon,* p. 122, 1885). Herndon also said that Abraham Lincoln never loved Mary. Mary had never liked William Henry Herndon, and she was still hurting from Lizzie's new writing profession.

In the meantime, Mary Todd Lincoln, the outgoing socialite, fell more and more into the twilight zone of madness. In 1875, she went totally insane. She was also into "spiritualism" which probably didn't help matters, since she didn't have all of her faculties intact. She thought that someone was trying to kill her. And with so many tragedies in her family, the poor woman thought that someone was trying to kill her remaining (and prejudice) son, Robert. "Her contemporaries said she suffered hallucinations, and she told them she hired two men to shoot her only surviving son *(USA Today,* Wed., 12-14-1983, p. 2A), Robert Todd Lincoln.

It will be years later in 1926 when the famous Adam Clayton Powell, Jr. from Harlem would encounter Abraham Lincoln's prejudiced son, Robert. Powell, Jr. was working at the San Remo Hotel during his summer from college. He said that Robert frequented this beautiful resort hotel and that Robert Lincoln despised Black people. Powell declared that whenever a Black man put his hand on Robert's car door, Robert would hit the man across his knuckles with his cane. So the manager asked Powell to take the job of opening Robert Lincoln's door. Adam Clayton Powell, Jr. was light-skinned enough to fail-for-white. When Powell, Jr. opened Robert's car door, he was satisfied to see this white-looking hand on his door instead of a black one. The manager of the hotel gave Powell a raise in salary for helping keep the racist old Lincoln man satisfied (Powell, Adam by Adam, p. 33). Is it possible that Robert slapped the Black hands because he felt that his father had freed them from this type of work? Doubtful. Too many attest to Robert's aloofness, coldness, and prejudice. Although Abraham Lincoln loved his son, he was not as close to Robert Todd as he was to his other sons, Eddie, Willie, and Tad. Robert Todd stated that during his early childhood, his father was often away from home working on court cases and political speeches. Being reared under the thumb of his mother, Mary Todd, Robert became a cold, introverted person. William Herndon said that Robert Todd Lincoln was definitely a "Todd." He said that Robert was nothing like his father, Mr. Lincoln. "He is a Todd and not a Lincoln," Herndon admonished (Oates, p. 97, 1977).

When Mary Todd Lincoln and Robert returned to Chicago from overseas, Robert was forced to hire someone to watch his mother. Mrs. Lincoln was insanely positive that someone was trying to steal her money, so she sewed $57,000 onto her underwear. She went on elaborate shopping sprees spending exuberant amounts of money on unneeded housewares, perfumes, and jewelry. She told a hotel manager that someone was talking to her though the walls, telling her that the South Side of Chicago was on fire. Who lived on the South Side of Chicago in 1875? Robert soon had his mother committed to the state mental asylum in Batavia, Illinois. This asylum used "treatments" as varied as cod liver oil to marijuana. After the courthouse proceedings — and with enough sense to be embarrassed, she went to the hotel were she was staying and tried to kill herself by pill overdose. Fortunately the pills the pharmacist had given

her were only sugar pills. A year later she was released from
the asylum as sane. Six years later on July 16, 1882 she died.
His-story says that the autopsy on Mrs. Lincoln revealed
that she had a brain tumor. After Thomas Jefferson's death,
the census bureau listed Sally Hemings as white to "protect
the honor of the President." She was an African, Black. Were
white people again trying to protect another late, great president by stating that Mrs. Lincoln had a brain tumor? How
was she during her last six years outside of the asylum?
State Journal, Illinois, July 17, 1882: The public has known for
some time that Mrs. Lincoln was in ill health, but nothing
had appeared to indicate that her death at any early day
was probable (Sandburg, p. 324, 1932). Well, whatever, she
was already listed on page 596 of the 1875 "Lunatic Record"
of Cook County Court, Chicago, Illinois. Mary Todd's dear
Mr. Lincoln was not around to vindicate her this time.

MR. LINCOLN IS GONE, OR IS HE?

When so many tell the same story, there must be some
truth to it. "He [Lincoln] made simplicity and candor a *mask*
of deep feelings carefully concealed" (Oates, p. 99, 1977). Lincoln suffered from mood swings that worried his family and
friends. One minute he would be melancholic, the next second he would be talking with gaiety. In the mist of a conversation, Lincoln was apt to stop all verbal communication and
stare absently out of a window. He would then shock everyone by repeating a poem entitled "Mortality" by William
Knox. Lincoln's face would be full of despair and misery. The
ones present would look on with worried amazement. Lincoln told a Congressman one day that he had been a "fatalist"
all of his life (Oates, pp. 100 & 293, 1977). Herndon said that
Lincoln had a "double consciousness." Although Lincoln did
think mostly of mortality, he sometimes had peculiar
thoughts of immortality. Carl Rowan, in his recent book,
Breaking Barriers, is amazed by the number of politicians who
become careless and self-destructive regarding their safety
even when they already understand that they may be in the
midst of danger. He said, "Perhaps it was not prudent for
John Kennedy to go to Dallas and ride around in a convert-
ible when he knew the level of hatred that existed there" (p.

307). As mentioned, Abraham Lincoln was melancholiac, and "melancholiacs are strongly inclined toward suicide" (Menniger, p. 42). Lincoln was certainly aware of the hatred surrounding him during the Civil War. On the day of the President's murder, many people, including Stanton, had declined The Lincolns' request to accompany them to Ford's Theater. The rejections were odd, especially when so many would seize the opportunity to accompany the President of the United States and his wife on a night out on the town. Lincoln felt that he did not want to go out this night anyway, but Mary Lincoln insisted. So he went. Why? He didn't want to hear Mary's mouth? Or was Lincoln so deeply secure in his feelings of immortality this particular night that he felt no evilness as he usually did? It is true; the only reason that he did not want to go to the theater this night was because he had already seen the play, "Our American Cousin" (Gross, p. 133). Mary Lincoln's awareness that she forced her husband to attend the play, may have pushed her completely over the edge. After Lincoln's death, she begged the doctors to kill her so that she could join him. Mary Todd was already mentally unstable; she never recovered from her husband's death.

The newspapers said that it was the most traumatic day in the history of the Republic. On April 15, 1865 in newspapers from North Carolina to Connecticut, they read: "Terrible Loss to the Nation," "Great, Awful Calamity," "The President has been Killed." But many papers read: "He Still Lives."

One hour before the twenty-six year old John Wilkes Booth shot the President, he stood in front of Ford's Theatre reading a bulletin about a benefit celebration that would be given in honor of an actress who had a starring role in the play, *The Octoroon*. (This title relays and replays to us what was on the minds of the people during this era. They were aware that hundreds of Africans were failing-for-white during this time and now. This phenomenon gives reverence and reason to assume and question that some of the Presidents of the United States may have been in this *failing* group.) Booth moved on to a bar called Taltavul's and ordered whiskey and water instead of his usual brandy; he usually drank a quart of brandy a day. Some drunkard in the bar told Booth that he would never be as good an actor as "your father was." Booth's father was an actor also. Booth smiled, acknowledged the drunk man, then quietly and calmly said, "When I leave the stage, I will be the most famous man in America." Booth had been very depressed since the Confederates had lost the war.

An hour later, Harry Hawk was the only actor on the stage at Ford's Theater. At this point in the play, there was a comic scene. Booth entered the presidential box and shot President Lincoln in the head. Lincoln's guest, Major Rathbone tried to subdue Booth. Booth stabbed him in the arm. Booth then jumped onto the stage below and in the process, he broke his left leg. He hopped off the stage, jumped on his horse and escaped — some say for another fifty years. In the meantime, a doctor by the name of A.F. Africanus King (an expert in the study of malaria and African colonization, [Lehrer, pp. 246-247]) ran to Lincoln's side and tried to revive him. Dr. Africanus King helped carry Lincoln across the street to the Peterson House. This doctor's name is hardly ever written in the Lincoln literature, and rarely, if ever, mentioned on television documentaries. Mary Lincoln and her son, Robert, waited tearful and torn in the front room of the Peterson House. Some years after Lincoln's assassination, Mr. Peterson, the owner of this boarding house, committed suicide. He was found on the grounds of the Smithsonian Institute.

The room where Lincoln lay in Peterson's house was so morbid, so quiet. I imagine the silence in the room was so loud that Stanton broke it violently when he whispered, "Now, he belongs to the ages" (Bishop, p. 298). The beloved President died at 7:22 a.m. on April 15, 1865. The body of Lincoln was walked back to the White House in a closed hearse surrounded by an honor guard of soldiers.

When neighbors in Springfield approached Sarah Bush about the death of her stepson, documentaries state that she said: "I thought it in my heart that something would happen to him and that I should see him no more." What Sarah actually said with her facial expression calm and showing no visible emotion, was, "I knowed [sic] when he went away that he would never came back" (Bishop, p. 300).

Across the street from the White House, on the far side of Pennsylvania Avenue the Africans stood in the rain. Some bowed their heads and wept. One man said, "If death can come to him, what will happen to us?" (Bishop, p. 300-301).

After Lincoln's death, Mary Todd presented to Frederick Douglass as a gift one of Lincoln's walking canes. She thought that Lincoln would like this gesture since Douglass had done so much for the Union cause.

Young Willie Lincoln was exhumed so that he could be buried in Springfield, Illinois with his father. Lincoln's body lay first in the the East Room of the White House, then in the Rotunda of the Capitol.

Some days later, two young boys, the nephews of a Confederate chief of secret services, watched Abraham Lincoln's funeral procession from their second floor window on April 25, 1865 as the funeral carriage rolled down New York's Broadway; these young boys were Theodore Roosevelt and his younger brother, Elliott, who would become Eleanor Roosevelt's father. It is so ironic that besides the nine newspaper clippings, the two pair of eye glasses, the wallet, and the handkerchief, that Union man Lincoln had in his pockets on the day of his death, that he had but one bill; it was a lone $5.00 Confederate bill.

Jefferson Davis humiliatingly disguised himself in women's dress in order to escape prison. He tried to make his escape to Ervinville, Georgia. Many northern papers attested to the fact that he had dressed like a woman in hopes of escaping (Jakes, p. 4). Others say that he did not dress in female clothing. In May of 1865, Confederate Jefferson Davis rode through Augusta, Georgia on his way to Federal prison. An eight year boy watched through the curtains at this pitiful scene that he would never forget; this boy was Woodrow Wilson.

By June of 1865, there were over two hundred thousand freed Africans. In the Carolinas having one-eighth black blood made you all black. (Jakes, p. 22). After some Africans were freed and were able to legally marry, they took on new last names. Many of them self-named themselves "Lincoln;" some of them choose names like "Washington" and "Sherman." A lot of these Africans choose other white people's names. Unfortunately during the time when we could have changed our names to anything we wanted, we didn't know, or we had forgotten our griot teachings. This was an excellent opportunity to get back to our African selves, through having our true African names. But as many of us know, things happen for a reason. And maybe, just maybe at this time, with the society being extremely racist, it helped to unite the races — if only in names. Of course, the Africans made the sacrifice, again. The entire premise of this book, however, is how Blacks and whites have physically united and the results and consequences of these unions.

A CLOSED CHAPTER

Due to the lack of a true and accurate account of Abraham Lincoln's psychological background and his-story, I can only do an analysis from the available research and combined written literature, and assess and analyze from this standpoint. My research shows that Abraham Lincoln possessed a borderline personality disorder which was in remission much of the time, i.e., he was a functional citizen of 1800's America with mental problems that were hidden much of the time; he was acting through life. I have psychohistorically analyzed him as a borderline personality with dissociative states of mind, which is a milder form of alternate or multiple personality syndrome (MPD). From these analyses, signs point to Lincoln being a seriously abused child, perhaps sexually. Not only do I regret, in some way, that I deduced from literature and psychohistorical research that Lincoln was possibly abused by his father (or someone) because of the sheer hideousness of such an act, but also because there has been so much insensitive coverage and sensationalism about the subject lately that many may disregard these analyses as serious and think of them as only an attention-getter. I can assure you that this is not the case. After reading these true accounts, you have probably figured for yourself that they are true to the best of the writers' knowledge which was gathered from the referenced literary works herein. Abraham Lincoln had deep inbred psychological scars, and it is time for these scars and problems to be addressed. However, I and anyone else, can only make professional assumptions and analyses because of insufficient clinical data and information from Lincoln himself. No one can be absolutely sure of anything in this psychological and sociological case. We will all assume, presume, and analyze now and forever reasons for Lincoln's mental state of mind.

A more in-depth study of the psychological ramifications of Abraham Lincoln would yield rich returns in social history, psychohistory, psychology, sociology and the political sciences. No attempt has been made here to provide a totally thorough account of Lincoln's psychological problems and his politics as a possible mulatto/African. I have, however, drawn from a djambalaya of past and present history and psychological analysis and theories to ascertain an adequate amount of information about Lincoln's psyche and life.

A few Blacks and many whites still hold Lincoln in exceptionally high esteem. This dark man had to live his life as a schizoid, on the outside or borderline of reality, not knowing whether nor how to be himself. He was inconsistent and split in policy and self. But when the assassin's bullet split Lincoln's head, the bullet also integrated his mind and his body, and made Mr. Lincoln whole again — as in conception, as in birth. He is now the immortal whole/integrated, dark-skinned President.

> It would not be rebound to Lincoln's honor to have it proved that he is part Negro. For then on the ground of a natural sympathy with his own race we might find excuses for facts which we could never pardon a white man.
>
> *Chauncey Burr*

> I see the President almost everyday. I saw him this morning about eight-thirty, coming into business. We've gotten so that we exchange vows — very cordial ones. *I see very plainly, Abraham Lincoln's dark brown face*, with its deep cut lines, the eyes always to me with a latent sadness to [their] expression.
>
> *Walt Whitman*

Lincoln, Abraham — had a homely face and dark skin. His hair was black and coarse, and stood on end.

The World Book Encyclopedia (1975)

It seems clear that those whites who said Lincoln was a Negro are right.

J.A. Rogers

Lincoln's behavior and sometimes his words and actions, indicated that he was aware of his Black Self to some degree. We are not blessed onto this physical Earth without some genetic memory as to who we are, who our true ancestors are and where we've been spiritually.

Auset BaKhufu

I am nearly six feet, four inches tall, lean in flesh, weighing about one hundred and eighty pounds; dark eyes, dark complexion, with coarse black hair, and … no other marks or brands [are] recollected.

****

… and inasmuch as it becomes a necessity that there must be a difference, *I am in favor of the race to which I belong having the superior position.*

Abraham Lincoln

Abraham Lincoln, *Library of Congress.*

Abraham Lincoln's wife, **Mary**.

At the time of Lincoln's murder, the play ***The Octoroon*** was being presented. In the back of the sign is *Ford's Theater, Washington, D.C.*

1934 **Eleanor Roosevelt** and **Lorena Hickok** in San Francisco, *(UPI/Bettmann)*.

Under the Veil, Abraham Lincoln, caricature by *Volck*, September, 1862.

Robert Todd Lincoln, Abe's multiracial-looking son.

Abraham Lincoln depicted in an 1861 *Vanity Fair* cartoon sporting an Afro.

Lincoln's African hairstylist (barber), **William Florville.** This picture was taken on November 25, 1860. *Courtesy of the Illinois State Historical Library.*

Marian Anderson sings in front of brother Lincoln's Memorial, 1939.
Courtesy Library of Congress.

gossip break

This is a good time to take a seven minute deep-breathing and meditative-thoughts rest. The following is a good break.

The man at the printing place told me that George Bush's son is married to a Black woman and that they have a child; I didn't care, and it's also hard to believe. Later my brother told me that the man was probably referring to Bush's Puerto Rican daughter-in-law. Who knows? Who cares? Then the man tried to tell me something about Quayle. He then commenced to babbling on about Bush, Bush's daddy, Prescott, and their connection with the CIA. I was no longer listening.

People are forever asking me if George Washington had African blood. I don't know. In the midst of one of these conversations, a friend of mine asked me if I thought Mrs. Bush looks like George Washington? Well we do need a woman in the presidential seat — one day soon. Fulani, perhaps?

In his lectures around the world, Dr. Ben oftentimes refers to the 39th vice president of the United States, Spiro Agnew, as "cousin Agnew." Dr. Ben is an African; so what does he mean? I found that Spiro Agnew was born in Baltimore, Maryland to his Greek immigrant father who had by the time of Spiro's birth "shortened the family name from the original Anagnostopolous" to Agnew (Van Doren, p. 16). Spiro the Greek said after the rioting over the death of Dr. Martin Luther King, Jr. that he "never did think Martin Luther King was a good American." Now it is a fact that Agnew said this, but was the statement a compliment or what? There is a lot of related his-story/ourstory between the Africans and the Greeks. Go to your local African bookstore. Purchase some books and read.

Many who know that I'm writing this book and understand the content have been bugging me to please print this little bit or that little about this or that White House affiliate. One such affiliate is Arnold Schwarzenegger. Bush appointed him chairman of the President's Council on Physical Fitness and Sports in 1990. One of my students, one of my relatives, and two friends have said please note that Schwarzenegger's last name implies double black.

"Schwarze" means black and so does "Negger." I've heard this before. However, I found that Schwarzenegger literally means, black farm hand. Now, let's go on.

Many big newspapers and other media are following in the footsteps of supermarket magazines like *Globe* in covering their news. They are now, according to *Emerge* Magazine, name dropping. *Emerge* said they found it interesting that the big media moguls did not follow in *Globe's* footsteps when they alleged that the presidential hopeful, Bill Clinton has fathered a seven-year male child by a Black woman. *Emerge* says that *Globe* quoted black activist Robert McIntosh as saying that "Bill Clinton has been with [many] black women...." (*Emerge*, May, 1992, p. 21; *Globe* Magazine, February 18, 1992; *Star* Magazine, January 28, 1992. Remember this is gossip). We do have melanocyte sense receptors, and Bill Clinton is receiving many Black votes. He even hobnobbed with Arsenio Hall on his show, and played a mean saxophone number. Blow Bill Blow. Do Black voters feel for some reason that Bill Clinton may be willing to look out for the well being of Africans for personal reasons? People who saw the multiracial child's picture in the *Globe* Magazine, said that, "The child looks just like Bill Clinton." I've only seen a very blurred picture that was faxed to me. Is the *Globe* story true? I don't know. None of us know. But I do know that there is a lot of talk about Clinton's "sins," whereas it seems that John F. Kennedy has been totally forgiven for his. Could this be because Kennedy's sins were white (as far as we know) and some of Clinton's alleged sins were not? And if it's true that Clinton has fathered a Black male child, he'd better concentrate on raising him (*and running this country*) instead of insulting our Sister Souljah. Is he jealous because she has a band and he doesn't? Or was this an appeal to whites that he was an "ok" white person? George Bush doesn't seem to think so. But what does he know?

Clinton's running mate, Al Gore, has admitted that he and his wife both smoked marijuana when they were younger (Ross, *Fall From Grace*, p. 281); whereas Clinton says that he never inhaled, and Sister Souljah affirms that she has never indulged.

While writing this piece on Clinton, I thought about the many Baby Boomers, and some who tip the scale (i.e., ages 44-47) who have expressed to me that they are having problems with hoarseness recently. Maybe the speakers mentioned above, and perhaps you too, may one day be able to benefit from the *Ancient African Throat Formula for Hoarseness* on page 154. The formula is an excerpt from my forthcoming work, "Healing: Herbs, Health, and Spirituality."

A friend of mine read my "gossip break" section and said, "it doesn't seem to be too much gossip here; it's all true." I told him that perhaps this section does transcend gossip, but gossip doesn't necessarily mean that the information is untrue. Gossip is "who cares?" conversation.

For the curious: This section was written before the November 3, 1992 election.

THROAT FORMULA FOR HOARSENESS

1. Start the day with a healthy breakfast of fruits, grains, and fibers. No meat.

2. After, or with, your breakfast, drink a cup of Licorice tea. This tea is best if brewed from the Licorice root. This naturally sweetened tea will restore the voice.

3. If hoarseness persists after an hour or so, gargle with golden seal powder (by breaking the capsule, or buy the actual golden seal powder from your natural health store) and sage. Be sure the water is hot enough for tolerance, but not scalding. Drink more licorice tea. Aloe Vera juice is good also.

4. Throughout the day, vitamin C (about 10,000 milligrams) and some vitamin E (five 400 IU) are essential.

5. Eat healthy meals during the day. And after each meal, take one teaspoon of Lobelia herb. If you like vinegar, then you can tolerate Lobelia. Eating fresh garlic with meals can do wonders for hoarseness. Parsley freshens the breath, please.

6. Another very good tea to drink and sip during the day (or the next day, if necessary) is an equal combination of peppermint, spearmint, cinnamon, and licorice. This remedy makes a delicious healing tea.

It may be necessary to repeat some of the above remedies. But before doing anything, check with your doctor.

ALTERNATIVE

7. If the hoarseness persists, mullein smoked in a peace pipe may be necessary ... but it must be *inhaled*. No kidding. And if this fails, the flower herb Hops can be used. But it slows down the sex desire, and therefore may not be desirable for some people. Jefferson surely would not have chosen this remedy.

HANNIBAL HAMLIN

15th Vice President U.S.A.

Hannibal Hamlin was born August 27, 1809 in Paris, Maine. He was the vice president to Abraham Lincoln during Lincoln's first term in office. Although he is rarely mentioned in the Lincoln literature, Hamlin served in this governmental capacity and in this very important period in American history from March 4, 1861 to March 3, 1865, leaving this position just one month before Lincoln's untimely death. In some of the most celebrated books on Lincoln, Hannibal Hamlin's name isn't even mentioned.

Hannibal Hamlin was the son Dr. Cyrus Hamlin and Anna Livermore. Dr. Hamlin was trained at Harvard College Medical School. He then settled in Livermore, Maine in 1795, where he quickly became a town favorite, a ladies man, and the talk of the town. This town had been founded by Deacon Elijah Livermore. Elijah Livermore resented Dr. Hamlin's intrusion on his territory, but later consented to a truce with the young Dr. Hamlin. The good Doctor later married Livermore's daughter, Anna (Hunt, p. 3).

The Hamlins are said to have descended from Teutonic clans ... living along the river banks and lakes of old, old Germany. According to the vice president's own grandson, Charles Eugene Hamlin, "The Hamlins are believed to have been Teutonic tribes, ... and when Germany emerged from *barbarism*, Hamlin became a family name" (Hamlin, p. 1; italics added). However, Hannibal Hamlin's grandfather, Eleazer Hamlin, traces the family lineage only as far up as young England. James Hamlin of Devonshire was the first of the Hamlins to leave the East for North America. He was Hannibal Hamlin's great, great, great grandfather (Hunt, p. 2). Eleazer was a big, muscular man who lived his life like a ginseng drinker. He fathered seventeen children with two wives. He was educated and he was a nonconformist. For example, he despised "the nomenclature that had been handed down and preserved with a clannish-like tenacity in the Hamlin family for many generations." In the family

annals, Eleazer found many Biblical and symbolic-type
names like Zaccheus, Deliverance, Job, Ichabod, Tobiatha,
and others. Eleazer was well read on war history and
admired Scipio Africanus, the African general. Eleazer
decided to never use the nomenclaturic names again. So, he
named his *first son for this general*. But the entire family
insisted on calling the young man simply and clearly,
"Africa." He named his other sons after other countries, and
when he had twins he named them "Hannibal and Cyrus, in
honor of the Carthaginian [African] and persian generals"
(Hamlin, p. 8). So when Hannibal Hamlin's father had his
last son, he named him after his twin brother, Hannibal and
the heroic African general Hannibal, the great Carthaginian
warrior. Hannibal, the African warrior, was in charge of a
military force of about 40,000 and several elephants. He conquered Rome as no one else ever had. He was a fearsome
and genius warrior.

WHAT ABOUT THAT SURNAME?

Much of the literature on Hannibal Hamlin and the documentation on his said African ancestry harps mostly on his
first name. But what about his more important surname?
How did this particular surname derive for this family?
Hamlins are found in many countries. Oftentimes, the family name is changed in spelling as time progresses. There
are, of course, many ways in which the Hamlin's ancestors
spelled their name, depending on where they were at the
time — Hamlin, Hamline, Hamlyne, Hamelin, and so forth.
Hannibal Hamlin's grandson Charles Hamlin expresses that
the American Hamlins descended from the English branch
of the family. What other branches of his family were there?
Was one branch possibly the mythological Ham, son of
Noah, from Cush (known today as Ethiopia)? Ham was the
so-called cursed one in the family, persecuted because of his
beautiful Blackness. The religion called Judaism, and other
religions after them, such as Christianity, has made this
myth very real for many people. Hamitics are a people who
proclaim their genetic origin as descending from Ham, the
Black. They called their language Cushitic.

The name "Ham" comes from the Hebrew word, "Cham" which in turn derives from the Kemetian (Egyptian) word "Kam," with all three words meaning "Black." Dr. Charles Finch writes, "That Ham is the eponymous ancestor of black African peoples is so universally accepted as to require no further demonstration" (Finch, p. 133; See Dr. Yosef ben-Jochannan's books: *Black Man on the Nile and His Family; AFRICA: Mother of Western Civilization,* and *African Origins of the Major Western Religions).* It was in 1856, while Hannibal Hamlin was United States Senator, that Brigham Young, the Mormon lecturer, stated in the *Journal of Discourses* that, "The Negro — The seed of Ham, which is the seed of Cain descending through Ham, will, according to the curse put upon him, serve..., and be a '"servant of servants"' to his fellow [white] creatures, until God removes the curse...." People like Brigham Young (Black and White) really believe this nonsense (the curse), even to this day.

Are the HAM-lins descendants from this ancient African branch? "Ham-LIN." Lin means -linear, lineal. Lineal means to be in direct line of descent from an ancestor. In essence, *lineage,* direct descent from a specific ancestor. So, did the James, Eleazer, Cyrus, Hannibal Hamlins come from the "family-Line of Ham?" They may very well be a family in a syntax of African survival, or at most, survivals in words formed from historical myths. Since the Hamlin family has apparently failed-for-white for so many years, it is unlikely that their real family name was taken away from them; therefore they remained the Hamlins from ancient times.

AFRICAN ANCESTRY

Hannibal Hamlin was said to be of African ancestry by many people when he was campaigning with Lincoln for vice president. These two men, both said to be of African ancestry, won the position of the highest office in the land. *The Philadelphia Bulletin* stated on July 8, 1891 that some of the campaign buttons with Lincoln and Hamlin's faces on them gave the vice president such a "swarthy complexion" that perhaps these very medals or buttons confirmed the belief that circulated in the South that one of his parents was a mulatto, and that he was named in honor of the great

Carthaginian to flaunt his African descent before the world. *The Philadelphia Bulletin* contended that it was all a lie. Hamlin's own grandson begs to differ as stated earlier.

J.A. Rogers lists Hannibal as one of the presidents "said to be a Negro" (Rogers, *The Five Negro Presidents*, p. 9). In the *Dictionary of American Biography*, Johnson and Malone write, "Hamlin had a stocky, powerful frame and great muscular strength. His complexion was so swarthy that in 1860 the story was successfully circulated among credulous Southerners that he had negro blood" (p. 197). J.A. Rogers also states in his book, *Your History*, that "Hannibal Hamlin, Civil War Vice President of the United States with Abraham Lincoln was generally believed in the southern states to have been a mulatto. This was openly written in the press and stated in Congress. Hamlin's very Dark Skin" and his facial features, especially his chin area, "caused many Northerners to believe the story also" (p. 78). An 1800's writer by the name of George T. Strong was a guest at a dinner party in which Hannibal Hamlin was also a guest. Strong wrote of Hamlin: "Hamlin impresses me favorably, ... He seems a vigorous specimen of the pure Yankee type. His complexion is so swarthy [dark] that I cannot wonder at the demented South for believing him a mulatto" (Hunt, p. 152).

Although Frederick Douglass never dined with the Lincolns, Hannibal Hamlin invited Douglass into his home as a dinner guest. He said that he invited Douglass to his home not because Douglass had done such great things, but because he was simply a man that he admired for himself. The color of a person's skin did not matter to Hamlin. Hamlin says that he was proud to see Douglass and other Blacks building their own businesses and organizations (Hamlin, pp. 528-529).

HAMLIN'S YOUTH

Hannibal Hamlin is said to have grown up in a wholesome home environment. He was a child full of energy and affection with a very independent nature. "Hannibal Hamlin's first recollection of his childhood days was when he was three years old. The War of 1812 had broken out, and he saw a company of soldiers march away from Paris Hill."

The soldiers later returned with many stories. The battle at New Orleans were his favorite tales, and Andrew Jackson became a hero to this young boy (Hamlin, p. 20). Hannibal Hamlin would later become a Jacksonian Democrat.

The Hamlins were a well-to-do family and were able to provide their children with a good education. Hannibal's father was on the school's town committee. Hannibal was a powerfully built boy for his age. One old friend of "Han's" described him as "tall, straight, supple, and dark as a young Indian. He was warm-hearted, affectionate and magnetic; his black eyes twinkled with fun and life. Han was always our leader" (Hamlin, p. 20). Friends and relatives described Hannibal Hamlin as sincere and honest. His grandson described him as a born "Nimrod." Others said that Hannibal was an uncommonly powerful person and very athletic. Hannibal's brother, Elijah, was "taller and darker than Hannibal himself" (Hunt, p. 16). Hannibal also, like Jackson and Lincoln, got into his share of boyhood fights.

A YOUNG MAN

Hannibal Hamlin attended the Hebrew Academy in preparation for college. Suddenly, his father died and the family ran into financial problems. Hamlin found it necessary to forgo his college education for a while and work to help the family. For a brief period he, again like Lincoln, was a surveyor. During other brief periods, Hannibal became a printer and a school teacher. Hannibal had a partnership as owner of a newspaper called the "Jeffersonian." Hannibal later began to see that the funds coming in for this newspaper simply were not enough for two people. He eventually sold his share, made a career change and decided to study law. So he bid good riddance to his business partner for a better and more exciting life. He became a student in the law office of Fessenden & Deblois in Portland, Maine. When he returned to Paris Hill in 1833, he was immediately admitted to the bar. He later relocated to Hampden, Maine where his interest turned to politics.

ROME AND THE "PANIC" WAR

On December 10, 1833, Hannibal married Sarah Jane Emery, the daughter of a Judge. The couple had one son, Charles. When Sarah died, Hannibal married Sarah's sister. Hannibal Hamlin represented Hampden in the legislature from 1836 to 1841, and again in 1847. In between these years, Hannibal Hamlin served as speaker. Benjamin Brown French, clerk of the House, wrote that Hamlin would make as good a speaker as any (Hunt, p.32). Mr. French was a politician who was very grateful to Hamlin for the rest of his life for securing him the position of clerk of the House, but he also seemed to respect Hamlin for his political views and amicable personality.

Hamlin was considered a conservative politician. He also opposed slavery, but only to a certain degree; he felt that slavery was an institution beyond the legislative authority of the government. On January 12, 1846, Hamlin made a long speech against war. "He was a lover of peace but not a pacifist." If war was extremely necessary, he would concur. He said that "Rome had her Punic war, but it was reserved for us to have our *panic* war." He was making reference to the joint resolution on Oregon (Hunt, pp. 32-33). It was during this time that Hamlin considered himself a Jacksonian Democrat. In 1848 Hannibal Hamlin was elected to the United States Senate.

I TAKE MY COMPLEXION FROM NATURE

John Holmes was a Senator from Maine and an opponent of Hannibal Hamlin's. In a debate, Holmes made a comment about Hamlin's "swarthy complexion." Hamlin replied, "If the gentleman chooses to find fault with me on account of my complexion, what has he to say about himself? I take my complexion from nature; he gets his from the brandy bottle. Which is more honorable?" Because of Hamlin's deliberate control over this situation, he was to be called "the Carthaginian of Maine" for the remainder of his life (Hamlin, pp. 56-57).

HAMLIN'S WIVES, SARAH AND ELLEN

Hannibal Hamlin's first wife, Sarah, thoroughly enjoyed the Washington social scene when she was able to travel with Hannibal to the Capitol. In February, 1854, she described with excitement, "a great jam" at the magnificent home of Secretary of War Jefferson Davis. After this party she then went to another "jam" given at the National Hotel "where there was lots of dancing and refreshments" (Hunt, p. 84). This lady, said to be a little wild, a little different by some, was unknowingly having the last of her good times. Sarah died on April 17, 1855 from consumption (body tissue waste and symptoms of tuberculosis). One year and five months later, on September 25, 1956, Hannibal Hamlin married Sarah's half-sister, Ellen Vesta Emery. She was not as outgoing and outspoken as Sarah. Hamlin married this plain-looking, but "good-natured" woman, who was young enough to be his daughter, in Judge Emery's home in Paris Hill, Maine. This is the same year that Hamlin become disgusted with the so-called democratic policy toward slavery and renounced his allegiance to this particular party. Although Hamlin abhorred slavery, he felt that to be an abolitionist was not his personal answer. He believed that the abolitionists were too careless and thoughtless regarding the "rights" of landowners, who were usually and mostly slaveholders (Hunt, p. 18).

THE TWO DARK MEN AND
THE HIGHEST OFFICE OF THE LAND

Around the time that Lincoln and Hamlin began their joint campaign for the highest office in the American land, African-Americans were becoming more and more outraged over their offensive, disgraceful, horrendous, and continuous plight in America as an enslaved people. All over the South, in Robeson County, North Carolina; Cherry Hill, South Carolina; Richmond, Virginia, and other southern areas, Africans were striking back. Political prisoners (slaves) on Jefferson Davis' plantation set his mansion on fire. This act of violence does not mean that these Africans were not sensitive toward humanity; they were dealing with inhumane people; they were not dealing with sensitive humans, and enough was enough. Was Jefferson Davis' lover a part of this honorable rebellion? Davis, president of the Confederacy, had a brother by the name of Joe. Joe had a daughter with an African-American woman (a Black enslaved person). Jefferson Davis later became the lover of his own mulatto niece — his own brother's daughter. J.A. Rogers records that there were masses of escaped political prisoners who killed whites (so-called slave masters) on plantations. Henry Berry Lowry from North Carolina was one of the most heroic leaders of these groups whose level of consciousness had raised to a point of race pride and equality, or else. Rogers points out that many of these Blacks thought that their plight was about to change because of the Civil War, plus they had heard that the "Vice President, was a Negro." Rogers quotes from *The Chicago Democrat,* June 4, 1861 that:

> The constant theme in the South for the last two months has been the election of the Abolitionist Lincoln and the free Negro, Hamlin, to the Presidential chair and the consequences that were to result from the events. The slaves heard all this and they have told it to their companions and the news has spread to the plantations with the celerity which is so remarkable a feature of slave life.

Rogers verifies that "Hamlin was much more hated in the South than Lincoln. Not only was he outspoken against slavery but his skin was darker than that of many who were called Negroes … Hamlin was for emancipation from the start. Lincoln later praised him highly for it" (Rogers, *Africa's Gift to America,* pp. 154-156; Jefferson Davis as molester of his niece, Reference: Rogers, J.A., *Your History,* p. 78).

Hannibal Hamlin stated to a law associate that he would fight slavery at every opportunity he received. Lincoln had supposedly made a similar statement when he was a young man. Lincoln and Hamlin worked shoulder to shoulder on the issue of overthrowing the institution of slavery. Lincoln's main objective, of course, was to save the Union. Lincoln and Hamlin had a good working relationship and Lincoln always understood where Hamlin stood on political issues. They became comrades. Hamlin had no problem speaking his mind to the President, and they did not always agree. Hannibal Hamlin did not believe that Africans were an inferior people. He knew the African to be brave, patient, and generous by nature. It is not unnatural that Hamlin would have such a penetrating insight into this character. This characterization has been in the past and present an advantage sometimes, but mostly a detriment to the Black race considering the fact that Blacks have to live in such a discriminatory, uncivilized, and violent society. Whites have killed more people on the face of the earth than any group of Black people ever have. Hamlin affirmed that Africans, i.e., Africans/Blacks, had proven their fighting abilities when necessary. Hannibal Hamlin also said that it is a "totally gratuitous assertion" upon the part of anyone who feels that Blacks are inferior. He admonished, "They are as brave and as fearless as any other of the races of human beings" (Hamlin, pp. 420-424). His statements reverberate as being quite defensive. Hannibal Hamlin's own son was a soldier in the Civil War ... among the Black division.

At a Bangor patriotic rally in July, 1862, Hannibal Hamlin described himself in his own words. Hamlin said in response to a Governor Samuel Kirkwood from Iowa that, "We want to save, as much as possible, our men, [even] if it is done by men *a little darker than myself*." (Author italics). The Governor from Iowa had made a similar statement, but in a crude manner. Kirkwood had said that he wished to see "some dead niggers as well as white men," before the end of the Civil War (Hunt, p. 162).

Again during Hamlin's political campaign for vice president he was the target of what most political writers called "smears" or "mudslinging." Southerners were repeating the story that Hannibal Hamlin was a Negro. Robert Barnwell Rhett an editor of a southern newspaper, *The Charleston Mercury*, said in a speech in Charleston, South Carolina that, "Hamlin is what we call a mulatto. He has black blood in him ... The 'Black Republicans' have put a 'renegade Southerner' on one side for President, for Lincoln is a native Kentuckian, and they put a man of colored blood on the other side of the ticket for Vice President of the United States *(New York Tribune*, July 26, 1860 & Hunt, p. 121). One racist white man asserted that "Hamlin looked, acted, and thought so much like a Negro that dressed differently, he could be sold South as a field hand!" (Hunt, p. 122). With many forces against him, Hamlin was nonetheless elected as Lincoln's Vice President.

On May 20, 1860, a band and a procession of well wishers formed at the "Washington House" residence of Hannibal Hamlin to serenade him. More than 900 people attended this occasion. Hamlin received a cheering and thunderous applause, then he made a few remarks with no interruptions (French, p. 323).

As mentioned in the Lincoln chapter, Hamlin arrived in Chicago, Illinois on November 22, 1860 to meet the President-elect of the United States. Lincoln and Hamlin shook hands and were immediately at ease with each other. They casually discussed anti-slavery principles. Lincoln had planned to discuss the Cabinet with Mr. Hamlin, but word soon got out that the Presidents-elect were in the Tremont House Hotel, and an impromptu reception resulted for the two men. Hamlin said of Lincoln's hair that he could not help but notice it's "curiously woolly appearance." These two men tended to hold some of the more intimate and innermost biological circumstances of life in common.

Hamlin was not elected for a second term with Lincoln. Andrew Johnson maneuvered that bid. Charles Hamlin and others felt that there was a political conspiracy surrounding this incident. A resolution was introduced calling for the renomination of Lincoln and Hamlin, again as a twosome. L.C. Cameron, the introducer of this resolution, was aware that this idea would be tabled. "This was done to remove the responsibility for Hamlin's defeat from his shoulders and to protect Lincoln" (Hunt, p. 258, #38). Lincoln, supposedly, wanted a Democrat on the ticket for the new election. It was in the minds of many southerners that if a man can be vice president, then he can become president. So some conspired to make this reality exist no more. Literature highly suggests that there were many more people than we will ever know who knew about the planned assassination of President Lincoln.

As mentioned in the Lincoln chapter, Hamlin declared to his relatives that Andrew Johnson was drunk when he was inaugurated into office as Vice President of the United States. Hamlin said that Johnson had drunk whiskey and made a public spectacle of himself on this March 4, 1865. Johnson had stated that he was feeling ill. A little more than a month later, President Lincoln was murdered on April 15, 1865. On the evening of April 14, 1865, Hamlin's daughter, Sarah, her husband, her brother Charles Hamlin and his wife went to see the play, *Our American Cousin* at Ford's Theater. Sarah was having a wonderful time and noticed that Mr. Lincoln and his wife Mary Todd were sitting in the state box decorated especially for the President. The actors were leaving the stage, and the on-stage scenes were being changed when all of a sudden, Sarah heard the loud pop of a gun. She had seen no flash, but she immediately realized what had happened. As mentioned in the Lincoln chapter, others state that a lone actor was on stage and that during a comic scene, the audience was laughing when Booth shoot the president. Anyway, the entire audience was paralyzed with fear and sadness. Many were happy and some knew about the conspiracy. The assassin ran off the stage as many people yelled, "Seize him! Catch him! Lynch him!!" Sarah's husband, George, turned to his wife, and said, "it is a man who boards at the National … & *who looks just like Wilkes Booth —*." Hannibal Hamlin's family stated that Hamlin mourned Lincoln's death as if he had lost his very best friend (Hunt, pp. 199-200; Hamlin, p. 499).

HAMLIN SHOULD BE IN THE WHITE HOUSE

Hamlin was devastated over Lincoln's murder not only because he lost a very good friend, but also because Johnson was now President of the United States! His horror was not because of jealousy, but more for the state of the country. There were many who felt that Hannibal Hamlin should "have been in the White House" as President of the United States at this time (Hamlin, p. 499). Hamlin and his family both felt that had he won the vice presidential seat over Johnson that he would have undoubtedly been assassinated just as Lincoln had been assassinated (Hunt, p. 265). Hamlin had never trusted Andrew Johnson. What was to become of this Reconstructive period for America? Hamlin wrote Johnson about his concerns. Johnson ignored the ex-Vice President's advice. Much of what Lincoln had started as a Reconstruction plan came to an abrupt halt.

Andrew Johnson declared that he would carry out Lincoln's plans to reconstruct the lives of a people who had lived as slaves and also those who had owned slaves. He lied. Johnson was determined to get on the good side of those who were against Lincoln's plan. He returned their land and put them back in charge of discriminatory acts that ricocheted, somewhat. Many whites were very fearful that African-Americans (ex-slaves) would gain some aspect of economic, political and/or social freedom. These fears were expressed during the Lincoln campaign in the south when racist southerners admonished that Lincoln and his mulatto running mate, Hannibal Hamlin, would encourage blacks to marry whites, and urge black men to rape white women (Handlin, p. 137). Therefore because of so many baseless fears by many whites, the Black Codes were designed. Blacks could not hold firearms; they were not allowed to socially mingle with whites; they could not own real estate, and they could not vote. "Johnson, Hamlin declared bluntly, was guilty of high crimes and misdemeanors" (Hunt, p. 205). It was around this time that Jamaican national hero, George W. Gordon was unjustly arrested and sentenced to death.

Blacks and abolitionists were sick and tired of Johnson's stupidity. Ideas on the issue of Black Codes in America continued and opinions were divided, but Congress finally decided to pass the Civil Rights Act of 1866; this act gave slaves (i.e., political prisoners) citizenship. Then Congress passed the Fourteenth Amendment which gave African-Americans the right to vote. Angry white mobs reacted violently to this amendment. They burned black schools and churches (the same thing their descendants will do a hundred years later in the 1960's — Who is civilized and who isn't?).

SOJOURNER TRUTH & FREDERICK DOUGLASS

It was in 1866 when Frederick Douglass was running around with a bunch of white women, two being Elizabeth Cady Stanton and Susan B. Anthony. Anthony stated in this same year that if there has to be a choice as to who should be allowed to vote first, most certainly it should be the white woman over the Black man, for the white woman is more intelligent. Still Douglass continued to "hang" with them. He went to a restaurant with one of them, and was told that he could not come into the establishment with a white woman. He slapped the man around, and was allowed to go in and eat with his white woman. Multiracial Douglass stated that, "you people are not much lighter than I." It is possible that Douglass' attitude in this area is one reason why Sojourner Truth found some fault in his deliverance of speech. From the reading and research done on this remarkable woman, she would have preferred a statement coming from Douglass more in the content of: "I am human, just like you people." Frederick Douglass stated that Sister Sojourner was always trying to "trip him up" in his speeches. She tended to always ask him straight-forward questions that to many listeners would at first seem to be "off-the-wall." Most would think about the question later, and realize that the question made a lot of sense. That was Sister Sojourner Truth's genius. Anyway some time before Douglass married a white woman, the Sister and Brother did make amends. Douglass said that Sister Sojourner Truth had some sort of "wild enthusiasm" and a "strange compound of wit and wisdom, and flint-like common sense" (McFeely, p. 97). Douglass also said that Sister Truth was "distinguished for insight into human nature, remarkable for independence and courageous self-assertion" (Ortiz, p. 144). Truth understood from her "insight into human nature" as Reuter does in his 1918 dissertation, *The Mulatto in the United States*, that the mixed-blood person sometimes has a difficult time deciding which identity or self to be or become. "The problem of the mulatto, then, is not something unique ... it is the problem of mixed-blood wherever blood has been made the basis of caste." And the United States is one of those places. Reuter states that it is ironic that a mixed-blood person can not pass on "his merits as an individual, but must *pass* as a member of the opposite race [white]." The white man hates the mixed-blood group for presumingly tainting the white race, while the black race envies the group for their supposedly superior blood. "Between these two groups, one admiring and the other despising, stand the mixed-bloods" (pp. 18-19 & 103). It is the 1990's, and most of the "admirers" are now simply neutral.

SOME MORE CONSTRUCTION

The Reconstruction Act of 1867 was formed in March of this same year in order to successfully carry out the Fourteenth Amendment. African-Americans being permitted to vote gave a tremendous advantage to the Republicans. This is the same year that the President of the United States, Johnson, who is said to have been illiterate, said that no one should try to deny that Blacks are very far inferior to white people. He said that Black people learned in slavery all that they will know of civilization. So, not only was he illiterate, he was also ignorant. He continued, "When first brought from the country of their origin they were naked savages...." Now this is ignorance of the severe type.

MR. & MRS. S

Thaddeus Stevens of Pennsylvania was a Whig congressman from 1849-1853, a Republican congressman from 1859-1868, and an abolitionist leader. He was also the chairman of a committee to impeach Andrew Johnson in 1868 of which Hannibal Hamlin played a significant part. Some people during this time attributed Stevens' "Negro" sentiments to his involvement with Mrs. Smith. The club-footed Stevens was said by some to be the lover of, or married to, his beautiful quadroon housekeeper, a Mrs. "Lydia Smith, or 'Mrs. Stevens,' the widow of a Black barber from Gettysburg (Davis, Burke, *The Civil War*, p. 162; Rogers, *Sex and Race*, vol. II, pp. 224-226, and Jakes, p. 10). Stevens died on August 11, 1868 and had requested that he be buried in a "Negro" cemetery, where "all God's children are equal" (Dennis, D., *Black History*, p. 106). Benjamin Brown French was a very good friend of Thaddeus Stevens. Mr. French documented in his diary on August 15, 1868 that as he passed through the Capitol yard, he saw the remains of Thaddeus Stevens being escorted by a company of colored Zouaves. "There was very small attendance ... I saw my good friend no more ..." (French, *Witness to the Young Republic*, pp. 576-577).

ULYSSES S. GRANT

While in Cairo, Illinois, Grant wrote his wife inquiring into the health and well being of his animals. Grant, who was fond of Egypt, named one of his favorite horses "Egypt" and kept the animal on the White House grounds. Although Hannibal Hamlin was not interested in the 1868 nomination of Ulysses S. Grant, he did respect him as a military man and he liked Grant's personality. Hamlin was now a well known and respected Senator, and he disapproved of the many political mistakes during the Grant administration. Nonetheless, he did began to have more faith in Grant as a president during Grant's eight years in office. The two men began to agree on more issues as time passed. Hamlin was impressed that "Grant was sound on Reconstruction" (Hunt, pp. 208-209).

SOJOURNER AND ULYSSES

On March 5, 1870, the Fifteenth Amendment was passed by Congress to protect African suffrage. Many Blacks were elected to government positions during this uplifting period. On March 31st, Sojourner Truth met President Grant. They were very formal with each other initially, but later they relaxed as the conversation about freedom for Blacks continued. He signed her book, *Book of Life*. Did he sign it "aunty" as Lincoln did? This meeting took place one day before the actual signing of the Fifteenth Amendment. In 1871, Truth decreed that the only real freedom Blacks would have in America was to live on their own territory in the West. She probably opted for the West because the weather is more conducive to the health, well being, and protection of the melanin content in African peoples. Now it is fine for us to understand this, but we must also have some common sense and genuine spirituality about ourselves. Just having the weather isn't going to get it. No matter where we reside, we must learn to carry ourselves as Sister Truth. She petitioned a white audience in New York to aid in settling former political prisoners (slaves) in the West. She told this audience, "You owe it to them, because you took away from them all they earned." Little support came from Washington, D.C., and the plan was never adopted (Krass, pp. 162-163). Between 1868 and 1896, 113 African-American legislators served in Louisiana. In South Carolina, many ex-slaves served on the Legislature; there were 50 Black members and 13 white members. The whole idea of Reconstruction and the freedom of Africans living in America caused Ulysses S. Grant to win the 1868 Presidential election. And under Grant, Reconstruction flourished. Howard University, Fisk University, and Moorehouse College were established. The real hue-mans (Africans) in America were being educated and accepted by some whites as citizens and human beings, somewhat. The ku klux klan resented this with a violent vengeance. They began to plunder and kill excessively. Ku klux klan members, of course, were in every sector of government, state, and local businesses. African-Americans were prevented from voting successfully by being arrested before the voting dates, and being given incorrect information as to where the voting would take place. Blacks obtained weapons and fought back. Grant had to send federal troops into some southern areas to restore order. In 1898, through the "Grandfather Clause," African-Americans were hindered again in their efforts to live a productive life. Many racist white people were running scared and desperate to regain what they considered power. Their brutal actions still affect America today.

Reconstruction ended in 1877 according to his-Story. It ended around the 1880's or has it ended? Ourstory shows (and knows) that it took a little longer to "reconstruct" African life during this era, which is an ongoing struggle.

Sojourner Truth was struggling with her health during this reconstructive period, and rumors abound that she had journeyed-on-to-the-ancestors. However, she was living in Battle Creek, Michigan. Her hair had turned gray when she was around fifty years of age, and in her eighties, her hearing and sight was now almost gone. Then suddenly in 1877, Goddess Truth's health mysteriously improved. Her hearing returned, her sight improved dramatically, her gray hair turned black again, and the wrinkles on her face disappeared. What herb did Sister Truth get her African hands, body, and soul on? Aloe? Ginseng? Soybean? Vitamin A extract? Gota Kola plant? Olive Oil? Garlic? Was it meditation and a new sense of well-being? Sister Truth told a friend that the "Lord had put new glasses in the window of her soul." She said that, "It is the mind that makes the body" (Krass, p. 166); it's the Truth. This Dutch accented, African Goddess of Wisdom was eighty years young when her melanin was positively reactivated.

HANNIBAL'S MELANIN

Hannibal Hamlin had a habit of going without a coat even in some of the coldest weather. A news reporter who interviewed Hamlin during his old age commented that Hamlin had very dark skin. The reporter said, "He is such a brown color that it has been suggested that early in life he must have been dipped in some brown liquid which has left upon his skin a coat which renders him impervious to heat or cold" (Hunt, p. 224; *Cincinnati Gazette*, July 11, 1891).

THE MOORS AND MEZEE

By the 1880's, Hannibal Hamlin was known as the "grand old man" of the Senate. He was aging and beginning to show his first signs of heart disease. Just five years prior to this time, Hamlin had legally adopted his daughter's son, Arthur Hamlin. Sarah's marriage did not work out, and Hamlin saw to it that she and her son no longer carried the last name of Sarah's husband. This was an unusual legal move considering the times. On June 30 of this year, President Garfield appointed Hannibal Hamlin Envoy Extraordinary and Minister to Spain. Before Hamlin accepted, Garfield was shot and died in September. Hamlin of course took the position. He was accepted into the Minister of Spain position on a temporary basis and without the usual referral committee. Hamlin sailed for Philadelphia with his wife, Ellen, on November 5. They sailed to London and Paris, and then on to Madrid, Spain. Home again, sort of...

The Moors, an African people, invaded Spain in 711 C.E. They were led by Tarik, an African Moslem from Morocco. During their reign, they introduced the common bath to the Europeans, starting with Spain, then they taught the French and Portuguese. Mathematics, botany, astronomy, history, and law were mastered by the Moors in Spain. The Moors stood supreme in the art of shipbuilding, irrigation, and metal work. This later group of indigenous Africans of the high cultures have preserved much of the African ancestors' teachings in the many works stolen by the Greeks and Romans from the Egyptian and Nubian Mysteries System. These very teachings are misnomered "Greek Philosophy" by Europeans and European-Americans (ben-Jochannan, *Black Man of the Nile;* Stanley Lane-Poole, *The Moors in Spain,* 1887).

Hannibal Hamlin was an educated, well-read gentleman. Seeing as how he was so interested in the humanity of the races, it would not be surprising if he were aware of a Moorish/African heritage. Moor literally means "Black." The Moors of Berber ancestry were the conquerors of Spain. They conquered Spain in the 8th century A.D., as mentioned above, and reigned for thousands of years intermingling with the Spanish socially and intimately, making the Spanish a darker brown than they already were. Being Minister to Spain could have been one way for Hamlin to make contact with his ancestral self. It would not be unusual for Hamlin to have learned the truth about Moors during his academic years, especially since during the 1800's much of the history and literature studied in the school system had not been as distorted as it is today. You see, then there was not as much for the white man to fear or lose as it is today. Whites in 1800's America had subjected Africans to inferior status and illiteracy, so the truth in history books stood as it was, in some cases.

Hamlin met the King and Queen of Spain, and essentially enjoyed his time as Minister. Hannibal Hamlin was Minister to Spain from 1881 to 1882. Hamlin retired to his home in the United States in 1882 to do some farming which he had put off for years to "politick" for America. This is the same year that Mrs. Mary Todd Lincoln succumbed.

FREDERICK DOUGLASS CHANNELS TO THE FUTURE

It was two years after Hamlin's retirement that elder Frederick Douglass married his white secretary, Helen Pitts. Douglass had stated that he could have more intellectual conversations with Helen than with his deceased African wife, Anna Murray. Douglass said that he married his first wife out of love and respect for his mother (who was raped by Douglass' sire), and married his second wife because his father was white (although this person never treated Frederick Douglass as his child). Douglass' children were disgusted with him for marrying this woman, but fortunately they could still communicate with their father — somewhat.

Two years later in 1886, Frederick Douglass gave an extremely enlightening speech in acknowledging the 24th anniversary of the Emancipation Proclamation in Washington, D.C. The speech was entitled: "Southern Barbarism." This speech could have, however, been titled: "Los Angeles Rebellion 1992."

> The American people have this lesson to learn;
>   That where justice is denied,
>   where poverty is enforced,
>   where ignorance prevails,
>   and where any one class is made to feel
>   that society is an organized conspiracy
>   to oppress, rob, and degrade them,
> *neither* persons nor property will be safe.
>
> *Frederick Douglass*

DOUGLASS AND THE LAND OF THE PHARAOHS

It was during the late 1880's that Frederick Douglass was writing and expressing to his sons his interest in the science of the human race. Douglass has many books of this subject-type on his bookshelf in Cedar Hills, southeast Washington, D.C. In 1887, Douglass decided that he wanted to visit Kemet and see the "Land of the Pharaohs." He visited and studied its splendor in February of the same year. He and Helen visited Cairo first. Douglass wrote his son that the people in Kemet are definitely more African than European. They are more African in color, conduct, and features, he asserted. He wrote that, "It has been the fashion of American writers, to deny that the Egyptians were Negroes and claim that they are of the same race as themselves. This has, I have no doubt, been largely due to a wish to deprive the Negro of the moral support of Ancient Greatness and to appropriate the same to the white race" (McFelly, pp. 331-332).

Frederick Douglass was commissioned, like Hamlin, to be Minister to another Black land, Haiti. Frederick Douglass and his wife of five years sailed for Haiti on the Civil War battleship in October, 1889. Frederick Douglass was the only person on the ship who did not get sick. Upon arriving at the Port-au-Prince, however, Mrs. Douglass begin to feel a little better. She stated in a letter that the first person she saw from the Haitian land was a young man with a molasses cake (she wrote that she thinks it was molasses cake) on his head who was wearing a short garment. Mrs. Helen Pitts Douglass wrote that the young man lifted the front of this short garment "to wipe his face, and the natural man was revealed" (McFeely, p. 334). Is Helen a descendant of Pauline Bonaparte? Was the young man so exciting to her that she felt it necessary to visually rape him and to write about him too? Apparently so. I hope this young man's father and mother had taught him to run like hell before "someone" cries rape! Anyway, Frederick Douglass, ex-enslaved person, was now Minister to the land that had one-hundred years before been seized by Toussaint L'Ouverture from Napoleon and other white men who *thought* themselves slaveowners. Napoleon Bonaparte had sold his Louisiana territory in order to fight this war and still lost. Frederick Douglass said that no one had done more for the Revolution and freedom of Africans than Toussaint L'Ouverture and his comrades — not William Garrison, not John Brown, not even David Walker's Appeal. L'Ouverture was on a serious mission. The Haitians were saddened when Douglass left his post as Minister to Haiti.

HANNIBAL HAMLIN DIES

In 1891, two years after the Douglass' Haitian voyage, a man about the same complexion as Frederick Douglass succumbed to his dis-eased heart. Hannibal Hamlin died. How strange America is. One Black man was an enslaved person in the United States, and the other Black man was Vice President of the United States, all because one said I'm this, and the other said I'm that — Yin and Yang; South and North; Black and White. Like Jefferson, Hannibal Hamlin died on Independence Day, July 4th. He was 81 years old.

President **Abraham Lincoln** discussing the *Emancipation Proclamation* with Vice President **Hannibal Hamlin**.

Moorish warrior, **Moor** means black.

Sojourner Truth *(Courtesy Smith College, Sophia Smith Collection).*

Frederick Douglas with his grandson **Joseph** *(Courtesy Library of Congress).*

WARREN G. HARDING

29th President, USA

Born seven months after the death of Abraham Lincoln, Warren G. Harding was born on November 2, 1865 on a farm in Corsica, Ohio. Harding was President of the United States from March 4, 1921 to August 2, 1923, and was said to have been one of the worst presidents that the United States has ever had in office. It is not surprising to read so much about Hardings' inadequacies which was written mostly in his-story form. He was not in office long enough to really prove what type of President he might have been. Harding died before his four-year term was up, and it is doubtful that he would have been given an eight-year opportunity.

BLACK HARDINGS

It is widely documented, and a well-known and definite fact to many White and Black elders in Hardings' hometown, that Warren G. Harding was a Black man. Research indicates in all probability that he was indeed of African ancestry. J.A. Rogers, ourstorian/historian and anthropologist in the 1940's, met and talked with a Mrs. Eva Thornton Wells, a brown-skinned and proclaimed African-American, who said that she was a descendant of Warren G. Harding. "Mrs. Wells is the granddaughter of Daniel G. Harding, a cousin of President Harding's father." Rogers goes on to explain "How Negro Strain Gets into the White Group" (Rogers, *Sex and Race*, vol. II, pp. 257-258).

Harding died a mysterious death on August 2, 1923 in San Francisco, California. He was the sixth President of the United States to die while in office, and the fifth known president said to be of African ancestry.

Warren G. Harding and his family have never been considered white people in their hometown community of Marion, Ohio (Coyle, p. 337; Russell, p. 531). William Estabrook Chancellor also states this as fact in his book, *WARREN GAMALIEL HARDING: President of the United States. A review of facts collected from Anthropological, Historical and Political Researches*, Sentinel Press, 1922. Some years after Harding's death, an old Ohio countryman stated that he had not been interested in politics and voting since the 1920's. He said, "That was an election … And Harding was a nigger." William Chancellor says in his book that, "Socially, a man is what his neighbors report. He has to take their classification or get out from among them. When they call him a negro, it does no good to sue them for slander; they still think so" (Chancellor, p. 35). From the time that Harding decided to get involved in politics, and even before, he and his family had been said to have "Negro blood." One author states that the book by Chancellor "proves" that Harding was an African man. Andrew Sinclair, a white author, states that the darkness of Harding's skin was the *only* obvious hint that Harding may be Black. (Sinclair, *The Available Man: Warren Gamaliel Harding*, pp. 36, 144, 169, 259). This is a rather obvious hint. Andrew Sinclair goes on to state on pages 171 & 172 of his book that:

> The news correspondents of Marion were filing up to five thousand words a day on the story [of Harding's Black ancestry]; but little of it was printed, because of *decent* editors. Harding was ready to come out with an official denial, but he remained true to his philosophy of simply ignoring the *unpleasant* … The interest of the episode was that anyone should have thought it even an issue that Harding could have been a mulatto. Americans were, on the whole, a *mongrel* race. Negroes were among the oldest Americans.

All italics in the above statement are the author's of this book. What's so *decent* about not printing that someone is or may be Black? And what's so *indecent* and *unpleasant* about being Black, Sinclair? Africans (Blacks, African-Americans) have been written about in this light for hundreds of years. Some of these writers were not and are not even aware of their bias.

It is true that Africans are among the most ancient people to have lived on the soil now called America. Dr. Ivan Van Sertima, the author of *They Came Before Columbus*, and other ourstorians/historians have asserted and proved that there was an entry in Columbus' diary stating that Blacks were among the natives when Christopher Columbus (Cristobal Colombo) accidentally found his way to the land here. To Africans and their fellow brown friends, the land of America is an "Old World" — not a "New World." It was a new world only to Columbus and other Europeans (i.e., white people) "conquering" up a his-story for themselves. Erik Erickson seems to have understood the concept of whites creating their own his-story when he stated at a Thomas Jefferson Lecture: "Jefferson's times [and before] demanded some self-aggrandizement in the service of the new, almost instant ancestral past which American history had to create" (Erickson, p. 55). Columbus named the people on the land during his era "Indians" because he thought that he was in India (ben-Jochannan, *African Origins of Major Western Religions*, p. 335). It is ironic how the name stuck. These history mythology writers' arrogant premise seems to be: "If we have not been there, then it has not been discovered."

I DON'T DENY IT

Harding himself never denied his ancestry, perhaps because his wife, no matter how unstable she seemed to be, was always on hand to see to it that he did not humiliate him-Self any more than America had already ridiculed and humiliated him. She likely told him that to openly deny your ancestry is definitely to deny yourself. When the Republicans were about to issue full-fledged denials of the allegations or truths about Harding's dark ancestry, Mrs. Harding stopped them. Harding told a friend of his that, "One of my ancestors might have jumped the fence." J.A. Rogers states that when Hardings' sister, who was a policewoman and later became a teacher in Washington, D.C., was to speak to a group of African-American women in Washington, D.C., she was literally "kidnapped" and sent away from the area until her brother's campaign was over. She looked very ethnic/dark (Rogers, *Sex and Race*, vol. II, pp. 254 & 257). "It is reported that when Republican leaders called on Harding to deny the "Negro" story, he said, '"How should I know. [sic] One of my ancestors might have jumped the fence …"' [sic] (Rogers, *The Five Negro Presidents*, p. 12). A similar statement was made by Billy Carter, the brother of the 39th President of the United States, Jimmy Carter. On April 8, 1977, Billy said, "We all left a nigger in the woodpile somewhere." This comment was made in reference to a question asked of Billy about an Oakland, California African-American politician who also had the last name, Carter.

FAMILY AND FRIEND VIEWS

Warren G. Harding's father was born in 1844 in the family log cabin. He believed in freedom and liberty as the highest virtues. Like Warren G. Harding's grandfather, his father was an avid abolitionist. He "felt that the institution of human slavery violated the law of God, and that the Negro should be freed of his shackles" (Kurland, *Warren Harding, Betrayed by Friends*, p. 4) — *before whites discover me and those shackles are snapped on my own feet*, Harding's father may have been thinking. Although the Harding men supposedly believed in freedom (assumingly for everyone — here's the usual contradiction), they violently fought the Indians from reclaiming land which was once the Indian's land anyway (Kurland, p. 4). Now if this is true, these Harding men were apparently light enough to really fail-for-white, or maybe they acted so white in their violence, attitude and demeanor that the Indians and the Blacks that they were fighting simply assumed they must be white. It would be easy to assume this about Andrew Jackson. It would not be unusual or odd that many of the Blacks and the Indians who the Hardings fought had the same complexion as these Harding men since the Harding's were known to be of dark skin, i.e., a swarthy complexion as many writers and historians describe this skin color. Harding's father also fought in swarthy Lincoln's Civil War. Upon his return, he began the study of medicine, and on November 2, 1865 his first child, Warren Gamaliel Harding, was born (Kurland, p. 4).

Warren G. Harding received "a highly patriotic version of American history, … he grew up with an implicit faith in the American dream" (Kurland, p. 5). Both the patriotic version of American history and the American dream have been to the detriment and psychological confusion of most African, African-American, Black, Creole, mulatto, quadroon, octoroon (whatever an African may wish to call him or her self here in America) people. Many of the latter four have "failed-for-white."

Harding was known for telling Blacks that he too was Black. Wendell Dabney, an African-American editor and a paymaster in the city of Cincinnati, said that Harding had been known as a Black man long before any circulars appeared attesting to the fact (Rogers, *The Five Negro Presidents*, p. 12). William Estabrook Chancellor, the white professor of Economics, Politics and Social Sciences of Wooster College, Ohio and the author mentioned above, investigated the Harding family genealogy. He produced a detailed book on them, claiming that Harding's great-grandmother, Elizabeth Madison, was a "Negress" and that his great-grandfather, George T. Harding, had Negro blood. Chancellor interviewed elderly residents of Marion, Ohio, who knew the Harding family. He secured affidavits from them, which can be found in FACT magazine, January-February, 1964. (Other references: Rogers, *The Five Negro Presidents*, p. 12; Sinclair, p. 170; Russell, p. 530; Chancellor's, *WARREN GAMALIEL HARDING: President of the United States.*) Sinclair states that Chancellor was from "old, slave-owning Virginian stock." Chancellor said that Warren G. Harding was a "big, lazy, slouching, confused, ignorant, affable, yellow and cringing like a Negro butler to the great." He went on to say that Harding "was loose on sex morals, like all Negroes." Chancellor also stated in his book that the Black man in general has no sex morals and will not lift a hand to help another black man. On the other hand, he states that the black and colored woman does not practice sex looseness, and that she is virtuous "according to white standards" (p. 31). Statements such as these coming from a racist, whether the statements are degrading or complimentary, are not worth anger nor a smile of approval. How does he know of the virtue of Black women anyway? Did he try? Chancellor also sounds like a person who is rather jealous and fearful of Black men. Still, his research and other literature shows that it is possible that Harding was of African ancestry. Chancellor went on to say that he thinks that

Harding's color strain comes from his paternal side. Chancellor was eventually dismissed from his post at Wooster College because of his research into President Harding's ancestry (Sinclair, pp. 170-171). This act was more than likely geared toward white people's fears that they may have appointed a Black man into the White House.

The book: *Warren Gamliel Harding, President of the United States,* The Sentinel Press, 1921, which is based on the research of William Estabrook Chancellor, is a relatively rare book. All of the copies except for two or three were allegedly bought by the agents of the Department of Justice and destroyed (Sinclair, p. 313). Gaston Means, the author of *The Strange Death of President Harding,* wrote in reference to Chancellor's book, "I myself had helped light a bonfire that burnt up the entire edition of this book — copyright and all — bought at a price. And the plates for this book were destroyed also" (Means, p. 139-140). During the past forty to fifty years, it has been found that some copies are in the hands of Ohio residents as well as in the New York Public Library. Princeton University and the Ohio Historical Society also have copies (Sinclair, p. 313; Rogers, *The Five Negro Presidents,* p. 12). Although copies of this book are limited, I am fortunate that I had no problem securing one of the copies. This borrowed copy did not come from any of the sources mentioned above.

The Harding family moved to Marion, Ohio when Warren Harding was seventeen years old. Harding attended Iberia College from 1879 to 1882. This college is now Ohio Central College. "This institution was founded in order to educate the fugitive slaves" (Chancellor, p. 75). By midwestern standards, this was an inferior college which offered an inferior education (Kurland, p. 6). This religious college is the only academic career listed in Harding's book of educational credentials. "The school had a very general collection of studies. They took an illiterate and gave him lessons in reading. They took a big boy or girl who wished to become a rural teacher and taught him [or her] some United States history, grammar and arithmetic. William Chancellor states that, "This was the course that Warren pursued" (Chancellor, p. 75).

EDUCATION/RELIGION

Harding's mother, Phoebe used to preach the teachings of Methodist religion. She eventually become a Seventh Day Adventist, and her son became a Baptist (Kurland, p. 5). Warren Harding never became devout in any of these religions, though he did have faith in his belief that any American person who was righteous, well mannered, respected others, and simply worked hard in America would in turn be respected and could prosper.

In 1883, Harding returned from Iberia to the family home in Marion to teach school. He said that it was one of the most difficult jobs he had ever had. At least during this American era, he could be respected as a teacher, but like today, he was not likely to prosper financially in a teaching position. After his "education," he took many odd jobs. Was Harding taught in his Iberian school that in 1878, one of his brothers, J.R. Winters, received a patent as the inventor of the fire escape ladder, and that in this same year, Liberia (Africa) had been named the location for free blacks? He could have liberated his mind and himself by accepting his ancestry and being proud of it. It is a wonder if he learned that one of his great sisters had "passed on to the ancestors" (i.e., died). Sojourner Truth, the marvelously inspirational poet and freedom fighter succumbed in Battle Creek, Michigan in 1883. Six years after the death of Sojourner Truth, Harding was in Battle Creek, Michigan himself — in a mental institution.

DILIRIUM TREMENS

Warren Harding was said to have delirium tremens (Sinclair, p. 170), and similar to Lincoln, he also suffered severe depressions. Harding was once found crying on the White House lawn (Ross, p. 159). Harding, again similar to Lincoln, had a history of mental disorders that was traced back to age twenty-four when he suffered a nervous breakdown and was institutionalized in a mental hospital in Battle Creek, Michigan. From this time on, Harding checked himself into many mental institutions to secure his emotional stability (Garrison, p. 59; Sullivan, p. 155; Ross, p. 159).

FLORENCE KLING DE WOLFE

At age twenty-six, Harding married Florence Kling de Wolfe. She had an extremely demanding personality and was said to be more masculine than feminine. Many people in Marion, Ohio wondered what Ms. de Wolfe had to gain by marrying Harding who was said to have "Negro" blood. "Harding was a tall, well-built young man, and was sought after by many of Marion's eligible young ladies" (Kurland, p. 7).

Florence's father, Amos Kling, was adamantly against her marriage to Harding. Florence didn't care; she was getting a handsome husband, and she knew that Harding was getting the support and respect of many of Marion's influential businessmen. Many authors and researchers feel that this marriage was a marriage of apparent convenience, not only because Florence was five years Harding's senior and had a very prejudiced father, but because she was quite unattractive. Florence had been married before — to a drunk, and from this union they had a son, who was adopted by Florence's more than prejudiced father. He adopted Florence's son and cared for him as his own. His adopting the child was probably to assure that the child become a "good, white American," and not go off and marry a "Negro" as his mother did. Chancellor states on page 225 of his research book that some believe that the Klings were "originally" Jews. Dr. Francis Cress-Welsing, the author of *The Isis (Yssi) Papers: The Keys to the Colors,* states in her many lectures around the country that many Jews have been known to have taught their children that it is pertinent to "whiten" the family "down" in order to be more socially and economically accepted. Instead Florence choose to "Blacken" the family "up," to the disbelief and bewilderment of her father. Her father had no reason to worry; she never had a child with Harding.

BROTHER HARDING

Harding was referred to as Brother Harding by many Blacks and Whites in and around his hometown of Marion, Ohio (Russell, pp. 92 & 98). "Brother" so-and-so has always been used frequently in African-American communities. De-coding. One of Harding's newspaper foes "complimented" Harding by printing in one of his issues (a rival newspaper) a silhouette of Harding and explaining in the "caption that because of the color of the subject he could not reproduce the features. Upon seeing this black caricature Harding threatened to kill" this newspaper rival. Author Frances Russell laments that through his reading and research on Warren G. Harding's personality that Harding's "innate dread of physical combat kept him from doing more than threaten." But Harding's father, George Tryon, actually got into a fist fight with Mrs. Florence Kling Harding's father, Amos. Just a few weeks after this black caricature appeared in the rival paper, George was walking past Amos Kling's house when George heard Amos call him a "nigger." Tryon knocked Kling to the ground (Russell, p. 97). This Black man did not stand for and accept being called this derogatory word by white (or Jewish?) Kling.

The legend of Harding's "Negro" blood was whispered all over Ohio. Flyers ran rampant and these flyers were usually connected with Chancellor's name. One such flyer was headed: *The Right of the American People to Know*. Then it showed Harding's family tree as being:

Amos Harding (Black), West Indian Negro — Wife, Huldah Harding, colored.

George Tryon Harding lst, colored — Wife, Ann Roberts, colored.

Charles A. Harding, colored — Wife, Mary Ann Crawford, pass-for-white

George Tryron Harding, 2nd — Wife, Phoebe Dickerson, white

So the issue of the Harding family possibly being white apparently began with Mary Ann Crawford being light enough to "fail-for-white," and with white Phoebe Dickerson who was the wife of light-skinned Black (or mulatto) George Tryon Harding. The marriage of Phoebe to George Tryon Harding II was objected to by a Dickerson family member because he said that Phoebe's husband-to-be was mulatto, having "Negro" blood. The above information was verified by an Ohio resident, Mr. Elias Shaffer of Akron,

Ohio, who had known the Harding family for fifty years. He attended the same school as George Tryon Harding, II, and he knew George's father, Charles (Russell, pp. 403-404). Chancellor described Charles Harding as having curly, kinky hair, dark complexion, a big body, and a big nose. And although Chancellor was incorrect in this information, he named Harding in his writings as "our first Negro President." (Thomas Jefferson was the first President of African ancestry — according to white people's statements and documentation. See the Jefferson chapter.)

Just before Harding, who was Republican, was elected President of the United States, many Democratic papers stated that Harding was a "Negro." Many papers were distributed stating that George Tryon Harding, Warren G. Harding's father, was an obvious mulatto; "he has thick lips, rolling eyes, and chocalate skin" (Rogers, p. 11). Young Warren Harding's playmates referred to him as "nigger" on many occasions, and his father-in-law would not accept him as his son-in-law because he said that the Hardings were mixed with negro blood (Sullivan, p. 154). One of Harding's ancestors, Elizabeth Madison, was well remembered by eight older people still living in Blooming Grove, Ohio as late as 1920. All of these older people stated that Elizabeth was Black. She was so dark that it was thought by some of the neighbors that she must have been a Moor. A Blackmoor, or a very dark woman from Scotland, "say of the black Picts?" (Chancellor, p. 37).

ISSUE: Warren G. Harding, Black — Wife, Florence Kling, white (Russell, pp. 530 & 403). Children: None (Kane, *Facts About the Presidents*, p. 193)

After Harding's death, the Post Office Department of America issued the 1 1/2 cent stamp first with Harding's portrait in Black, then later with his portrait in Brown. Either way, in America, you are considered Black. The Harding family did not complain.

HARDING'S DARK SISTER

There were, and continue to be, many stories about the Hardings having black blood running through their veins. Warren G. Harding's sister, Carolyn Harding Votaw, was said to be the darkest in the family. When William Estabrook Chancellor was city school superintendent for Washington, D.C., Senator Foraker took interest in "minority" people. He mailed a letter of reference to Chancellor asking that he hire a teacher that he knew and that she was a "quardroon." Foraker asked that this teacher be placed in a Black school. She was Warren G. Harding's sister. Carolyn was a teacher in Washington, D.C., teaching in a Black school, and living in a Black neighborhood (Chancellor, p. 41; Rogers, *The Five Negro Presidents*, p. 12; Russell, p. 530). Before she began her American teaching career, Carolyn had worked as a religious missionary. She returned from one such trip in 1909 full of daring enthusiasm and stories about her adventures in India. Having worked in India, Harding's sister probably saw many whose faces looked a lot like her own. This is a land full of Africans who are called Bonda people and Dravidians. Africans in India are one-hundred million strong. These Africans just happen to live in India, just as people who are called Black Americans are Africans who just happen to live in America.

There are many Black families with the last name Harding in Ohio, U.S.A. Some of them claim relationship with Warren G. Harding (Russell, p. 530). "President Harding, it says, was named after his uncle, Warren Gamaliel Bancroft, a Negro preacher" (Rogers, *Sex and Race.* vol. II, p. 257).

HARDING'S MARRIAGE

Although it seems as if Harding did not profit much sexually by marrying Florence, he did gain a certain amount of prestige and social acceptance. Some historians and writers state that Harding was sexually and emotionally frustrated in his marital union with the overly aggressive, unattractive Florence. Many of his psychological crises stemmed from his confused feelings of self and being, in addition to his strange union with Florence — of which he eventually had some serious affairs.

In most of the so-called "official" documents on facts about the Presidents of the United States, it is stated that the Hardings had no children, although Mrs. Harding had a child, and so did Warren G. Harding. Warren G. Harding is said to have liked children, but he never saw his biological child that he had through an extramarital affair with Nan Britton, and no thanks to Florence, he hardly ever saw their grandchildren (Florence's son's children) because she didn't want to be reminded that she was a grandmother.

Florence had begun to wear a collar brooch to cover neck wrinkles by the time her grandchildren were born. When Harding was President of the United States, Florence had contemplated having her son's wife adopt Nan Britton's young daughter, Elizabeth, so that Harding could be near his biological child. But she got angry and reneged on this thought forever when in one of their arguments he threatened to get impeached and run away with his child. In this same conversation, Harding told Florence that he had never loved her, that he was sick of the presidency. He said that going crazy would be better than this life. Mrs. Florence Harding lamented, "I hate Warren Harding with a hatred greater than my former love and affection" (Means, pp. 242-243). She was rejected, disgruntled, angry, and hurt during the past few weeks before Warren G. Harding's death.

When young Warren G. Harding became interested in politics, wife Florence was more than happy to keep his newspaper, "Star," running and profitable. She was a good businesswoman on the personal and career front. One of the workers at the *Star* stated that it was a well-known fact that the Hardings had African ancestry, but W.G. (Harding) had outgrown it (Rogers, *Sex and Race*, vol. II, p. 255).

When Harding became President, Florence said to him, "Well, Warren Harding, I have got you the Presidency; what are you going to do with it?" (Sinclair, p. 295). Harding seemed more than willing to have the public believe (or perhaps it was true) that his wife "wore the pants" in the house. This way, he said, he could turn all of the public pests and problem business deals over to his wife and still keep his friends, the love of the public, and especially his political supporters. Harding seemed to have an emotional need, as a public and private person, to be liked.

THE SMOKE-FILLED ROOM

One writer states that Harding lived a lie from the moment he became president, which was by default. He seemed to be a decent compromise candidate and won. Harding was called to a meeting in suite 404-406 on the thirteenth floor of the Blackstone Hotel in Chicago. This meeting room has gone down in history as "the smoke-filled room." He was asked if there was any reason for him to renege on the offer to become President of the United States; in essence, "are there any skeletons in your closet?" he was asked. Harding's answer was a simple "no." This answer came after 10 minutes of absence in another room. No one knows for sure what Harding did, whether he called his lady friends, his father, his wife, or anyone at all. It is presumed Harding telephoned Nan Britton, his young mistress who was in Chicago at the time with their "love" child, Elizabeth. (My research shows that this child was referred to as "illegitimate" 99.9% of the time. My question and Nan's is: "What is an 'illegitimate' child?" — See: *The President's Daughter*, by, Nan Britton, 1927). A child is a child! And all of them "Legit."

Of course Harding had to also consider the situation with his more mature mistress, Mrs. Carrie Phillips, the wife of an old friend and department store entrepreneur, Jim Phillips (Ross, p. 158; Russell, p. 166). The Phillipses had two children, a son and a daughter. Carrie was not very easy to handle and had to be bribed with money, a car and a lustrous trip to keep her mouth shut.

Warren G. Harding had spent fourteen lonely years in his marriage of compromise and convenience before he finally began the strange affair with his wife's "friend," Mrs. Carrie Phillips. Mrs. Phillips was considered attractive (according to white people's standards of beauty). Harding was the Lieutenant Governor at this time, and the other spouses were not aware of the affair. Through all the lying and deceit, the couples still double dated a lot. As fate would have it, the Phillips' young son died. Jim Phillips began to have emotional and mental problems and was committed to the same mental institution that Harding was in at age twenty-four. Both men had nervous disorders. Mrs. Harding was hospitalized to have a kidney removed, which left the vulnerable Mrs. Phillips, and the sexually frustrated Warren Harding alone. No holds barred, an intimate affair began which lasted fifteen years. Four years into this affair, the couples took a vacation cruise to the Mediterranean and Egypt together. Whenever Harding and Carrie could find time alone, they did. The two couples returned to America on a nine-day boat called the *President Lincoln*. Upon their return Harding continued what he called his "Alexander Hamilton Speech — entitled: Prophet of American Destiny." Alexander Hamilton was the mulatto Secretary of the Treasury during the Thomas Jefferson years, and Harding was probably more than knowledgeable of this fact.

At some point, Carrie started pressuring Warren G. to divorce the domineering Florence and marry her. He could not afford to do this considering his interest in a successful political career. Furthermore, no matter how overbearing and asexual Florence may have been, Harding did not want to see her hurt. Florence eventually suspected an affair between her husband and somebody and hired detectives to track them down. She was devastated to learn that her beloved was having an intimate relationship with one of her best friends. She knew there was somebody, but not Carrie! The Hardings' dull home life became interesting warfare.

MISTRESS NAN

Harding become intimately interested in Nan Britton when she was only fifteen years of age. Harding was forty-seven. She used to sit on his lap. Florence had already seen that this child might pose an even bigger problem and asked Nan's mother to keep her child off of her husband's "bulging lap" (Sullivan, p. 161). When Nan turned twenty in 1917, a real affair started. By 1919 they had a daughter, Elizabeth Ann. Elizabeth Ann was later adopted by Nan's sister and her husband. Elizabeth Ann was married to Henry Blaesing in 1938 and later lived in Glendale, California. She named her first child "Warren."

When Warren G. Harding became president of the United States, Nan Britton could not attend the inauguration. But she eventually got the opportunity to not only visit the White House, but to also make love to Harding in a White House closet. This was a small, five-foot-square closet in the ante-room (Britton, p. 173). This affair took place simultaneously with the Carrie Phillips relationship. Florence's concerns became very true.

FRONTYARD EMOTIONS RUN DEEP

Like Rachel Jackson (Andrew's wife) and Mary Lincoln (Abe's wife), Florence Harding (Warren's wife) too had mental and emotional problems. She was extraordinarily possessive and protective, not only because Harding was said to have had many affairs, and not only because he was said to have heart problems, but because this was simply a part of her personality. After Florence learned that Harding was dating Mrs. Carrie Phillips, Mrs. Phillips one day visited the Hardings on their front porch. Mrs. Harding threw a cleaning utensil then a trash can at Carrie. Now this sounds like a relatively normal, immediate reaction for a woman scorned, but this action took place many weeks after she discovered that her husband was "seeing" Carrie. Carrie also seemed to be a little crazy herself because she didn't duck or run until she saw a piano stool coming at her head. Harding must have been some brother, for although Carrie retreated, she still had the nerve to blow a kiss at him — right in Florence's face! In another interesting incident at the Marion, Ohio fairgrounds, Mrs. Carrie Phillips sat calmly in the amphitheater, while Mrs. Harding sat on the platform with her Warren. She called him "Wur'ren." Mrs. Harding being a nervous-type person seemed restless. While Harding spoke to the crowd, with hundreds of people crowded into the amphitheater, Mrs. Harding would get up, walk to the end of the platform, and shake her fist at Mrs. Phillips. Warren G. simply acted as if he didn't see his strange wife and carried on with his speech (Russell, p. 402) probably hoping that he would not lose votes because of his wife's ridiculous antics.

HARDING AND THE PHILLIPSES

When Harding eventually ran for president, Jim Phillips'
store had no Harding campaign banners draped around its
windows like other Ohio store owners. When Harding
became President, Carrie threatened to publicize love letters
that Harding had written to her. Occasionally, passages
from their letters to each other are not so security tight, and
are published. For example in 1976 the *Washington Post* ran a
piece from a Harding/Phillips letter: "Oh, Warren, Oh,
Warren — when your body quivers with divine paroxysms
and your soul hovers for flight with mine." And also in a
1911 letter, Harding had written Carrie saying, "I love you
garbed, but naked more," and in a poem, he had written,
"Carrie, take me panting to your heaving breast." Harding
brought Carrie a Cadillac as a "hush-up" gift. Carrie also
was paid $20,000 by the Republican National Committee,
plus $2,000 a month. She and her husband, Jim, were also
given an imperative and free trip around the world. They
remained abroad until Harding's death. On their return
from their leisurely Republican-sponsored trip, it was written that Jim sold out his interest in the department store.
Afterwards, Carrie Phillips convinced her husband to
legally place his property and their house totally in her possession. During the Depression years, Jim lost all of his
money. Carrie then put him out of the home which once
belonged to him. He died of tuberculosis in 1939. He was
living a lonely life in the Hotel Marion in a back room. Carrie Phillips died in 1960 in Marion, Ohio an eccentric recluse
(Ross, pp. 164-166; Sullivan, pp. 159-161; Murray, pp. 529-
530; Russell, p. 644).

AND OTHER AFFAIRS

As mentioned, Harding had started dating Nan Britton in
the midst of his affair with Carrie Phillips. Nan Britton had
his child, Elizabeth Ann on October 22, 1919. Nan stated in
her book, *The President's Daughter*, that Harding would come
to her for love, and often cry to her that his wife gives him
hell. His exact statement to Nan was, "She'd raise hell!" (p.
132). That statement sounds so Black male. The last sentence

is written with a smile — out of understanding and African communitive love, and *not* Black male bashing! Our men say this beautifully: "Man-n-n, she'll raise hell." And they are usually right — about whatever it is. Nan said that Harding was her hero, a darling, her love. Many people tried to discredit Nan's book as untrue, but whenever the "discreditors" would look for proof, their "investigations merely seemed to confirm her story" (Russell, p. 642; Gaston Means' writings).

Warren G. Harding was a friend of Nan's father. When Harding was U.S. Senator, Nan wrote him a letter asking him if he could find her a job. He met her in Manhattan and suggested that she live in New York instead of Washington. That way, they could be more discreet in their illicit affair.

EAST ST. LOUIS - NEW YORK

During Harding's love triangle, more important affairs were taking place. A few days before Nan Britton lost her virginity to Harding, there was a race riot going on in East St. Louis, Illinois. African-American's homes were vandalized and burned. Forty-eight people died (40 African-American and 8 white). There was a March of Protest on July 28, 1917 on New York's Fifth Avenue. Banners carried by African-Americans read: "MAKE AMERICA SAFE FOR DEMOCRACY." At this time, there were no U.S. anti-lynching laws in existence. Harding was on "shaky ground" here. (And it is a possibility that six years later, in 1923, poor Harding did experience a type of lynching.)

Two days after the New York demonstration on July 30, 1917, Nan Britton lost her virginity (they say) to Harding in a hotel overlooking Broadway, near Fifth Avenue. By 1919, the two had started having sex in the Senate office. This is where Nan thinks their child was conceived. Harding never met his daughter. Many of Harding's relatives believed Nan's story, but were not willing to offer any finances in support of their beliefs. So Nan wrote *The President's Daughter* to supplement her income. Some white writers said that if she really loved Harding, she would not have written the book. They're crazy; the girl had been used long enough — or rather they had used each other long enough. Gaston

Means believes that Nan carried on this affair because of the prestige, power and the pleasure — not necessarily because she was head over heels in love. Nan completed her book in 1927 with the help of a friend, Richard Wightman, whose wife later sued him for divorce, naming Nan Britton as the person who broke up her family by having an affair with her husband.

BUT WHO IS SHE?

As a senator, Harding had also written several love notes to another old flame who too threatened to publicly divulge the content of her letters. It is also said that she was in Paris at the same time as Harding. It seems that this is the same woman who Nan Britton mentions in her book (pp. 11-12). This woman's real name is not used. After Harding became President, Mrs. Florence Harding warned this woman to never come to the White House. The lady ignored Florence, and came to the White House whenever she pleased (Means, p. 57). It is not documented as to whether any of these women believed the stories about Harding's African ancestry.

HIS-STORY

Research has shown that many historians today apparently believe it true too that the Hardings have African ancestry, because Harding is the only President with Black blood running through his veins who they readily and abundantly make mention of African ancestry whether they are in agreement or not. As for the other Presidents they simply ignore these assertions or truths, or they adamantly deny that they're true. Harding, like Hamlin, has been a very much overlooked and underpublished president, yet in almost every piece of literature, his African ancestry is noted. As mentioned earlier, many writers and historians consider Harding a total failure as a president. The meager literary findings seem to be an indication of what and how American historians feel about this man. He seems to be relatively insignificant to them. But to write about Harding too extensively will only intensify the possibility that white Americans have voted a Black man into the White House, and many, if not most, whites simply cannot accept this, yet. It is too bad for them, philosophically and with their warped psychological concerns, that they have already voted six, and perhaps seven (or eight!), African-American Presidents into the White House. Frances Russell said, in so many words: So what if Harding had African ancestry. Black people were on American land before everyone. We are all mixed. So what is the big deal with Warren Harding?

HANDSOME HARDING

Harding has been described by many historians and writers as very handsome, tall, well-built, and very brown with features like an athletic god. One author described him as superbly handsome with a bronzed-tanned face and the features of a god (Sullivan, p. 153). Harding was often described as looking like a god. One of Harding's friends and employees described Harding as having "the regal look of a King! Warren has a very handsome appearance. Once seen — he could never be forgotten .... Warren Harding was an amazingly handsome man." These words were spoken by two men: Harry Daugherty and Gaston Means (Means, p. 47).

Many white writers and historians who wrote about Harding were and are relentless in slandering him. Many political writings about him are negative. They write that his personality is nice; his body and his face are gorgeous, and not much else. We must learn to read between the lines. Simply reading the way these writers phrase their sentences about the Hardings, shows any African in tune with his or her blackness and ourstory (history) that these people wholeheartedly believed Harding to be Black. The signs are clear.

1912

Many people said that Harding was over his head as a President (Ross, p. 158), and some wrote that he was inadequate. Another white author writes, "It is generally agreed that Warren G [sic] Harding was one of the most inept and probably one of the most corrupt Presidents to have held office" (Williamson, p. 154).

When Harding was an Ohio politician, "The presidential contest of 1912 threatened to destroy the Republican party as a national political force ... Moderates in both parties were anxious to restore the shattered unity of the Grand Ole Party, and in Ohio, Warren Harding became a powerful voice urging reconciliation." They reunited. Although Harding wanted to be considered a peacemaker, he could stand his ground and put his foot down when he felt it totally necessary (Kurland, pp. 11 & 23).

In 1912 another strong political voice was preparing for a greatness which, of course, exceeded Harding's voice for African-Americans by leaps and bounds. Ourstorian/Historian Carter G. Woodson completed his so-called "formal" education with a Ph.D. from Harvard University. Although it is found in most literature that Carter G. Woodson was the offspring of former slaves (perhaps mulatto; perhaps Indian?), J.A. Rogers contends that Woodson was mixed (*Sex & Race*, vol. II p. 390). Carter G. Woodson knew that he was a strong African man living in America; Harding did not. As mentioned, Harding choose to fail-for-white and hide behind a white mask; Carter G. Woodson did not, and fortunately could not. He was a man in love with his race. Fourteen years later in 1926, Dr. Woodson initiated "Negro History Week," now known as Black History Month. "This celebration was initially designed to commemorate the birthdays of Abraham Lincoln and Frederick Douglass." "Dr. Woodson ... was keenly conscious of symbolism in the American psyche." "It was Dr. Woodson's hope that, through this special observance, all Americans would be reminded of their ethnic roots" (*Negro History Bulletin*, vol. 45, No. 2, April/May/June, 1982). Lincoln too?

WORLD WAR I

During the summer of 1914, World War I began in Europe. Senator Harding advocated the necessity of strengthening the U.S. Military as preparation in case war broke out (Kurland, p. 12). In 1914, a very young Dwight D. Eisenhower was in the U.S. Military academy, preparing for a very American military career. He would become the sixth President of the United States mentioned in this book as having African ancestry (see the next chapter; also see his 1916 military picture on p. 308).

A NORMAL NOMINEE

In June 1920, Harding became presidential nominee — Republican Party. He was ecstatic. His campaign was managed by Harry Daugherty. Harding's problems with the public deciding that he was virtually an imbecile started when he made a statement, after becoming a nominee, that, "America's present need is not heroics, but healing; not nostrums, but normalcy; not revolution, but restoration ..." (Kurland, p. 18). Many so-called intellectuals reprimanded Harding for his "illiteracy." They said that there is no such word as "normalcy." They felt that the most appropriate term to be used in that particular statement should have been "normality." But research shows that there is such a word as "normalcy," and either form is appropriate for the statement. The word has been used as far back as 1857. The word "normalcy" is also used in a book written in 1894 entitled, *Social Evolution*, by B. Kidd. The word (normalcy) is used throughout English and American literature and mathematical writings. The American Heritage Dictionary states that "normalcy" is widely employed in standard usage, though disapproved by some as a needless alternative to "normality;" they say that it is coined outside of the "normal" pattern of the language. It is further stated that the word is "unacceptable" to 59% of the Usage Panel (American Heritage Dictionary, H.S. ed., Houghton Mifflin Co., Boston, 1982). Who is the Usage Panel? Most whites have never understood, nor accepted, African-Americans' colorful use of language and words. It was fresh in the minds of many of these so-called intellectuals that even though it had been affirmed by some that Harding was not a Black man, they couldn't be sure. *"He is rather dark,"* they were likely thinking. So these white "intellectuals" stayed on the safe side, and maintained that Harding's intelligence must be restricted and not within the limits of their own. Woodrow Wilson, 28th President of the United States, leaving office in March, 1921 wanted to know of Harding: "'How can he lead when he does not know where he is going?'" "More than anyone else, Warren Harding was aware of his intellectual limitations" (Kurland, p. 20). It is unfortunate that Harding allowed these people to interpret his intelligence, as many of us have done, and continue to do so even today. One drop of black blood is all it takes for one to be labeled Black (and therefore inferior according to white American standards). Warren G. Harding suffered the same type of stereotyping problems in his early years of school as many young African-American brothers of today and yesterday. He himself, up until and during his years as President of the United States, felt inadequate in his writing skills. He was the first president to employ a speechwriter, feeling himself poor in this area of academia. This feeling of inadequacy may well have been initiated by teachers in his community who did not award him the same halo effect (i.e., the brilliance, the trust, and the glory attributed to a person idealized, and viewed with an unseen virtuous, shining, round light above his/her head, like an angel) as they did many of their white students — believing that Harding was a Black child and could not learn as fast and wasn't expected to do so. "Warren and his brother and sisters were reared and treated as colored people" (Chancellor, p. 22). One of Harding's friends stated that "Harding was notoriously clumsy when he tried to write his own speeches" (Garrison, p. 208). Harding was probably more nervous than anything else, perhaps regressing to early childhood school "daze" and becoming again fixated in that particular time of life whenever he attempted to write a speech. In William Chancellor's book, he wrote that Harding hardly ever knew his lessons, and that his school friends always called Harding "Nigger," especially when they went swimming together (p. 75). Becoming a teacher, an insurance salesman, an auditor, and an editor of his own newspaper didn't validate Harding's own adeptness about his writing. This seems to be an example of massive brainwashing — unless Harding was simply being crazy like a fox (Uncle Tomming). He could have been thinking, *"I'll allow these white boys to write my speeches for white America; they probably can word it just white enough, while my own writing might put too much brown spice in it and then I'll give myself away."* As seen earlier, Harding definitely did not have a problem writing to Carrie. And it's no telling what type of spicy brown notes and letters he sent to young Nan to get her so crazy. It's too bad that she naively destroyed her letters, but at least she had the good sense to write the book.

VICTIMS OF THE IMMIGRATION RESTRICTION ACT

Harding really failed-for-white when he showed his three-quarters of white blood by doing a very "white" thing. He endorsed the Immigration Restriction Act of 1921 which was signed to legally close the doors to a select group of Europeans into America. It was not restricted to Anglo-Saxons. This restriction was only for the so-called poor and persecuted Europeans. They were Italians, Slavics, and Jews. Whether he realized it or not, many Italians, Slavics, and Jews' actions in history have been just as white (although all three are a dark people) as the Anglo-Saxons' actions by fighting against the freedom of Africans in war, in enslavement, and media exhibitions (The Nation of Islam, Historical Research Department, *The Secret Relationship Between Blacks and Jews*, vol. 1, 1991). Originally, the word "slave" was applied to white people. The word "slave" comes from the word "Slav", a Russian people captured by the Germans. Therefore Harding, at this time, may as well have invited the other races into Amerikkka also — since he, or somebody, was apparently trying to maintain some type of white American "status quo." It was a very "slavish" act for Harding to give approval and sign papers to keep out so-called undesirables. The famous writer, F. Scott Fitzgerald, wrote in a letter this same year (1921) that "The negroid streak creeps northward to *defile* [Author italics] the Nordic race. Already the Italians have the souls of blackamoors. Raise the bars of immigration and permit only Scandinavians, Teutons, Anglo-Saxons and Celts to enter ... I believe at last in the white man's burden. We [white people] are as far above the modern Frenchmen as he is above the Negro."

Harding was a victim in America. "As long as white supremacy exists, **all** non-white persons are **victims** of White Supremacy. Those who willfully and deliberately **cooperate** with White Supremacy are Victims, as well as those who **resist** it" (Fuller, Neely, *The United Independent Compensatory Code*, p. 40). Kurland stated on page 27, "While he was not racially biased, Warren Harding [like most of his fellow Americans (author insertion)] felt that it was wise and proper to preserve the ethnic *status quo*." What is the definition of an American to these people? A person who fears any other race? A person who makes claims of ownership in barbaric ways — like Americans did during the Jefferson-Jackson-Lincoln/Hamlin days? A person who feels that s/he is superior enough to own another person? A person who has stolen land, and yet feels that s/he can still keep someone else off of the land? A person who feels that if another isn't white then that person has a handicap? Are Americans a people who hide behind white robes and/or white masks? Imagine the real African's place in the minds of "Americans" in America. Actually we don't have to imagine it; we still live it. Remember, even Brother Lincoln tried to deport Blacks. Lincoln was a victim. He failed in his deportation attempt and he also failed-for-white. All of these Presidents, said to be Black, had been slicked by the cunning of white supremacist attitudes.

TULSA, OKLAHOMA AND "HOW TO PASS FOR WHITE"

Three months into Harding's term as president of the United States, on May 31, 1921, the all African and very prosperous business district of Tulsa, Oklahoma was bombed from the air by angry white militant mobs. This act caused the total destruction of "Little Africa." This district was also fondly known as the "Wall Street" for Blacks. This was considered one of the nation's worst race riots, and it lasted 24 hours. Three hundred African-Americans were killed, and more than one thousand three hundred homes were burned to the ground. This community had produced some of the richest African-Americans in the United States. They operated their own banks, businesses, and more importantly, their own schools. This was a planned destruction of economic progress for African-Americans. This city, which became the first city to segregate telephone booths, boosted a ku klux klan membership of 3,000. When the very proud African people made an attempt to rebuild their community and their businesses, a city ordinance was passed that stipulated a new railroad would "have" to run straight through this Black economic district. Another whitewashed law was passed that made it impossible for these African-Americans to rebuild their homes. Many of these Africans had to resort to living in tents — even in the cold of the winter. Very few regained their prosperity, and today this area of the Tulsa African-American business district is a ghost town (*Tony Brown's Journal [Magazine]*, "The First U.S. City to be Bombed," First Quarter, 1986, p. 14; Cortner, Richard C., *A Mob Intent on Death*). This is so ironic, especially since there had not been a president said to Black in the white house since Lincoln. Harding was now in office as Chief Executive, and many people had read about the possibility of his being of African ancestry, and with a prosperous group of Africans in the city of Tulsa at this time, it was a wonder to many white racists what these "blacks" were going to do next? The violent acts of these white militant mobs (and their discriminatory attitudes or whatever their problem was) were arrogant, sick, murderous, and ultimately, fear. Walter F. White was a very light-skinned African-American living Tulsa, Oklahoma who, in this case, "passed-for-white" in order "to investigate the circumstances of the riot." He was an NAACP assistant secretary, and after his III (in-house infiltrated investigation), he later wrote an article in the October 18, 1919, *Chicago Daily News* stating what he learned. He found, of course, that there was a definite conspiracy to riot, destroy Black businesses and exploit African-Americans in general (Cortner, p. 179).

DEATHBED CONFESSION OF A PREACHER

In 1922 Harding made a speech while traveling in the South. He said that it was now the appropriate time for the Southern states to allow literate Blacks (he said Negroes) to vote. Here was a man whom white people had been telling all his life that he was illiterate, now here he was doing the same thing to so-called illiterate Blacks what white people had done to him, i.e., belittling them. What constitutes an illiterate person anyway? People who cannot read and write can still listen and understand much, and they can take someone whom they trust and who can read with them to the voting booth. But Harding's statement could indicate one other thing: that is, Harding did not consider himself

semi-illiterate as many of the historians and writers claimed
he was. Harding had already voted and apparently did not
consider himself totally limited in his intelligence. Harding's
contention and statement that Blacks should be allowed to
vote brought back the whispers and tabloids that Harding
was part Black — otherwise, why would he suggest that
Blacks had rights and a right to vote in America? Harding
did not feel that segregation should end, but he did feel that
Blacks had rights as Americans. This was a pretty strong
statement to make, because during this time there was a
serious resurgence of the ku klux klan. The ku klux klan
membership was four million (i.e., 4,000,000) in the United
States at this time. But we must learn and we must remember that according to Stephen Kennedy, a white male guest
on *Tony Brown's Journal* (the television talk show, 1989), said
that Harding had very strong associative ties with the ku
klux klan, and that they had even visited Harding in the
White House. Mr. Kennedy's exact words, on this segment
entitled, "Inside the Klan," were:

> "In the late forties, I was in the Manhattan area, and
> heard of a life-long imperial ... Chaplain of the
> klan, named Reverend Alden Young. And Rev-
> erend Young was in the hospital on his deathbed,
> and the only klansman who came to see him had
> wanted to borrow ten dollars. So he was down on
> the klan at that point, and on the other hand, the
> Catholic priest in the hospital had been nice to him,
> so he was getting religion at the last moment and
> was willing to tell me what he knew about the klan.
> And one of the things he told me was being a part
> of a five man imperial induction team, they initiated
> President Warren Harding into the klan, in a cere-
> mony, in the Green Room of the White House, and
> there were great details. They were so nervous, they
> had forgotten their klan bible and had to borrow the
> White House bible in order to administer the oath,
> and in deference to his being President, they
> allowed him to lean his, ah, elbow on the desk as he
> knelt on the floor and swore to obey every com-
> mand of the imperial wizard of the ku klux klan;

this is the President of the United States [pause] we're talking about. And as [his] token of appreciation, he gave each member of the team, ah, ah, war department in those days, a license so that they would not have to stop for red lights in the future ... As you say, America was literally kluxed; they had control of a half dozen state legislatures" during the Harding years. (Additional Reference: Kennedy, *The Klan Unmasked*).

So, reader, you decide. Was Harding cunning, klanning or scared? (See the paragraph on Harding as a Victim in America, p. 199).

RATINGS

"In 1948, Arthur M. Schlesinger, Sr. asked a group of fifty-five leading historians and political scientists to rate the presidents of the United States ... scale: ... E would indicate failure. Only two presidents received E ratings. One was Ulysses S. Grant and the other was Warren Gamaliel Harding ... Fourteen years later, in 1962, Professor Schlesinger took a second poll to see if the passage of time had altered the experts' opinion. This time, seventy-five experts were asked to rate the presidents ... Ulysses S. Grant and Warren Harding were rated as failures (Kurland, p. 3). As mentioned, we must learn to de-code white historians' purpose. For example, Schlesinger decided to wait until 1962 before doing another presidential poll. Who had just gotten out of office? Answer: Dwight D. Eisenhower (see the next chapter on Eisenhower). Dwight D. Eisenhower was not rated a failure (E), and I do not know what he was rated in this poll, but a "D" indicates below average on these political expert's scale. Harry S. Truman did not feel that Eisenhower, a Republican, did much as a President in the fifties. And during the twenties, although the Republican party lost their chance at gaining the trust of Africans living in America, Harding did attempt to examine the race relations question. "His request for an interracial commission died in a congressional committee; his proposal for an anti-lynching bill was killed by a Senate filibuster; his hope for an early military withdrawal from Haiti" as demanded by the African community, was stopped by the State Department (Murray, pp. 402-403). Harding received numerous threats stating that he was marked for death. So what's a Black President to do? Harding did not fret.

Kurkland, the author of: *Warren Harding - A President Betrayed By Friends*, writes that, "President Harding's historical reputation has increased in stature, ... His one notable failure was his inability to say "no" to his friends. It proved to be his one tragic fault" (p. 4). Harding did hire many of his friends into his administration. This decision was indeed tragic. Harding was known to be an honest man. The criminal actions of his "Ohio gang" friends, especially Secretary of Treasury Andrew Mellon and Attorney General Harry Daugherty, upset him greatly.

GETTING TIED & TIRED

Before his death, Harding seemed to be losing his jovial manner and confident demeanor. He was also beginning to look older than his age (Means, p. 260). Harding had much stress, strain, and depression from the scandals and corrupt administration during his term in office. Harding once stated that, "I knew this job would be too much for me ... I am not worried about my enemies. It is my friends who are giving me trouble" (Garrison, p. 74). "Before he left on his Western tour, Harding had a premonition of betrayal and of death ... he exploded with the words, "My God, this is a hell of a job! I have no trouble with my enemies. I can take care of my enemies all right. But my damn friends, my God-damn friends ..., they're the ones that keep me walking the floor nights!" (*The Autobiography of William Allen White*, N.Y.: Macmillan, 1946, p. 619).

Hardings' Interior Secretary, Albert Fall, was the first cabinet member to go to prison for crimes committed while in office. The head of the Veterans' Bureau was caught getting money from war surplus products, selling drugs to drug dealers, and taking kickbacks from purchasing agents. This man's assistant committed suicide and left a note for the president to read. Harding never opened it. Another personal aide to a high officer in the Harding Administration committed suicide. And others were convicted for taking bribes.

In 1924 and for a decade after, many scandals were exposed that started in the Harding administration. The Teapot Dome, for one, was a naval oil reserve in Wyoming that had been set aside for government emergency use. Then many people began to notice that in 1923, Albert Fall was living a little better than a public servant salary could afford him. Fall allowed a big oil company to tap into the Teapot Dome reserve in exchange for a little over a fourth of a million dollars and a herd of cattle. He got another $100,000 for illegally allowing Pan American Petroleum and Transport Company to tap into the Elk Hills reserve in California.

PARTY HARDY

His-storians continue to allege that Harding was of mediocre intelligence. Has anyone pointed out to them that it takes a lot of intelligence to become a Black president of the United States in 1920's racist America? Many say that he had great presence (Sinclair, p. 297) and looked a lot like a president. Sinclair says on page 298 of his book that "Harding clung foolishly" to worldly high powered people "because he was too weak to give up the nostalgic joys of his life, the parties of cronies, and the stories of the small-town smoking room. He was not ruthless enough to be President." In hopes of not stereotyping Harding, or Blacks in general here, being President is not going to stop any black person from not having some type of recreation, so it must be pointed out that Harding was the first President to have an official entertainment fund (Garrison, p. 210) to party. This is considered a compliment of good sense ... if one knows how to party (vacation, etc.) sensibly in order to keep the stress level down from being an African living in a racist America — and especially if you're the President.

Harding thought his tolerance of his old friends in office as an amiable weakness, not as a national disaster as many felt it was. Harding's cabinet member friends were referred to as a "gang." Murray, a more sympathetic, and perhaps truthful, Harding biographer, felt that Harding's personal life, partying, and golfing had little to do with his success or failure in administrative decision making. He states that it is unfair to epitomize the Harding years as the most destructive and bankrupt years of any other President. He states that the political records show otherwise. He asserts that "the Harding administration's achievements were rather impressive — the peace treaties, the Budget Bureau, the Washington Conference, agricultural legislation ... The period 1921-1923 was one of crisis and readjustment — these were years of tremendous economic and social change." This was true especially after the animosity of the Wilson administration (Murray, p. 533). According to white standards of politics, the Harding administration was very successful; although most of the literature does not attest to this fact. Harding as a calm, political mediator contributed to this success. Murray states that, "Harding, more than his two successors, was actually 'president of all the people'" (p. 535). Father of all peoples, as are all African men?

MARCUS GARVEY

These crises and social-change years during the Harding administration were important years for Africans who happened to live in America also. Many of these changes of lives and attitudes were due to the Honorable Marcus M. Garvey. Garvey moved from Jamaica to New York City in 1916. By 1920, he had geniusly, creatively, and lovingly started the Universal Negro Improvement Association (UNIA). This organization attracted the attention of Africans (and whites) nationwide and worldwide. The Garvey Movement was awesome. His philosophy was race pride, economical sufficiency and self-sufficiency. He dedicated many of his speeches and writings to "Africa for the Africans," believing that all Africans all over the world had a cultural, spiritual, and common-goal connection. In 1920, Garvey had formally established himself "Provisional President of Africa." He even appointed a cabinet.

In July, 1921, Marcus Garvey returned from a trip to Central America and the Caribbean. Upon his return, he recorded two brief speeches on a 78 rpm record. In his first speech he comments on the problems he had obtaining a return visa to the United States. In his second speech he talks about the "Explanation of the Objects of the Universal Improvement Association." Garvey was superior in speech-making and a great orator, yet these two speeches are the only known recordings of this marvelous man's voice. These recordings have been re-engineered from a second generation copy of Marcus Garvey's original record. (For more information on the copyright owners of these rare tapes and the sole distributor of these tapes, please see the Bibliography/Reference section in the back of this book under: Garvey, Marcus - Speeches).

In 1921, in Birmingham, Alabama, President Harding said in a speech, sounding a lot like Abraham Lincoln, that there are inescapable differences between the races which would cause them to never be able to live together equally. Marcus Garvey immediately sent a telegram, which was widely pub-licized, congratulating Harding on this statement. Concerned African-Americans adopted a resolution condemning Hard-ing for this racist statement and criticized Garvey for his endorsement. W.E.B. Du Bois and other African-American leaders were exceedingly upset and confused about this very serious issue. Then Garvey visited the ku klux klan in June, 1922. Concerned African-Americans were really outdone when Garvey agreed with the imperial wizard that Amerikkka is the white man's country. Then all hell broke loose again when Garvey made a statement in North Car-olina that white southerners should be thanked for "lynch-ing" race pride into the African-American. Du Bois called Garvey a name; then Garvey called Du Bois a name (Clarke & Jacques, *Marcus Garvey-and the Vision of Africa*, pp. 225-226). And this went on and on. Although we all possess a certain genius within us — still, in any event, it might take the intelligence of the African genius, God of Kemet, and Philosopher, Imhotep, to understand all of the Honorable Marcus Garvey's views and actions. The actual visit to the klan headquarters was simply too much for many histori-cally-ignorant and average-thinking citizens to understand. But we must keep in mind, that one way to keep an enemy down is to infiltrate their quarters and get a better look and understanding of their work and purpose. In order to get a better and more in-depth understanding of Garvey, the Man, one needs to sit at the feet of Elder Dr. John Henrik Clarke,

African leader ourstorian/historian, writer and poet for
months and listen ... without interrupting.

These events occurred the same year that Garvey was
arrested and indicted wrongly in a conspired mail fraud case.
The U.S. Government was threatened by the additional social
and political changes that Garvey may be able to erect. In
May 1923 the Honorable Marcus M. Garvey went to trial in
New York City. The case against him was politically inclined,
with mail fraud as a cover. Garvey stated that he was confined in the Tombs prison for several months awaiting a decision from the Appellate Court. Marcus Garvey said, "It was
through the good office of President Harding that I was
allowed out on bail; when the question of bail came up the
trial judge ... insisted on a bond of $50,000, but President
Harding prevailed with the district attorney, Colonel Hay-
wood, and I was released on a bond of $1,500" (Clarke, p.
149). Good office? Did Garvey feel a connection with Harding
in some way? Why did Harding do this for Garvey? (See Bib-
liography-Reference section under Garvey, Marcus - Mail
Fraud Transcripts, on how to obtain more information and
the actual transcripts pertaining to this case.)

Anyway, in June, 1923 Garvey was convicted, and
received the maximum sentence of five years in prison. This
is usually the plight of an African man living in America
who understands deeply who he is and shows it. Two
months later, August 2, 1923, Warren G. Harding died.

THE DEATH OF WARREN HARDING

When Harding died, he was "mourned more than any
other President since Abraham Lincoln" (Sinclair, p. 283).
Harding died (or was murdered) in 1923 before the major
White House Administration corruptions and Harding's
"gang" were exposed, which was in 1924. Harding did see
enough to spiritually weaken him to a point of looking older
than his age and asking for a resignation as president of the
United States. Harding's death is a mystery because many
historians and writers have alluded to the possibility of Mrs.
Florence Klinger Harding poisoning her husband's food.
Gaston Means said that Mrs. Harding stated to him "indirectly" that she did this to save Harding from the embar-

rassment of the recent White House administration scandals that were about to surface. But some historians and writers feel that Mrs. Harding perhaps did this because her husband had had extramarital affairs and she was resentful, rejected and dejected. I concur with the last theory, in addition to the genetic or familial environmental possibility that she too harbored (consciously or unconsciously) the same type of racial feelings as her father, and therefore, it wasn't very difficult for Mrs. Harding, who had her own psychological problems anyway, to simply think: *"Do away with the nigger."* Some of her psychological problems stemmed from a seemingly severe type A personality (e.g., nervous, excitable, hyper); her husband's obvious lack of interest in her as a woman; being a woman who never cared much for her own biological child for the sake of a love that was not returned; a father who disapproved of her husband and therefore disapproved of her; another woman birthing her husband's child, while she had no children with him herself; the fact that her husband desired her best friend, and not her; and last, the fact that her dignity and respect were about to explode because of the scandals of the Presidential Administration while she served as First Lady of the White House. Mrs. Harding fumed after discovering that Warren Harding had fathered a child, "... I ought to kill them both ... That's what I ought to do ... They deserve it ... They are not fit to live ..." (Means, p. 124). In a book entitled: *Secrets of the White House,* by Mrs. Jeffray, published by Cosmopolitan Book Corporation, much light is shed on the personality of Mrs. Harding. Mrs. Jeffray was a White House housekeeper during six administrations. She had obtained the experience to be considered an expert in the study of White House wives. Mrs. Jeffray was able to study Mrs. Harding's idiosyncratic behavior and strangeness "at very close range" (Means, p. 291).

Gaston Means said that he was a private detective for Mrs. Harding and was assigned officially to her while she was First Lady. She petitioned him to prove that Harding could not have children, and therefore couldn't be the father of Nan's baby. She stated that she had already proven that she was fertile, because she had already birthed a child. What Mrs. Harding apparently did not take into consideration was that she was older now and she also had some medical problems. Neither did she consider the fact that if the man wasn't into the act of making love seriously and was perhaps doing this out of husbandly duty, then the "spirits," the Gods, the "cosmos," bad timing, whatever, or even Harding's will and determination that this should not happen possibly caused Mrs. Harding to not become impregnated. Warren Harding probably thought the possibility of the child being darker than the public expected would definitely "blow his cover," or mask. In addition to this, statistically, the probability of Florence Harding conceiving was perhaps against her since Harding possibly found all types of reasons not to make love to her often. Gaston Means stated that he couldn't imagine the couple even making love. He too felt that Harding was apprehensive about having a child with his wife because of his Negro "taint," and that he probably felt safer having a child with a mistress. At this time, Harding was also older with health problems. He had heart ailments, arterio-sclerosis and a blood pressure above 200 (Chancellor, p. 224). Anyway, Means found all of Harding's medical records, and they all indicated that Harding could have many children, and with Nan being a young vibrant, healthy, and willing woman, she and Harding apparently had no problem getting pregnant, and this was only after fifteen or sixteen months of lovemaking without living together. Mrs. Harding wouldn't hear of it and told Means that she would get their personal physician, Sam Sawyer, to make a written statement that she could bear children and therefore that meant that Harding could not. Means thought that this woman was losing her mind. And she probably was at this point in her unstable life. She went on to tell Means that Dr. Sawyer had already informed them that Harding could not father a child because of some complications of mumps in his youth. Harding's father, who was a physician, had medical records that proved otherwise, and they were in the possession of Gaston Means. When he tried to show them to Mrs. Harding, she refused to look at them. This is a perfect example of "white-folk denial syndrome;" this same sort of syndrome is going on today regarding the truth about the history of the world and Black folks' place in it.

CALVIN COOLIDGE, 30th President of the U.S.

Calvin Coolidge succeeded Harding as President of the United States. He proudly admitted that his mother (and therefore so does he) has some dark mixed blood ancestry, i.e., Indian. Coolidge said that he has Indian blood running through his veins (Stevens, p. 10). There is no substantial information to support the two rumors that I've heard recently that Coolidge was actually of African ancestry, except for the fact that: "By 1800, the New England Indian was hardly any longer an Indian" because they mixed often with Blacks or whites. Calvin Coolidge was born and raised in Vermont, a New Englander he liked to call himself. "The mixture of blood arises far more frequently from connection with Negroes than with whites," as confirmed in the works of many hard-writing ourstorians. Most Indians from the northern East coast to the southern East coast are now largely African, i.e., African-American (Morse, J.E., *Report to the Commissioner of Indian Affairs,* 1829; Rogers, *Sex and Race,* vol. II, pp. 355-357. Also see: Van Sertima's work; and Katz, L., *Black Indians: A Hidden Heritage).* India/Indio means black, dark.

Calvin Coolidge's mother's maiden name was "Moor," meaning black. (For more information on the Moors, see the Hamlin chapter.) Victoria J. Moor was born in 1846, Vermont. She died when Coolidge was only twelve years of age. A probing inquiry from a reporter asked Coolidge to reveal "the man behind the mask" to him. The reporter/writer, William Allen White, went on to write that "There was a man behind the mask ... Behind the mask he had a private life. Coolidge revered his mother. He said of his mother: "She was of a very light and fair complexion with a rich growth of brown hair ..." (Kent, Z., *Calvin Coolidge — Encyclopedia of Presidents,* p. 13; McCoy, D., Calvin Coolidge, pp. 296-297 & p. 5) Any genetic (Indian, African or whatever) or any psychological element could have been behind Coolidge's mask.

When Calvin was a young boy, his grandfather wished to impress upon him the importance of owning land. So loving a practical joke, old grandfather granted a young Calvin Coolidge forty acres (Kent, p. 17) minus the mule. Calvin

Coolidge's life and personality are very similar to that of Abraham Lincoln's, minus the sick father. Coolidge's father was very good to him. Of course, he was his biological father, too. Calvin Coolidge also had a three letter nickname, "Cal." He was sickly, like "Abe." He had a sister who died at a young age. After his mother's death, he had a mother-figure (an aunt) who taught him the importance of education. He was an introvert. He was a lawyer. He was president. His wife was from a well-to-do family, and an extrovert. He was witty. And he absolutely adored his dark mother; he always carried a picture of her. J.A. Rogers stated that the famous African-American dancer, Josephine Baker, looks more Indian than most Indians (Rogers, *Sex and Race*, vol. II, p. 357. See the pictures of Josephine Baker and Victoria Josephine Moor Coolidge on page 219 of this book).

After the Coolidge administration, Charles Curtis became the 31st vice president of the United States. This was during the Hoover administration, although there was a drive against Curtis as Hoover's running mate. Curtis also had "Indian" blood. J.A. Rogers was a young historian during this time, and noticing everything of color around him, he noticed that, to him, Curtis looked more Black than white or Indian (Rogers, Sex and Race, vol. II, p. 363). There were several articles written to attest to Curtis' Indianness. One article was titled, "From teepee to White House" (*Digest*, Nov. 12, 1927). Another article was titled, "Heap Big Chief" (*American Mercury*, August, 1929). Curtis was one of Harding's poker playing buddies. Neither Calvin Coolidge nor Charles Curtis have been named as one of the six presidents titled for this book, but I've conversed with so many Black people who are forever trying to impress upon me their unAfricanness because of their so-called Indian blood.

Calvin Coolidge pardoned Marcus Garvey from the Government's mail fraud scam in 1927.

THE YEAR 2014

When the new president, Calvin Coolidge and his wife, Grace Coolidge, arrived in the White House in 1923, Mrs. Harding was destroying papers. Although as many as 325,000 Harding documents remain, it is believed by some researchers, writers, and historians that Mrs. Harding destroyed most of her husband's letters, documents, and other papers. The remaining papers are available for researchers at the Ohio Historical Society. Harding's love letters to Carrie Phillips will be available in the year 2014. Nan Britton's book about Harding, *The President's Daughter*, can be found in many large community and university libraries.

NANCITIS

Donald Regan, chief of staff to Ronald Reagan wrote that Nancy Reagan conferred with astrologer Joan Quigley about President Reagan's schedule. Quigley wrote that Nancy Reagan used many of her ideas. She was angered when Mrs. Reagan denied that she used Quigley's ideas in important presidential and political decisions. Mrs. Harding also used to seek out the advice of a so-called psychic by the name of Madame Maria. This woman would later on declare that the White House national government revolved around her psychic powers and the advice that she had given to Mrs. Harding. According to a housekeeper, Mrs. Harding was said to have been the dominant power in the White House, not Warren Harding. Madame Maria told a superstitious Mrs. Harding that the President would die by poisoning at the hands of an enemy close to him (Sinclair, p. 295). Was this intimate enemy his own wife? Was this an innocent or evil suggestion that an already emotional and fragile mind could not handle?

A PRESIDENT'S STRANGE DEATH

Mrs. Harding was said to be the only person in the San Francisco, California hotel room with President Harding at the time of his death. Harding's death took place one day after returning from a trip to Alaska. He did indeed have a rather strange death. It was first reported that he died of a heart attack, then it was later stated that he died from food poisoning. If so, was this an intentional poisoning?

Dr. Sawyer said that the cause of death was a cerebral hemorrhage, but when other doctors arrived at the scene, they disagreed (Russell, p. 591). It was later stated that Dr.

Sawyer was also in this hotel room when Harding died. There has been many questions regarding Harding's death. His death was a shock to the public and he was mourned deeply and widely.

Gaston Means stated that he had a private conversation with Mrs. Harding whereas she indicated *indirectly* that she had "something" to do with Harding's death. She told Gaston Means that everything was closing in on her and her beloved Wur'ren. There were White House scandals and rumors concerning the Department of Justice. More and more associates were now aware of the Harding/Nan Britton affair and their child, and Mrs. Harding had also caught Harding depressed and writing a letter to Nan Britton. Mrs. Harding intercepted the letter. Then she said something very strange to Means; she said, "No — I have no regrets." (Means, pp. 260). She told him that she was alone with Harding for about ten minutes in the hotel room, and that it was time for his medicine. She told Means that she gave him his "medicine," then Harding lay back on his pillow. Harding suddenly opened his eyes wide and looked directly into Amos Kling's daughter's face — his wife, Florence Kling de Wolfe Harding. Means asked Mrs. Harding, "You think — he knew?" She answered, "Yes, I think he knew. Then — he sighed and turned his head away — over — on the pillow … After a few minutes — I called for help. The papers told the rest" (Means, pp. 260-261). Please note that research and literature indicate that Gaston Means seemed to have had some mental imbalances also. This does not negate the fact that many of these incidences ring true for various research and historical reasons.

After Harding's funeral in Marion, Ohio, Florence Kling Harding left immediately, walking determinedly with her mourning mask thrown back, her head held high, with no tears in her eyes. She was accompanied by Dr. Sawyer. Amos Kling's daughter had finished her crying, and was headed for Washington to finish destroying those papers.

On September 24, 1924, Dr. Sawyer died in a manner almost identical to that of the death of Warren G. Harding. Did he have to be silenced about something? Mrs. Harding was at Sawyer's home when he was found dead. What was she doing there? And adding to these strange occurrences or coincidences, exactly eight weeks after Sawyer's death, Mrs. Harding was found dead in Sawyer's Marion, Ohio home as well.

HARDING FINALLY RESTS

Warren G. Harding was buried under two tons of black granite stone on his hometown land. As far back as the 1700's the Hardings were erecting gravestones for their family members made of marble and specifically in the shape of the an obelisk. It is said that this attested to the "substance" of George Harding (Russell, p. 25). The indigenous and African name for an obelisk is "Teke-nu."

The original and first Teke-nu was erected in the Before Christ (B.C.) era, in Ancient Kemet by the Goddess Aset (Isis) in honor of her perfect-Black Brother, Asaru (Osiris), the god of resurrection. According to Dr. Yosef ben-Jochannan, Dr. Charles S. Finch, III and other great scholars of ourstory, many features of Christianity derived from the teachings and worship of Asaru, the African/Egyptian God (See: ben-Jochannan, and Finch — Bibliography and Reference section). I wonder if Warren G. Harding was fortunate enough to "go on to these ancestors?"

From left to right: President **Warren G. Harding**, his wife **Florence de Wolfe
Harding, Mrs. Grace Coolidge** and Vice President **Calvin Coolidge** *(Courtesy
Library of Congress).*

"Coolidge with Indians", Calvin Coolidge, front row, third from the left
(Courtesy, Library of Congress).

Te-Ke-nu (Misnomered) Washington Monument and Obelisk *(BaKhufu Archives 1992)*.

MARCUS GARVEY

The Garvey Paper's Project, Professor Robert Hill *(UCLA)*.

Carter G. Woodson.

An African woman living in India, the ***Bonda Woman.***

Victoria Josephine Moor, Calvin Coolidge's mother and **Josephine Baker,** the 1920's famous dancer.

Lincoln blessing brothers **Harding** and **Coolidge** through the mask of time. A Harding campaign picture, July 30, 1920 (*Courtesy Library of Congress*).

220

Carrie Phillips, Harding's girlfriend.

Warren G. Harding and his Black uncle, **Oliver Harding**, *Abbott's Monthly, September, 1932* and *J.A. Rogers' Pamphlet cover (The Five Negro Presidents)*.

DWIGHT D. EISENHOWER

34th President, USA

Dwight David Eisenhower, whose given name is David Dwight Eisenhower, was born October 14, 1890 in Denison, Texas. Eisenhower would later affectionately be called "Ike" by many. Both names will be used interchangeably throughout this chapter. Eisenhower was President of the United States from January 20, 1953 to January 20, 1961. It had been twenty years since the United States had a Republican president in office. Eisenhower asserted that the Democrats had been in office too long.

Eisenhower was very much loved by many who thought he was one of the greatest presidents that the United States has ever had. But like Harding, there were others who said that Eisenhower was one of the worst presidents that the United States has ever put into office. One author said that Ike did nothing in his whole eight years in the White House. He said that Ike showed that the country does not "need" a President (Parmet, p. ix). However, with the numerous positive historical and literary documentation available on Eisenhower, this tells us, or rather implies, that much of the American public feels he was one of the best leaders ever.

Dwight David Eisenhower was born on a thunderous and stormy Texas day in his parents' home. David Jacob and Ida Stover Eisenhower were the parents of Dwight "Ike" Eisenhower. Dwight Eisenhower's father carried a double Beta Israel (Jewish-type) name. Dwight's parents were said to be of German and Swiss ancestry, respectively — maybe. David and Ida Eisenhower had seven sons, Arthur, Edgar, Dwight, Roy, Paul, Earl, and Milton. Roy died when he was almost two years of age. The Eisenhowers had no daughters.

Although the ancestry of Eisenhower's mother as the carrier of the most recent African blood in the Eisenhower family is the main premise of this section, it would be remiss to exclude the possibility of Eisenhower's paternal side as having a background of African ancestry also. As the research on Eisenhower's father's background began, the information found made the "possibility" prevalent. One might say, "But anything is possible." And I would like to express to One that, "I agree."

Eisenhower states in his autobiography, *at ease: Stories I Tell My Friends, page 56, that his parents did not talk a lot about their ancestors who arrived in America on the "good ship"* Europa in 1741. *(Author's note: Europa was an African Queen from whom Europeans designated the name of their country, Europe.)* Eisenhower expressed that his parents were aware of their past, but were concentrating more on their present survival and responsibilities. He mentions on this same page that the name "Eisenhower" translates essentially to "iron" and "hewer." He states that, in original German, it should be pointed out that eisenschmidt means "blacksmith," whereas "Eisenhower" was more like an iron artist, e.g., the making of weapons, armor, or other metal ornaments (p. 56). If "Eisenhower" means "iron artist," then it also means "blacksmith," for a blacksmith is a person who works with iron or metal using a hammer and/or forge to shape weapons and many other ornaments such as horseshoes. Word clues are a literary substance that can led one to the truth. Blacksmithing was a trade that many political prisoners (slaves) perfected and were able to buy their freedom with funds from this trade. Professor Franz Boas, an American anthropologist, was convinced as he wrote that Africans were the first in iron technology and culture. He confirms:

> "Neither ancient Europe, nor ancient Western Asia, nor ancient China knew Iron, and everything points to its introduction from Africa. At the time of the great African discoveries toward the end of the past century, the trade of the blacksmith was found all over Africa, from north to south and from east to west. With his simple bellows and a charcoal fire reduced the ore that is found in many parts of the continent and forged implements of great usefulness and beauty.
>
> (The Atlanta University Leaflet, No. 19 — Reference, see: Jackson, p. 63)

MEDU NETCHER

With my enormous interest in Kemet (Egypt, Africa), and since I'm studying the ancient language of the Gods and Goddesses called Medunetcher (better known as hiero-glyphs to many), I thought it would be interesting to research that area of the Eisenhower name also. I instinc-tively realized that this name would somehow be connected to this ancient language (as most things are anyway). What I found was interesting ...

𝕌 (h ꜥ w). In the Medunetcher language, this symbol denotes a weapon, axe. It's shape is similar to a shield. The word, hꜥ w, is pronounced "shew," like "hew." It means the carrier of metal, iron, copper and bronze (weapons; the axe). The symbol is a determinative and dates back to Dynasty III in Kemet. This symbol (determinative) is placed at the end of the Old Kingdom Medunetcher word "axe," pronounced "hew." Definition: Carpenter, to use the axe; to hew. The instrument used for hewing wood was made from iron or metal. In Dynasty XII, "axe" became ꝫkhw, pronounced **ah-q-howe(r)**; this sounds very similar to Ei-sen-hower. The Medunetcher connotation is written ⟆⟐⟐. The "a" and the "e" are often used interchangeably; so are the "w" and the "u." Note the more modern-type axe (determinative) at the end of the Medunetcher word (BaKhufu, "The Mystery Teachings of the Temple of Ast" [notes]; Gardiner, *Egyptian Grammar*, pp. 490 & 511).

JOSHOWER/JOSHUA

Dwight D. Eisenhower's paternal ancestors have spelled their name several ways, such as, Eisenhauer, Isenhauer, and even Joshower (Joshua) — all of which means literally "iron hewer" (Davis, p. 12) from ancient times. The ancient use of iron and iron smelting began in Africa, dating back as far as Dynasty III - Kemet (as mentioned above), 200 B.C. in Nigeria, and 650 B.C. in Nubia (Van Sertima, p. 263). Early Iron Age technology was utilized by many Africans in Cen-tral Africa of which many of these so-called Bantu-speaking Africans were descendants of peoples from the Cameroon. Their Iron Technology dates back to the seventh century

B.C. (Van Noten & Raymeakers, *Scientific American*, June, 1988, p. 104). The word clue, "Joshower" (mentioned above) is pronounced "Joshua." Remember the interchange of usage for the "a" and "e," and the "w" and "u."

Joshua was born in Kemet and was the son of Nun. He succeeded Moses. Joshua fought in battle with blades of armor. Before Joshua ordered the job of hewing water and wood to his captured enemies, this chore had been attributed to his own congregation. (See: The Old Testament - Joshua, 1:14, 6:19, and 9:27 for information on Joshua and his tribe as hewers of iron, wood, and water.) Ahmed Osman, the author of *The House of the Messiah*, contends that the ancient military leader "Joshua was modeled on the Pharaoh [of Kemet], who lived about 1,350 years before Jesus" (*Washington Post*, "Author Says Jesus Was Really Tutankhamen," by: Heathcote, Graham, Religion Section, May 30, 1992, Gll). Most Jewish and African professors speak favorably of Osman's argument; most white ones do not. Osman, like Sigmund Freud, and many others before and after the two mentioned, also claim that Moses was actually Akhenaten of Kemet.

Many black and white theologians and writers have harped on the fact that Moses married an Ethiopian woman. So what? He was Black too. (Ra)Moses spent more than thirty years in Pharaoh's temple. He lived with the Black Egyptians "passing" as pharaoh's grandson. He looked African and was referred to as an Egyptian. Solomon also married an Ethiopian woman. All three, Solomon, Joshua and Moses, were Black men.

Joshua and Moses are the subjects of two age old African-American (not "Negro") spirituals: "Joshua fit de Battle of Jericho ... and the walls came tumbling down," and "Go Down Moses," respectively. The latter song starts with: "When Israel was in Egypt's land ... Way down in Egypt's land; Tell old Pharaoh, Let My People Go!" Dr. John Henrik Clarke contends that Pharaoh wasn't holding anyone, and anyone could have left on their own free will anytime that they pleased, just as they had walked in on their own free will.

Jesus was also a Black man — an African. The many pictures drawn of him do not show it, but this white image is now being challenged through Africentric writings — and drawings.

Frederick Douglass said in 1849 that Africans will never have "impartial" pictures drawn of them at the hands of white artists. It seems impossible for them to draw a black person like they actually see [or know] them; they always have to "grossly exaggerate" their features. Douglass went on to say, "'I am black but comely,'" is as true now as it was in the days of Solomon." Dr. Clarke contends that the dark and beautiful woman, Solomon's love interest, in "The Song of Solomon" probably said, "I am Black *and* comely," because during the days of Solomon and certainly today, there is no reason to apologize for being Black and Beautiful! Dr. Clarke goes on to assert that: "There is no proof in existence that Moses was a Jew. There is no proof in existence that he came out of the House of Levi" (Melanin Conference, April, 1988, City College, Harlem, New York).

AFRICA, GERMANY

During the 1700s and 1800s, in Germany (the Eisenhower's ancestral land — as far back as they know, or have written), there were so many German and African interracial relationships that there was a section called German Africa. Finally, in 1912 the German Reichstag legalized marriages between Africans and Germans (Rogers, *Your History,* p. 39; also J.A. Rogers, *Sex and Race,* 3 volumes). In the United States, there were so many German immigrants living in the Texas area during the Civil War that many of the Africans learned to speak the language fluently. There were German schools, churches, newspapers, and other organizations. Marcus Baum was a German Jew who served under General Kershaw. Baum made a reputation for himself as being loyal and brave. Other German soldiers "behaved gallantly at Egypt Station, Tennessee, ... before becoming prisoners of war (Davis, *The Civil War,* pp. 99 & 101). I had even heard rumors that Hitler was of a dark (Jewish) ancestry, and immediately disregarded the story as ludicrous until I read in the *Washington Post* a book review on a recently published book entitled, *Adolf Hitler,* by John Toland. The review states that according to CIA files, which have just recently become available, Hitler and Himmler (the commanding chief of the Final Solution) had always surrounded themselves with "tall, blond, blue-eyed subordinates." The reviewer said that the contents of the book also mention that "… Himmler planned to weed out dark Germans (like himself and Hitler) by "having sexual contact only with blonde women. The review goes on to state that:

> Similarly, Hitler's family tree, which appears in an early page, bears on his hatred for Jews. His paternal grandmother was Maria Anna Schicklgruber; his paternal grandfather is described as follows: "UNKNOWN, could be Johann Nepomunk Hiedler; his brother, Johann Georg Hiedler; or a Jew from Graz named Frankenberger of Frankenreither."
>
> (*Washington Post,* Sun., Feb. 16, 1992,
> Book World Section, p. 12.)

If these allegations are true of Hitler or Himmler, then these men also suffered from the same or similar type of psychological sickness as did the presidents referred to in this book. As mentioned in the Hamlin chapter, by reading old literature, one is more likely to find the truth, as long as decoding is understood. In some cases, possessing this talent isn't even necessary because the truth simply jumps off of the pages right at you. What follows here is another case (though spiked with some racist statements) of German and Jewish mixture. During Lincoln's term as President of the United States, in 1862, Karl Marx wrote in a letter to Friedrich Engels that an acquaintance of theirs descended from African people because this friend's head structure, his hair type and his obliging mannerisms proved it. Marx said, "It is now entirely clear to me that, as his cranial structure and hair type prove, Lassalle is descended from the Negroes who joined Moses' flight from Egypt (that is, assuming his mother, or his paternal grandmother, did not cross with a nigger). Now this union of Jewry and Germanism with the negro-like basic substance must necessarily result in a remarkable product. The officiousness of the fellow is also nigger-like" (Karl Marx, 1862, in a letter to Friedrich Engels). So Marx admits here, abet offensively, that the ancient Egyptians (sometimes called "gypsies" if they were wanderers) were Africans, and that Jews and Germans are "substances" from them. Marx did have the insight (or biological innateness) to see the "remarkable product" however.

JOSHOWER'S MENNONITES

Eisenhower's "Swiss-German" ancestors and parents were followers of a religion called Mennonites. The Greek misnomered "Memnon" comes to mind when discussing the name of this religion, Mennonites. The indigenous, African name for Memnon is "Pharaoh Amenhotop III." He was the Father of the original Theosopher on Monotheism (ben-Jochannan, *Abu Simbel - Ghizeh*, p. 242; reference: Freud, *Moses and Monotheism*). The Mennonites were a persecuted cult in their homeland of Germany, so Dwight D. Eisenhower's ancestors, the Eisenhauers, hastily relocated to Switzerland. They would later sail to Philadelphia, U.S.A. on the *Europa, as mentioned above.* Eisenhower's great grandfather moved to Elizabethville, Philadelphia, where his son, Jacob (Dwight Eisenhower's paternal grandfather, who also carried a Beta Israel name), would later build a beautiful spacious, nine room, red brick home, which still stands today. Jacob had a son by the name of David, who would later become the father of the thirty-fourth president of the United States. Jacob named his next son who was born in 1865 Abraham Lincoln. Abraham (a Beta Israel name) was a feisty person who would later become a veterinarian and who would eventually relocate to California. In March of 1878, the family sold their beautiful home for $8,500 and moved to Abilene, Kansas. "Wild Bill" Hickok was the town marshall. As residents of Abilene, the Eisenhower family was a part of a religious group called the River Brethen, a division of the Mennonites. The River Brethen were said to be a very organized group. Jacob's wife, Rebecca, came from a family of well-established River Brethens also. Jacob was scholarly and read as many books as he could. He opposed slavery and felt that the Civil War would cause a moral problem. Many authors refer to him as a pacifist, as David and Ida would later be considered. Jacob wanted his son, David, to establish himself as a farmer as his life's work. David wouldn't hear of it, and was determined to become an engineer. So with his father's blessing and money, he attended Lane College. At

Lane college, he met a nice-looking girl named Ida Elizabeth Stover. Ida and David both studied Greek and literature. Their studies began to demand less of their attention as they found themselves falling in love. They were married in 1885. (See David and Ida's wedding picture at the end of this chapter. This same picture can also be found in *Life Magazine*, April 28, 1952, p. 112, and also in their son's book: *at ease*.) The Eisenhowers lived an average life. They worked hard for their money and simple lifestyle, and were proud to be able to send their boys even to the local public schools.

HANNIBAL AGAIN

Dwight Eisenhower would become a very good athlete but not a very studious young man. He did enjoy mathematics and history classes though. At West Point, Eisenhower was somewhat of a mathematical wizard. Mathematics is a subject that we all should aspire to learn and understand, and to least understand its importance and stop running from it. Hannibal could not have been the military genius that he was without the understanding of important mathematical strategies and logical thinking; learning to think ahead is also very important. There are some people (adults!) still asking the question: "How can you help the people in the community by studying math?" This is a very sad question to have to ask anyone. Anyway, Hannibal was Ike's favorite war hero, and Eisenhower would call upon the strategic intelligence of this very popular African man the rest of life. Did young Eisenhower realize that this expert warrior was an African man? I think so. Eisenhower admits that he could have read literatures on the philosophies of life, but he preferred the armor and warrior literature of war.

During the Punic Wars, if Ike had wanted to be a part of Hannibal's military regime, he would have been obliged to fess up to his true ancestry, because Hannibal did not accept too many white people into his military camp. He said that most of the Europeans he tried to train like a true warrior were too slow to learn, and that they were afraid of the elephants (Reference: ben-Jochannan, *Africa: Mother of Western Civilization*, p. 534, plus Dr. Ben's other books).

1896-1898

In 1896, there was another type of war developing. It was a court war: Plessy vs. Ferguson. This was the controversy over separate railroad accommodations for Blacks and whites. When Eisenhower was a young schoolboy of eight years, with his history books, paper and pencil in hand, it is improbable that he learned about the Plessy vs. Ferguson controversy, or about the inventor of the pencil sharpener. He was an African-American by the name of J.L. Love. Love received his U.S. patent for the pencil sharpener on November 23, 1897. Eisenhower felt that he never acquired a very good penmanship — stating that his hands were made more for the gun and the axe than for pencils (Eisenhower, *at ease,* p. 95). A year later, in 1898, Abraham Lincoln Eisenhower, Abilene's veterinarian and Dwight's very lively uncle, sold his practice and moved to the sunsets of California. He sold his house to David and Ida. It was a modest two-story white-framed house on south Fourth Street with a three-acre tract. It provided a family garden and this is where Dwight D. Eisenhower learned how to plant and garden. Ida carefully planned how the garden would be used. The family raised its own produce and the boys sold it. When Dwight and his brothers did a good job working the garden fields, David would surprise them with baseball gloves and other sports paraphernalia (Neal, p. 13).

DWIGHT EISENHOWER'S FATHER OR THE SPIRIT OF RELIGION OR THE RELIGION OF SPIRIT

In the process of providing for, teaching and raising their children, David and Ida decided to relinquish their ties with the familial River Bethren group and searched for their own religions ... and spirituality. One of the groups they joined was called the Bible students. Sometimes they had prayer meetings at their house, and Ida played the piano as the group sang hymns; she loved music. Ida would eventually become a member of this religious group.

David Jacob Eisenhower's spiritual quest (and he has been given the benefit of the doubt here) led him to what many historians and theologists refer to as "mysticism."

David was uncomfortable reading a Bible in the English language. He said that reading the English version made him nervous (Eisenhower, *at ease*, p. 78). He always preferred to read the Greek Bible — of which the language, if not the actual contents of the Bible, was getting closer to the source of truth than his English bible version. He loved reading about travel, and it was imperative that he read about people who could think for themselves. His son, Edgar, said that his father read as though he were trying to retrace his steps back into his "ancestral self" (Miller, p. 65). One expression of David's readings and belief was a huge wall chart which he drew of the Kemetian (Egyptian) Pyramids of Ghizeh. This pyramid drawing was ten feet high and six feet wide. According to David, the chart contained prophecies for the future as well as testimony of some biblical events. Captivated by the "unusual" drawing, the Eisenhower sons spent hours "studying" their father's artistic creation (Neal, p. 13). Mysticism to many is a simple, yet complex "African Education System" to Africans — and others — who have studied their history, their true history (ourstory), extensively. Studying ourstory is pertinent to the understanding of truth, justice, and liberty for all. And this is a "mystery" for many and any people — yellow, brown, tan, black or white.

"Egypt, though subordinated to the Christian and biblical traditions on issues of religion and morality, was clearly placed as the source of all 'Gentile, or secular wisdom ... Greek civilization and philosophy derived from Egypt." The Greeks studied in Egypt (Bernal, Martin, *Black Athena, pp. 121). As you continue to read this chapter, you will see that Dwight Eisenhower, too, felt the first Holy Land (Egypt) was a special place.* Even so, he still seems to have had a "head problem" with his father. For example, in 1903 (two years after the birth of the great author and anthropologist, Zora Neale Hurston) when Eisenhower's hometown was flooded, Dwight's father, David, mentioned to him that the Ancient Egyptians considered the flooding of the Nile a Godsend. Dwight's thoughts were that he didn't care what his father thought, a flood was a flood, and their hometown was a mess (Eisenhower, *at ease*, p. 86). Dwight D. Eisenhower hardly ever spoke of his father. One of Dwight's best friends stated that, "It just wasn't his favorite subject." Dwight devoted a seventeen-page chapter to his mother in his book, *at ease;* he did not do the same for his father (Miller, p. 63). Dwight seems to have loved his father; it is questioned as to whether he liked him. David Eisenhower has been described as tall, muscular and broad-shouldered, with thick black hair, dark eyebrows and deep-set penetrating eyes. Dwight's father had large powerful hands and [in his young adult age] a large prominent chin (Ambrose, p. 16) similar to the looks of Hannibal Hamlin's chin during his young adult age. (This newfound comparison is interesting, although it has nothing whatsoever to do with whether either one of these men were Black or White.) Dwight Eisenhower's brother, Milton, said that Dwight's mind was very similar to his father's mind. They both tended to be totally logical — as logical as mathematics.

David Eisenhower did not seem to be a happy man. He also tended to be in a constant state of deep thought and few words, but he did discipline his boys when he felt that they needed it. David was well read, and Dwight admired his father for his love of education and his penmanship; although Dwight Eisenhower seemed to have negative feelings about his father as a good businessman. His father's failures in business encouraged Dwight to aspire to be the best that he could be. David Eisenhower's business did not necessarily fail; his business partner was a weak crook. After he had put up funds to get the business started, his partner could not face up to everyday business dilemmas. He stole the business money and ran. David Eisenhower never saw him again. Another story in the life of business partners.

While Dwight Eisenhower moaned the death of his father in 1942, he felt it impossible to find the time to attend his father's funeral. He did consign some quiet time for mourning. David Eisenhower, this nonconformist man of a few words, seems to have known more about the true history of the world than he cared or dared to discuss with his friends and family. Ida said after the death of her husband that she had never regretted marrying him. Was it necessary to say so?

IDA: IKE'S MOM

Dwight D. Eisenhower's mother, however, was a true love in her son's life. Dwight respected and admired his mother immensely. She had very ethnic looks and her ancestral background has been questioned. Literature (not genealogical research) points to her being from a Swiss background, and she could have been.

Elizabeth Link, Ida's mother, married Simon Stover in 1848. From the research that I gathered from the National Archives in Washington, D.C., 1810 - 1870 Census Data shows that there were numerous Black and white Links and Stovers in the Mount Sidney area of Virginia. After many attempts to secure the birth certificate of Ida Stover (or Sto-ever), I decided to cease my pursuit. Her parents' census information states that they were white, whether they both were white or not. Therefore, it is highly improbable that they would have anything different on their daughter's birth certificate. Ida was born on May 1, 1862 and named Elizabeth Ida Stover. She, like her mother, switched her name around too. David Dwight Eisenhower, Ida's son, would later do the same. Ida Stover is not listed in the 1870 census data, and the 1880 census data is lost. By the time 1900 arrives (the next census survey), Ida has left this Vir-ginia area, is married to David Eisenhower and lives in another state.

The Links owned, sold, and willed away many slaves. Before doing this, the old Links would give thanks to Amen (Link, pp. 786-787). Amen is an Ancient African God of Kemetian heritage. Many people continue to express their love for God by uttering Amen's name at the end of their prayers even today. Many of Eisenhower's ancestors, from his mother's side of the family, carried African names — names that were heard in and around the pyramids and temples in ancient times. Two female ancestors' names were Hypatia, i.e., Hypatia Link and Hypatia McGhee. Hypatia was an African mathematician and teacher. This great scien-tist has been portrayed in almost all of the modern history and mathematics books as a Greek white woman. She was not. There are no pictures of Hypatia, and the sketched drawings of Hypatia as a white Greek woman is simply a figment of someone's eurocentric imagination. Hypatia was an African scholar who was brutally murdered because of her spiritual beliefs and her very scientific and sophisticated mathematical theories and proofs. Hypatia is the initiator of the concept that we refer to as Sunday school today. She was killed by ignorant religious fanatics who were more interested in converting everyone, rather than promoting the importance of education. An educated person need not kill to be understood.

Another ancestor, a male, was named D. *Melanchthon* Link. Another male ancestor was named Nimrod. Nimrod from the Bible was the founder of Assyria and Babylon. Nimrod is mentioned in the Bible as being the son of Cush and the grandson of Ham. Cush and Ham were Black men as have been established by old history, ourstorians and others. "Nimrod ... founded the city in which Abraham was born, namely Ur, which is in the country of Chaldea ... The ancestry of the Israelites stems from Abraham, who was [also] black" and a descendant of Shem [Khem/Kem] (Hughley, p. 11). Cush (Kush or Kish) is also the ancient, African, and indigenous name for what is called Ethiopia today. This information is nothing new, but it is important to repeat and begin to place the ancestry of these presidents (and others), and events in another valid and evolutionary light. There were other given first names in the Link family: Moses, Noah, Solomon. Much of the information and other little known anecdotes mentioned throughout this book are significant events for people of serious study and who want to know the truth, and for those who are tired of hearing and reading continuous historical lies — no matter what color you are. Cush and Kemet is read about throughout **Genesis,** the BEGINNING of the Bible. Genesis, genealogy, genocide. Who is trying to destroy the beginning?

Below is a shortened version of a poem entitled, *Conquer with your African Mind,* 1988.

GENOCIDE!!
In our quest and BATTLE for real
Freedom
We will recapture our minds and
true African spirit!!

God/Amen has given us strength —
now give us Victory!
The Queens and Kings will rejoice
for their descendents
As We make promises in your name
O Amen/Aset/Asaru
We will praise you — as we rise
and shut the mouths
and stop the pencils
of liars!!

by: *Auset BaKhufu* ©

Dwight Eisenhower admitted to knowing less about his mother's ancestral background than his father's background (Eisenhower, *at ease*, p. 76). Her uncle, however, seems to have known more about Ida's background. The uncle of Eisenhower's mother, Paxson Rude Link, questioned the biological birth of Eisenhower's maternal grandmother, Elizabeth Link Stover (Ida Stover Eisenhower's mother), in his 1951 book, *Family of Links*. I've found no pictures of Dwight Eisenhower's maternal grandmother. And besides pictures of Eisenhower's mother, Ida Stover Eisenhower, there is scarce written and accessible evidence of these two women's true ancestry. But it must be remembered that pictures often speak louder than words. In essence, "what you see is what you get." However, there is a considerable amount of speculation, many questions, and sporadic statements and code writings by White and Black people alluding to the possibility of Eisenhower's African ancestry. Questions and speculative inquiries are warranted (please see the front cover and the pictures of Dwight Eisenhower and his mother on pages 304 & 308 of this book.) Many authors described Mrs. Eisenhower as having brown hair, full lips, and a ready smile. It is highly unlikely that she had surgery like so many Hollywood and television personalities of today who pay big money just to obtain these full lips. Eisenhower himself stated in his book, *at ease*, that many people had tried to analyze the character of his mother by looking at pictures of her. He stated that some of the analyses were sometimes "farfetched, even preposterous" (p. 78). What did these people say to prompt Dwight into using such curt and abrupt adjectives to describe their depiction of what they saw?

On February 20, 1992 and on February 27, 1992, I had the interesting opportunity to speak with one of Ida Link Stover Eisenhower's descendents who resides in the same Virginia town of which Ida was born. Don Link expressed to me that he had heard nothing in family conversations of any African ancestry on this side of his family. He also told me that a friend, a playmate, of Ida's had described Ida in a newspaper article as having golden hair and blue eyes. This friend said that Ida was very beautiful and very intelligent. He had a picture in his hand from a newspaper as he spoke with me, and he pointed out that she looked white. When I disclosed to Mr. Link that many people were saying that his ancestor had African blood, he laughed heartily and said: "I don't think so; but is that supposed to be something bad or negative?" My response, "Not to me, it isn't." His very proper and respectful attitude was, "So what if it's true?", although he does disagree with the research that points to the possibility of African blood on this side of his family. He also assured me that using his name in this book and stating what he communicated to me would be no problem. I thanked him then, and I thank him again for this information.

According to writer descriptions in books about the Eisenhowers, and to others who have seen Ida Eisenhower and pictures of her disagree that she was golden haired. Her hair was a dark brown, but Ike did say that his mother had blue eyes. She is described in one such book as having brown hair, full lips, and a wide grin (Ambrose, p. 16). Considering Ida's blue eyes, facial features, dark hair, and skin color, she appears to be of the Type 3-4 Melanin Racial Trait (Barnes, pp. 20-21). Ida was gray as she grew older, but at age twenty-three when she married Ike's father and later as a young woman with children in her thirties, she most definitely did not have blond or golden hair, unless it was a dark golden brown hair strain. Ida didn't seem to be the type person who, if she did have light-colored hair, would dye her hair. She was a very natural, intelligent, down-to-earth person. Eisenhower, himself, had ethnic features although he looked essentially white during his elder years. However, his younger pictures show ethnicity and more color. (See the front cover of *Life* magazine, April 28, 1952 and the picture on page 308 of this book.) Pictures of Eisenhower's mother, as mentioned, look "very ethnic" (i.e., Black/African, and perhaps Jewish, like David) especially in her youth. Now somebody is going to say that they were probably in the sun more during their youth. Go on.

In the book, *The Klan Unmasked*, by Stetson Kennedy, a white acquaintance of Kennedy's opined, "We have the worst men in the world at the head of the American Army ... Of course you know Eisenhower is a Jew" (p. 127). In the book, *Ike The Soldier: As They Knew Him* (1987), by Merle Miller, it is stated that while a military cadet at West Point, in the school's yearbook, the *Howitzer*, Dwight D. Eisenhower was referred to as the "Swedish-Jew." This author goes through literary pains to explain away the term Swedish-Jew used in the yearbook. Miller writes that Swedes were the subjects of a lot folk humor during this time, and that Jews outwitted Gentiles, and that since Ike displayed all of these qualities in his looks and mental attitude, he was given the name Swedish-Jew (pp. 43-45). *Life* magazine stated that the "Swedish-Jew *joke* has been used as an anti-Eisenhower *smear* by some lunatic fringe anti-Semetic groups" *(Life,* April 28, 1952, p. 117). Forty-two years ago, written in Kenneth S. Davis' biography on Dwight D. Eisenhower *(Soldier of Democracy, 1945, pp. 147-148), he cites the same Howitzer* source as Miller, but completely omits the sentence on Eisenhower's Jewishness. It is said that a smear campaign was started on Ike calling him a Jew, a Swede, and a German (Neal, pp. 280-281). If the "Black gossip" had left the African communities (and it did somewhat), then I guess it would have been called a "despicable/utterly unspeakable" campaign. Sources do, however, indirectly refer to Eisenhower as being Black/African. It is sad that having Jewish, German, Swedish, or African ancestry, to so-called Americans, is considered a "smear" against a person. Two main sources about Eisenhower's Africanness are J.A. Rogers' pamphlet, *The Five Negro Presidents (p. 13),* and Francis Russell's book, *The Shadow of Blooming Grove: Warren G. Harding in His Time,* p. xv, in which he compares Eisenhower to Warren G. Harding, who was said to have been of African ancestry or "Negro blood."

Another interesting element is the fact that although Eisenhower makes an effort to defend his mother's ancestry in his book, *at ease* (p. 76 — footnote) by stating that: "In spite of information given in the "'Book of Links,'", [Ida's uncle's book] ... (My grandmother [his mother's mother] was a Link.)" Meaning white? Meaning she was a member of the Link family, no matter what Paxson said? Eisenhower also fails to give correct book information. Eisenhower states that the name of Paxson Link's book is "Book of Links" written in 1950. Eisenhower even "mispelled" Paxson's name; he spelled it "Paxon." The name of the book is actually *"Family of Links,"* written in 1951, not 1950, by "Paxson" Link. Eisenhower could have written this in this way in order to confuse and mislead the search of curious readers or serious researchers. My research deduces that the writings and literature on, about, and by Dwight D. Eisenhower shows that Eisenhower was a very meticulous, precise, and careful literary dictator and writer.

One of the most valid sources of information is J.A. Rogers' pamphlet, *The Five Negro Presidents*, 1965. On page 13 of his pamphlet, he does not mention the name of this "Negro President." During the time that Rogers published this pamphlet, Eisenhower was still with the living, so Rogers was probably being a little careful and perhaps protective in this area. But from the way in which Rogers wrote his pamphlet and the obvious hints that he gives, Rogers shows, and my research and study indicate, that Eisenhower is indeed the president for whom Rogers referenced. If Rogers had not wanted anyone to know, period, then he would not have even written this at all — period. Eisenhower's mother being Virginia born was one of the hints that Rogers gives in his pamphlet. The other hint was that he named his five "Negro" presidents in order of their terms in office, and there was no president during Rogers' lifetime after Harding whose mother was Virginia born except for Dwight D. Eisenhower's mother. Rogers also affirmed in his pamphlet that many people asked him if this president was of African ancestry. He said that he himself had read of this possibility in only one source, and that was in the Baltimore Afro-American newspaper in Maryland, U.S.A. An editor of this newspaper stated to Rogers that the newspaper article was considered a "smear." A white woman in Paris told J.A. Rogers that this president's name had come up in in a French newspaper "on the topic of race intermixture." Rogers goes on to say that this president's mother does have African features and so does some youthful pictures of this president. I do not know of which pictures J.A. Rogers had in his possession, but please do, again, see the pictures of Dwight David and Ida Stover Eisenhower on the front cover of this book.

Dr. John Henrik Clarke who is one of the most respected African elders and well-known African ourstorians (and this term is used seriously) in the United States also concurred with my analyses, reasons, and research for stating that this is indeed the President for which Rogers references. Furthermore, before my research efforts were even mentioned, Dr. Clarke informed me, after I inquired about the fifth president in Rogers' pamphlet, that it was indeed Eisenhower who was rumored to be of African ancestry and that his mother was Virginia born. He went on to say that he used to golf caddy for Eisenhower, and that "although Eisenhower looked white enough, he did have ethnic features." I talked with another African elder, Mr. U.L. Farris who still lives in Denison, Texas (Eisenhower's birth town); he said of the numerous pictures in the Eisenhower museum there that, "Eisenhower has never looked like a white man to me." J.A. Rogers said that almost everyone who sees this president's mother's picture "has without prompting or knowing who she is says she is '"colored."' He said that all of these people were "amazed" when he told them who this lady was.

After showing Ida Stover Eisenhower's picture to people on the street, in the malls, in bookstores, to librarians, relatives, friends, my students, people of all colors and races, only two people (one African and one white) stated that they did know what race Ida might be; two others (of mixed race) said that she looked white, and five students (all African) between the ages of 12 and 16 stated that she looked "mixed." So after asking seventy-nine people what race/color this woman was, seventy answered "Black." Two Black women (one on the East coast the other on the West) stated, "I know my people when I see them!" One white man asked, "Who is this? An old picture of one of your relatives?"

I smiled. Our young African children are beginning to be very confused with the notion of mixture in this society. They do not yet understand that you either are or you aren't Black (physically, but especially mentally). Dr. John Henrik Clarke said that:

> The United States Census Bureau is experimenting with an idea that could be disastrous for African Americans. There will be a new classification on the census form. If you're racially mixed, you can put down mixed … These '"mixes"' can be used as a buffer … Who mixed them? … The slave ships didn't bring any West Indians, East Indians, or black Americans, … didn't bring any high yellows or low yellows. Those who mixed them are now going to put the mixes against the so-called unmixes. Where will that put us?" Within our own families, most of us have every color gradation under the sun. A cousin who is mixed is just as much a cousin as one who is unmixed. What these enemies of African people understand at last is … While European life is based principally on economics and class, non-European life is base [sic] principally on religion and culture. If they split African Americans along these lines, they can pit one against the other.
>
> *(African World Revolution, pp. 4-5)*

Ask your friends and relatives to look at Ida's picture. I asked 42 African people, 13 Hispanic people, 4 Asian people, and 20 white people from 1989 to 1992. Now that her identity is known, of course, many will have personal prejudges and see whatever they wish to see.

In 1990, I spread the word throughout the Virginia genealogical circle that I was looking for genealogists who might be able to aid in obtaining Ida's birth certificate, but to no avail. In the process though, I did talk with an older genealogist who, when I asked about the ancestry of Ida Stover Eisenhower, told me that she had heard a long time ago that somebody in the neighborhood was Ida's student, or was a teacher along with Ida. She said that this student or teacher had told her "children or someone" that Ida was "colored or something." This lady said that she had only heard this "rumor" once. I understand that anonymous sources are infamous, but felt this information pertinent to the content of the subject matter here. Furthermore, this conversation did take place, and there is never a reason not to write the truth.

Author Francis Russell *(The Shadow of Blooming Grove: Warren G. Harding in His Times*, p. xv) names Dwight D. Eisenhower as the President who most resembles Warren G. Harding. Warren G. Harding was the 29th president of the United States, and is said by many to be of African ancestry. Russell goes on to say that for all of Eisenhower's incompetencies and lack of aptitude, he still remains the "Little Father." Russell says that, "... both are very similar ... Both shared roughly the same cultural values, in life, in books, in music, in art. Both got themselves entangled in the syntax *jungles* of their mother *tongue*" (BaKhufu's italics). The mothers of both of these men were very religious, although Harding nor Eisenhower were forced to accept the religions of their mothers. Harding's mother was a Seventh-Day Adventist and Eisenhower's mother became a Jehovah's Witness after being a religious member of many other sects. Eisenhower states on page 305 of his book, *at ease*, that his mother was indeed deeply religious. It's interesting to note here that Lincoln's biological mother was also very religious. Mrs. Eisenhower struggled to understand the bible; she was unable to simply accept the dogma of any specific denomination or sect. As mentioned above, she eventually began to study with a local group known as The Bible Class. This class had no church nor minister; she liked this. This group would sing, pray, and discuss the bible and a periodical called, *The Watchtower.* This group eventually adopted the name of Jehovah's Witnesses, and they now have many Witness Halls and elder leaders and counselors. Some of these "elders" are as young as 40. Ida said that she could not accept the dogma of any specific denomination or sect, whereas David Eisenhower, her husband, said that he could not "go along with the sheer dogma that was so much a part of their [Jehovah's Witnesses] thinking" (Miller, p. 63). There is one thing for sure, and that is, if David was trying to study the Egyptian Mysteries, and Ida was studying under the Jehovah's Witnesses, then the two definitely had their philosophical disagreements.

Author of the book, *The Harding Era*, page 530, Robert Murray, thought it "curious" that Russell should compare Dwight Eisenhower with Warren Harding. He goes on to say that "Russell seized upon the Negro-blood story as the primary conditioning factor in the development of Harding's personality and "ridiculously" called it the "'shadow'" which hung over Harding's entire life." Is this an indication that Russell thought of the possibility of Black blood in Eisenhower's family background also? Is this why Murray thought it "curious" that Russell would compare these two presidents? I agree with Russell's reading and research conclusions that Harding's and Eisenhower's *"personal interests"* and "cultural values" were very similar. Did this author purposely omit feelings on the "genealogical similarities" of the two men? Otherwise, throughout his entire book, there was really no other reason to compare the two. Why not mention the other presidents whose cultural and personal interests were similar to Harding's? There were others.

Many wrote and referred to the six presidents discussed in this book as gods and/or fathers often. Are these men alluded to to as gods and fathers because of the conscious or unconscious mind of all of us who know that the first man to grace the universe was Black? All people, especially Africans, should learn to "code read" in order to learn the true history of the world.

"Another Ike? *The Most Celebrated General Since Eisenhower Has a Bright Political Future — If He Can Answer A Few Questions."* I found it interesting to read this heading in an article written in the *"Washingtonian"* magazine, politics section, Washington, D.C., April, 1991, vol. 26, no. 7, page 37, in reference to the African, General Colin Powell. The second column of this article, second paragraph states, "… Powell — now a military hero, the Joint Chiefs chairman who masterminded Desert Storm — is being called "'the black Eisenhower.'" Of course, the article directs most of its content to these men's war careers. This article also alludes to the possibility of General Powell running for President of the

United States in 1992. Of course, to refer to Powell as "the black Eisenhower" could be seen as "redundant."

I talked with Dr. Dan Ford, a respected African elder, entrepreneur and motivational speaker, who spent his childhood in Eisenhower's other hometown of Denison, Texas, about his views on the community of which Eisenhower resided in his early youth. He stated that his home and many of his African-American friends' homes were not too far from Dwight D. Eisenhower's house. He said that the community was a cordial one with many attitudes probably kept silent. An example he related to me about this neighborhood was this:

Dr. Ford said that when he was about seven years of age, he was walking through a white neighbors' backyard. This neighbor had a white visitor. This visitor looked out of the back window and informed her friend that a "nigger" was in her backyard. The neighbor looked and looked, exclaiming, "Where? Where!" The visitor pointed and said, "Right there!" Dr. Ford's white neighbor laughed and exclaimed, "That's no nigger; that's little Danny Ford." Considering Eisenhower's mother's intolerance for bigotry, it can be understood why it would be pertinent that she live in a somewhat "liberal" environment. Her descendent, Don, seems to be just as liberal-minded, intelligent, and friendly as she. Ike's mother was adamantly against war and violence. She resented the way white people had treated slaves and believed that the Civil War was the cause of her own mother's early death. One of Ida's relatives, Christopher Link, joined the Union Army on September 10, 1861; he was 39 years old and a sergeant for Co. E, 66th infantry for three years. His wife died suddenly and he asked one of his best friends, President Abraham Lincoln, if he could secure him with an immediate discharge so that he could return home to take care of his family. President Lincoln concurred with a personal letter of discharge. The letter was in the Link family for years until it was mistakenly burned (Link, p. 279).

So strangely or not so strangely, Dwight Eisenhower made war and violence his career. His father and mother abhorred war. Dwight served in the military from 1911 to 1948. His mother cried. Eisenhower said that his mother was well respected by most people who met her; he said that she was gentle and serene, had an open smile and had her "own strict pattern of personal conduct" and he adored her (Eisenhower, *at ease,* p. 76). The author of *Eisenhower for President?* stated that this "phase of the General's [Eisenhower] career which might profitably be analyzed for voters by Dr. Karl Menninger, or some other eminent psychiatrist, is the relationship he maintained with his mother. Never has a son shown more love and affection for his mother; yet he chose the one profession that was most abhorrent to her (Clugston, p. 19). Could it be that Dwight Eisenhower adored his mother for being, in a sense, a double mama? Black women are biologically, and therefore, scientifically and spiritually known as the Mother of all peoples and the universe (PBS Special: *Children of Eve; Newsweek,* "The Search for Adam & Eve, Jan. 11, 1988, pp. 46-52; BaKhufu, *The Mystery Teachings of the Temple of Ast* (notes); Dr. Yosef ben-Jochannan's works, and Cheikh Anta Diop's books on melanin). So Dwight was fortunate enough to have Ida as his mother on a "here-and-now/physical" plane as well as on a "universally biological and spiritual plane." This could have been an entity that he understood innately although not consciously. Did Dwight resent the fact that his mother claimed white, although he probably understood the necessity after so many family years of "failing?" Or did he subconsciously resent the truth — That he too was of color? So as much as he loved and respected his mother(s), he had to find a way to strike back and try to rid himself of the anger that he would never be able to express to anyone, ever! No one, but no one is going to convince me that in Texas, Kansas, West Point, Europe or someplace in this world some little smart alecky boy or girl, cadet, soldier, reporter or some adult in jest, humor, or anger did not ask Eisenhower if he or his mother was "colored or Negro." Ike was a young winning athlete and fighter and — good looking. A piqued loser might allege anything after a fight or game. An ignorant girl might say anything after being rejected. The more liberal-thinking European (in Europe) may have asked Ike about his ancestral background(s) not meaning any harm whatsoever. And an "irresponsible" teacher will ask or say anything period. Not understanding the beauty of blackness, Ike could only hold the trauma and hurt inside —

not even being able to express his feelings to his mother or father. Did Dwight D. Eisenhower have black blood, or even a wonderful double dose of black blood, running through his veins?

This next section continues to contrast Ike's military and political careers with surrounding African and African-American events during those periods. It is important not to forget Eisenhower's possible mixed heritage as you delve deeper and deeper into this biographical and psychological narrative.

Dwight Eisenhower was a West Point military student from June 14, 1911 until his graduation date, June 12, 1915. During his term as a student here, Harriet Tubman, leader of the Underground Railroad, journeyed on to the ancestors (died) on March 13, 1913. Eisenhower was a young man at West Point making military music, while some African-Americans were making their own special music. That is, on June 20, 1914, musical genius W.C. Handy wrote "The St. Louis Blues," and two weeks later, on July 3, 1914, five hundred African-Americans in Oklahoma made joyous music by sailing for West Africa during the "Back-to-Africa" movement. This expedition Back-to-the-Homeland was led by Alfred Sam.

Dwight D. Eisenhower's graduation from West Point took place six months after the birth of one of the most brilliant men in the world, Dr. John Henrik Clarke, who was born January 1, 1915. Eisenhower received World War I promotions that made him Lieutenant Colonel. Dr. Clarke would later become a Master Sergeant in the military. He always points out though that he was drafted. He asks, "What fool would volunteer?" Nineteen-fifteen is the same year that James Hamilton graduated from college and went on to pursue a law degree. Before he obtained his law degree, he was a soldier in World War I. He said that the discrimination in the armed forces was horrendous, and vowed to change things. This great African-American lawyer would later be called the "Man who killed Jim Crow." It was appalling for Hamilton, and for Dr. Clarke who served during a later military period, to serve the United States then have the horrible experience of learning about other African soldiers who were lynched in their uniforms after returning to civilian (or more like uncivilian) life in the United States.

MAMIE

Eisenhower was still a military cadet when he saw and fell in love with Mary (Mamie) Doud. Dwight had been invited to the officers' club in San Antonio where he was introduced to the daughter of a very rich man. Dwight was now stationed at Fort Sam Houston near San Antonio, Texas, not too far from Mexico. San Antonio is where the Doud family, from Denver, usually spent their winter vacations. Dwight wasted no time. These young people, Dwight twenty-four and Mamie nineteen, took a walk together. This is when Dwight learned that the pretty young woman already had a dinner date for the evening. He asked her to cancel her date. Mamie looked at this handsome, swarthy-skinned man and broke that date. Later on that night, they gazed into each other's eyes as they dined together, probably in a Mexican restaurant. Dwight loved Mexican food; his mother used to cook many Mexican dishes and had taught her son to do the same. Mamie wasn't in for a lot of cooking, so Dwight would eventually do much of the cooking. Dwight was only a young serviceman and could not afford the expensive restaurants for which Mamie was accustomed. She wasn't spoiled, and hung right in there with him.

Dwight and Mamie were married July 1, 1916 in high spirited, high society in Denver, Colorado. Mamie would not live the socialite life again for a while, for *she was in the Army now*. But, Mamie's father did send money to the newlyweds from time to time.

On their way back to Fort Sam Houston, the newlyweds visited Ike's parents in Abilene, Kansas. The elder Eisenhowers were unable to attend the wedding because it had been planned with very short notice. Dwight's mother thought that her new and first daughter/daughter-in-law was an adorable girl. The couple arrived in the early morning hours, and Ida Eisenhower cooked the happy couple "a good ole" fried chicken meal for breakfast. Eisenhower's mother was called a saint by her relatives and friends. She seems to have been a giving, loving, secure, hardworking, religious woman. From what I have read about her, she was a very likeable person.

Dwight and Mamie's army home became the social spotlight, the hangout. Their place was called "Club Eisenhower." They had some happy times before they were doomed to become hurt, bitter, and distant with each other. Their first child died at a very young age, and neither Dwight nor Mamie would ever recover from this hurt. Little Dwight Doud Eisenhower was born September 24, 1917 in Denver, Colorado; "Icky," as he was affectionately called, died on January 2, 1921 in Camp Meade, Maryland. The child had come into contact with, and acquired scarlet fever from the babysitter. The Eisenhowers went through a long and antagonizing "what if/if only we had ... syndrome" period. Eisenhower dove into his career, and the couple began to be very polite, cool, and distant with each other after this very stressful experience. Dwight and Mamie did manage to have another child. John was born August 3, 1923, one day after the death of the President of the United States; Warren G. Harding died strangely on August 2, 1923. Dwight Eisenhower never forgot to send his wife flowers on the day of their first son's birth for the rest of his living days. During the strain of such a stressful life, Mamie is said to have later developed a drinking problem (Williamson, *Derbrett's Presidents of the United States*, p. 176). Her daughter-in-law, nonetheless, explains this problem away by stating that Mamie had an inner-ear infection that made her dizzy, but many people preferred to think that Mamie was drunk (Lyon, *Eisenhower: Portrait of the Hero*, p. 604). Mamie told one biographer in 1974 that she has never had a drinking problem. It is stated that she had a low tolerance for alcohol. Mamie said that she lived with herself and could care less what people thought (Neal, pp. 254 & 463).

ROARING TWENTIES

Good and bad things were happening during these roaring twenties. It was 1923 when an influx of Africans from all over were migrating to Harlem. It was Renaissance Time! Some of the richest Black people in the world lived in Harlem during this time. Even people who were not so monetarily rich were experiencing rich lives. Education, Music, Entertainment, and Literature abound. Some of the chief places where African-Americans were living financially well besides Harlem were, Atlanta, Georgia; Washington, D.C., and Durham, North Carolina (Anderson, *This Was Harlem*, pp. 137-138). *Even so, Africans were still being brutally attacked mentally and physically all over the United States.* Many of the writers during this period were financed by white people who wanted these brothers and sisters to write about African people as a primitive people. Some did; many refused. Lynchings were still a part of the social and political order of some white people.

From 1925 to 1926, Eisenhower went to Command and General staff school at Fort Leavenworth, Kansas. It was, as indicated, a special time for Africans all over the world whether they realized it or not, for in May and July of 1925, two great men were born, they are, Malcolm X (El hajj Malik el Shabazz) and Patrice Lumumba, respectively. Malcolm X was born in Omaha, Nebraska, U.S.A., and his brother in African spirit, Lumumba, was born in Zaire, Africa. Unfortunately, both would later journey-on-to-the-ancestors by way of tragic deaths at the hands of conspirators. This is the same year that the great entertainer, Josephine Baker made her grand entrance and dance debut in Paris, France. A. Philip Randolph, who would later play an important role in the civil rights events during the Eisenhower administration, organized the Sleeping Car Porters' Union on August 25, 1925.

In 1928, Dwight Eisenhower attended Army War College in Washington, D.C. Here, I have learned that, Hannibal's war strategieswerestudied then and even today. After serving from 1929 to 1932 on the staff of the Assistant Secretary of War, Ike joined the staff of General Douglas A. MacArthur, Army Chief of Staff in Washington, from 1932 to 1934. And speaking of war ...

In 1929, Nigerian great grandmothers, grandmothers, mothers, daughters, aunts, nieces, sisters, and young women from a myriad of communities rose up against white British colonial dictatorship, like the warrior Nzinghas from whom they descended, and fought. This ourstory in survival is called the "1929 War of the Women." For more information about these very brave African women, read the book: *I Saw the Sky Catch Fire* (1992), by *T. Obinkaram Echewa*. On November 2, 1930, Ras Tafari was crowned Haile Selassie I, King of Kings, Lord of Lords, Conquering Lion of Judah (land of Judaism and Beta Israels). History classes would have been (and still could be) much more interesting, fun, and spicy if only the educational school system in the United States and abroad were not so prejudiced and naive. Study, learn; teach the children the truth; teach the children ourstory. It is time for ourstory/history to become everyone's story.

MURDERERS COME TO TUSKEGEE

It was 1932 in Tuskegee, Alabama when the U.S. government dispensed a deadly shot of syphilis to 412 African-American men to see what would happen if these men were not treated. They told these Black men that they would get burial insurance for participating in this experiment and that they would be treated for their illness, which they were told was a malady of "Bad Blood." The Tuskegee experiment agitators, so-called doctors, gave these men very painful spinal taps and told them that this was treatment. From this deadly lie, many of these African/Black men, of course, went blind, crazy, or died.

A NEW DEAL

Although Blacks in the United States during the 1930's were experiencing some horrendous times, as mentioned above, and some hard economic times, it is sometimes difficult to believe that during these turbulent years, there were also prosperous black businesses, and an economic and social Black pride that seems to be virtually unfounded today. Even so, there were some rich black and white folks who in the 1920's and early 1930's were now in 1931-1932 scrubbing floors in order to survive. This was the Great Depression. By the time Franklin D. Roosevelt was elected President of the United States, many Americans were without jobs. He promised a "New Deal."

THE SPRING AND SUMMER OF 1932

Zeni Miriam Makeba, fondly called the "Empress of African Song" was born in Prospect Township, South Africa on March 4, 1932. Her political views and protests toward a better life and freedom for all African peoples was to later cause her to have to take political refuge in the United States for a number of years. She adamantly spoke out against the apartheid system in South Africa.

During the summer of 1932, the veterans in America were taking a march to Washington, D.C. The World War I veterans of the United States were disturbed when they returned from war and realized that they were without jobs; their families were hungry, and they were not receiving any government support. This led to the March in Washington, D.C. called the *Bonus Army to Washington*. These veterans were holding Government Bonus certificates, and they were due to be paid in the future. But these veterans demanded that Congress pay them now. The veterans began to move to Washington from all over the United States. They brought their wives and their children with them. Over 20,000 of these veterans relocated to Washington, D.C. complaining, and rightfully so. They camped out by making shelters out of cardboard, trash can remnants, and packing crates. Most of these veterans and their families camped across from the Potomac River from the capitol on Anacostia Flats. The bill to pay off the bonuses was passed by the House, but the Senate defeated this bill. Some of the veterans were agitated and upset and decided to move on, but most of the veterans would not be moved and decided to remain and camp out in Government buildings near the capitol — downtown, Washington, D.C. Hoover was president of the United States, and he ordered the Army to evict the veterans. This army consisted of Major Dwight D. Eisenhower, who was the aide to General Douglass MacArthur and George S. Patton. The veterans lived up and down Pennsylvania Avenue, and these army officials used tear gas to clear the veterans and their families out of these buildings. Buildings were even set on fire by the army. They tear gassed these veterans along with their children and their wives. It was a horrible ordeal for these people, and the whole camp was ablaze with fire instantly. A very young baby died; an eight year old boy was blinded, and thousands of veterans were injured by the tear gas (Zinn, *A People's History of the United States*, p. 181). Some said that this battle was almost as violent as some of the war during the Civil War (Garrison, p. 157). Once the protesters were cleared from the federal buildings, they went on to Maryland and Anacostia Flats. Hoover was severely criticized for sending Eisenhower and the fellows to descend upon these ex-veterans who had risked their lives for their country (Zinn, p. 181). Sometime after I'd written this part of the book, I attended a Malcolm X celebration on Anacostia Flats — which is now a relaxing park. As I Buddha sat across from the Potomac River drinking my herb tea, eating injera (Ethiopian bread) and picking at my Egyptian olive-oiled salad, I looked over toward the White House and thought about these veterans, and the plight of my people all over the world.

On August 7, 1932, Abebe Bikila of Cush (Ethiopia) was born. This manchild would later, as a Man and during the Eisenhower administration, win the 1960 Olympic marathon while running barefoot! Zola Budd was not the first.

1933-1942

Franklin D. Roosevelt became President of United States in 1933. It was around 1934, as we progressed in the Lincoln chapter, that Eleanor Roosevelt was having a woman-to-woman heyday with her intimate friend, Hickok. It would be 1953 before Dwight D. Eisenhower would ignore Mrs. Roosevelt as an important person in the political arena.

On October 3, 1935, Bikila's homeland, Cush, was invaded by Italy which led to World War II. At the end of October, 1935, Kwame NKrumah enrolled at Lincoln University in Pennsylvania. Many Africans, home and in diaspora, were adversely affected by the Italian invasion. J.A. Rogers witnessed this white nationalist war first hand. Because of the Mussolini/Italian-Ethiopian War, more and more Africans were studying and becoming more conscious of their ourstory. (It is important to note here that Mussolini's granddaughter is now running for some political office in Italy. She is a lot like her grandfather. She stated on a recent [April, 1992] prime-time news series that maybe the murders of countless Africans and Jews ordered by her grandfather were necessary.)

On August 9, 1936, Jesse Owens won four Olympic gold medals in Hitler's war-torn Germany. During Summer breaks, Kwame NKrumah lived in Harlem. It was around this time that Dr. Clarke and NKrumah were attending some of the same African study groups. Kwame NKrumah and Dr. John Henrik Clarke both are leading African forces in the survival of ourstory and the African race in general.

Military officers had begun in 1936 to rule Japan. Japan did not have all of the resources necessary to become a big industrial country. Anyway, with the United States controlling the Phillipines, and Japan not being strong enough at the time to take control of the situation, America ultimately stood in the way of Japan's independent expansion. Six months before the Pearl Harbor incident, on June 10, 1940, in London, England, the honorable Marcus Garvey succumbed and journeyed on to be with the ancestors. He was, at the moment of his death, still working for the survival of African peoples, while the Japanese tried tediously to work for theirs. The Japanese were an independent surviving people, when suddenly they were demanded, two generations, before to trade with the West. It was during the late 1930's and early 1940's that Japan was still sending their youth to America, after two generations, to trade, study and continue their education. They studied architecture, engineering, mathematics, physics, everything. They were admitted to the Virginia Military Academy when African-Americans were not allowed to attend. The Japanese studied at this military academy — in America, although they were not new to the art of militia. The Japanese slaughtered the Russians in 1905. "Most of the Japanese staff officers at Pearl Harbor were trained at Virginia Military Academy" (Clarke, *African Revolution. pp. 268-269*). On March 27, 1941 a spy for Japanese Navy Intelligence, Takeo Yoshikawa, arrived in Honolulu Harbor. During an eight-month period, Yoshikawa collected enough information to assure a successful military attack on the U.S. which took place on December 7, 1941. The Japanese knew the habits and movements of the ships and planes stationed at Pearl Harbor before the attack (*Life,* **"Pearl Harbor: December 7, 1941 - December 7, 1991,]"** p. 30). During the time of the Pearl Harbor attack by the Japanese, a somewhat obscure figure, Dwight D. Eisenhower, was holding rank as a temporary Brigadier-General oversees. He was called immediately to Washington, D.C. and his life was about to change to that of a very public figure. Dr. Clarke states that, "a lot of the Japanese who built Japanese industry, which built the ammunition that struck America at Pearl Harbor, was trained at MIT, Massachusetts Institute of Technology, at a time they wouldn't let a black student in from America, the Caribbean or South Africa." Clarke continues, "most of the scrap that went into the bomb was bought from the Sixth Avenue El and the Third Avenue El stations" [United States]. The calculating Japanese were known for losing their text-books while studying in America. What they were actually doing was sending their textbooks back home to Japan, so that the others might learn the American teachings, strate-gies, and ways (Clarke, pp. 269-270). So, embarrassingly, America was attacked with their own ammunition. Many still wonder to this day how this happened.

On November 22, 1991 on a *20/20* special television show, it was revealed in an "eye-opening" document in recent National Archives that America was planning an attack on the Japanese before the Pearl Harbor attack, and Franklin D. Roosevelt was very aware of this. On this show a Mr. Lauchin Currie, who was a personal assistant to Roosevelt, stated that they were to "kill as many damned Japanese as we could; simple." He was making reference to the power-ful Lockheed bombers that they were to use. Secret volun-teer bombers had been secured and they had the blessing of the U.S. Government, the Secretary of the Navy, and the Secretary of the Army. This was top level stuff. The National Archive document number for this information is JB No. 355, serial 691, dated July 23, 1941 (ABC *20/20 - Television Special, November 22, 1991). After the Pearl Harbor tragedy, Roosevelt said, Pearl Harbor is a day that we will "live in infamy."* This may be true, and he had planned to do it to them first. Roosevelt got to work on this issue. In February of 1942, he quietly signed Executive Order 9066, giving the army permission to arrest every Japanese-American on the

West Coast of the United States and place them in concentration camps. The Japanese remained in these prison camps for more than three years (Zinn, p. 407). They later, in 1990, received monetary reparations for America's actions.

On May 27, 1942, Dorie Miller, a Navy cook on the fateful *Arizona*, was awarded the Navy Cross for his outstanding and heroic feats at Pearl Harbor. As a Black man in America's military, Mr. Miller was limited to kitchen detail, however, when the Japanese attacked Pearl Harbor, Dorie Miller fired the ship's guns continuously. This action vindicated the African-American military personnel somewhat, and made the way clear for the approval of African-American naval officers. But, in spite of the racial breakthroughs in the American military, Eisenhower did not abandon his prejudice. Ike said, in the same year that Miller was awarded, "My policy for handling colored troops would be absolute, equivotively treatment, but there will be segregation when facilities are afforded." Klan members were happy to hear a statement like this coming from such an authoritative military official. On July 16, 1942, a directive with Dwight D. Eisenhower's signature was delivered to all Red Cross facilities in London ordering that, "care should be taken so that men of two races are not needlessly intermingled in the dormitory or at the same tables in dining halls" (Kennedy, *The Klan Unmasked, pp. 259-260).* The Red Cross even kept Black blood segregated in the medical blood banks (Dennis, *Black History, p. 109).* Dr. Charles Drew, born in Washington, D.C. was the leading authority on blood plasma and the preservation of blood. He introduced to the world the Blood Bank. During World War II, England's soldiers suffered tremendously; they called on Dr. Drew to organize their military blood bank program. He saved many lives on and off the battlefield which motivated the British to encourage Dr. Drew to set up the first mass blood bank project. He became the first Director of the American Red Cross Blood Bank. Insulted and angered that blood from the races would be separated, *Class* Magazine states that, Dr. Drew resigned his position. Charles Drew declared that there is absolutely no scientific basis as to a difference in human blood from race to race *(Class,* p. 62). Other sources say that Dr. Drew was fired from his Red Cross position when he tried to end blood segregation (Zinn, p. 406). During times like this for strong African people anything may have happened. Dr. Drew was probably so enraged with anger that he was fired while he was resigning, or resigning while he was being fired. By the way, where was Eisenhower's blood?

J.A. Rogers states in his book, *Sex and Race,* that "The Negro strain is apparent among a considerable number of American Jews ... The Island of Jamaica has a considerable number of mulatto [Black] Jews, also (vol. I, p. 94). And although the leader of Berlin's German Youth Education Organization, Ewald Althans, may understand the ancestral connection of Africans and Jews, I wonder if he understands the compliment he pa id to Jews when he said: "To me the funniest thing I ever heard was that in New York, Blacks and Jews are fighting with each other. As if there's a difference between them" *(Emerge* Magazine, June, 1992, p. 28).

Many Africans, with the blood of their ancient ancestors (creators of the human race) still running through their veins, understand themselves to be a chosen people. However people who call themselves Jews, Semites of the Jewish religion and who consider themselves white, have referred to themselves as a chosen people for years also. Frances Cress Welsing states that although Jews claim they are chosen, they continue to debate on the issue as to what they were chosen to do. Dr. Welsing explains in her many lectures around the country that although Jews have lightened themselves down, they are still not treated as white people by white people. She theorizes that (BaKhufu's italics):

> The Semites of the Jewish religion were chosen to teach a very important moral, and that is, never disrespect or be ashamed of the *Black genetic heritage of Africa, and speak up for, own up to, protect and defend that heritage with your very life, should conditions and events ever call upon you to do so. Be proud to be Black and be proud to be non-white. This is a profound lesson in self-respect for all of the people in the world.*
>
> *The Isis Papers,* p. 229

Dwight D. Eisenhower was called upon, and whether Eisenhower is ancestrally and/or biologically German-Jew,

African-Jew, Swiss-African, Swedish-Jew or African period, he has disrespected himself immensely. Eisenhower's actions and attitude, being as contradictory as history has shown, like Warren G. Harding, presents Ike as a victim in America. Most signs point to the possibility of Ike as being of African-Jewish ancestry. Frances Cress Welsing also mentions in her book that Albert Einstein and Karl Marx have both been described as having African ancestry. Karl Marx had such dark skin that his own children referred to him as the Moor. Dr. Welsing states that there is a great resemblance in the appearances of Frederick Douglass and Karl Marx. (Please see page 307 at the end of this chapter.) Einstein was described in one of Dr. Welsing's references as having a prominent nose, swarthy skin, and frizzy hair (See pp. 224-225 of Dr. Cress Welsing's book for more references and information).

Very good sources of information pertaining to Africans of the Jewish persuasion (and vice versa) are Dr. Yosef ben-Jochannan's books, *We, the Black Jews; Africa: Mother of Western Civilization;* and *African Origins of the Major "Western Religions."* Also read: *The Truth About Black Biblical Hebrew-Israelites (Jews): The World's Best-Kept Secret! What Happened to the True "Black Jews" in the Year 70 C.E. (A.D.)?*, by Ella J. Hughley. Also see the Bibliography section of this book.

THE WAAC's

Four days after Ike's statement to separate the races, on July 20, 1942, African-American women were accepted into the Women's Army Auxiliary Corps (WAAC). One of these African WAAC's was just recently on a television special (March, 1992), and she stated that "General Eisenhower was forced" to accept them. This is the same year that Eisenhower began a close relationship with Kay Summersby, an Army WAAC. Kay Summersby Morgan, a white woman of Irish descent, wrote a book in 1976 revealing in detail the love affair that she had with Dwight D. Eisenhower while he was Supreme Commander of the Allied Forces in Europe. Kay Summersby, was Eisenhower's personal assistant and official chauffeur during World War II. She affirms in her book, *Past Forgetting*, that she loved Ike dearly. She began to write and dictate this book while dying from cancer. Her deathbed confession reads genuine. She states that she met Ike in 1942 while they both worked for the military services. Mamie could not escape seeing all of the photos of this young ex-fashion model hanging around her husband. The Eisenhowers were continuing to drift apart. Mamie also could not escape the rumors of a love affair between her husband and Kay Summersby. And a "love" affair it must have been, because Kay Summersby states in her book that they never were sexually intimate because Ike was apparently impotent — which, of course, could have stemmed from many things, e.g., guilt (i.e., love for his wife); age and/or stress. Ike also suffered from high blood pressure/hypertension. Neither did he understand the gift of his melanin content and how to utilize it effectively; more simply put, it is felt that in this case, Ike had been mentally "europenisized" by American paternalistic teachings and brainwashings. Freud calls this type of impotency, "self-castration," and as mentioned above, and in this case, I feel that my term, "europenisization" is more appropriate. Summersby wrote:

> Ike refilled our glasses several times and then, I suppose inevitably, we found ourselves in each other's arms in an unrestrained embrace ... Buttons were unbuttoned. It was as if we were frantic ... But this was not what I had expected. Wearily, we slowly calmed down ... "Oh God, Kay. I'm sorry. I'm not going to be any good for you ..." It was a bit embarrassing struggling back into the clothes that had been flung on the floor.
>
> *Past Forgetting,* pp. 171-172

After reading this, any healthy person can understand why this is past forgetting. Kay asserts that Ike lamented to her that "It [marriage] killed something in me ... For years I never thought of making love, and when I did, I failed." Kay goes on to say in her book that Eisenhower's "Hungry, strong, demanding" kisses made her weak with love for him. "I love you," Ike told Kay. Kay too admits that she "loved this middle-aged man with his thinning hair ... I wanted to ... feel the intensity of those eyes on mine, feel that hard body against mine" (Summersby Morgan, p. 178, 132 & 128). At this time, Kay was a young woman in her thirties whose fiance had recently been killed in war. She was possibly very vulnerable during this time, but in 1976, she continued to carry lingering memories and spoke fondly of her love for Dwight D. Eisenhower.

ROMANTIC TIMES IN KEMET

Kay simply could not forget the romantic times she and Ike spent together, especially a very memorable time in 1945 when they visited Kemet (Egypt) together, and Ike told her that it would mean a lot to him to have her with him when he visited the pyramids of Ghiza in Cairo. This is the year that Kay says she and Ike really fell in love. While in Cairo, Kemet, they shared marvelous lunches, dinners, and cocktail parties. Ike was always the center of attention, and Kay had a difficult time hiding the glow on her face displaying to the world the love she had for the military magnate.

After Cairo, the two love birds visited Wa'set. (Wa'set is better known to many as Luxor or Thebes, as the Greeks term it, and Luxor is an Arabic nomenclature.) Later on that night, Eisenhower and Kay Summersby went to view the temples, which Summersby refers to as "crumbling temples" in her book. Under the moonlight of Africa, they visited the rows of ram-headed her-em-achets (sphinxes). Summersby said that this night "seemed like a dream" to her. After wishing Kay "sweet dreams" and going to their separate rooms, the next morning, the love birds visited the sacred Valley of the Pharaohs/Valley of the Kings on the west bank of the river Hapi/Nile. Kay alleged that they got a look at the "primitive life" of the ancient and modern peoples, and she went on to refer to the children as "grimy" with flies everywhere. As one reads her book, it is plainly seen that she was just as "sincere" with her expression and impression of these people as the actress' Debbie Reynolds' racist remarks about Hispanic peoples. When Ms. Reynolds was asked by a Hispanic career woman what her suggestion would be for Hispanic women who were having difficult times finding jobs in the Los Angeles/Beverly Hills area, Ms. Reynolds remarked that there are plenty of people who need "maids." Reynolds went as far as to stereotype that all Hispanic peoples have a lot of children. And so what if they, or anyone else, do? Women like Summersby and Reynolds and many other innocently racist people have a very difficult time seeing beyond themselves. The Reynolds' spokespeople stated that her statement was blown out of content. How?

Back to Kemet. Summersby said that on this day, it was fiery hot, but she enjoyed learning about the history of the ancients by "a very learned guide" who could translate the "hieroglyphics." (*Author's note: It is impossible for the word hieroglyphic to be found on the tombs and temples in Kemet. The indigenous, African/Kemetian word for the Greek word "hiero-glyphic" is "medunetcher," which means the writings of the Gods.*) Anyway, Summersby enjoyed this tour and said that she felt as if she had "jumped across hundreds of centuries." She states that she experienced a wonderful type of tired-ness and wanted nothing more than a cold drink, a bath, and a bed. The next morning Ike did not have to entice Kay to take a luncheon trip with him to Jerusalem. They jumped on a plane, and by noontime, they were having lunch at the King David Hotel. Summersby states that after Kemet, the so-called Holy Land was nothing but an anticlimax. Had Kay understood that she had left the first Holy Land before noon, she would have understood her disappointment bet-ter. Kay said that Jerusalem was very commercial and not very impressive. Even Bethlehem was a disappointment to Kay and Ike. She said that the manger where Christ was (supposedly [author insertion]) born was nothing but a big "hunk of marble, and I was absolutely repelled by it." She goes on to say that, "None of Christ's long-ago agony com-municated itself to us [Summersby and Eisenhower]," but they did enjoy the Garden of Gethsemane. Kay kept a post-card that Ike gave her of this place until her death (*Past For-getting*, pp. 155-162). They jet-setted back to the spiritual land of Kemet.

DROPPING BOMBS

The fifth Pan African Conference was held in Manches-ter, England in 1945. The delegates, many of whom were destined to become leaders of independent African states, developed and planned the decolonization of the African continent. During this same year, Roosevelt died and vice president Truman became President of the United States. This is when Truman learned that Roosevelt had approved the development of the atomic bomb. By this time, the bomb was ready for use. Germany had invaded the Soviet Union in 1941. Japan was said to be an ally to Germany and Italy. World War II raged on. The war continued in the Pacific. Truman decided to drop the bomb on Japan, twice! The first time was in Hiroshima; the second time was at Nagasaki. Japan surrendered. The use of the bomb left a scar on the world. Albert Einstein had earlier signed a letter to Roosevelt stating that powerful bombs were possibly being made in Germany. Einstein had fled Germany because being from the Jewish community, he was not welcomed there; he was brown. In any event, because of the letter that Einstein and others had signed, Roosevelt authorized a highly secret project to make the first atom bomb. After the United States bombed Hiroshima and Nagasaki, Einstein regretted that he had ever signed the letter. Eight years later, Albert Einstein will sign another letter to President Eisenhower — pleading for the lives of Americans.

PATTY KAYKE

Ike's affair with Kay Summersby continued. Ike, the General, was promoted to the title of Supreme Allied Commander. He may have been considered a supreme military commander by most Americans, but Kay Summersby knew that he was not so supreme in another area. The war was on; he was making decisions that would cost people their lives, and he was receiving troublesome letters from Mamie. Anyway, Ike and Kay tried to consummate their love affair one more time:

The fire was warm. The sofa was soft. We held each other close ... I remember thinking, ... Wouldn't it be wonderful if this were the day we conceived a baby — our very first time. Ike was tender, careful, loving. But it didn't work. "Wait," I said, "You're too excited. It will be all right." "No," he said flatly.

"It won't. It's too late. I can't." He was bitter. We
dressed slowly. Kissing occasionally. Smiling sadly.
"Comb your hair," he said ... When I returned from
the bathroom, there was ... white wine [and] some
chicken.

Summersby, *Past Forgetting*, p. 238

MELANIN

As indicated, Eisenhower seems to have possessed a certain amount of melanin. For example, when Dwight D.
Eisenhower was fourteen years old, he skinned his knee and
got blood poisoning. The doctors knew nothing to do except
to amputate the leg. Ida and David, the parents, left the
decision up to their young son, and Ike was adamant about
not having his leg removed. He said that he would rather
die than be an amputee. Dwight's whole leg turned black.
The blackness travelled up to his pelvic area. To keep from
screaming, Dwight bit on a kitchen utensil; the pain was
excruciating. "Miraculously, when the swelling reached the
pelvis — when Dwight was supposed to die, in other words
— it quite suddenly subsided. Dwight recovered without ill
effects" (Link, p. 188; Reference: Eisenhower, *at ease*, p. 97),
even though "The doctor ... warned the family that they
would be responsible for the boy's death. Despite the doctor's grim predictions the black swelling subsided and
Dwight recovered ... it was nothing less than a miracle"
(Neal, p. 16). In essence, when the healer of melanin reached
Ike's genital area, the point when "medical authorities (?)"
said that Dwight "Ike" Eisenhower should have died, he
"miraculously" recovered.

*Human skin is furnished with the capacity to form a black pig-
ment called melanin, or "black G." It acts as a protective shield
over the areas beneath the skin. Melanin is a chemical in the pineal
gland; it is considered a "life chemical" and is found in various
organs and functional centers in the Black man* (Barnes, p. 1;
King, pp. 31-35).

As a young man, Eisenhower understood "something."
He was young enough and close enough to his natural state
to understand and use his *sense receptor* and chose not to
have his leg cut off. As we grow older, dubious, or paternal-

istic, environmental powers can sometimes influence our mental attitudes to the point of adversely affecting our bodies. In suppressing his melanonic senses, Ike, presumably and inadvertently, also suppressed his ability to be sexually intimate with Kay.

The pineal gland is located near the center of the brain. Bear with me now. Serotonin and melatonin are both chemicals found in the pineal gland. Serotonin is a neurotransmitter in the central nervous system. Melatonin is formed from serotonin and is highly concentrated in the "third eye," i.e., pineal gland. Melanin is involved in the development for "proper" sexual development in human beings (Schlesinger, Kurt, Biological Psychology, p. 477; Ref.; BaKhufu, See Bibliography section, Dissertation, 1985, pp. 19-21).

Even if Ike were not cognizant of nor understanding of the power of his melanin substance (no matter how little he may have possessed), he could have educated and enlightened himself with other natural ways to solve his sexual problem. For example, he could have used herbals. *Several good, stiff cups of ginseng tea, some gota kola tea or vitamins, and generous plates of salad filled with traditional lettuce, raw onions, celery and garlic capped with a little vinegar could have helped. Garlic? Eat a generous amount (1/4 handful) of parsley afterwards; it freshens the breath (BaKhufu, "Healing: Herbs, Health and Spirituality," 1992 — exact publication date pending, work in progress). Had Dwight Eisenhower been aware of, or prepared this remedy often, Kay, perchance, may have gotten her wish and had herself a little Ike.

Dwight D. Eisenhower apparently did not keep this problem forever, because just recently, in a March, 1992 newspaper, a Ms. Sally Fischer has admitted to having a sexual affair with Eisenhower while he was President. She states that she

*The author is not prescribing herbs nor medicines here. This is general information for the reader who may be interested in an alternative to medicine. Therefore you should see your herbalist, natural doctor or even your medical doctor before administering any new health alternatives for yourself; although it is your constitutional right to do whatever you feel best toward good health and the healing of your own body.

was a young executive secretary on Capitol Hill when she pursued Eisenhower. Sally said that she went after him because she liked bald men. Ms. Fischer said that she met Ike at a fundraising ball in Washington, D.C. She said they finally made love "one unforgettable night in the White House in 1955 ... Until that night I didn't really know why people had worn those 'I like Ike' buttons during the campaign. But after that night I certainly knew why I liked Ike!" Ms. Fischer exclaims. She went on to say that after that night, she understood why America won World War II. Sally Fischer said that she gives Ike "A definite 10" [in the sex department] (Tracy, Rick, "I Slept With Five Presidents," *Weekly World NEWS*, March 10, 1992, pp. 4-5). I am personally not an advocate of these types of papers; however, this does not mean that everything in such papers are not true. I do not know if I believe Ms. Fischer's story (if indeed it's her own story; I have not spoken with her personally), but if this rumor/story is true, then all I can say to Kay is, "I guess he was saving it for later." And I ask, "Mamie, where were you girl!?"

America liked Ike. Mike Wallace, the broadcast journalist, said that he remembered Ike as being a fatherly figure. Mr. Wallace stated that Ike gave a sense of stability and leadership to America. He remembers Ike as a man with very large hands, and thick fingers (*Class of the 20th Century, 1952-1955*, Television Special, 1992).

OTHERS LOSE

David Williamson, the author of *Debrett's Presidents of the United States of America*, states on page 174 of this book that: "Dwight D. Eisenhower, like Ulysses S [sic] Grant *(gv)* before him, was living proof that good generals do not necessarily make good Presidents." The fact that this author considers Eisenhower to have been a good general is questionable by some other authors. One such author is James Bacque who wrote the book, *Other Losses*. Bacque states that Eisenhower, while serving in World War II, was responsible for the deaths of many unarmed German soldiers. During World War II, Ike became a five-star General. Bacque asserts that Eisenhower allowed many of these German soldiers to be inhumanely starved to death, and others met other tragic deaths at the hands of Eisenhower's troops. Eisenhower was designated to be the Supreme Commander of Allied Expeditionary Force on December 24, 1943.

In early 1944, Ike was on his way to London to continue with his Army duties when Mamie said that she couldn't bear to lose him again, and asked him not to come back until his duties were over. Later on, Eisenhower asked General Marshall for permission to move Mamie to London with him. This request was denied by the Chief of Staff because it would show favoritism to a general when all of the other married American soldiers were lonely for their wives also (Miller, *Plain Speaking*, p. 178).

Dwight Eisenhower planned the D-Day invasion of Europe on June 6, 1944. It was during this turbulent war period that African-American women were fighting for their rights to be a part of some aspect of the American dream. On March 8, 1945, Phyllis Mae Daily became the first African-American nurse sworn into the Navy Nurse Corps. But the military was still segregating the races. "When troops were jammed onto the U.S.A. *Queen Mary* ... to go into combat duty in the European theater, the blacks were stowed down in the depths of the ship near the engine room, as far as possible from the fresh air of the decks, in a bizarre reminder of the slave voyages of old." "Was the war being fought to establish that Hitler was wrong in his ideas of white Nordic supremacy over 'inferior' races?" Zinn asks (Zinn, p. 406).

Martin Brech is a professor of Philosophy and Religion at Mercy College in New York; he stated that he witnessed many atrocities under the military command of Dwight D. Eisenhower. For example, he said that German P.O.W.'s were not only beaten and starved to death, but were denied water, when there was plenty of it, and forced to live without shelter. He said that they were very close to water and that many of these German P.O.W.'s were so thirsty that they took a chance at going under barbed wire fences to get to the water. In their attempt, they were savagely machine-gunned down by Eisenhower's American guards (Reference: see the book, *Other Losses*, by James Bacque, 1991). Eisenhower later made a statement that Germans had it coming to them after what they did to the Jews. He said that the SS troops should be given the death penalty without question, and that all of the German people were party to the holocaust project. Eisenhower went on to say that he would like to "see things made good and hard for them [Germans] for a while." Eisenhower also stated that he hated apologizing to Germans. This statement was made after several Germans had "accidentally" suffocated in box-cars while being shipped by Americans. Eisenhower finally agreed to apologize. In a 1944 letter to his wife, Eisenhower wrote that he hated Germans. He said that the Germans were beasts. In August, 1944, Eisenhower said while in the presence of the British ambassador to Washington that all 3,500 officers of the German General Staff should be "exterminated." He said that he would also exterminate all leaders of the Nazi party, in addition to members of the Gestapo (Bacque, pp. 194 & 23). American historian, Stephen E. Ambrose "categorically" denies these allegations about Eisenhower. His denial may be a bit biased. Ambrose is a historian and director of the Eisenhower Center at the University of New Orleans. Eisenhower's grandson wrote in his book that, "It was also ironic that Eisenhower, the son of German parents, would emerge as a historic leader of a holy war against Germany" (Eisenhower, David, *Eisenhower-at War 1943-1945*, p. 507).

Ike's allied campaign was going exceedingly well. When he and the rest of his crew heard that President Roosevelt had died, Kay Summersby stated that they were so busy that they did not have time to mourn his demise. Then they heard that Hitler had killed himself. She described this day in the military as "one grand happy mess" (Summersby, p. 220). Hitler had tried to design a strategy "to disrupt communications and create confusion in the Allied rear." Eisenhower called this strategy "Hitler's last bid." It is said that within this bid was a plot to assassinate Dwight D. Eisenhower and other Allied generals. This "Operation Greif," was headed by Lieutenant Colonel Otto Skorzeny, who by the orders of Hitler, "had kidnapped Mussolini from a mountain hideaway in northern Italy. Skorzeny was thought by some Allied intelligence officers to be the most dangerous man in Europe. The German soldiers under his command wore captured American uniforms and carried false identification papers." After all of the trouble they went through to learn American ways, pronunciations, and accent, many of these German soldier plotters were captured, drilled, then killed by Ike's American soldiers while Ike was in semi-hiding (Miller, pp. 725-727). On May 7, 1945, Eisenhower accepted the surrender of the German army at Rheims.

According to other records, even though the American allies were supposed to be providing safe shelter for the Jews for whom they were rescuing from the Germans, the Jews were cramped in small spaces with only bread and coffee as their diet. When Eisenhower heard of this problem, he took care of it. These Jews had been labeled "displaced persons." General Patton had hired Germans to oversee the displaced people. Eisenhower and Patton had a major disagreement over this matter, and although Eisenhower owed Patton a lot for his very successful military career, Eisenhower still did not hesitate in demanding that Patton to get rid of the German overseers (Lyon, pp. 379-381). Dwight Eisenhower returned to America a hero.

Dr. Linus A. Hoskins made an interesting point when he confirmed the unwarranted arrogance of white leadership and name makers in reference to wars; he notes in this book, *Decoding European Geopolitics:*

> ... that when the Western European allied nations fought against the Central European powers between 1914-1918, that is called World War I. When the Western European allied nations/forces fought against the Eastern European Axis powers between 1939-1945, this is called World War II and at the end of World War II when the head-on conflict between "Russian regionalism and American interest in the balance of power in Europe" was "aggravated by the universalist rhetoric of Communist dogma versus American democratic universalism and free trade capitalist ideology," this far-reaching hostility between the two superpowers is called the "Cold War"; but when non-Europeans from North Korea fought against non-Europeans from South Korea between 1950-1953, this is *only* regarded as the Korean War, [sic] when non-Euro-

> peans from North Vietnam fought against non-
> Europeans from South Vietnam between 1957-1975
> [sic] this is *only* regarded as the Vietnam War ...
>
> (1990, pp. 3-4)

During World War II, Eisenhower was given the opportunity to become the person in charge of finding homes for
German-Jews in the event of disaster. Although this offer
was made before the 1945 Jewish holocaust, tragedy was
already running rampant for Jews and more disaster was
expected. Eisenhower learned through friends that a "group
of people" were willing to pay him $60,000 a year to search
the world for homes for conceivably millions of German
Jewish refugees (Hargrove, p. 47). Hitler was already at war
with the Jewish citizens in Germany. Eisenhower did not
accept the job. Why did this "group of people," who were
willing to pay Eisenhower so well (at the time, 1939) choose
him for such a task? Was it because they too had some incli-
nation about Ike's ancestral background — more than he
was admitting or dismissing? Did this group feel that Ike
would have intimate and emotional reasons for doing a
good job at finding them a homeland?

Many Jews, including Germans, were descendants of the
ancient African Jews from Gondar, Ethiopia — negatively,
but better known as the "Falacha" Jews of today. These
proud people prefer the name Beta Israel. The Black Jews,
Beta Israel, Children of the House of Israel, lost control of
Ethiopia during 840 C.E. under Queen Judith (Dr. ben-
Jochannan, ...*Western Religions*, p. 325). Judith I was the
Queen of the Black Jews who put the line of Solomon off the
throne. She ruled Ethiopia from 937-977 A.D. (Rogers, *Your
History*, p. 67). Dr. Ben states in his many works that there
are today Black Jews living in Brooklyn, the Bronx, Queens,
Manhattan, Chicago, Philadelphia, Washington, D.C. and
other American areas. Their name preference is "Black
Israelites." There is no reason to be confused; many of these
brothers and sisters are studying ourstory just as you are.
"Jew" is not a very ancient word. Jews are known to have
come from the community of Judah, whose people practiced
the religion of Judaism. Judaism is a religion and not a race
(Hughley, p. 9). Dr. Yosef ben-Jochannan is an African-Jew,

born in Africa — Gondar, Ethiopia. Dr. Ben, as he is affectionately known in African communities all over the world, is a historian (i.e., ourstorian), Kemetologist, lawyer, and writer. Dr. Ben being a Beta Israelite (Jew), and the Children of the House of Judah being African, is an example of ancestral backgrounds (and shades of color) and how they may or may not change as time goes on.

Jackie Robinson, on April 11, 1947, signed a professional baseball contract and became the first African-American to play the sport "professionally." Roy Campanella also played baseball in the South and with an interracial team. Robinson was later to become a political activitist for Black causes during the Eisenhower presidential administration.

Dwight Eisenhower was on the Army Chief of Staff from 1945 to 1948. He retired from the Army on February 7, 1948, then secured an office at the Pentagon for a while. On February 28, 1948, Sergeant Cornelius E. Adjetey became the first martyr for national independence of Ghana.

It is almost certain that Eisenhower, being the athletic enthusiast that he was, was aware of the great presence of Jamaican-born track star Herb McKenley. Mr. McKenley set a new world record for the 400-yard dash on June 2, 1948. Ike became the president of Columbia University in New York on June 7, 1948. Two years later, he purchased his famous Gettysburg home in Pennsylvania. By this time, Ike's affair with Kay Summersby was over.

X-KAY

Ike had coolly but politely accepted Kay's few visits to the Pentagon, but he was very irritated and annoyed when Kay showed up in New York City where he was then president at Columbia University. He told her that there was nothing that he could do, and with tears in her eyes she understood that it was really over (Summersby, p. 246).

Around this time in 1948, Eisenhower announced before the Senate Armed Forces Committee, that "Armed Forces are not concerned with social reform." He went on to add that a "certain amount of segregation is necessary in the Army." Ultimately, when campaigning for the presidency of the United States, he announced his opposition to civil rights legislation by the Congress. After the klan heard this, they were ecstatic and campaigned actively for Ike, they respected and relished in Ike's brainwashed viewpoint (Kennedy, *The Klan Unmasked*, pp. 260-261).

Ike arranged for Kay Summersby to become an American citizen. She relocated and lived in New York very comfortably from her military savings and the first book that she wrote entitled: *Eisenhower Was My Boss*, 1948, of which she left out many important and intimate details. She states that she deliberately kept Eisenhower's life as private as possible while writing this book. Others did the same. Summersby states that, "In those days anything that could have been construed as a *shadow* on the General's character would have been seized upon as a political weapon" (p. 16). She "tells all" in her second book, *Past Forgetting*.

Kay states in *Past Forgetting* that when she lived in Washington, D.C. and had attended political social functions, many male political officials were very nervous when she chatted with their wives, because Kay was the only female in attendance who knew all of the high officials' girlfriends and mistresses. She never told. But she may as well had, because Mamie Eisenhower had already learned of the liaison of her own husband and those of other military officials. She obtained this information from wives whose husbands were overseas, who in turn told them. Men do gossip. And it doesn't matter that they may be holding a pipe, a gun, or something else, their chatter (and some of their writing) is still no more than gossip.

Besides Kay Summersby, other military personnel attested to the fast that Ike and Kay were very close. It has been stated in the literature that Ike saw to it that Kay was kept as comfortable as possible, and she seemed to have been a very important part of his life. But after Eisenhower was called back to the Washington, D.C. area, Kay continued to wait for her new duties somewhere near him; they never came. She was devastated. Ike apparently felt that his career was more important. Forsaking personal happiness can sometimes be a sign of overcompensation for another unfulfilled area in one's life or personality. Kay mentions that Ike had never been ashamed of his simple and country upbringing, and that Ike seemed to be a man who had not had a lot of comforting during his lifetime. But would he have been really happy with Kay Summersby? He had children with Mamie; he couldn't even be intimate with Kay. Although his statements to Kay show that his problem may have very well stemmed from many things, including the war, an improper diet, the lingering stress from the sudden death of his three-year-old child, or even Kay's beauty; who knows? And who knows whether Mamie and Ike were ever intimate again? It doesn't matter, when Eisenhower died, Mamie was his wife.

Harry S. Truman stated to his biographer that Eisenhower had written a letter saying that he wanted to come back to the United States, divorce Mamie Eisenhower, and marry Kay Summersby. Dwight D. Eisenhower's request was denied. Eisenhower had written this letter-request to General Marshall. Marshall wrote back telling Eisenhower that if he did such a thing that we would make his army, and therefore political, life a "living hell" — forever! (Summersby Morgan, p. 12; Neal, p. 177).

Marshall's official biographer, Veris C. Pogue, said that he doubts very seriously if Eisenhower and General Marshall ever exchanged such correspondence. Eisenhower's son, John S. Eisenhower, went on to say that Harry S. Truman was a "liar." But what else would a loyal son say who loves both parents dearly? Summersby, herself, stated that she was unaware of such a letter, and was very pleased to hear about the letter. Of course, she wished to believe that there was such a letter. We must also keep in mind that Truman did not care for Ike a lot. Truman claims to have destroyed the letter. Dwight D. Eisenhower's son, John, admonished, "I don't give a damn what Truman thinks." He went on to say, "I found myself wondering why anybody pays attention to Truman's foul mouth railings" (Neal, pp. 176-178 & 458-459). Seeing as how Truman did not care for the man, would he have destroyed such a damaging letter? Maybe, or maybe not.

When Kay Summersby visited Washington, D.C. one summer, Mamie spoke to her, but treated her with a cold shoulder. Mamie asked Dwight's biographer, Kenneth Davis, not to mention Kay in his book. Mamie, in many of her numerous letters to her husband while he was overseas, makes many references to Kay in her letters. There were numerous rumors circulating around the U.S. that Ike and Kay had a romance going, and this created many strains on the Eisenhower's already shaky marriage. Mr. Neal states from numerous sources that Kay Summersby was a fashion model and motion picture actress before becoming Ike's driver in London and in North Africa. He states that Kay was beautiful, with high Garbo cheekbones, long flowing hair, and a model's slender figure. In Neal's book, an Eisenhower assistant, Butcher said, "Kay was a diversion to Ike." He also said that, "She was a breath of fresh air [to Ike]. She was witty and charming. As a driver during the Blitz, she had been through a lot of danger ... Ike appreciated that." For example, Kay Summersby barely escaped death in December of 1942 when she was in route to join Eisenhower in North Africa. Her ship, the *Strathalen*, was torpedoed by a German submarine and sank. Kay arrived in North Africa in a lifeboat.

Mamie had heard a lot of gossip about this romance from other military wives whose husbands had "leaked" information. Her letters soon began to put Dwight D. Eisenhower on the defensive. He wrote her back from Algiers February 25, 1943, saying, "Fear not about WAACs taking care of my house ... I love you all the time — don't go bothering your pretty head about WAACs." Eisenhower wrote his wife that he had no emotional involvement and would never have any emotional involvement with any WAACs, Red Cross workers, nurses or drivers (Neal, *Eisenhower: Reluctant Dynasty*, p. 176). Even so, Mamie was skeptical about what she was hearing from Ike, and from the looks of things, she should have been. He wrote his wife that she was the only person he loved and wanted and that her love and their son were the greatest gifts of life to him (Miller, *Plain Speaking*, p. 177).

Dwight D. Eisenhower's son admits that the relationship between his parents across the ocean was not always very smooth. Eisenhower wrote to Mamie on September 25, 1944 that "of course, maybe we've both changed, and we've been through a lot together. How could we not change in our own certain ways. He said one thing for sure is that we should keep our sense of humor and that there's no problem that is separating us, it's just distance that is separating us, and that will one day change. She wrote back: "I do love you, but you must keep in mind that I take a beating every day from things I hear." So they went back and forth in their letter arguing. She also made a statement to Ike that, "I understand that when you blow off steam, you don't really think about sometimes what you are saying." She went on, "and I know you can't think of me as such a black-hearted creature as your language implies [in your letters]." It is not known whether Mamie might have had a suspicion about Ike's likely dark ancestry.

Eisenhower's son John said in 1977 that, "nobody can bear witness that an incident between his father and Summersby did not happen." He said that his letters to his mother established beyond any doubt of his that divorce never crossed his father's mind. John declared that Kay Summersby was just one of the crowd. He said that Kay was very attractive. She was his bridge partner and a very amiable person. John Eisenhower did say later on that had he found written evidence of an affair between his father and Summersby, that he would have destroyed the letter, or deposited it at the Eisenhower library with a 50-year seal (Neal, p. 460; Miller, *Plain Speaking*, p. 178).

THE PRESIDENT

It's 1949, and not too far from the Capitol of the United States, the White House and the Pentagon, on October 29th, Alonzo G. Moron from the Virgin Islands became the first Black president of Hampton Institute in Virginia. Meanwhile, Ike was being groomed into becoming the 34th president of the United States.

It is said by many authors that Eisenhower's weak characteristic traits began to show when he became president of the United States. Many people, authors, politicians and others, discuss in their books, articles and lectures that Ike's actions during and surrounding the controversial Civil Rights movement were not sufficient. Martin Luther King, Jr. was disgusted with Eisenhower's inept attitude on these important matters. King believed that many racial problems could have been avoided had Ike exercised his executive leadership with a stronger arm. For example, during his first term as president, Eisenhower desegregated the armed forces, and although he supported equal opportunity for every citizen, he however thought that the individual states, not the federal government, should decide whether to desegregate schools. Eisenhower's leadership is thought by many blacks to have been deficient regarding the segregation issue. Frederick Morrow, the first readily identifiable Black to work as an immediate aide to a president of the United States, went on to state that it was very shocking to hear Eisenhower at a news conference inadvertently admit that he had some problems understanding some phrases of civil rights legislation. This statement was detrimental to the Eisenhower administration and Morrow, being Black, had to take the blame. He received many phone calls from citizens demanding an explanation to Ike's statement.

The Eisenhower administration also refused to ratify the convention against genocide. This law drafted by the U.N. in 1948, states supremist acts committed with intent to destroy, in whole or in part, a national ethnic, racial or religious group or sect is against the law. This covenant, by 1951, had been ratified by enough nations to make it a law of the world, but the United States of America refused its signature of the original document until very recently. The Metholist Federation of Social Action said, "The failure of the United States senate to sign the genocide convention caused the whole world to question the American motivation, to doubt her purpose to build world brotherhood, cooperation and justice." There was a great deal of rejoicing in the klan klubs on April 5, 1953 when Republican Secretary of State John Foster Dulles shocked the world by blatantly announcing that the Eisenhower administration had no intention of ratifying either the United Nations Covenant on Human Rights nor the U.N. Convention on the political rights of women (Kennedy, *The Klan Unmasked*, p. 262-263). This nonaction of the Eisenhower administration contradicted the so-called democratic philosophy of America, and some actions of the Eisenhower administration baffled Americans' belief of a democracy in America.

It was also during this year that Eleanor Roosevelt had been working at the United Nations under the Truman administration for years. It was only government protocol that she should write a resignation letter every year, to be happily reassigned by Truman to her official position at the U.N. However, during the new Eisenhower administration, her position was abruptly curtailed when she received a curt note from Eisenhower accepting her routine resignation letter! In the short note, Ike didn't even acknowledge her services as being anything important. This unrelenting worker for the people was very disappointed. Eleanor Roosevelt was a humanitarian and felt that people were people. For instance, Eleanor liked hot dogs, so she saw no reason not to serve them to the Queen and King of England when they visited the White House. Her mother-in-law almost fainted. Eleanor campaigned vigorously for Adlai Stevenson against Eisenhower in the 1956 campaign. When Stevenson lost, she was terribly disappointed. A few years later, in 1962, at Eleanor Roosevelt's funeral, President John F. Kennedy said that Eleanor's "timeless idealism" ... and "her memory and spirit will endure." Adlai Stevenson said that Eleanor Roosevelt "would rather light a candle than curse the darkness." Harry S. Truman in his own tacky way asked Eisenhower (at the funeral!) why he never used Eleanor's services. "Eisenhower shrugged his shoulders and walked away" (Whitney, *Eleanor Roosevelt*, pp. 1, 97, 100, 113). Even if Eisenhower had an answer to Truman's question, I'm sure his Momma had taught him better than to answer such a question at the person's funeral, especially if the answer was negative or demeaning. This is a question that Truman should have asked before Mrs. Roosevelt's death.

Didn't Harry Truman have anything better to do with his time than to hassle Eisenhower? It is written that he and Bess had an extraordinary sex life. When they missed each other, they really missed each other. After returning from a long presidential trip, Harry and Bess broke a bed.

McCARTHYISM

Many citizens also had a problem with Eisenhower's failure to take a firm stance against McCarthyism. Henry Fonda, the famous actor, also worked hard for the Adlai Stevenson campaign committee. He disliked McCarthy to the point of losing well-known friends like John Ford and John Wayne. John Wayne sounded a lot like Lincoln when he said, "I believe in white supremacy until the blacks are educated to a point of responsibility. I don't believe in giving authority and positions of leadership and judgement to irresponsible people" *(Playboy* magazine [a John Wayne Interview], May, 1971). Henry Fonda was a Democrat, and had once smacked a young Jane Fonda across the face for uttering the word "nigger." While watching McCarthy hoopla on television one day, Henry smashed his television screen *(T.V. Guide,* "Remembering Dad," by Jane Fonda, January 11, 1992, pp. 6-11). From his book, *African Origins of the Major "Western Religions,"* Dr. ben-Jochannan writes:

> Senator Joseph McCarthy was a post [World] War II U.S.A. Senator, who made his national fame through investigations and public exposures of the U.S.A. Communists during his tenure on the Un-American Committee of the Senate. This Committee and the Senator met with public ridicule and the censure of this colleagues in the Senate. It also led to the destruction of the public life of hundreds of government employees; such as Alger Hiss (a high positioned State Department official) and Professor J. Robert Oppenheimer (one of the fathers of the Atomic Bomb).
>
> #12, p. 316

An acquaintance of Stetson Kennedy's by the name of Appleby said that, "The biggest Kluxer of all is Joe McCarthy. He may not be a member of the klan, but he would certainly make a good one!" Stetson Kennedy agreed with him. "McCarthy makes the grand dragon look like an earthworm by comparison ... He is pulling every trick in the ku klux bag and then some ... McCarthy was cut out to be a barroom bouncer, but he's got the makings of another Hitler including big money backing. Unless we get together and cut him down to size mighty quick, he just might turn out to be a greater curse on the world than Hitler ever thought of being." (Kennedy, *The Klan Unmasked,* p. 270). Many celebrities were being scrutinized and blackballed by

McCarthyism. Joe McCarthy ridiculously accused Harry Belafonte and Lucille Ball (and some other television professionals wrongly accused) of having Communist affiliations. He even had some of Eisenhower's generals under scrutiny.

WORLD DJAMBALAYA, 1952-1953

It is fitting and not surprising, considering the content of this book and understanding the importance of the visible and invisible concept of Sakku/psychology, that Dwight Eisenhower would accept his nomination as President of the United States while standing beneath a masterfully drawn silhouette of Abraham Lincoln (Picture: *Life Magazine*, vol. 33, p. 28, July 21, 1952). Eisenhower went into office stating that he would clean up the mess that was left by Harry S. Truman (Ross, p. 185). I've been informed that Truman was apt to use the words "kike," "Jap" or "nigger" whenever he pleased. Ironically, or maybe not so ironically, Truman was known to have done more for Civil and Human Rights than Eisenhower ever did; although Ike's very Being probably forced him to think about or maybe want to do more in the area. At any rate, Truman was rewarded for his efforts by the Negro Newspaper Publishers Association and the Interdenominational Ministerial Alliance of Greater New York in 1949. A relative of mine said no matter what he did, Truman was as racist as they come. And it is paradoxical that a year after Truman received all of his humanitarian awards, Dr. Charles Drew, mentioned above, died from a lack of blood when he was taken to a white hospital, and they would not treat him by use of his own blood plasma preservation invention when he needed blood because he was African-American, Black. Several sources state that he would have survived had this white hospital treated him.

Truman understood Ike's value as a political figure for the U.S. Government and harbored a certain and curious resentment or jealousy of the younger military man. They had a mutual dislike for each other. They blamed each other for many political disasters. When Eisenhower was paid $650,000.00 for his book, *Crusade in Europe*, Truman was livid. Ike was also given special tax treatment for his book. Truman, of course, was upset with the IRS when his memoirs did not get the same favorable tax treatment (Garrison, p. 233). Harry S. Truman sarcastically referred to Eisenhower as a demigod. (*A demigod = the child of a goddess or god who was intimate with a human being.* People seem to be intent on referring to these men as Fathers and gods.)

In the meanwhile, in 1952, a group of African-American women called The Daughters of Isis (Goddess of Kemet) were preparing young African women for greatness. They had teas to fund charities and educational programs that were usually held at the Masonic Temple in Washington, D.C. (*The Washington Afro-American*, Feb. 1952). This is the same year that J.A. Rogers was being praised for his work and research on African ancestry in the white race. He had just self-published *Nature Knows No Color-Line* (1952). He was especially applauded in *The Crisis* newspaper for his chapter on "The Negro as a Moor." In the MotherLand, the Mau Maus, an organization of Africans in Kenya, were using powerful revolutionary tactics in order to gain Freedom against white British colonial rule. Mau Mau literally means "The Hidden Ones" or "Do it quickly." They were committed to driving the white man out of their country. The British arrested Jomo Kenyatta, who was called "Burning Spear." He was suspected of master-minding this Act for Freedom. Whites had moved in on Kenya in the early 1900's — seizing the Africans' land and their homes; it was now 1952, and that's a long time. Enough is enough.

Two months later in America, Truman and Eisenhower were able to pull off a very interesting and amiable show during Eisenhower's inauguration into the White House on January 20, 1953. The two men shook hands and smiled at each other. It is interesting to note here what Americans consider priority in their lives. For instance, just one day before the presidential inauguration, January 19, 1953, on the "I Love Lucy" show, the birth of little Ricky seemed to be much more important than Eisenhower. (I wonder what my Mother was doing on this day; it was her birthday.) On this day in American history, 44,000,000 people watched "I Love Lucy" while only 29,000,000 people watched the presidential inauguration of Eisenhower. Had more Americans been given more details about Ike's personal and genealogical background, he probably would have had just as many people watching him as Lucille Ball and The Clarence Thomas-Anita Hill Show combined. The Eisenhower administration had a hectic eight years in front of it. Problems started early for Ike.

Eisenhower's vice president to be, Richard M. Nixon, had accepted monies from a big business company in California; this deal with Nixon and these business people was called the "slush fund." Eisenhower had considered dropping Nixon from his bid, but decided against this after Nixon "eloquently" made an attempt to defend himself during a public relations type speech over national television. He explained the fund and how he planned to utilize the money. He did admit to receiving a gift from a business person in Texas; the gift was a dog. Nixon in turn gave the dog to his daughter; they named the dog "Checkers". As Nixon told the world, "No matter what you do to me, this [the dog] is one thing that I'm going to keep!" (Ross, pp. 185-186; Garrison, p. 197), Eisenhower felt the man brave; he decided not to drop Nixon from the presidential bid. While Nixon survived this political scandal, Eisenhower had other staff members who were not so fortunate. Nixon would get his share of scandal much later during the Watergate controversy.

It was during 1953, under the Eisenhower administration, that Indians were told to give up their identity and assimilate with the whites in America. This issue was called the "Termination policy." Indian tribal officials gathered in the East room of the White House to meet with Eisenhower. He "was in a good mood; he loved Indians. And he welcomed his guests with fine words and bad jokes, as Presidents have done ever since the defeat of the tribes. It was an ancient white ritual." One elder Indian blessed the President with a peace pipe. The Indians knew that the racist white men would like that. Some even dressed in Indian headdress, beads and turkey feathers. In politeness the Indians concealed their humor at the pitiful supremist attitudes of the white men in the White House. They had come to discuss the "Termination Act." Unfortunately, eleven Indian communities were to be totally destroyed, and the Interior Department had adopted laws and regulations to divide up the Indians' territory and lease the land to white people (Stein, pp. 158 and 213-215). America, America.

Julius and Ethel Rosenburg were Jewish-Americans who were accused of being spys and planning to conspire to give sketches of American atomic weaponry to the Soviet Union. There was a widespread campaign and protest when the United States Government decided that this husband and wife team should be executed. Albert Einstein wrote a letter to Roosevelt appealing the decision; Einstein and Pope Pius XII felt that this was a hideous and severe punishment. There was an appeal to President Truman just before he left the presidential office; he turned it down. Then there was another appeal written to the new President, which was Dwight D. Eisenhower; he also turned the appeal down. With McCarthyism running rampant, Civil Rights issues being overlooked, and the KKK on the rise, Eisenhower gave permission to Judge Irving R. Kaufman to proceed with a sentence of execution to the Rosenburgs. Ike was in hot water with America. Eisenhower agreed with Judge Kaufman that the Rosenburgs had unforgiveably betrayed the country. He said that he must secure the country. Eisenhower also felt that to undermine the Judge's sentence would cause adverse reaction from the general United States' citizens. On Thursday, June 18, 1953, the Rosenburg's wedding anniversary, Egypt became a republic. The next day, Friday, June 19, 1953, the Rosenburgs were executed — one day after their fourteenth wedding anniversary, and one day before the Jewish Sabbath (Zinn, p. 382; Lyon, *Eisenhower: Portrait of a Hero,* p. 524-6).

MASKED BALL

Almost a year and a half later on January 7, 1955, singer Marian Anderson, who sang outside on the front steps of brother Lincoln's Memorial in 1939, made her debut in "Masked Ball" at the Metropolitan Opera in Washington, D.C. Blacks and the struggle for equality continued all over the world.

"PROGRESS?"

In April, 1955, Dr. Jonas Salk developed the polio vaccine. A year later, an oral vaccine was developed by Dr. Albert

Sabin. Actor Richard Dreyfuss, while hosting a television show *(Class of the 20th Century)*, called the development of the 1956 vaccine "progress." It was not mentioned on this program that Salk and Sabin became bitter enemies. Although Sabin's "discovery" was somewhat safer than Salk's "discovery," the charge that these vaccines were safe was not altogether true. The general public was not informed about the dangers of this vaccine nor other vaccines and drugs on the medical market then and now. It was mandatory in some areas that everyone, especially children, be given the polio shot. One newspaper in Massachusetts reported 2,027 cases of polio against only 273 the same time in 1954. The Washington Bureau reported that Polio was on the Rise. They issued a report stating that all sections of America have had more polio problems since Salk's vaccine was developed. "The damage to children taking the polio vaccine is well documented ..." And this was not because people were getting naturally sicker (Allen, Hannah, *Don't Get Stuck! The Case Against Vaccinations and Injections*, pp. 145-150; also see: Lehrer, Steven, *Explorers of the Body*, pp. 400-404).

It was recently reported by Tom Curtis in the April 5, 1992 issue of *The Washington Post* that a polio vaccine experiment was done in Africa with the possibility that this "contaminated polio vaccine" which was "administered from 1957 to 1960 to at least 325,000" Africans may be the cause of the AIDS spread in certain areas in Africa today. The article goes on to say that it is possible that the AIDS spread among American homosexuals may "have been accidentally started in the mid-1970's by an experimental treatment for herpes lesions used in New York and California."

OUR CHILDREN, OUR CHILDREN

Sadly, children died needlessly in other ways in 1955 also. For example, on August 28, 1955 a young 14 year-old African-American manchild from Chicago named Emmett Till was brutally murdered by two white men. Emmett was visiting relatives in Mississippi. Emmett had gone into a store, and on a bet with friends, he had said "Bye Baby" to a white woman behind the counter. The young man did not know just how detrimental this statement directed toward this white woman would be for him. He was in the deep south of Money, Mississippi. Emmett Till was later found at the bottom of the Tallachatichie River with a very heavy cotton-gin fan tied around his innocent neck. He had already been beaten and shot through the head. His anguished relatives were devastated. Emmett's mother insisted on having an open casket funeral for all the world to see just how barbaric and uncivilized some white people will become because of racist attitudes and conscious or unconscious fears of even the youngest of Black men. Young Till's face was swollen and totally disfigured. Roy Bryant and J.W. Milam killed this woman's child. These white men were not convicted. Not one word from the Eisenhower administration was said about this tragedy that Africans continue to moan over today.

ATTACK

Eisenhower suffered a series of heart attacks as he grew older. He had his first heart attack on September 24, 1955. As mentioned earlier, Eisenhower did suffer from stress, high blood pressure/hypertension. *Food for Thought: According to Francis Cress Welsing, M.D., the active skin melanocytes are capable of releasing large quantities of the amino acid, dopamine, to certain nerve endings which may be part of the mechanism by which higher blood pressure levels are manifested in pigmented (i.e., melanized) peoples than in people who lack color, i.e., white peoples* (Welsing, *Urban Health, The Journal of Health Care in the Cities*, "Blacks, Hypertension, and the Active Skin Melanocyte, June, 1975, p. 65). *It has been found that people of African and other skin pigmented "descent" shows a higher incidence of hypertension (which can cause heart attack) than white people* (Chobanian & Loviglio, *Heart Risk Book, pp. 11 & 25-26, Stamler, J., et al., "Hypertension in the Inner City — see the reference section). And, according to Welsing, this malady is often directly attributed to the stress that People of Color experience from residing in a racist society. Dr. Welsing points out that this sensitive cell in People of Color is not a reflection of negative functioning, but more a reflection of "the extreme destructiveness and negativity of the social system organization ..." (p. 72; also read the Lincoln chapter for more information on this subject and melanin as a sense receptor, e.g., Invisibility/knowingness.).* This "Food for Thought" is not an indication that because Coolidge, Eisenhower or anyone else who may have died from a   heart attack is Black, for that would be absurd. But the indication or suggestion isn't so absurd for a person subsisting under the stress of living two lives or a lie. Recent studies concur with Dr. Welsing's research findings. Dr. Robert Murray, Jr., a professor at Howard University's College of Medicine, contends that racism plays a significant part in the high blood pressure and hypertension of African-Americans. The way African-Americans react to stressful and discriminatory situations in America "have a significant effect on their blood pressure" *(Ebony,* "Why Hypertension Strikes Twice As Many Blacks As Whites," by Haynes, Karima, September, 1992, pp. 36-41). It is theorized that for a Black person failing-for-white, and in fear of being discovered, the stress level could be tremendous. Every heart attack victim is not of African ancestry. Eisenhower was almost eighty years old when he died.

THE ELECTION OF 1956

During the Adlai Stevenson/Dwight D. Eisenhower campaign, Groucho Marx, the famous comedian, was asked his opinion about the impending election for the President of the United States. He gibed, "It's the only country in the world where the people can go on the radio and kid the politicians — and where every four years the politicians go on the radio and kid the people" (Kup, p. 76).

Psychologist Abraham Maslow considered Adlai Stevenson to be a person that he termed "Self-Actualized," i.e., a person who has met profound personal achievements in life, a person who is satisfied with his or her life, and can therefore better serve the needs of others (See the Lincoln chapter). Although Eisenhower's heart attack did cost him some votes in the election of 1956, he went on to win the election against the self-actualized Adlai Stevenson (Garrison, p. 80) with many African-Americans, help. But not Grandma's.

Before I was born, my elementary student sister had asked my paternal grandmother who she was voting for. Grandma told my sister, "Don't tell your Daddy, but I'm

voting for Stevenson." My sister never understood why
Grandma Lucetta asked her not to tell. After the completion
of this research, I think both of us understand — a little better, anyway. Well, for one thing, Grandma wasn't one for
violence and militarism, and on the other hand (and from
her community of Little Haiti in Durham, North Carolina),
she felt that the Black one who makes it can "sometimes" be
worst than the white one period. Grandma read *Life* magazine, and was willing to think for herself. Even political
sophisticates such as the editors of *The Crisis* newspaper
supported Eisenhower; Val J. Washington, the assistant to
the chairman of the Republican National Committee stated:
"In 1860, Abraham Lincoln, allied with the party which
championed freedom for the slaves, was best equipped to
act in the interest of this minority. In 1952, Dwight D. Eisenhower, standing with the party whose position on Negro
rights is an honest one, ... is best fit to serve the interests of
Negro Americans as President of the United States *(The Crisis,* October, 1952, p. 487). Did Val really believe this? Or did
she and other Blacks feel an indistinguishable responsibility,
connectedness, or Link toward Eisenhower?

MS. PARKS

On December 1, 1955, Rosa Parks became the first
African-American person to be widely recognized for refus-
ing to sit at the back of the bus. This particular incident
ignited the Montgomery, Alabama bus boycott. Before Ms.
Parks, many other African-Americans with darker hues
(whose friends and relatives I've personally spoken with)
had simply and literally been thrown off the bus. Ms. Parks'
strength and work in the civil rights movement before and
after the bus incident have aided tremendously in the Struggle. Two months after Ms. Parks' heroic feat, on February 2,
1956 Autherine J. Lucy became the first African-American
student to attend the University of Alabama. She was ultimately expelled for her own safety and has just recently
(1992) received a master's degree. Congratulations to Mrs.
Autherine J. Lucy Foster for her perseverance.

NASSER

On July 28, 1954, when the British agreed to evacuate the Suez Canal, Egyptian President Mohammed Abdul Gamal Nasser celebrated with a cheering crowd. Two years later, Eisenhower was pacing up and down a White House room when one of his assistants, Mr. Larson, entered. It was July 20, 1956 and relations with Nasser had reached its most critical point. The previous day, Allen Dulles, had told the Egyptian ambassador that the United States' offer to help finance the Aswan Dam in Kemet/Egypt was to be considered withdrawn because of Egypts long delays and impossible counter-proposals (Larson, pp. 8-9). Carl Rowan, the author of *Breaking Barriers*, said that a key source told him that Eisenhower and Foster Dulles considered Gamal Nasser a menace. "Allen and Foster Dulles both were warning Ike that war was possible" (Rowan, p. 146). Subsequently, on the site of the old Aswan Dam, a new Dam was constructed. What had started out by Nasser to be a "Monumental Idea" became an "International Project." Later, the consequences of this project were horrible for the many Nubians who were killed during the tragic construction of this new Aswan (Senu'wet) Dam. This project flooded homes, destroyed belongings, and caused many deaths. These proud Nubians who had been living around this Dam for thousands of years and surviving from what the Dam contributed to their livelihood refused to move. They died; they journeyed on to the ancestors (ben-Jochannan, *Abu Simbel - Ghizeh*, p. 102). Dr. Clarke says that Nasser was one of the shining lights of African survival. Nasser died in 1970. His death is still a mystery with the CIA being in suspect.

PROOF?

In his diary dated November 6, 1956, E. Frederick Morrow, the Black man who worked in the Eisenhower administration, had been traveling all around the United States giving campaign speeches promoting Eisenhower's second term. He mentioned that he had given his last few speeches in Memphis and Nashville, Tennessee, then in Durham, North Carolina, New York, and New Jersey. Eisenhower had a regular African-American following in all of these places (Morrow, p. 104). It is interesting that both Black people and KKK members were eager to be convinced that Dwight D. Eisenhower was the best candidate to represent them as President of the United States.

Morrow said that there had been numerous questions during the many conventional meetings about Black people's part in Eisenhower's political arena. Morrow was the person who instituted an African-American speaker to get the convention off and started. This speaker would be used to second the nomination of President Eisenhower and to make an inspirational speech. Morrow said that there was a real need for an intelligent and dynamic Black ("Negro") woman who would look "unsuspectingly" Black on television screens; "rather than some lightskinned person who might be mistaken for white" (Morrow, p. 87). Well, there were thousands of African women who more than met this criteria. Dr. Helen Edmonds, a professor of history at North Carolina College in Durham was one of these women. Morrow submitted her name for consideration. Morrow contacted Dr. Edmonds immediately. She was delighted and, of course, she accepted. "The North Carolina delegation was adamant against her appearance. It felt that this smacked of the kind of social equality that it was not ready to accept or abet. The paper stated that one member of the delegation said that he would walk out of the convention and go back home rather than have a Negro woman appear." Morrow and Larson both mentioned that the whole question and the whole area of the talk about Black and white situations in this administration were very delicate. Eisenhower himself was uncomfortable using the terms race and discrimination. (Morrow, pp. 87 & 90). But the White House had taken a firm stance for once and Dr. Edmonds delivered an excellent speech. I spoke with Dr. Helen Edmonds on Saturday, March 7, 1992. She is a delightful woman. She told me that she had heard nothing about Eisenhower being of African ancestry. She related to me that she had never seen Eisenhower's mother, the picture in the 1952 Life magazine or otherwise. Dr. Edmonds went on to advise me to write about something else; that way, she lovingly cautioned, I would be accepted as a serious historian. I related to her that

I am a psychologist and an educator. She said, "I hope you change your mind." She told me, as John Hope Franklin had, that, "You nor J.A. Rogers can prove that these men are Black." I am not, and I do not think Rogers was, trying to *prove* anything to anyone; it's just that no one, but no one has proven to me nor Rogers that any of these men were white.

RACE AND COLOR, AS USUAL

Morrow said that officials in the State Department had deep, negative feelings about race and color, and they communicated these feelings to others especially during their duties abroad. Morrow alleged that it was very difficult for many of the people in the State Department, especially the southerners, to be objective when dealing with black countries. This attitude abroad communicated itself to Africans who are very outspoken in their denunciation of the paternalistic and racist attitude they experienced when they visited the United States State Department personnel. President Sekou Toure, from Guinea, Africa, visited the United States while Ike was in office. Morrow said that on the surface the visit was a success. But there were many great struggles behind the scenes. He said for example that President Toure wanted to visit an important southern city. It was some personnel staffs' thoughts that Atlanta should be the place for this special visit. While Atlanta had all the usual and racial problems that afflicted southern communities during this time, it also is the home of the great Atlanta University and several Black colleges. Black businesses also thrived in Atlanta, and this was another reason the staff-in-charge thought it would be the best city for Toure's visit. Morrow said that he knew that the State Department was the culprit in causing the officials of Atlanta to later reject the idea on the grounds that the reception for Toure could not be a friendly one. In other words, the social aspects of the visit made it necessary to veto it. Therefore, the southern city chosen was none other than Durham, North Carolina. Morrow said that Durham was not necessarily a good substitute but it would do. I personally disagree with Morrow's assessment and perception of Durham. In Durham, despite the fact that President Toure visited Duke University and the University of North Carolina in Chapel Hill, only the Black institution which was North Carolina College (now called North Carolina Central University located in Durham) gave him an honorary degree. Many African-Americans and President Toure's delegation were angry about the blatant oversight of the non-black universities. Morrow writes, "Going to the white universities was merely a token gesture, and it would have been prolific of them to bestow an honorary degree upon this distinguished visitor" (Morrow, p. 289). I agree. We are Parents of Fools.

CIVIL RIGHTS

Dwight D. Eisenhower was president of the United States when the civil rights revolution of the mid-fifties began. Eisenhower was a Republican, but he finally felt that segregation had no place in the Federal Government of the U.S. He took steps to integrate a navy yard, the armed forces, and veterans hospitals. He also forwarded the integration of Washington, D.C.'s public schools. Yet, outside the spear of direct federal authority, Eisenhower was hesitate to act toward other civil rights issues. His philosophy of government was that, state should have control of those areas where federal and state powers overlapped. School integration was one of those "overlapped" areas. Eisenhower doubted that federal laws would be effective in changing social attitudes. He said, "I don't believe, you can change the hearts of men with laws or decisions." When the Supreme Court ruling of 1954 was announced, President Eisenhower refrained from public comment — just as he had done during the Emmett Till tragedy. Following the racial outbreak in Little Rock, Arkansas, where nine black students were attempting to attend classes at Central High School, Eisenhower seemed to have shifted to a more supportive stance on this particular educational/civil rights issue. Eisenhower and Arkansas governor, Orville Faubaus, found themselves in verbal confrontation. Faubas believed that forcible integration would threaten public order. Faubas then tried to secure the national guard to prevent these nine students from attending Central High. The federal court overruled Faubas and forced him to withdraw these guardsmen. But within three weeks, white hysterical and militant mobs were standing around screaming and yelling at these Black students. The militant mobs even went so far as to attack cameramen and news reporters. On September 24, 1957, Eisenhower apparently felt it in the best interest of all concerned to send paratroopers into Little Rock to enforce the court's order to integrate the schools, and most likely to save lives. It should be kept in mind that this date was the second anniversary date of Ike's own life being spared by the Supreme Being. September 24, 1955 is the date that he had his heart attack, which was one month after Emmett Till's untimely death. In Ike's mind, especially on this day, the decision to send help to Little Rock probably was not a hard one to make. (Eisenhower had had plenty of time since January to make this decision. During this month, Ike had even refused a request from Dr. Martin Luther King, Jr. to visit the South and make a public statement that he would do all he could to uphold the Supreme Court school decision. The White House wrote back that it would be impossible for the President to honor Dr. King's wish at the time [Oates, *Let the Trumpet Sound: The Life of MLK*, p. 109]). However, in September, Ike sent thousands of paratroopers into the South to assist Blacks. He was the first president to do this since Reconstruction (Dennis, pp. 325 & 340 and Oates, p. 125). Why?

TO DADDY

In honor and in the memory of my father (1923-1991), I enjoy telling the story about one day in 1957 when I was his tiny little girl. Daddy took me into an ice cream parlor to get my favorite favor. All of the African-Americans were standing while they ate their ice cream. Of course, I didn't know any better (or maybe I did) and climbed onto one of the stools at the counter while Daddy ordered the ice cream. The attendant behind the counter placed a sign right in front of me. From just recently coming out of the womb (the environment had not yet gotten to me) and therefore still very African, I couldn't read english. Anyway, you know what the sign said. My father stood but he didn't eat, and all the other African-Americans stood. My father told this white man that he was not taking his daughter off the stool.

Daddy said, "It's just not right; she doesn't understand." The man shook his head from side to side, and said, "I sure hope the boss doesn't come in." My father stated, "I hope he *doesn't* either." (Maybe he and the white guy both had said *"don't."*) Anyway, my father was shocked when I was about nine or ten and tried to relate this story back to him. This is the day when I learned the essence of the story I just disclosed to you. I sit wherever I please now, as then, and that's usually in an African-owned environment. Looking hard and long for these African-owned places or environments are sometimes necessary, but pertinent to our economic, mental and spiritual survival. I asked Daddy when I was nine or ten, "Why didn't the Black people just take the ice cream home and eat it? Why did they want to stand around in the white man's store? Why didn't they make their own ice cream?" Daddy looked at me and smiled — a little. He then put on a very thoughtful, serious face, and said nothing. After a long while, Daddy said, "We do make good ice cream don't we?" I was glad when Daddy spoke, because I was wondering if he would ever come out of his Thoughts. It was my turn to smile, because I then thought about our next door neighbor's homemade ice cream that I loved. It could have been sold for $$$Millions.

BLACK ECONOMY

Before the famous 1961 lunch counter sit-ins, Clara Luper, an African-American teacher in Oklahoma City had already led many lunch counter sit-ins. Because the news reports were not widespread, the news did not reach very far. But why did we allow ourselves to give up our own restaurants and economic power to eat with some people who did not want to eat with us? Sister Betty Lou's Soul Food Cafe went out of business because we wanted to eat at Missy Jane's Hors d'oeuvre Place. We had some flourishing shoe shops, shoe repair shops, restaurants, corner grocery stores, plumbers shops, pastry stores, laundry shops, sewing shops and other businesses. We gave almost all of it up to mingle socially and give our money to another community while our own communities went down. I do understand the invisible, and things tend to always happen for a reason. We'll get our true selves back one day soon. These hardships have given us strong, hard backs and strong clever minds. Economic power and security, though, would have assured the social mingling later because African-Americans would have established, discovered, invented, and marketed **something** that somebody else would have wanted and/or needed, without it being stolen from us as many of our inventions have been today. Others would have wanted a piece of our pie. Even to get our 40 acres and a mule now would help — especially if we work together! But since times have changed, somewhat, and things are a bit more "sophisticated," monetary reparations (like or more than the Japanese received) would be nice. Of course, the Ultimate Solution is Self - sufficiency, efficiency, determination, work, and Buy Black. It's not too late. But we must work together and stop crying about attitudes, person- alities, opinions and who has what and did or did not do whatever! All of us have differences; this does not mean that we cannot work together. We can work for white people all of our lives, then get a company, a store, a group, a school, or an organization of our own, and we then commence to complaining about every little thing. This nonsense must stop in order to survive as a people.

Marcus Garvey's wife said, "Stand on your own two Black feet, and fight like hell for what's yours" [in America and Africa]. She and her husband advocated African togeth- erness, and this is the only way that we can regain and reclaim our true selves and economic power. Someone once asked Dr. John Henrik Clarke why his people had not pulled themselves up their bootstraps like every other race? Dr. Clarke replied, "Because somebody stole our boots, you ...." He made this statement in reference to his facts that African people are the richest people on the face of the earth, yet the poorest. Africans are rich in culture, oil, ore, gold, land, and spirituality. All other peoples pimp off the Africans' (and this means Africans all over the world) wealth for their own selfish development because African people do not today understand the need and demand for Nationhood in order to survive as a people. Well, Africans are now making grand efforts and heeding to the words of Mrs. Garvey and other strong African leaders like Dr.

Clarke who understand that knowledge and economic stability is Power. We now have some Homegirl potato chips, some X potato chips and some packaged soul food from Glory Foods. Who needs Lays or Bel-Air? We don't. Please buy from and support these African-American entrepreneurs. More and more Africans are starting their own businesses and providing more jobs for Africans. Africans are going to soon understand who they are, take their appropriate place as a people on this earth, manufacture and buy some kente cloth designed leather boots with gold shoestraps, and kick somebody's ...

THE LITTLE ROCK NINE

The Little Rock Nine, the Arkansas heroic nine, are today well and successful. Many of them are still working and lecturing continuously for the Cause. Ernest Green became the first African-American to graduate from Little Rock's Central High School in Arkansas on May 8, 1958. Some good things were happening in the Motherland around "The Little Rock Nine" time, too. On May 15, 1957, Andre Marie Mbida became the premier of Cameroon. On December 13, 1957, Daniel A. Chapman became Ghana's first Ambassador to the United States.

ROBINSON, BELAFONTE, RANDOLPH

Eisenhower helped persuade Congress to pass the first federal civil rights law — again since Reconstruction. The Civil Rights Act of 1957 allowed the Federal Government to bring suits for citizens whose voting rights had been violated (Dennis, Ethel, p. 340).

In November of 1958, one thousand Africans and whites descended upon Washington to march from the center of the city to the Lincoln Memorial to listen to speeches discussing the tragic situation in Little Rock, Arkansas. The crowd also listened to speeches about the country's undemocratic resistance to integrated schools. A delegation of marchers came to the northwest gate of the White House with a petition that they wished to deliver to Eisenhower. They were denied admission only and supposedly because their request for an ordinance with the president had not been granted. The march to Washington was lead by Jackie Robinson of baseball fame, Harry Belafonte of television fame, A. Philip Randolph of the Brotherhood of Sleeping Car Porters fame, and others. The Black community was partially divided on the usefulness of such a march. Ten days before this march, the attorney general had called and asked Morrow if he knew the purpose of the march. The attorney general felt that the only reason for the demonstration was an opportunity for "radicals" to get out of hand. Morrow told Jackie Robinson that since the President was adamant about taking this thing on through, (in reference to the Supreme Court making a positive decision that Blacks would attend integrated schools) that there was no reason for the march. He also told Robinson that he could really jeopardize his life if he went on with the march because he had heard that the march had been infiltrated with Communists (Morrow, p. 242).

BIRTH OF A NATION

Morrow stated that he had represented Eisenhower at the birth of a new nation of Ghana in March of 1957. He said that what's so ironic about this situation is that when president Kwame Nkrumah, the prime minister of Ghana, came to visit the United States, Morrow was left off the guest list for the dinner. Many Black newspaper reporters questioned this action. When Nkrumah arrived at the airport, he was given a nineteen gun salute and met by the vice president. At this point Morrow was in the receiving line when Nkrumah got off the plane. That afternoon after he arrived, Eisenhower gave an official White House luncheon for this very prominent African guest. Morrow was invited to be a guest at this noonday function, but not at the formal night-time dinner. (Morrow, pp. 241-242 & 263).

SCLC

On another side of politics, SCLC was organizing a drive called the Crusade for Citizenship to demonstrate that a new African-American determined to be free, has emerged in the U.S.A. This action was to promote a southern-wide voter registration crusade to start on none other than brother Lincoln's birthday, February 12. It was 1958. African peoples continue to use their inner spirit and knowingness to make the invisible, visible.

SLOW PROGRESS AND ORIENTAL RUGS

Even with these steps toward equality, acceptance, and integration, by September of 1959, almost two years after all of the political and educational efforts, only six Black students were studying in all of Little Rock's non-black (white) high schools, and throughout the South. Though integration won a moral victory, the actual benefits were very small. Many so-called high officials and southern lawmakers showed little concern in the area of civil rights for others; although unlawful acts of violence, scandal, or embezzlement for them seemed to be readily acceptable. For example, in 1958, during Ike's second term, and after being in office for five years, House Chief of Staff, Sherman Adams was accused of manipulating monies and securities; he was also accused of manipulating the Civil Aeronautics Board. Adams accepted money, coats, and oriental rugs for his home and other gifts that should not have been accepted as a political figure. Although Adams could not prove that he was not wrong in these incidences, he still came out to say that if there had been any errors made, it was because of his "inexperience." Eisenhower stood by Adams, and issued a statement saying, "A gift is not necessarily a bribe; one is evil; the other one is a tangible expression of friendship."

PARENTS OF FOOLS

Prince Edward County in Virginia went so far as to close down its public schools entirely in 1959 rather than have their white children study with Black children. These racist people were willing to and did pay more money for their children to go to private schools instead. Certainly many white people could afford this additional expense after so many years of discrimination, inhumane practices and economic plundering toward African-Americans. African-

Americans received no instruction in Prince Edward County for years (Dennis, p. 326). It is so ironic that Black children, the offspring of the originators of math, science, writing and teaching in general would in this day and age not be allowed to learn. Below is a poem that has been slightly revised so that parent discretion will not be necessary. You can find the 1988 uncensored cut-out poem on page 336 of this book.

PARENTS OF FOOLS

Sitting in the airport
in between states
reading my Black history
whew, my head has
a swimming ache
Just read here that we're the
Chosen Ones
For we were the first
to grace this earth!
You mean to tell me that we're the
Parents of Fools?
My God, all my white chillin
One sitting across from me now
… lookin' like he attended
snob adult preschool …
Undeserved, sanctified, superior acting cool.
I'm moving (ah), roughly gathering
my stuff
These Kriminals, outcast from Europe,
den lied
kicked us all up side our heads
and hides!
In my new seat developing my own
Superior Stance,
I saw from my … white child
a curious, defeated,
disgusted-looking glance
UMP!
Just read here that Cleopatra was Black
how happy she must have been so proud

African and Exact
Ah? What? Queen of Sheba too?
Go on, Black Sisters and do-the-do!
Oh no; Here comes another one
walking toward me with a
survey book.
How dare this ... child (of mine?!)
interrupt me with her
(pale) look!
No. No, I'm not interested dear
I have a book here
getting my mind in gear
for an African Worldwide Cure!

Auset BaKhufu, © 1991

(MORE) PROOF

On January 5, 1959, some of the earliest fossils proving
that the earliest man was African were found in Olduvai
Gorge, Tanzania, Africa. Then, as now, the parents of the
world were fighting for the right to be equal, to be free, to be
at peace and alive. Three months later on April 15, 1959
African Freedom Day was declared at the All-African People's
Conference in Accra, Ghana.

ALL SPACES ON THE PLANE ARE SPOKEN FOR

Morrow relates to us interesting African ourstory surrounding the Eisenhower period in the White House. He
documents on January 15, 1960, p. 290 of his book: *Black
Man In the White House,* that the Cameroons in North Africa
came up for independence on January 1, 1960. A few days
after this independence, President William V.S. Tubman
was to be sworn in again as president of Liberia. In preliminary discussions at the White House and the State Department, Morrow had been told that his wife would travel
along with the delegation on this special African trip (particularly since an Air Force airplane would be used as trans-
portation). In the event that commercial airplanes would
have to be used, the wives of these delegates would not be
able to make the trip. After about six days, Morrow called

the State Department because he had not heard from them; he needed a briefing on the best way to dress and other pertinent travel information for this trip. He called the State Department for information and was shocked when he learned that his wife could not occupy him on the trip, because: "All the spaces on the plane had been spoken for." The person from whom he received this information told him that only the wives of certain members of the delegation had space on the plane. Ironically enough, Morrow stated, these "certain members" turned out to be the wives of all the white male delegates only (p. 290) and none had Black wives. None of the Black delegates were permitted to take their wives. Morrow furiously had his name removed from the delegation. There was no way that he was going to disrespect his African woman too!

THERE IS A DIFFERENCE

Morrow said that he had a difficult time resolving the conflict of being two personalities at once — a Black person and an American. There is a difference. He said that as long as he was to hold the job as Assistant Presidential aide that he would have this unique conflict (pp. 218-219). Morrow seemed to have had too much love, devotion and loyalty for a president who didn't seem to have a clear understanding of true civil rights among races. Morrow's two selves were no more or no less mental and contradictory than those of all the presidents mentioned in this book. Had he seen pictures of Ike's mama in the 1952 *Life* magazine or elsewhere? Had Morrow looked into Ike's eyes and seen or felt a strange comradary? I don't know. In a conversation with Dr. Clarke, he told me that Eisenhower would never even look him in the eye. He couldn't trust a person like this. Dr. Clarke stated that "a person becomes a human being when they can look another person directly in the eye."

STORMY YEARS

Congress passed a second Civil Rights Bill in 1960. This bill created the right for African-Americans to enroll as voters, and it provided permanent penalties for white mob acts and bombings that were designed to obstruct court orders, e.g., not to kill young black children in churches. However, African-American leaders were not satisfied with these acts because the provisions still allowed leaks; there continued to be leaks and loopholes which allowed racist and discriminatory acts to occur. These types of loopholes were utilized all over the world.

On March 21, 1960 seventy-two Africans fighting for their freedom by protesting apartheid were killed in Sharpville, South Africa. Racial violence seemed to be a way of life during these stormy years.

BAY OF PIGS

One author stated that the action that the United States took in the Bay of Pigs project should be one of the most shameful episodes in American history. Eisenhower initially was not enthusiastic about the Bay of Pigs invasion, but later on, he and the rest of his assistants decided that it was really justifiable self-defense against communist aggression, and therefore, against Fidel Castro. Eisenhower stated that he was willing to take any steps necessary for the Bay of Pigs project to succeed (Wyden, p. 21, also see captions under the picture insertions in this book: *Bay of Pigs: The Untold Story*).

Fidel Castro seized control of Cuba in 1959 after carrying on a two year war against the corrupt government of Fulgencio Batista. Castro sought an alliance with the Soviet Union in 1960 (Zinn, *A People's History of the United States*, p. 426). In April, 1960, Eisenhower secretly authorized the Central Intelligence Agency (CIA) to arm and train anti-Castro Cuban exiles in Guatamala. This was a planned strategy for future invasions of Castro's Cuba (Schesinger, p. 103; Zinn, p. 432).

A memo written to Allen Dulles recommended that thorough consideration be given to the "elimination" of Fidel Castro. The CIA had drafted a top secret policy paper and this project or paper was called: A Program of Covert Action Against the Castro Regime (Wyden, pp. 24-25).

Ike was partially sympathetic towards Cuba, but stated that he simply did not know enough about the situation to make a clear judgement (Wyden, p. 24). Dulles and others knew that most of them wished Castro dead (Wyden, p. 25). On a recent television talk show, Norman Mailer, best selling author of the new book, *Harlot's Ghost : A Novel of the CIA*, stated that if the United States has already admitted to seven or eight attempts on Castro's life, then it was probably more like fifteen or sixteen attempts on Castro's life. I heard on a television documentary, May 13, 1992, that Norman Mailer has a FBI file because of his firm stance on telling and writing the truth about America.

Although Kennedy was in office when the Bay of Pigs Project was executed, he had been attacking the Eisenhower administration for allowing communism to get so close to America, i.e., eight air jet minutes away from the coast of southern United States (Wyden, p. 66). The CIA plan to invade Cuba at the Bay of Pigs and the plan to encourage Cubans to rise up against Castro blew up in the United States' face. The Kennedy Administration and the United States were faced with witnessing a Communist regime being born only eight jet minutes away from America. However, putting an end to the CIA secret war did not mean the end of the paramilitary activities which would later aid directly or indirectly in the death of Patrice Lumumba (Prados, *Presidents' Secret Wars: CIA and Pentagon Covert Operations Since World War II*, pp. 216-217 & 233-235).

PATRICE LUMUMBA

"The Congo was another of those crises that began in the twilight of the Eisenhower administration and lingered long into the Kennedy's ... The Eisenhower administration did not favor Lumumba and did what it could to encourage opposition ... such CIA operations as this one against Lumumba actually occurred" (Prados, pp. 232 & 234-235). With Eisenhower just out of office and Kennedy recently in office, on February 15, 1961 Africans born in America and their brothers and sisters residing in other places protested the slaying of Congo Premier Patrice Lumumba by disrupting a United Nations session in New York City. This is the same year that Dr. Franz Fanon, the African Algerian author of *White Masks, Black Skin* and *Wretched of the Earth* succumbed. He was also a politician and an advocate for ourstory. He advocated that Europeans were the enemy; he was married to a white woman. Fanon was living in Bethesda, Maryland when he died.

Since Dwight D. Eisenhower's death, his son, "John, has spoken out when his father's reputation has come under attack. The 1975 Senate hearings on Intelligence activities revealed CIA assassination plots against such foreign leaders as Cuban Premier Fidel Castro and the late African Revolutionary Patrice Lumumba." Ike's son apparently feels that his father would have told him about secret CIA assassinations that he urged or assigned. John Eisenhower insinuated that since his father did not tell him about these assassination plots, that his father is innocent of any wrongdoing in the matter. "The Committee did not implicate Ike in the assassination plots and the Senate report indicated that the murder of undesirable foreign leaders was to proliferate during the Kennedy administration." They said that undesirable foreign leaders was to be carried out (executed) during the Kennedy administration, not during the Eisenhower administration (Neal, p. 458).

"As a result of the Cuban operations [sic] secret warriors succeeded in creating a cadre with military skills, … Cuban pilots later flew B-26 bombers for the CIA in the Congo" (Prados, p. 217). In early August, 1960, Dwight D. Eisenhower ordered the CIA to assassinate Patrice Lumumba. Five months later, Patrice Lumumba, one of Africa's greatest men and leaders was brutally murdered by enemies: western enemies, American enemies, and African traitors. Robert H. Johnson was a member of the national security council from 1951 to 1962. He was later to relate to the Senate Select Committee about a conversation during an Eisenhower administration meeting and the conversation that occurred during a NSC meeting which was held August 18, 1960. Johnson said, "At some time during that discussion, President Eisenhower said something — I can no longer remember his words — that came across to me as an order for the assassination of Lumumba who was then at the center of political conflict and controversy in the Congo. There was no discussion, the meeting simply moved on. I remember my sense of that moment quite clearly because the President's statement came as a great shock to me" (*Church Committee Report*, p. 55; Kondo, *A Crash Course in Black History*, pp. 14 & 37; Info.: *Upscale* magazine, "Crash Course," Book Mark section, p. 83, February/March, 1991).

Patrice Lumumba was the first prime minister of the Republic of the Congo in Africa. His ancestral community was a branch of dynamic Africans from the family of Central Congo. Lumumba attended school in Africa, and rapidly became a leader. In 1959, he was seen as the only truly national figure on the Congo political scene. (Note: for the children — On September 5, 1960, Leopold Sedar Senghor, politician and poet was elected President of Senegal.)

Maya Angelou, a famous African-American activist, poet, and author, related her horror in one of her books after hearing about the assassination of Lumumba. She said that she and a friend met on 125th Street in New York. Her friend proceeded to tell her that she had learned of the assassination from Congelese diplomats. Her friend (I think her name is Rosa) stated that this tragic news would not be publicly announced until later. It would be announced by Adlai Stevenson, who was then the United States delegate of the United Nations. Ms. Angelou said that she felt completely numb. As she walked sadly along the streets of Africa/ Harlem, New York, she saw Malcolm X at a microphone. He was saying, "All of you under the sound of my voice is a soldier." He continued, "The Black man has been programmed to die by his own hands, his brother's hands, or the hands of the blue-eyed devil!" Maya said that everybody shouted and stamp their feet. The policemen patted their guns. I'll never forget reading this. Reading this passage from Ms. Angelou's book is when I learned who Patrice Lumumba was. I had not been taught in school that he was one of my heroes. Maya played an important role in the United Nations disruption in February of 1961.

"In Zaire, formerly the Congo, Casey met the leader Joseph Mobutu. CIA ties with Mobutu dated back to 1960; this is the same year that the CIA had planned the assassination of Congolese nationalist leader Patrice Lumumba. On August 25, 1960, a cable to the CIA station chief from then DCI Allen Dulles stated that Lumumba's 'removal' must be an urgent and prime objective and under existing conditions, this should be a high priority of our covert action" (Woodward, Bob, *Veil: The Secret Wars of the CIA, 1981-1987, p. 268)*. As mentioned, Lumumba's death in 1961 was that of horror to many Africans in Africa and Africans in diaspora as well. Dwight D. Eisenhower played a big part in the fate of Africans. Carl Rowan, the author of the recently published book, *Breaking Barriers,* states that Eisenhower was a liar and a gradualist who, in his view, compromised "away the freedom of America's black people" (pp. 230 & 145).

NO NEGRO SHALL COURT MY DAUGHTER

Dwight Eisenhower was known to stress "his distaste for the word 'discrimination,'" but added that "as one who had lived in the south," he would "be sure to make it clear that the social equality of political and economic opportunity did not mean necessarily that everyone has to mingle socially — or that a Negro should court my daughter." Arthur Larson, the author of, *Eisenhower: The President Nobody Knew,* said that Eisenhower was a man who seemed to be extremely uneasy when anyone used the word racial (Larsen, p. 126). Why was he uneasy? Freudian slips can be interpreted in many ways. In this case, Ike made Freudian slop. He puked and told all over himself. Eisenhower had no daughters. Is this an unconscious or conscious implication that it's all right for the Eisenhower men to marry or be intimate with Black women? Why would he say daughter instead of son? He had two sons; no daughters. His father had seven sons; no daughters. Ike and all of those brothers; no sisters. It would be unusual to think daughter when such is so far and intimately removed from one's life. Did an Eisenhower man marry a Black woman? Why couldn't he bring himself to say that he wouldn't want a Negro to court his son? Did he feel that he would be disrespectful toward someone he loves dearly had he actually said this? Had Eisenhower used the word son instead of daughter, the insinuation would have been that a Black woman was not good enough for his son. Ike could have been thinking, *"If she's good enough for Dad, and honorable enough to be my son's grandmother, then a Black ("Negro") woman must be good enough for my son(s) to marry."* So it was important that Dwight Eisenhower choose his words carefully; therefore the noun "daughter" instead of "son" was used to complete the racist statement made by Eisenhower. Like Lincoln, Ike was confused, and after reading through the "invisibility" of this analysis, I hope you're not — confused.

SLICK, CUNNING — "LINCOLN PHILOSOPHY?"

The Eisenhower administration believed in what they termed the "Lincoln Philosophy." Eisenhower said that he had noticed that in Lincoln's public speeches a certain level of style was always preserved, although privately Lincoln could be very "brawdy." This philosophy began to be called the "Lincoln Formula" in the Eisenhower administration (Larson, pp. 134-136). Although Eisenhower's vice president was not of an African heritage, like Lincoln's vice president, there still is one final point of interest about the Eisenhower administration and the black choice. Appointments within the executive branch served several "firsts" including Frederick Morrow, the author of *Black Man in the White House*, and the first recognized African-American to serve on a president's immediate staff, as mentioned earlier. Morrow was Arthur Larson's assistant on the speech writing team for a period of time. Morrow felt that the Republicans lost a million dollar opportunity by not capitalizing on his presence in the White House. J. Ernest Wilkins was also appointed. Eisenhower proudly pointed out that "Wilkins was the first Negro in United States history ever to sit officially at the president's cabinet table." There is a now disclosed story to this very proud statement made by Eisenhower. Larson said that he and Secretary Mitchell, a non-black, had a rule that neither one of them would ever both be out of town at the same time, because this would place Wilkins at the table at the cabinet meetings. One day after Wilkins had been appointed assistant secretary, Larson was on his way back from an out-of-town business trip. Mitchell was also out of Washington. The cabinet was due to hold its regular meeting the following morning, and before Larson could leave to get back to Washington, he received a rather strange phone call from Mitchell's administrative assistant. The administrative assistant commanded to Larson, "Don't return to Washington until tomorrow night, and don't ask any questions." Larson did as he was told. So Eisenhower was noted for being the first president to have a "Negro" at a cabinet meeting (Larson, p. 131). Slick and cunning? Yeah.

"The Underestimation of Dwight D. Eisenhower" is the title of an article in the *New York Post* (*Esquire* Magazine), 1967. The writer says of Eisenhower that, the picture that emerges here is "that of a man whose very intelligence, was deliberately concealed behind *masks* of assumed confusion." Kempton, the writer, alleges that Eisenhower was cold in his relations even with his closet associates. "He was a master of deception." The article continues: "The Eisenhower who emerges here intermittedly free from his habitual *veils* is ..., indifferent to any sentiment, is calm when he was demonstrating the wisdom of leaving a bad situation alone as when he was moving to meet it on those occasions when he absolutely had to." Kempton concludes by stating that Eisenhower was the great turtle of which the world sat for eight years. He said that the public laughed at Eisenhower. They gossiped about Eisenhower, "and all the while the public never knew the cunning *beneath the shell*." (Larson, Eisenhower: *The President Nobody Knew*, p. 199). Bill Moyers, Broadcast Journalist, said that Eisenhower could be deliberately deceiving. He said that when he first heard President Eisenhower speaking, he immediately thought that here's a President who cannot express a complete thought; here's a President who is not grammatical. Moyers said that Ike would go through one hundred semi-colons in a two minute span just to make one point. Then he realized that the President was cunning the listening audience in order "to prevent the press from hussling his priorities." Moyers said, "This is an act. Eisenhower could put a sentence together as grammatically and effectively as Harry Truman or John F. Kennedy; he just chose not to" (T.V. Special Documentary, *Class of the 20th Century: 1952-1955*, 1992).

EISENHOWER'S DEATH

Dwight D. Eisenhower died of a heart attack on March 28, 1969. His last words were: "I've always loved my wife.

I've always loved my children. I've always loved my grand-children. I've always loved my country." And although he didn't think of it or was simply to weak to say so, it does seem surely that he always loved his parents and brothers too. Kay Summersby expressed that she was very proud of Ike when he became President of the United States, and felt relieved when Ike finally died after numerous heart attacks and stomach pains. She stated that, "He had suffered too long" (Morgan, p. 250). Ike had been a national hero to many. After Ike's death, Mamie spent her time reading, watching soap operas, and thinking about her very public husband. Mamie asserted that Ike is now at peace with friends in Abilene. She also stated that she hates it when the cold white snow covers the head of her beloved husband's statues.

There had been no President like Ike, a writer stated, since Abe Lincoln (Morgan, p. 229). Perhaps not, for Harding didn't seem to have the same type of "American political" charisma as Lincoln nor Eisenhower.

David J. Eisenhower and **Ida Stover Eisenhower** *(Dwight's parents).*

Eisenhower standing on Michigan Avenue, Chicago, 1911.

Ike's girlfriend, **Kay Summersby** *(Library of Congress).*

The pyramids of **Ghiza Cairo, Kemet (Egypt)** *(BaKhufu Archives)*.

Goddess Hypatia, author's depiction.

Frederick Douglas and **Karl Marx**.

Dwight D. Eisenhower, "What you talking 'bout, Auset?"

Dwight D. Eisenhower and his wife, **Mamie**, 1916.

NAME WITHHELD

This next, and seventh, president said by some to be of African (Black) ancestry will not be named in this book. After careful research and a few moderately angry white historians and librarians and some amused ones, there seems to be no published research or literature stating that this president is of African ancestry.

The first time there was mention to me about the African ancestry possibility of this president was in the form of a question. A friend of mine asked if this president had black blood — or something to that effect. My reply: "I do not know." The second time I heard of the possibility was in an African study group. This was enough to get me curious, especially since, third, I had overheard an overzealous political, history-buff acquaintance of mine mention to a friend of his a few years back that he doesn't care what anyone says, "this man has some black blood somewhere in him. But who cares? He claims white!" I agree, but I was still curious. I found only one statement attesting to the possibility. The fourth time I heard a remark suggesting that this man may be of color was in a Washington, D.C. library when a white man stated to a person who accompanied him that both this "president and his wife look ethnic" (in a picture). We were in the same Biography section of the library. I did not see this particular picture, but I did find some pictures myself. A few of these pictures does show a possibility of African ancestry. Since the fourth time someone made mention of this president's ancestry, and indeed several times since that time, many African-Americans have given me this man's name as the seventh (or eighth) president who has African blood. The three reasons for their assertions are essentially the same: "I've heard it somewhere;" "He seems to be nicer," and "He looks like it." Pictures sometimes speak louder than words.

Though there have been many African peoples who are white enough and have white enough features to fail-for-white (and have completely), this man can go either way. I did find one picture where this president and his wife both look Black. This may be the same picture for which the man in the library referred.

So far as I can recollect, the basis for the speculation is on facial features and behavior. As mentioned, this man's pictures, to those very familiar with African physiognomy, does show some African features. I can say one thing for sure and that is: If this man is indeed of any little bit of African blood or melanin, he's blessed, and I would hope that no one Black nor white would consider it a "smear" to be so.

This president's father is said to be a racist, his mother a liberal, and all of them known to "like Blacks ..." whatever that means.

CONCLUDING REMARKS

It is usual for white writers to condemn offhand the statement that any President could possibly have any degree of Negro strain, whatsoever. But it is not possible, with the tracing of ancestry, to find whether one is "pure" white.

Joel A. Rogers

No anthropologist, ourstorian nor historian has a definitive word on such a debatable issue as the race of the presidents mentioned in this book. However, I agree with Lyndon Johnson when he said that "Washington, D.C. was founded on rumors, and most of them are true." But if your mind is fixated within the realm of "White president or No president" then you will never understand the persistent ninety percent chance that America has already voted at least six Black men into the White House. No one has proven to anyone that any of these presidents are genetically and biologically white. It has, however, been proven over and over again to everyone that they were *mentally* white. The truth about the DNA testing on Abraham Lincoln would give good cause for America to seriously rethink the entire historical concept of race and politics. Educational psychologist Asa Hilliard, Georgia State University, Atlanta, said, "Never has white been separated from the influence of Africa, even in Europe. There are millions [of white people] living in America who think they are white but are actually Black" (*Tony Brown's Journal*, 1988). As mentioned in the Preliminary Treatise, no one is trying to claim these people as their own; the statement Hilliard made is simply a fact.

These presidents harbored white personalities, which is called the host or dominant personality in their cases. Their white personality had prime control over the mind most of the time. Andrew Jackson is the only president mentioned within the contents of this work known to physically injure people of color. Abuse of any type is abuse, but we must remember that there are even people today who still do not understand this. And if these men could fool themselves into thinking they are white, then they could definitely fool themselves into thinking that just because they did not strike a person of color physically that they have not abused them. They were also protecting themselves, for to abuse a person of color would be to abuse themselves, although these presidents did cause much pain for African-Americans in many other ways.

Andrew Jackson killed people of color. He seemed to have had a continuous psychological breakdown. Jackson was so traumatized by many of the events and experiences of his childhood that in his young and adult life, he had eventually turned to, what I consider to be, murder. He murdered not just for the American status quo, but seemingly as an act of mind clearing. In essence, he killed himself long before he died. He was very destructive.

For most of these presidents their black selves were mild alternates which denote a personality other than the original, or more appropriately for this theory, the host/dominant personality, which was white. This black and white personality is complex and is integrated with its own unique behavior patterns and social relationships. The healthy personality is an entity with a firm, persistent and well-founded sense of one self and a characteristic and consistent pattern of behavior and feelings in response to given stimuli. This personality must have a range of functions, a range of emotional responses, and a range of significant life history of its own existence. In America, a person must function as Black or White, Jewish or Hispanic, Latino or Japanese, Spanish or Mexican, Korean or Indian, German or Italian, or whatever. But a combination of any of these peoples poses a sociological problem when trying to live a productive, problem-free life in American society. With these men, their black existence, their black selves, did not have significant lives and a history of their own; therefore these "selves" were just as confounded and confused as the white "selves."

White people's idolation of these presidents reveals to us more about the unconditional love and innate feelings, and the truth of the world and history/ourstory than is readily recognized. Children almost always love, in addition to rebel against, their parents at some point during their growth. I think that immature whites (and you can be any age) are now at the puberty/rebellion stage. But accepting the truth will set everybody free. Dr. Hollis Lynch said in 1978 that according to American standards, these presidents are Black. He said this testimony is not farfetched at all. "It is very likely that these men had African ancestry" (*Tony Brown's Journal*, 1978 & 1988). Dr. Lynch was making reference to the presidents mentioned in J.A. Rogers' pamphlet, *The Five Negro Presidents*, 1965.

In the year 2000, the United States will be in critical need of a real Black/African-American President. I appeal to the strong Brothers between the ages thirty and sixty-five to please think about this seriously, and begin to prepare yourself(ves) to campaign for this office and win. This is not a paternalistic nor chauvanistic request, because women, especially Black women, have a much more important responsibility than being president of the United States in the year 2000 and beyond. This does not suggest that we should never run for President. Read about these inspiring responsibilities in my next work: "The Mystery Teachings of the Temple Ast." The Original Woman (not First Lady) in the Black House in the year 2000 will understand these teachings.

If Africans/Blacks are going to live in America, fine. Stop complaining and invest in it with a full understanding and plan to get your fair share of it. Campaign for President. It is time for the children of America (Whites) to stop mentally and physically abusing the Parents of the World (Blacks). Being president will not solve all of the problems in American society, but developing other economic and political strategies will help, and we do not need this book to prove that a Black man can be President of the United States. We already know it. Everybody already knows it.

It is felt that most of the presidents referenced here are of African ancestry, and it is complimentary enough in saying so, but Africans in America have enough problems without trying to claim Blacks who do not want to be Black; therefore, I proudly and hastily give all Six (seven or eight) of these mentally deprived men back to the white race.

I've been "alive" serious throughout this work — my Africanness and profession demand it.

Maát/Hotep.

BIBLIOGRAPHY AND REFERENCE LIST

Adler, David A., *Thomas Jefferson: Father of our Democracy*, Holiday House, New York. 1987.

Akbar, Na'im, *Chains and Images of Psychological Slavery*, New Mind Productions, New Jersey, 1985.

Allen, Frederick Lewis, *Only Yesterday and Since Yesterday: A Popular History of the '20's and '30's*, Bonanza Books, N.Y., 1986. Originally *Only Yesterday*, Harper, 1931.

Allen, Hannah, *Don't Get Stuck! The Case Against Vaccinations and Injections*, Natural Hygiene Press, Florida, 1985, pp. 145-150 (For more information on the Salk and Sabin Vaccines - polio).

Ambrose, Stephen E., *Eisenhower-Soldier, General of the Army, President-Elect, 1890-1952*, Garden City, New York.

Ibid. The Supreme Commander: The War Years of General Dwight D. Eisenhower, Garden City, New York, 1970.

American Heritage Dictionary, H.S. ed., Houghton Mifflin Co., Boston, 1982.

Anderson, Jervis, *This Was Harlem (1900-1950)*, Farrar Straus Giroux, New York, 1982.

Aptheker, Herbert, *A Documentary History of the Negro People In The United States (1933-1945): From the Beginning of the New Deal to the End of the Second World War*, The Citadel Press: Secaucus, New Jersey, 1974.

Amen-Ra, Jehuti El-Malik, Reference: *Shattering the Myth of the Man Who Freed the Slaves: A True Account of Abraham Lincoln's Failure to Free Enslaved Africans in America*, Fourth Dynasty Pub. Co., Silver Spring, MD, 1990.

Baber, Adin, *Sarah and Abe in Indiana*, Moore Publishing Co., Durham, N.C., 1970.

BaKhufu, Auset (p.k.a. Janet Barber), Dissertation: "A Comprehensive Study of Multiple Personalities: Why Aren't Blacks in Therapy?" 1985.

Ibid. Unpublished Graduate Paper: "The Counseling and Treatment of Adult Multiple Personalities," 1985.

Ibid. Unpublished Graduate Paper: "A Study of Incest and Rape Perpetrators' Psychological Motivations and the Agony of the Victims — Treatment For All." 1985.

Ibid. Health and Psychological References: "Healing: Herbs, Health and Spirituality," and "The Mystery Teachings of the Temple of Ast: Nut, Goddess of the Universe — Uzit/Auset, Mother of the Earth" (Works in Progress by the author, 1985-1992. Exact publication dates are pending.)

Balsiger, D. & Seller, C., *The Lincoln Conspiracy*, Schick Sunn Classic Books, Los Angeles, California, 1977.

Banneker, Benjamin, *A L M A N A C (Banneker's 1795 Almanac)*, Also see: Howard Eves, Univ. of Maine, Orono, *The Mathematical Teacher*, 1962.

Barnes, Carol, *Melanin: The Chemical Key to Black Greatness*, BLACK GREATNESS SERIES, Houston, TX, 1988.

ben-Jochannan, Yosef and Clarke, John Henrik, Reference: *New Dimensions in African History - From the Nile Valley to the New World: Science, Invention & Technology*, Africa World Press, Inc., New Jersey, 1991.

ben-Jochannan, Yosef, *Africa: Mother of Western Civilization*, Black Classic Press, Baltimore, MD, 1971 (1988).

Ibid., "*African Origins of the Major 'Western Religions,'*" Alkebu-lan Books, N.Y., 1970.

Ibid., "*Black Man on the Nile*," Black Classic Press, Baltimore, 1989.

Bennett, Lerone, Jr., *Before the Mayflower*, Penguin Books, Inc. Maryland, 1973.

Black History for Beginners, Reference. By Denise Dennis & Susan Willmarth, Writers and Readers Documentary, 1984.

Boritt, Gabor, "The Case of the President's Feet," (Abraham Lincoln), *Horizons-U.S. News & World Report*, Nov., 28, 1988, by Lew Lord, pp. 64-65.

Bovill, E.W., *The Golden Trade of the Moors*." Oxford Univ. Press, London, 1978.

Britton, Nan, *The President's Daughter*, Elizabeth Ann Guild, Inc., New York, 1927.

Brodie, Fawn, *Thomas Jefferson: An Intimate History*, New York: W.W. Norton, 1974.

Brooks, Noah, *Abraham Lincoln and the Downfall of American Slavery, 1894.* AMS Press, Inc., New York, 1978.

Brooks, Stewart M., *Our Murdered Presidents: The Medical Story*, Frederick Fell, Inc., N.Y., 1966.

Brown, Tony, References: "Inside the Klan" and "Black and White." Tony Brown's Journal, the Television Series,

Tony Brown Productions, Inc., New York, N.Y., 1986. "The Five Negro Presidents," 1988 (See: the Conclusion of the book).

Buell, Augustus C., *History of Andrew Jackson*, I, 38.

Bumann, Joan & Patterson, John, *Our American Presidents*, Willowisp Press, Inc., Worthington, OH, 1989.

Burk, R., *The Eisenhower Administration and Black Civil Rights*, Twentieth-Century America Series, 1984.

Burke's Presidential Families of the United States of America, "Lineage of President Coolidge," London, Burke's Peerage Limited, 2nd ed., 1981.

Calhoun, A.W., *Social History of the American Family*, vol. II, p. 300, Cleveland, OH, 1918.

Callender, James Thomson, *The History of the United States for the Year 1796*, Philadelphia: The Press of Snowden and McCorkle, 1797.

Carter, Paul, *The Twenties in America*, Harlen Dividson. Inc., IL, 1975.

Catterall, Helen Tunnicliff, *Judicial Cases Concerning American Slavery and the Negro*, Octagon Books, New York, 1968.

Cecil Textbook of Medicine, "The Marfan Syndrome," by Byers, Peter H., Wyngaarden & Smith, W.B. Saunders Co., Philadelphia, 1988, pp. 1177-1178.

Census Index (U.S. Federal), Virginia 1870, 1850, 1830, & 1810, as mentioned in the content of the book, Washington, D.C.

Chancellor, William Estabrook, *Warren Gamaliel Harding: President of the United States (A Review of Facts Collected From - Anthropological, Historical and Political Researches)*, The Sentinal Press, 1922.

Chase-Riboud, Barbara, *Sally Hemings* (The Hemings-Jefferson Affair — a semi-fictional account), Viking, 1979.

Chobanian, Aram & Loviglio, Lorraine, *Heart Risk Book: A Practical Guide for Preventing Heart Disease*, Bantam Books, N.Y., June, 1982 (For this book or more information about this book, contact Boston University Medical Center, John Hancock Mutual Life Insurance Company, or your local HMO.).

Churchill, W. & Vander Wall, J., *Agents of Repression: The FBI's Secret Wars Against the Black Panther Party and the American Indian Movement*, South End Press, Boston, MA, 1988.

Civil War Times, November/December, 1991, Vol. XXX, No. 5, pp. 19-67.

Clarke, John Henrik, *African World Revolution: Africans at the Crossroads*, African World Press, Inc., Trenton, New Jersey, 1991.

Clarke, John Henrik & Garvey, Amy, *MARCUS GARVEY and the Vision of Africa*, Vintage Books, New York, 1974.

Class of the 20th Century, Special Television Documentary, 1992.

Class Magazine, "Dr. Charles Drew," by: Donna Henry, March/April, 1992, p. 62.

Clugston, William George, *Eisenhower for President?*, Exposition Press, New York, 1945.

Coit, Margaret, *Andrew Jackson*, Houghton Mifflin Co., Boston, 1965.

Concise Dictionary of American Biography, Hopkins, Joseph, "Hannibal Hamlin," p. 393, Scribners, N.Y., 1964.

CONVERSATIONS (Private, one-on-one) Between the Author and: Dr. John Henrik Clarke, Bro. Asamoah NKwanta, Dr. Dan Ford, Mr. U.L. Farris, Dr. John Hope Franklin, Mr. Fred Barber, Mrs. Almanda Barber, Mr. Don Link, Dr. Helen Edmonds, Ms. Jean Barber Rogers, Ankh Mi Ra, Mrs. Barbara Taylor Bragg, Sis. Kandaky Ashby and Dr. Wade Nobles — from January, 1990 to October, 1992.

Cortner, Richard C., Reference: *A Mob Intent on Death*, Wesleyan University Press, Middletown, Conn., 1988.

Cotterill, R.S., *The Southern Indian*, p. 189, 1814.

Cox, LaWanda, Reference: *Lincoln and Black Freedom*, Univ. of Illinois Press, Chicago, 1985.

Coyle, David C., *Ordeal of the Presidency*, Maywood College Library. By Public Affairs Press, 1960.

The Crises, "Discrimination in Africa," p. 372, June/July, 1952; "The Republican Case," p. 487, October, 1952, and "Book Reviews - J.A. Rogers", p. 535, October, 1952.

Cumston, C.G., *The History of Medicine*, Dorset Press, New York, 1987.

Cunliffe, Marcus, *American Presidents and the Presidency*, American Heritage Press, N.Y., 1972.

Current Medical Diagnosis and Treatment, A Lange Medical Book, Appleton and Lange, Norwalk, CA, 1992.

Curtis, Jane, *Return to these Hills: the Vermont years of Calvin Coolidge*, Curtis-Lieberman Books, Woodstock, Vermont, 1985.

Davis, Burke, *The Civil War: Strange & Fascinating Facts*, Wings Books, New York, 1982.

Davis, Kenneth, *Soldier of Democracy*, Doubleday Doran, Garden City, N.Y., 1945.

Dennis, R. Ethel, *The Black People of America*, McGraw-Hill Book Co., New York, 1970.

The Descendants of the Presidents, Tucker, R. Whitney, "Warren G. Harding," p. 149, Delmar Printing Co., Charlotte, N.C., 1975.

Diagnostic & Statistical Manual of Mental Disorders (DSM-III), 3rd edition, American Psychiatric Association, Washington, D.C., 1980 (and 1987 - revised).

Dictionary of American Biography, Fraunces to Hibbard. "Hannibal Hamlin", pp. 196-197. "Charles Hamlin (H. Hamlin's third son)", p. 194. Johnson, Allen and Malone, Dumas, Charles Scribner's Sons, New York, 1931.

Dictionary of American Portraits, (4,000 pictures of important Americans from earliest times to the beginning of the 20th century), Dover Publications, Inc., New York, 1967.

Diop, Cheikh Anta, *Civilization or Barbarism: An Authentic Anthropology*, Lawrence Hill Books, N.Y., 1991. (Please see other scientific, masterfully researched and written works by Dr. Diop.)

Dissociation, Reference: (The Official Journal of the International Society for the Study of Multiple Personality and Dissociation), vol. II, No. 4: December, 1989. Richard P. Kluft.

Donald, David, *Lincoln's Herndon: A Biography*, Da Capo Press, Inc., New York, 1948 (by Alfred A. Knopf, Inc.)

Du Bois, W.E.B., *Black Reconstruction in America 1860-1880*, Atheneum, N.y., 1962 (1935).

Ebony Magazine, "Was Abe Lincoln a White Supremacist?" Bennett, Lerone Jr., Vol. XXIII, February, 1968, pp. 35-38.

Ebony Magazine, "Why Hypertension Strikes Twice As Many Blacks As Whites," Vol. XLVII, No. 11, September, 1992, pp. 36-41.

Ebony Magazine, Sociopsychological Reference 1: "Trapped in the Body of A White Woman" (Oregon teacher reveals pain of "'living Black and looking White,") by Kathleen

Cross, vol. XLV, No. 12, October, 1990, pp. 70-74. Reference 2: "Is Skin Color Still a Problem in Black America?"(Sociologists and Psychologists were interviewed.) vol. XL, No. 2, December, 1984, pp. 66-70.

The Economist, "Abraham Lincoln: Dreaded Abe Wins Case," (American Survey section), 1991, p. 31.

EISENHOWER: American Hero, Historical Record of His Life, by the editors of: American Heritage Magazine and United Press International, 1969.

Eisenhower, David, *Eisenhower at War 1943-1945,* Random House, New York, 1986.

Eisenhower, Dwight D., *at ease: Stories I Tell My Friends,* Doubleday & Co., Inc., Garden City, N.Y., 1967.

Eisenhower, John S.D., *Strictly Personal - A Memoir,* Doubleday & Co. Inc., Garden City, N.Y., 1974.

Emery, Noemi, "Alexander Hamilton: An Intimate Portrait." N.Y., G.P. Putnam's sons, 1982.

Encyclopedia of Medicine (The American Medical Association), Random House, New York, Clapman, Charles B., 1989, p. 664.

Erikson, Erik H., *Dimensions of a New Identity: Jefferson Lectures 1973,* W.W. Norton & Co., Inc., New York, 1974.

Faber, Doris, *Dwight Eisenhower,* Abelard-Schuman, New York, 1977.

Fairbank, C., *How the Way was Prepared,* Chicago, 1890.

Fanon, Frantz, *Black Skin, White Masks,* Grove Press, Inc., New York, 1967.

Ibid. Reference: *The Wretched of the Earth,* Grove Press, Inc., N.Y., 1963.

Fell, Barry, *America B.C.: Ancient Settlers in the New World,* Pocket Books, New York, 1976.

Franklin, John Hope, "Runaway Slaves," *American Visions Magazine,* February 3, 1991, pp. 30-31.

French, Benjamin Brown, *Witness To The Young Republic: A Yankee's Journal, 1828-1870,* Univ. Press of New England, London, 1989. (French knew Abe Lincoln and Hannibal Hamlin equally well. He was at Lincoln's bedside when he died. He, like Thaddeus Stevens, supported Hamlin for reelection for vice president to no avail; Andrew Johnson won.)

Freud, Sigmund, "Collected Papers," *The International Psycho-analytical Library, no. 8,* N.Y. - Basic Books, Inc., 1959.

Ibid. "Moses and Monotheism," Vintage Books, N.Y., 1967.

Fuller, Neely, *The United Independent Compensatory Code/System/Concept,* Washington, D.C., 1957 - 1984.

Gardiner, Sir Alan, *Egyptian Grammar,* 1927. Griffith Inst., Ashmolean Museum, Oxford, 3rd ed., 1988.

Garrison, W., *A Treasury of-WHITE HOUSE TALES,* Rutledge Hill Press, Nashville, Tennessee, 1989.

Garvey, Marcus (Audiocassette: "LOOK UP, YOU MIGHTY RACE! Two short speeches by Marcus Garvey. **A & A Distributors,** the sole legal distributors of the audiotape of Garvey's actual voice — the only known recording. Also available: The Garvey Mail Fraud Transcripts. Write P.O. Box 1113, Temple Hills, MD 20757 for more information). RESEARCHER: Professor Robert Hill, The University of California-Los Angeles, The Marcus Garvey Papers Project.

Gladwell, Malcolm, "Ethics Panel Clears Plan to Test Lincoln's Remains: Experiment Seeks to Determine Whether He Had Marfan's Syndrome, a Tissue Disorder," *Washington Post,* May 3, 1991, p. A3.

Gould, Stephen Jay, *The Mismeasure of Man,* W.W. Norton & Co., New York & London, 1981.

Gray, Paul, "Whose America? Who Are We? American kids are getting a new — and divisive — view of Thomas Jefferson, Thanksgiving and the Fourth of July," *Time Magazine,* July 8, 1991, pp. 12-17.

Gross, Anthony, *Lincoln's Own Stories,* The Sun Dial Press, New York, 1940.

Gunn, John, "Crash Course: 150 Important Facts About African Peoples," *Upscale Magazine,* Book Mark Section, February/March, 1991 p. 83. Re: Kondo.

Hamilton, Charles, V., *Adam Clayton Powell. Jr., The Political Biography of an American Dilemma,* Atheneum, N.Y., 1991.

Hamilton, J.G. de Roulhac, "The Many-Sired Lincoln," *The American MERCURY,* vol. V, No. 18, June, 1925, pp. 129-135.

Hamilton, Milton W, "Augustus C. Buell, Fraudulent Historian," *The Pennsylvania Magazine of History and Biography* (1956), LXXX, pp. 478-492.

Hamlin, Charles Eugene, *The Life and Times of Hannibal Hamlin*, Published by Subscription, by H. Hamlin's Grandson. Riverside Press - Cambridge, 1899.

Handlin, Oscar and Lilian, *Abraham Lincoln, and the Union*, Little, Brown and Co., Boston, 1980.

Harris, Middleton, et al., *The Black Book*, Random House, N.Y., 1974.

Harvey, P., *Reminiscences of Daniel Webster*, n. 77, 1882.

Hazard, Thomas Robinson, *The Jonny-Cake Papers of "Shepard Tom" Boston*, 1867 & 1915.

Hemings, Madison, "Pike County [Ohio] Republican," 1873.

Herndon, W.H., *Herndon's-Life of Lincoln, The History and Personal Recollections of Abraham Lincoln as originally written by WILLIAM H. HERNDON and JESSE W. WEIK with introduction and notes by Paul Angle*, The World Publishing Company, Cleveland and New York, 1892.

Ibid. *Lincoln: A True Story of a Great Life*, The Bobbs-Merrill Company, Inc., Indianapolis & New York, 1892.

Ibid. *The Hidden Lincoln - Letters From Herndon* (the originals), Springfield, Illinois, 1865-1891.

Hertz, Emanuel, *The Hidden Lincoln: From the Letters and Papers of William H. Herndon*, The Viking Press, Inc., N.Y., 1938.

Hoskins, Linus, *Decoding European Geopolitics: Afrocentric Perspectives*, African-Amer. Affairs Monograph Series, Kent State Univ., OH, 1990.

Hoover, J. Edgar, *Masters of Deceit* (Communism), Pocket Books, Inc., N.Y., 1961.

Huggins, Nathan Irvin, *Frederick Douglass: Slave and Citizen (the life of)*, Little, Brown and Co., Boston, 1980.

Hughley, Ella J., *The Truth About Black Biblical Hebrew-Israelites (Jews): The World's Best-Kept Secret! * What Happened to the True "Black Jews" in the Year 70 C.E. (A.D.)?* Ms. Hughley asks and answers. HUGHLEY PUBLICATIONS, P.O. Box 261, Springfield Gardens, New York, 11413, 1982.

Hunt, H. Draper, *Hannibal Hamlin of Maine*, Syracuse University Press, New York, 1969.

Hyman, Dick, *Washington Wind & Wisdom*, The Stephen Greene Press, Lexington, Mass., 1988.

JAMA (Journal of the American Medical Association), (1) "Marfan's Syndrome Starting to Yield Secrets," by, Kirn, Timothy, vol. 260, No. 21, December 2, 1988, p. 3108. (2) "Marfan Syndrome gene search intensifies following identification of basic defect," by, Randall, Teri, vol. 264, No. 21, pp. 1642 & 1645.

Jackson, John G., *Ethiopia and the Origin of Civilization*, Black Classic Press, Baltimore, MD.

Ibid. *Introduction to African Civilizations*, (Introduction by: John Henrik Clarke), The Citadel Press, Secaucus, New Jersey, 1970.

James, Marquis, *The Life of Andrew Jackson*, Garden City Publishing Co., N.Y., 1940.

Jefferson, Isaac, (Dictated to: Charles Campbell), *Memoirs of a Monticello Slave*, Univ. of Virginia, 1951. The memoirs of a man who was enslaved by Thomas Jefferson.

Jeffray, *Secrets of the White House*, Cosmopolitan Book Corp.

Jellison, Charles, A. "James Thomson Callender: Human Nature in Hideous Form." *Virginia Cavalcade*, vol. 29, no. 2, 1979.

JET Magazine, "Old Hickory," (Andrew Jackson), p. 19, Weekly Almanac section, vol. 79, No. 26, Johnson Publications, Chicago, IL, April 15, 1991.

Kane, Joseph Nathan, *Facts About the Presidents: From George Washington to Ronald Reagan*, The H.W. Wilson Co., 4th ed., New York, 1981.

Kennedy, Stetson, Reference: *Jim Crow Guide to the U.S.A*, Lawrence & Wishart Ltd., London, 1959.

Ibid. Reference: *The Klan Unmasked*, Florida Atlantic University Press, Boca Raton, 1954 & 1990.

Kent, Zachary, *Calvin Coolidge (Encyclopedia of Presidents)*, Children's Press, Chicago, 1988.

King, Richard, *African Origin of Biological Psychiatry*, Seymour-Smith, Inc., 1990.

Ibid, "Black Dot, Black Seed," *Uraeus: The Journal of Unconscious Life*, Parts I & II.

Kondo, Zak, *A Crash Course in Black History: 150 Important Facts About Afrikan Peoples*, Nubia Press, Washington, D.C., 1988.

Krass, Peter, *Sojourner Truth: Antislavery Activist*, Melrose Square Publishing Co., Los Angeles, CA, 1988.

Kurland, Gerald, *Warren Harding: A President Betrayed by Friends*, SamHar Press, Charlotteville, N.Y., 1971

Kush, Indus Khamit, *What They Never Told You In History Class*, Luxorr Publications. 1983.

Ladies Home Journal, "Diseases Your Doctor May Miss" (Health Section), June, 1990, pp. 104-108.

Lane-Poole, Stanley, *The Moors in Spain*, T. Fisher Unwin (London), 1887.

Larsen, Arthur J., *Crusader and Feminist (Letters of Jane Grey Swisshelm. 1858-1865)*, Hyperion Press, Inc., 1934.

Larson, A. *Eisenhower: The President Nobody Knew*, Charles Scribner's Sons, New York, 1968.

Leary, Warrene, "A Search for Lincoln's DNA," *The New York Times NATIONAL*, Sunday, Feb. 10, 1991, p. 28 L.

Lefton, Lester A. *Psychology*, Allyn and Bacon, Inc., Boston, 1979.

Lehrer, Steven, *Explorers of the Body: Dramatic Breakthroughs in Medicine from Ancient Times to Modern Science*, Doubleday & Co., Inc., Garden City, New York, 1979.

Leigh, Wendy. Reference: *Arnold: An Unauthorized Biography.* Congodn & Weed, Inc., Chicago, 1990.

Lewis, Lloyd. *Myths After Lincoln*, The Press of the Readers Club, New York, 1941. Harcourt, Brace, and Co., 1929.

The Liberator, vol. VIII, p. 152, September 21, 1838 (Thomas Jefferson).

Life Magazine. Reference: Collectors Edition — Pearl Harbor: December 7, 1941-December 7, 1991, Fall, 1991, vol. 14, No. 15.

Life Magazine, "Lincoln: The power of words in times of war," See: Wills. pp. 22-34, vol. 14, No. 2, February, 1991.

Life Magazine, "The Young Eisenhower: Eisenhower of Abilene," April 28, 1952, pp. 111-120.

"Lincoln: Trial By Fire," (Television Documentary), American Heritage Publication, produced in association with Warner Communications Co. (A David L. Wolper Production), Historian, Bruce Catton; narrated by Cliff Robertson, 1992.

"Lincoln's Devotional," Religious Tract Society, Channel Press, Inc., Great Neck, N.Y., 1957. Introduction by, Carl Sandburg.

Link, Paxson Rude, *The Link Family*, (Eisenhower's maternal ancestors) Paris, IL, 1951.

Long, Richard, *Black Americana,* Chartwell Books, Inc., N.J., 1986.

Lyon, Peter, *Eisenhower: Portrait of a Hero.* Little, Brown and Company, Boston, 1974.

Mailer, Norman, *Harlot's Ghost: A novel of the CIA.* Random House, New York, 1991.

Malone, Dumas, *Jefferson and His Times: The Sage of Monticello,* vol. 6, Little, Brown and Co., Boston, 1981.

Mapp, Alf J., *Thomas Jefferson: A Strange Case of Mistaken Identity,* Madison Books, N.Y., 1987.

Marryat, F., *Diary in America,* vol. 1, p. 251, 1839 (Jefferson).

Masson, Jeffrey M., "Freud and the Seduction Theory," *The Atlantic Monthly,* February, 1984, pp. 33-60.

McCoy, Donald R., *Calvin Coolidge: The Quiet President,* University Press of Kansas, 1988.

McFeely, W, *Frederick Douglass,* W.W. Norton & Co., New York.

Means, Gaston, *The Strange Death of President Harding,* Gold Label Books, Inc., Guild Publishing Corp., 1930.

Means, Sterling, *Ethiopia and the Missing Link in African History, 1945.* Hakin's Publications, Philadelphia, PA, 1980.

Medved, Michael, *The Shadow Presidents,* Times Books, 1979.

Meier, August & Rudwick, Elliott, *From Plantation to Ghetto,* American Century Series, New York, 1966.

Menninger, Karl, *Man Against Himself,* Harcourt, Brace, & World, New York, 1938.

Miller, Merle, *IKE THE SOLDIER-As They Knew Him,* G.P. Putnam's Sons, New York, 1987.

Monte, Christopher F., *Beneath the Masks,* Holt, Rinehart and Winston, New York, 1977.

Morgan, Kay Summersby, *Past Forgetting: My Love Affair With Dwight D. Eisenhower,* Simon and Schuster, New York, 1973.

Morin, R, *Dwight D. Eisenhower: A Gauge of Greatness,* Simon & Schuster, N.Y., 1969.

Morrow, E. F., *Black Man In The White House,* Coward-McCann, Ino., New York, 1963.

Murray, R., *The Harding Era,* U. of Minnesota Press, Minneapolis, 1969.

National Archives, Records Administration & Information, Washington, D.C. 20408.

National Enquirer, "Wily Washington was a Super Spy, by George," by, Fenton, Peter (referencing the book: Honorable Treachery. by O,Toole, G.J.A.), April 21, 1992, p. 19.

Neal, Steve, *The Eisenhowers Reluctant Dynasty,* Doubleday & Co., Garden City, N.Y., 1978.

Neely, Mark and MccMurtry, R. Gerald, *Insanity File: The Case of Mary Todd Lincoln,* So. Illinois Univ. Press, 1986.

Negro History Bulletin, (Carter G. Woodson), April/May/June, 1982, vol. 45, No. 2.

Nevins, Allan, Reference: *The Emergence of Lincoln,* 2 vols., Charles Scribner's Sons, N.Y., 1950.

Ibid. "Ordeal of the Union: Fruits of Manifest-Destiny, 2 vols. (1847-1857), Charles Scribner's Sons, N.Y., 1947.

The New England Journal of Medicine, (1) "Immunohistologic Abnormalities of the Microfibrillar-Fiber System in the Marfan Syndrome," by, Hollister, et al., vol. 323, No. 3, July 19, 1990, pp. 152-159. (2) "Location on Chromosome 15 of the Gene Defect Causing Marfan Syndrome," by, Kainulainen, et al., vol. 323, No. 4, October, 4, 1990, pp. 935-939. Newsweek. "The Lincoln Syndrome," by, Seligmann & Witherspoon, p. 81, October 8, 1984.

New York Evening Post, "Betsy Walker Affair [with Thomas Jefferson]," April 5, 1805.

The New York Times, NATIONAL, "A Search for Lincoln's DNA," by Leary, Sunday, February 10, 1991.

Nobles, Wade, "African Philosophy: Foundations for Black Psychology," pp. 23-36. *Black Psychology,* ed. Reginald Jones, Univ. of Berkely, Harper & Row, Publishers, N.Y., 1980.

Oakley, J. Ronald, *God's Country: America in the Fifties,* Dembner Books, New York, 1986.

Oates, Stephen, *Abraham Lincoln: The Man Behind the Myths,* Harper & Row Publishers, New York, 1984.

Ibid. Let the Trumpet Sound: The Life of Martin Luther King. Jr., A Plume Book, New York, 1982.

Ibid. With Malice Toward None: The Life of Abraham Lincoln, Harper & Row, Publishers, New York, 1977.

O'Rourke, P.J., Reference: *Parliament of Whores* (a lone humorist attempts to explain the entire U.S. Government), Atlantic Monthly Press, New York, 1991.

O'Toole, G.J.A., *Honorable Treachery: A history of spying in the U.S.*, 1992.

Pasteur, Alfred B., and Toldson, Ivory L., Reference: *Roots of Soul: The Psychology of Black Expressiveness*, Anchor Press/Doubleday, Garden City, N.Y., 1982.

Parmet, Herbert S., *Eisenhower and the American Crusades*, The MacMillian Co., N.Y., 1972.

Peterson, James A., *Lucey Hanks*, Peterson (publisher), 1973.

Powell, Adam Clayton, Jr. *Adam By Adam, The Autobiography of Adam Clayton Powell. Jr.*, The Dial Press, New York, 1971.

Prados, J. *President's Secret Wars: CIA and Pentagon Covert Operations Since World War II*, William Morrow and Co., New York, 1986.

THE PRESIDENTS, Funk & Wagnalls Special Edition-Saturday Evening Post, The Curtis Publishing Co., Indianapolis, IN, 1989.

Preston, D., *Young Frederick Douglass: The Maryland Years*, The John Hopkins University Press, Baltimore, Maryland, U.S.A. & London, 1980.

Professional Guide to Diseases, "Genetic Disorders," 3rd ed., Springhouse Corp., PA, 1989, p. 12.

Quarles, Benjamin, *Lincoln and the Negro*, Oxford Univ. Press, N.Y., 1962.

Ibid. The Negro in the Making of America, Collier MacMillian Publishers, London & New York, 1969.

Remini, Robert V., *Andrew Jackson*, Harper & Row Publishers, New York, 1966.

Reuter, Edward Buron, *The Mulatto in the United States*, Haskell House, 1969. This book was first published in 1918 on the mixed-blood in the United States and the rest of the world and the nature of race intermixture. This book includes information on Blacks and multiracial (mulatto) people in the sciences, the arts, business and other professionals.

Rogers, J. A., Pamphlet: *The Five Negro Presidents* — According to What White People Said They Were, H.M. Rogers, FL, 1965.

Ibid. Nature Knows No Color-Line — Research Into the Negro Ancestry In the White Race, H.M. Rogers, FL, 1952 & 1980.

Ibid. 100 Amazing Facts About the Negro-with Complete Proof, H.M. Rogers, FL, 1957 & 1970.

Ibid. Sex and Race, vols. I, II, & III, The New World-H.M. Rogers, FL, 1942 & 1970.

Ibid. Your History: From the Beginning of Time to the Present, "Hannibal Hamlin," p. 78. Black Classic Press, Baltimore, MD, 1983.

Rowan, Carl T., *Breaking Barriers: A Memoir,* Little, Brown and Co., Boston, 1991.

Rubel David, *Fannie Lou Hamer: From Sharecropping to Politics,* Silver Burdett Press, 1990.

Russell, Francis, *The Shadow of Blooming Grove: Warren G. Harding in His Times,* McGraw-Hill Book Co., New York, 1968.

Sandburg, Carl, *Abraham Lincoln: The Prairie Years and the War Years,* Dell Publishing Co., New York, 1925.

Ibid. Mary Lincoln: Wife and Widow, Harcourt, Brace & World, Inc., New York, 1932.

Schlesinger, Arthur M., *EISENHOWER,* Chelsea House Publishers, New York, 1986.

Ibid. Jackson, Chelsea House Publications, New York, 1986.

Ibid. Jefferson, Chelsea House Publications, New York, 1986.

Schlesinger, Kurt. *Biological Psychology,* William C. Brown Company Publishers, Dubuque, Iowa, 1982.

Seligmann, Jean with Witherspoon, Deborah, "The Lincoln Syndrome," *Newsweek* Magazine, October 8, 1984, p. 81.

Sennett, Richard, Reference: *The Psychology of Society,* Vintage Books, N.Y., 1977.

Simon, John Y., *"House Divided: Lincoln and His Father,* Louis A. Warren Library and Museum, Fort Wayne, Indiana, 1987.

Sinclair, Andrew, *The Available Man: Warren Gamaliel Harding,* The MacMillan Co., N.Y., 1965.

Sinkler, G., *The Racial Attitudes of American Presidents from Abraham Lincoln to Theodore Roosevelt,* Doubleday/Anchor Books, New York, 1972.

Sports Illustrated, "Marfan Syndrome: A Silent Killer," by, Demak, Richard, pp. 30-35, Feb. 17, 1986, vol. 64, no. 7.

Stamler, J., et al., *Symposium: hypertension in the inner city.* Published by Proforum, A division of Modern Medicine Publications (Also see the Welsing article in *Urban Health).*

Stampp, Kenneth, *The Era of Reconstruction: 1865-1877*, Vintage Books, New York, 1965.

Ibid. The Peculiar Institution, Vintage Books, New York, 1956.

Steiner, Stan, *The Vanishing White Man*, Norman: University of Oklahoma Press, 1987.

Sterling, Dorothy, *Black Foremothers*, The Feminst Press, New York, 1979.

Stevens, Rita, *Calvin Coolidge, 30th President of the United States,* Garrett Educational Corp., Ada, Oklahoma, 1990.

Stuckey, Sterling, Reference: *Slave Culture: Nationalist Theory & the Foundations of Black America*, Oxford Univ. Press, New York, 1987.

Sullivan, Harry Stack, *Clinical Studies in Psychiatry*, Norton, N.Y., 1956.

Ibid. The Interpersonal Theory of Psychiatry, Norton, N.Y., 1953.

Ibid. Schizophrenia as a Human Process, Norton, N.Y., 1962.

Sullivan, Michael, *Presidential Passions: The Love Affairs of America's Presidents — From Washington and Jefferson to Kennedy and Johnson*, Shapolsky Publishers, Inc., New York, 1991.

Summersby, Kay (See: Morgan, Kay Summersby).

Swisshelm, Jane Grey, *Crusader and Feminist — 1858-1865*, Hyperion Press, Inc., Westport, Conn.

T.V. Guide, The Grapevine Section, p. 16, January 25, 1992 (Haley's Digging Up Some More Roots — [about Alex Haley's maternal family tree]).

T.V. Guide, "If Abe Lincoln were campaigning for President today, he wouldn't win," by: Ken Burns (Documentary creator of the Civil Wars), p. 13, January 25, 1992.

T.V. Guide, "Remembering Dad," (Henry Fonda's dislike for Joseph McCarthy, etc.), by Fonda, Jane, January 11, 1992.

Time Magazine, "Whose America? (Who Are We? American kids are getting a new — and divisive — view of Thomas Jefferson, Thanksgiving and the Fourth of July) by Paul Gray, pp. 13a

Tabers Cyclopedia Medical Dictionary, F.A. Davis Co., Philadelphia, Pennsylvania, 1989. Reference.

Truth, Sojourner, *Book of Life*, Battle Creek, Michigan (Published for the Author, 1878). *Narrative of Sojourner Truth*, Katz, Ayer Co., Publishers, Inc., Salem, New Hampshire, 1988.

Ullah, Ibrahim Khalil, "Thanksgiving For Whom?" *Moorish Guide-Moorish Science Temple of America Inc.*, vol. I, No. XI, November, 1982, Chicago, IL, pp. 6-7.

U.S. *News & World Report*, Reference: "The Case of the President's feet [Lincoln]," by Boritt, pp. 64-65, Nov. 28, 1988.

U.S. *News & World Report*, Reference: "Early Man: The Radical New View of Where We Came From," September 16, 1991, pp. 53-59. (The front cover is graced with an African man.)

Ibid. Reference: The Roots of Language: How Modern Speech Evolved From a Single, Ancient Source, November 5, 1990, vol 109, No. 18, pp. 60-70.

Urban Health (The Journal of Health Care in the Cities), vol. 4, No. 3, June, 1975, "Blacks, Hypertension, and the Active Skin Melanocyte," by Welsing, Frances Cress, pp. 64-72.

Van Sertima, Ivan, *They Came Before Columbus: The African Presence in Ancient America*, Random House, New York, 1976.

The Virginia Magazine of History, "Letters From Andrew Jackson to R.K. McCall," vol. 29, pp. 191-2.

Walden, Carl, *Who Was Who In Native American History: Indians and Non-Indians From First Contacts Through 1900*, Facts on File, 1990.

Wallace, Douglas & Cann, Rebecca, "The Search for Adam and Eve — Scientists Explore a Controversial Theory About Man's Origins," *Newsweek Magazine* (The front cover displays a drawing of an African male and female), pp. 46-52, January 11, 1988.

Ward, John William, Reference: *Andrew Jackson: Symbol for an Age*,

The Washington Afro-American, "Daughters of Isis Sponsor Tea For Charity," p. 7, February 9, 1952. (The indigenous African [Ancient Kemetian] name for "Isis" is "Ast" [Auset]).

The Washington Post, "Adolf Hitler," (Book World Section), p. 12, February 16, 1992. A review on the book written by John Toland titled: *Adolf Hitler*, 1992.

The Washington Post, "A Look at ... The Origin-of-AIDS Debate. Did Polio Vaccine Experiment Unleash AIDS in Africa?" by Curtis, Tom, April 5, 1992.

The Washington Post, Reference: "Buffalo Soldiers (Forgotten Black Heroes of the Old West)" Magazine Section, pp. 14-21.

The Washington Post, "Ethics Panel Clears Plan to Test Lincoln's Remains," by Gladwell, May 3, 1991 (A3).

The Washington Post, "Father of Harding Dies After Stroke: Mrs. Votaw at Bedside," November 20, 1928.

The Washington Post (Magazine insert), Reference: The Harding chapter (Information on Nancy Reagan), July 26, 1992, p. 11.

The Washington Post, "Should Researchers Probe Abraham Lincoln's Genes?" (Health-Forum), p. 18, October 21, 1991.

Webster's New Twentieth Century Dictionary, Unabridged, 2nd ed. - Deluxe color, Simon and Schuster, N.Y., 1983.

Webster's American Biographies, Van Doren, Charles, G. & C. Merrian Co., Publishers, Springfield, Mass., 1974.

Weekly World News, "I Slept With 5 Presidents" (Sally Fischer), by: Rick Tracy, pp. 4-5, March 10, 1992.

Welsing, Frances Cress, Reference: "The Concept of the Color of God and Black Mental Health," *Black Books Bulletin*, vol. 7, No. 1, pp. 27-9 & 35.

Welsing, Frances Cress, *The Isis (Yssis) Papers: The Keys to the Colors*, Third World Press, Chicago, 1991.

White, Deborah Gray, *Ar'n't I a Woman? (Female Slaves in the Plantation South)*, W.W. Norton & Co., New York, 1985.

White, Richard Grant, *Book of the Prophet Stephen, Son of Douglas. Wherein Marvelous Things are Foretold of the Reign of Abraham*, New York, Feeks & Bancker, 1863. This book has been referenced by some old-time Lincolnites as "scurrilous anti-Lincoln propaganda."

White, William Allen, *The Autobiography of William Allen White*, N.Y.: Macmillan. 1946.

Whitney, David C., *The American Presidents*, Doubleday & Co., Inc., Garden City, N.Y. 1978.

Whitney, Sharon, *Eleanor Roosevelt*, Franklin Watts/an Impact Biography, New York, 1982.

Wills, Garry, "The Power of Words in Times of War, " (Inspiration through the words of Abraham Lincoln), *LIFE Magazine*, February, 1991, pp. 22-34.

Williamson, David, *Debrett's Presidents of the United States of America*, Salem House Publishers, Topsfield, MA, 1989.

Wilson, Amos N., *Black-on-Black Violence: The Psychodynamics of Black Self-Annihilation in Service of White Domination*, Afrikan World Infosystems, New York, 1990.

Ibid. Psychological Reference: *The Developmental Psychology of the Black Child*, Africana Research Publications, N.Y., 6th ed., 1987.

Wilson, Rufus R., *Lincoln In Caricature*, Horizon Press, N.Y., 1953.

Windsor, Rudolph R., *The Valley of the Dry Bones*, Windsor's Golden Series, Philadelphia, PA, 1988.

Woodson, Carter G., (Author of *Mis-education of the Negro*), "Beginnings of the Miscegenation of Whites and Blacks," *Journal of Negro History*, October, 1918.

Ibid. "Negroes and Indians in Massachusetts," *Journal of Negro History*, January, 1920.

Woodward, Bob, *VEIL: The Secret Wars of the CIA 1981-1987*, Simon and Schuster, N.Y., 1987.

Woodward, C. Vann, ed. *Responses of the Presidents to Charges of Misconduct*, New York, Delacorte Press, 1974.

Woodward, W.E., *The Way Our People Lived*, E.P. Dutton & Co., Inc., New York, 1944.

World Book Encyclopedia. Reference: Dwight D. Eisenhower, Warren G. Harding, Hannibal Hamlin, Andrew Jackson, Thomas Jefferson, and Abraham Lincoln. Field Enterprises Educational Corporation.

Wright, Bobby, *The Psychopathic RACIAL Personality* (A major source for understanding ourstory and his-story), Third World Press, Chicago, 1984.

Wyden, Peter, *Bay of Pigs: The Untold Story*, Simon and Schuster, New York, 1979.

Zilversmit, Arthur, *Lincoln on Black and White: A Documentary History*, Wadsworth Publishing Co., CA, 1971.

Zinn, Howard, *A People's History of the United States*, Harper-Perennial, New York, 1980.

Illustration and Picture Credits

JEFFERSON: 27 Jean Antoine Houdon (Paris, 1789). **28** (Top) Self-portrait (1700's), Library of Congress; (Bottom) New York Public Library. **29** (Top) Courtesy Thomas Jefferson Museum. **JACKSON**: **45** (Top & bottom) Library of Congress. **46** (Top) Schomburg Collection, New York; (bottom) Photo courtesy Kenneth Wiggins Porter through What's A Face Productions. **LINCOLN**: **147** Library of Congress. **148** (Top) Library of Congress; (Bottom) Courtesy Lincoln Museum/Illinois State Historical Library, Springfield, Illinois. **149** (Top) UPI/Bettman; (Bottom) Volck, 1862. **150** (Top) Library of Congress; (Bottom) *Vanity Fair*, 1861. **HAMLIN**: **175** (Top) Charles Hamlin; (Bottom) What's A Face Productions (The Moors of Spain). **176** (Top) Courtesy Smith College Collection; (Bottom) Library of Congress. **HARDING**: **216** (Top & Bottom) Library of Congress. **217** (Top) © BaKhufu Archives; (Bottom) The Garvey Papers, UCLA, Professor Robert Hill. **218** (Top) Schomburg Collection; (Bottom) What's A Face Productions. **219** (Top) Courtesy Library of Congress and The Schomburg Collection; (Bottom) Library of Congress. **220** (Top) Library of Congress; (Bottom) *Abbott's Monthly* (1932) & J. A. Rogers' *Five Negro Presidents* cover. **EISENHOWER**: **304** Courtesy The Eisenhower Library. **305** (Top) The Eisenhower Library; (Bottom) Library of Congress. **306** (Top) © 1987, BaKhufu Archives; (Bottom) "Hypatia" © 1992, BaKhufu Archives. **307** (Top) Library of Congress; (Bottom) Associated Press © 67-29932. **308** Courtesy The Eisenhower Library.

Cover and computer graphics, page layout and typesetting by Gibril's Fire, Perfect Secretary, and PIK².

Index

If you are researching or studying, please take notes. This index is not all inclusive.

334

WE ARE THE PARENTS OF FOOLS

Sitting in the airport
in between states
Reading my Black history
Whew, my head has
a swimming ache
Just read here that *we're* the
chosen ones — for we were the
first to grace this earth!
You mean to tell me that we are
the parents of fools?
My God, all my white chillin
— one sitting beside me now
with an ole nasty-looking drool
undeserved, sanctified, superior-
acting cool
I'm moving, shit! roughly gathering
my stuff
these Kriminals-outcast from Europe-
den lied
kicked us all up side our heads
and hides!
In my new seat developing my own
superior stance,
I saw from my white mutated child
a curious, defeated, disgusted-
looking glance
Whoops! just read that Cleopatra*
was Black
How happy she must have been so
African, proud, and exact.
Ah? What? Queen Sheba too? Go
on Black sisters and do-the-do!

Oh no, here comes another one-
walking toward me with a
survey book.
How dare this pale child (of mine?!)
interrupt me with her
ugly look!
No, No, I'm not interested dear; I have
a book here — putting my mind in
gear for an African worldwide cure!

Auset BaKhufu
Copyright © 1988 by Auset BaKhufu

*Cleopatra was mulatto, African with a mixture of Persian, who is
known for her love of Africa/Egypt.
SHEBA, *fully* African of Ethiopian origin.

338

NOTE PAPER